For Liann Kiyoko and Lennon.

— CONTENTS —

Introduction 6
My Own "Divorce Story" 7

PART 1
Divorce: An Overview 35

Chapter 1
Divorce Happens in Three Acts 36

Chapter 2
Getting to "Reasonable" and Doing it Quickly ... 94

Chapter 3
A Personal Story 107

PART II
The View From The Clouds (50,000 Feet) 117

Chapter 4
The Rule of Reasonability and The Range of Normal 118

Chapter 5
Reasonability in Action 152

Chapter 6
The Three Property Rules of Family Law 160

Chapter 7
Dispute Resolution 179

Chapter 8
Outcomes and Resolutions 221

Chapter 9
Dealing with Difficult Questions in a Negotiation 232

Chapter 10
Mindfulness, Negotiation and Strategy 260

Chapter 11
Fiduciary Duties 271

KEEP YOUR SANITY. STAND YOUR GROUND.

~~BITTER~~ *Better* DIVORCE

A Handbook for Getting through the Most Difficult Time in Your Life

DR. M. JUDE EGAN, PH.D., J.D.

Better Divorce:
A Handbook for Getting Through the Most Difficult Time in Your Life

M. Jude Egan, Ph.D., J.D., Certified Family Law Specialist, Certified by the State Bar of California

Copyright © 2025

All rights reserved. No part of this book may be reproduced in any form or by any electronic or mechanical means, including information storage and retrieval systems, without permission in writing from the author, except by a reviewer who may quote brief passages in a review.

For permissions, inquiries, or more information, contact:
M. Jude Egan, Ph.D., J.D.,
805.332.3984
426 Barcellus Ave Suite 304 Santa Maria, CA 93454
jude@judeeganlaw.com
www.judeeganlaw.com/

This is a work of nonfiction. Every effort has been made to ensure accuracy, but the author and publisher assume no responsibility for errors or omissions. Any references to third party products, companies, or trademarks are for informational purposes only and do not constitute endorsement.

Published in 2025

ISBN 979-8-218-65817-5

Cover design by Shivaal

Interior design by Marcy McGuire

PART III
THE VIEW FROM THE WEEDS (TRUDGING THROUGH THE DUST) . 289

Chapter 12
Child Custody and Visitation 290

Chapter 13
Child Support 317

Chapter 14
Spousal Support 356

Chapter 15
Applying the Three Property Rules of Family Law to Property
Division 375

PART IV
STEPPING BACK JUST ENOUGH TO SEE THE FOREST
AND THE TREES 441

Chapter 16
Getting What You Want in Your Divorce 442

ABOUT THE AUTHOR 464

INTRODUCTION

DIVORCE IS DEEPLY emotional, whether the emotion is anger, sadness, a feeling of having been betrayed, or the shame of having done the betraying. Everyone who divorces must process their emotions in their own way. I hope to one day write a follow up book in partnership with an expert in psychology and/or therapy to help people manage these emotions and understand that they are not alone.

This book is not a guide toward healing from your divorce; nor is it a paean to collaboration or a manual on how to "fix it" with your spouse. There are many books on how to try to get along after a bad marriage, and for ways to collaborate on divorce outcomes that feel good, but are not "fair" (fairness can have many connotations, from "divide everything in half" to "each keeps what they earned" to "ensuring that each partner has what they need," but a negotiated divorce outcome may not comport with any of these). This is not a guide to the nuts and bolts of how to move your divorce along either.

This book is unique in that it a) teaches you about the law in a more overall sense and b) in so doing, gives you real strategies to protect yourself in your divorce. Armed with information about how the law works, you will be in a stronger bargaining position going into settlement negotiations (and you should absolutely settle the majority of your divorce).

MY OWN "DIVORCE STORY"

I REMEMBER THE first night I spent alone in my little granny flat in one of the canyons outside Arroyo Grande, CA. My daughter was all of 18 months old. I had packed a few things from the house and bought a few things from IKEA. My parents visited for a few hours but eventually had to go. I sat there with a sucking feeling in my chest, wondering what the f**k I had done leaving my family—even though staying was not an option. I was alone without cable or internet, with crappy cell reception, sitting on my bed with my photographs and Netflix DVDs (it was 2008) wondering how I would get through the long dark night. I sobbed inconsolably into a couch pillow, clueless as to how, or if, I could move beyond the feelings of hurt and ache and loss.

In the years to come I would confess to friends and clients that the pain of not having your child with you every day is like a gaping hole in your chest that never heals. You learn to deal with the grief, to find the finest joy in the moments you have together—and you eventually look forward at times to solitude. You fill your life with things, different things: a new partner, stepchildren, work, solitary hikes, writing, every cable TV show imaginable. Slowly you crawl out. Slowly and painfully.

The emotional side of a divorce can be fraught with self-doubt and wondering if there was anything else you could have done to save your marriage, especially as the reality of "getting divorced" sets in. Normally, you have half of the money and half of the items, often sell the family home and see your children about half of the time. I try to urge potential clients to try everything to save themselves from worrying whether they did enough to try to save their marriage by trying everything they can to do so. This will save them grief as they process the loss of their marriage later. But we all grieve differently. Sometimes anger is easier than sadness. And sometimes the marriage is beyond repair by the time they are sitting across the table from me.

I have often viewed my role as divorce lawyer as akin to the Greek Ferryman, Charon, who takes the dead across the River Styx into Hades. The dead must pay the Ferryman or risk standing on the shore for eternity. They stand at the shore in a sort of purgatory full of anxiety and sadness, wondering what is to come in the Underworld on the other side of the River. The Ferryman is the guide across treacherous waters, the one who brings them to the opposite shore where they cross into life after death. And divorce is a type of death. Maybe the analogy is not perfect. Charon is taking them into a type of Hell (although the Greeks conceived of Hades differently than we conceive of Hell), but I think of the afterlife as a place of your own making. You walk through it or you get stuck there – that choice is yours alone. All I can do is help you get across the River.

The lawyer's job as Ferryman and guide is to get you there as quickly and as painlessly as possible. This doesn't mean the anxiety disappears, but at least you know you are travelling with an experienced guide. A good guide gets you across the River and has a plan for you to follow to do it.

This book lays the foundation for that plan so that rather than spending $45,000 stumbling through your divorce, you start with a map and a strategy for navigating it. The little secret about divorce is that almost no matter what happens on your journey you will arrive in the same neighborhood at the end. You can spend years and a small fortune being led around in circles by an attorney (or by your own inaction) or you can use strategy and dogged determination to get through the ordeal as quickly and as reasonably possible. And if you take away nothing else from this book, *remember to get through your divorce as quickly as possible—without being taken advantage of in the process.*

The reasons for this admonition are: 1) Divorce is expensive and it gets more expensive the longer it takes; 2) Divorce is stressful and it gets more stressful the longer it takes; 3) usually, it is better to leave a few dollars "on the table" (i.e., giving them to your soon-to-be-ex-spouse) then to fight for them. As to number 3, why? Because when you focus on the 50 cents of yesterday's dollars, it will cost you 10 cents for each 50 cents (or more) and it will take away from tomorrow's dollars and your overall happiness and enjoyment of life. People who fight out their divorces to the bitter end, end up with half of the stuff (at a cost of 15% of or so of the value of their half of the stuff), have a hard time forming new intimate partnerships, have difficulty running businesses or working in their jobs, and have a harder time parenting their children. The stress and pain of the high-cost and the anxiety of appearing in court often just wears people down. I counsel all of my clients to move through the divorce as quickly as reasonably possible without giving up the farm in the process.

It is hard to "win the divorce" but it can be done if a) you received the one-half of the property that you wanted b) you have reasonable visitation/timeshare with your children c) your lawyer doesn't take half of your 401(k) and d) you survive the process with your emotional faculties relatively intact. The law requires that you get (a) and (b). The law says 50% of the "stuff" to each party. The law also requires "continuing care and contact" between each parent and the children. While the particular judge's view of "reasonable" visitation (often 80-20) and your own view of "reasonable visitation" (often 50-50) may not line up, the law supports reasonability in timeshare. While nothing is a given, as you will see below, if you can end up with between 35% and 65% custodial timeshare with your children, I believe this to be reasonable in most circumstances (there are exceptions: drugs, crimes, violence, mental health problems and very young children or children who are late teenagers) and because you will learn a lot from reading this book, you should be able to keep your attorney's fees low and escape with your emotional and mental faculties intact.

················· PRO-TIP ·················
People who leave everything up to their attorney end up at their attorney's mercy.
··

In my almost two decades of being a divorce lawyer, I have learned that people who leave everything up to their attorney end up at their attorney's mercy. They are unaware of the value of the fights and the agreements, they take advice blindly, and they eventually spend tens of thousands in attorneys' fees. Conversely, people who micromanage their attorney without information or knowledge end up going through three or four attorneys, looking suspicious to the court, and spending tens of thousands in attorney's fees anyway. Clients who ask their lawyer to explain things so they can make educated decisions tend to push through the divorce more quickly and at less cost.

I recently had a conversation with a very famous self-help book author at a dinner party. I told him I was a divorce lawyer, and he did what everyone does when they find out I am a divorce lawyer—he told me his divorce story. He explained that his ex-wife hired the meanest lawyer in the state (I can vouch for this because I have met her and I think she is the meanest person in the country, easily making her the meanest lawyer in the state). He offered his wife 50% of all his future earnings and half of their property. He said he thought it was fair because they started with nothing and built everything together. The lawyer told him this was not happening. Ultimately, his wife spent more than $1 million in fees to extract a $9 million settlement out of him. Yet, two years later he sold one of his companies for $63 million, of which his wife did not see one penny. He told me: "I guess you have to say she was a good lawyer. She deposed me for 5 days, copied thousands of pages of documents, hired forensic accountants who looked at every bank statement for over 25 years. She was really thorough."

No, she was not a "good lawyer."

Granted, she was mean; she was thorough; she got every piece of information in existence about this now famous author. But she squandered a probable $100 million deal that would have been split between Husband and Wife for the rest of their lives in favor of $9 million now. It's true they probably did not know that one company would sell for $63 million just two years later or that his book empire would generate another $100 million in earnings, but this writer was already famous when they divorced. Was $9 million now worth a bet on $100 million in the future? And at the cost of $1 million in fees?

He then told me something that rang very true and is something worth reflecting on. He said, "I love my ex-wife very much. We had been together all our lives. Every book I wrote and every talk I gave had her at the heart of it. I called her in the middle of all of this and asked her, 'Why are we doing all of this spending and stress on lawyers? Don't you just want half of what we have built forever?' She told me, 'I hired a lawyer, and I am just going to let her decide." The divorce took three years and cost more than $30,000 *per month*! And the ex-wife came out so much the worse for it.

Divorce is a complicated business, and it is worth having a lawyer. But you cannot let the lawyers decide how much you will spend on their bill and how long your case will take. A lawyer is not an Emergency Room doctor who needs to do everything they can to save your life, often without explaining every action in detail; your lawyer has time, you have time, to make informed decisions about what actions you want to take and how much you want to spend. Drive your lawyer forward and get to the end of your case as quickly as you can while not being taken advantage of. Translated this means you should get about half the stuff (including businesses, pensions, and retirements), spend a *reasonable* amount of time with your children (*between 33% and 67% of the time*), and pay or receive a reasonable amount of support based on what the computer program or statewide support calculator says that support should be. That is a reasonable outcome.

················· PRO-TIP ·················

Reasonable Divorce Outcome *(Anything else is bunk)*

- Approximately One-half of the stuff (including businesses, pensions, and retirements),
- Reasonable timeshare with children (between 33% and 67% of the time),
- Reasonable child and spousal support (pay or receive) based on what the statewide support calculator says that support should be.

··

I will say repeatedly throughout this book that there is a range of reasonable outcomes in any divorce case, and that you should consider any offer to settle the case within that range. You should, however, reject any offer within the range of reasonable outcomes that contains a term that you cannot live with. As my client said to me just the other day, "I am going to give her half of everything without any problem, but if she wants to change the custody and visitation schedule with our kids, I am going to see a judge." That was where he drew his line. That was his hill to die on.

In a divorce (or child custody) action, there are only two alternatives: an agreement or a trial. If you know the basics of the law (not every detail, but how the law works conceptually) and you know the items you will never give up willingly, you can develop a range of possible negotiated outcomes: outcomes you may achieve in court by litigating, and outcomes you are willing to accept by agreement.

This book will help you reality-check those items you believe you will never give up willingly—because if those things cannot be won in court and your spouse will never give them to you by agreement, then you must revise your list. Otherwise, like Leonidas leading his army in the movie *300* against the entire rest of the world, you will win nothing but a moral victory for defending your beliefs in a losing cause. There is honor in fighting a losing battle, but those battles are best fought when an attorney is not on your personal payroll.

I have a basic discomfort for mediation and collaborative law with respect to family law, and it is why I believe that through targeted divorce negotiation and a basic understanding of the law you can and should always settle your case (or most of it).

Let me explain the difference between "traditional divorce mediation," "collaborative law" and "targeted divorce negotiation" as I use the terms in this book.

Traditional Divorce Mediation

Traditional divorce mediation is a process where two parties, usually without lawyers meet with a neutral mediator to try to resolve disputes. The mediator will help them complete their financial disclosures and income and expense declarations so that the mediator can get a read on the assets, liabilities, income and expenses. Then, the mediator will attempt to facilitate agreements between the parties. My problem with traditional divorce mediation is that it tends to prioritize all potential positions, some of which may be totally untenable under the law. The mediator's job is not to teach the parties the law, but to try to reach agreements. Husband in a 35-year marriage just does not want to pay alimony. The mediator will hear this position, whereas a judge would never even listen to this argument. Adding lawyers does not tend to help in traditional divorce mediation because lawyers posture over untenable outcomes because there is no judge to tell them to knock it off.

In traditional divorce mediation, as in collaborative law, the marital bully tends to keep bullying through tears, yelling, anger, guilt, shame, etc. Again, because there is no judge, bullying behavior does not get punished and bullies tend to be rewarded in the process. Finally, mediation is a sunk cost with no guarantee of a dispositive outcome. In other words, you might spend 3 months and $20,000 on mediation and have it fail and have to start all over again because one party walks away from mediation never to return.

Collaborative Law

Collaborative law is, to my mind, a fabulous method of dispute resolution, in theory. In collaborative law approaches, both parties get a lawyer who they agree will not litigate their case for them if the collaborative process fails. Both parties are paying $500 per hour for their lawyers. They bring in experts of all kinds to help with disputes. They will have a CPA, a custody analyst, perhaps speak with teachers and principals and even psychologists. Collaborative law can cost many tens of thousands of dollars for each side. While collaborative outcomes are often more "legal" than traditional divorce mediated outcomes, they are demonstrably more expensive. Bullies still tend to "win" in collaborative processes and either side can still simply walk away and start over with litigation. Now, you may have spent 4 months and $50,000 and have nothing to show for it as you hire a litigation attorney to push your case in the courts.

If you pay $35 for this book and settle your divorce case fairly for you, your soon-to-be ex, and your children, you can save yourself $50,000 or more. If you don't settle your case, the book will have cost you the equivalent of a 6-minute phone call to the lawyer you will hire to litigate for you.

Targeted Divorce Negotiation

The book will give you a set of conceptual tools for how to approach targeted negotiation in your divorce case. Targeted negotiation is a process where you and your spouse (with or without lawyers) focus on legal issues only: alimony, child support, child custody, division of assets and debts. Targeted divorce negotiations recognize that divorce is really several different negotiations in one. Dividing assets and debts is one type of negotiation. Determining timeshares for children is another type of negotiation. Support normally follows timeshare. If you cannot resolve everything through targeted divorce negotiation, resolve as much as you can and litigate the rest. You may shave days off a potential trial (you can have a support hearing in a couple of hours, while a custody and timeshare trial may take a week and cost tens of thousands of dollars with experts on both sides and lawyers with 4-inch thick binders full of text messages).

I call upon some of the great work done by negotiations experts, including the authors of the book *Getting to Yes*, Professors Fisher and Ury to give us some foundation in negotiation, but I also point out that divorce negotiations differ from classic negotiations because there are multiple, distinct issues in a divorce negotiation and there is truly no one winner or one loser (the more time it takes to resolve your divorce, typically the more both parties "lose" because typically there is only a finite amount of money and a finite amount of time for your children to be young and when we burn up time and money, we burn up resources). In *Getting to Yes*, the focus is always on understanding your Best Alternative to a Negotiated Agreement (BATNA), which is normally litigation.

If you know that failing to reach a negotiated agreement leads only to litigation, then you can analyze your future costs (attorney's fees) and risk of loss (the chance that you will have to pay damages, multiplied by the likelihood that you will pay damages) and get a pretty good idea of what your settlement range is. For example, if you have been sued for $100,000 and there is a 50% chance you will lose and have to pay $100,000 and it will cost you $10,000 in attorney's fees, then you should settle for $60,000 (the expected loss = $50,000 or 50% chance of losing * $100,000 + $10,000 in attorney's fees).

But divorces differ from traditional one-off negotiations because there are a range of issues, each of which you could win or lose. I discuss this in much greater detail below, but I teach you to develop a range of possible outcomes from your Worst-Case Alternative to a Negotiated Outcome (if you lose all issues on the table) to your Best Case Alternative to a Negotiated Outcome (if you win all issues on the table), with a Range of Reasonable Outcomes being your settlement territory (basically anything within the range from you WCATNA to your BCATNA). I urge you to take any offer seriously that falls within this range. Certainly you can nibble and try to do better than an offer that is close to your WCATNA to push it toward your BCATNA, and we can expect that the most likely outcome is that you each end up with half of the marital assets, all of your separate property assets, a reasonable timeshare with the children (33%-67%) and a support payment commensurate with your respective earnings. If we already know the outcome will *most likely* look a certain way, then we can drive toward that outcome in our negotiations.

Targeted divorce negotiation recognizes basically three areas: property division (including reimbursement and separate property claims), custody and visitation, and child and spousal support. I try, in any targeted divorce negotiation, to start with the least emotional issues first. Usually, big ticket property items are easiest. Once the parties understand that we are going to divide 50% of the community interest in everything they own, including pensions, retirement accounts, bank accounts (even ones in one person's name alone), credit cards (even ones with casino debt), medical debt (even elective surgeries and breast implants), vehicles (even the vintage VW bug you've been meticulously restoring), and couches, kitchen items, camping gear, and every other blessed thing you own, they get to it quickly. I try to start with the idea that the person who wants the thing the most should get it in their column for a value and then see where we are at that point in terms of payment made to the other spouse. I tell people to divide things up first by just who likes or wants it more, then hold out that agreement at arm's length and see if it "looks fair enough." I get my clients thinking early and often that a few thousand bucks is not worth fighting over when I'm charging $500 per hour.

Targeted divorce negotiation, therefore, understands that each of you is going to get roughly half of the assets. It starts by asking about the largest assets: does either party want to purchase the house from the other party for half of the equity value? Are there reimbursements owed to either spouse because they had separate property money that went into the down payment or improvements? It asks whether one spouse could trade their interest in the house for their spouse's interest in their pension or 401(k) or other assets. It looks quickly at vehicle values (normally Kelly Blue Book "private party good"), RV values, bank account values and divides those. You know that you drive the BMW and your wife drives the Explorer; targeted divorce negotiation accepts that that is not going to change (we all personalize our vehicles), we just need to put values on things in each column. Normally, you can divide the community and separate property in a couple of hours – perhaps fewer than that if you do not get into who gets the dishware and camping equipment.

If there is a community property business, it asks: who will keep and run the business? How will we get a value for the business? What do we do about profits and dividends or capital calls and losses? Does someone have a license to practice or work (law, medicine, contractor, architecture, CPA, etc.)? What should we do about the business?

Does either side have reimbursement claims? Did one party or the other use separate property money to buy the house? Did their parents give them a big gift or loan? Did either party get an inheritance and remodel the bathroom? Did someone have $100,000 in an IRA before marriage? We deal with those claims next. When I say that we will divide the community property portion of all assets and liabilities in half, what I mean is that we will divide the portion of the asset that was earned, purchased, saved or acquired during the marriage with community property income, assets, or credit. We do not divide the separate property – it returns to the spouse whose separate property it was. Much, much more on this below.

Then, targeted divorced negotiation focuses on custody and visitation of children. As I mentioned, the law requires "continuing care and contact," somewhere between 20% and 80% to each parent. We live in a world where judges are increasingly moving to 50-50 timeshares. It is also not uncommon for Dad to ask for

50-50 and Mom to ask for 80-20 and the parties to settle on that midpoint of 65-35 (roughly 5 overnights out of 14 – something like Dad has the kids afterschool on Wednesdays to school drop-off on Thursday and alternate extended weekends from Friday afterschool to drop-off Monday at school, keeping the kids until Tuesday is Monday is a holiday). My personal position is that anything 35% or above (up to 65%) is reasonable unless there are drugs, crimes, violence, mental health issues, or the children are either very young or very late teenagers. If any of these is present, then it may take a deeper look to get to a reasonable solution.

Finally, we look at support and perhaps attorney's fees. In California, child support is calculated based in part on income differential, tax filing status, percentage timeshare with children, etc. Child support is always calculated by formula. Alimony is not supposed to be calculated by formula, but there are formulas out there to make calculation easier. Support normally follows custodial timeshare.

Targeted divorce negotiation, so long as you understand certain nuances, can be done by two reasonable people in about 4 hours, perhaps 8 hours over two sessions if there are complexities to the situation. Targeted negotiation can also resolve certain issues and preserve other for future negotiation or trial. Decisions on selling or buying out the home, dividing pensions, dividing vehicles, furniture, and bank accounts can be easily done in one short negotiation with good financial disclosures, a reasonable understanding of the law and parties keeping emotions in check long enough to get through the process. It can save tens of thousands of dollars in doing so.

Let's do a touch of math to understand. If you each have $500 per hour lawyers, the cost of a targeted divorce negotiation will be 8 total hours apiece or $4,000 each, plus $2,000 of paralegal time to prepare. Each side spends $6,000. You resolve 80% of your issues, leaving 20% of issues for a trial. Instead of a 5-day trial at a cost of $10,000 per day apiece, you get a one-day trial. You will have spent $16,000 to resolve your case completely or $32,000 total. If you went to trial, you would likely spend closer to $60,000 on a five-day trial apiece. You spend $32,000 instead of $120,000 and get a better, more controllable outcome.

In addition, most of my clients spend about $3,000 per month when I am on retainer. This is not because we try to run up the bill during the representation but because invariably things come up that take lawyer time while you wait for a trial. The waiting period to get a 5-day trial is likely 18 months in most courthouses, while the waiting period for a one-day trial is probably 4 months. So, assume $3,000 per month for four months is $12,000 plus $16,000 – your divorce costs $28,000. If you litigate everything in a 5-day trial, it's $60,000 plus $3,000 * 18 months = $114,000 to EACH SIDE. This is ungodly money and most people truly don't have that much money to spend on their divorce and they should not spend that much unless the other side is wholly and completely unreasonable and you absolutely must.

In a targeted divorce negotiation, if you don't agree on a value for the home, then you agree on a process to get the value for the home. Each of you picks a realtor to say what they think they could sell if for and split the difference if there is one – or agree that if the difference is more than 3%, you will pay an appraiser to give a value or ask one realtor friend to give you a value or pay the appraiser (or just sell the house and split the equity and let the market decide its value). Then, once you have the value, you know how much it will cost to buy out your spouse. If you might trade the home equity for the pension, agree to get a pension value by using an actuary to give that value and meet again in two weeks with both values in hand.

This book teaches you several different foundational elements required for a targeted divorce negotiation. I am trying, with a little investment from you in time spent learning the basics of the law and how to look for reasonable outcomes, to save you money. If we follow the example above, your divorce will have cost you $28,000 versus $114,000. For $35 (the cost of a 6-minute phone call to your lawyer) and 15-20 hours of reading time in the evening instead of watching *Gilmore Girls* reruns, you save yourself (and you soon-to-be-ex-spouse) $172,000. This is not just real money, it's *really* real money.

What the Book Teaches

First, I teach you how a divorce is scripted (it takes place in three acts).

Second, I teach you what "reasonability" means and how important it is in a divorce, including the Range of Normal Outcomes.

Third, I teach you the Three Family Law property rules so that, conceptually, you understand how your case will or should resolve.

Fourth, I focus on negotiating strategies and techniques, and why it is so important for you to understand the basics of Family Law before you begin to negotiate. This includes a chapter on Mindfulness—not mindfulness in the sense of how the yoga practitioners and meditators think of it (although that cannot hurt you in any way here), but mindfulness in the way it is conceived by Navy fighter pilots and air traffic controllers–an intense focus on the task at hand. This is what I wrote my doctoral dissertation on at UC Berkeley and Los Alamos National Laboratory, and I think I have something to say about this.

Fifth, I talk about the duties owed between spouses—more like general partners in a business that is ending than like two people who were in love.

Sixth, I delve into Custody and Visitation, Child and Spousal Support, and Property Division in separate chapters so that I can do a deeper dive into the laws of each.

Finally, I give you strategies for comporting yourself in negotiations and in court, whether you have a lawyer present or are representing yourself.

I pepper each of the sections with anecdotes based (loosely) on cases I have worked on, and I provide "Pro Tips" whenever I am able. I also will give you tips on how to manage your lawyer, if you have one, to save both time and money. This is especially true if you are the high-earner.

You should have an almost singular goal of resolving your case as quickly as reasonably possible. The book helps you work through the math to show that, in many instances, it is more rational and reasonable to settle leaving a few dollars on the table than to continue fighting for things with only nominal value.

Why Write This Book?

I started writing this book with a former client in mind. I had known him for many years, even prior to his family law problem. He is a smart man, college educated but without an advanced degree. He was successful in his career and had over $2 million in assets to divide with his wife of almost four decades, despite adopting 4 kids and having his wife not earning money outside the home during their marriage – all of their children had gone to college and they were beginning the years of less financial commitment to their children and more focused on beginning to think about what semi-retirement would look like for them. He had met someone else, so his wife wanted vengeance and was spending ridiculous money on her lawyer and was refusing to negotiate even the most basic issues. He called me regularly, pleading, "Jude, what is going on? How can she be doing this to me?" I reassured him that every offer she made was well-outside the Range of Normal Outcomes, and that every offer we made was well within the Range of Normal Outcomes and tried to explain "normal outcomes" and what the "range" might be. And I reminded him that when another party is acting irrationally, sometimes the only option is to litigate.

And as expected, despite all his bluffing and posturing, her lawyer completely caved within the first five minutes of the Divorce Trial; the other lawyer made an opening toward settlement in his opening statement, and I asked the judge for a brief recess so that the two lawyers could talk. She obliged and about 35 minutes later we recited a full agreement on the record. We ended up signing an agreement that saved my client $350,000 in cash—just as I predicted it would. Not because I am the Oracle at Delphi, but because the law would not allow any other result. My client's wife paid her lawyer $60,000 to watch him roll over the minute I handed him our evidence binders.

Since that case, I have been practicing an additional number of years and so I have expanded beyond just thinking of him as I write. His case, however, symbolizes some of the most extreme position-taking I have ever come across – an utterly irrational approach taken by the ex-wife, one that could never be a litigated outcome (meaning an order by a judge after a trial), even if they had won every single issue in front of the judge. This couple could have easily divided their wealth in two for about $3,500. Instead, all told, it cost them about $60,000 apiece.

This book is for people educated enough to understand that it makes no sense spending tens or hundreds of thousands of dollars on a divorce on issues that can be 90% resolved in an hour or two through a targeted divorce negotiation

··············· **PRO TIP** ···············

Virtually all divorce issues can be resolved in somewhere between 4 and 8 hours of dedicated and focused time. Each side would prepare a balance sheet of all assets and liabilities and, armed with the law, can sit down and make an agreement regarding almost all property, custody and support issues. Only when people take extreme positions is this not possible. Most of the time, in my experience, when someone is taking an extreme position, it is the lawyer's fault for either a) not explaining the law to them (and the Range of Normal Outcomes) or b) posturing in order to increase the lawyer's fee. This book is meant to be the antidote to both.

··

Although it is true that courts are leaning more toward shared custody and that women have more earning power in the market than ever before, men still largely pay support and women still largely have majority custody of the children. Men still largely want to keep their pensions/retirements and women still largely want the family home. Men still largely ask for more time with their children, while women try to juggle work and children.

I believe that men and women take different positions in a divorce because they feel different things from the divorce. Where a man (or the more masculine partner) feels that he is losing his family, a woman (or the more feminine partner) feels that she is losing her protector and provider. These "gender" roles are more about the masculine and feminine way-of-being in the relationship, than they are about whether someone has a particular body part, but I see this play out over and over: men fighting for more time with their children; women fearful of being bullied or not having enough resources to keep a home for their children. This may well be the subject of a future book. For now, suffice it to say, this book focuses on what a divorce outcome will and should look like and how to get there quickly and while minimizing your investment in attorney time and resources.

The example I gave above involved a man, but this is a book for both sexes. The lessons taught are as directly relevant to a woman (or to the person who feels they have lost their protector and provider and does not want to get bullied) as they are to a man (or to a person who feels like they have lost their family and reasons for providing). Throughout the book I attempt to use either gender-neutral language, or to move back and forth between genders in my hypotheticals and my case examples. Rarely is gender truly important to my case examples.

I also note that in the several years of drafts of this book, there have been several new developments in family law. The family law is an interesting place for an academic like me to have found himself being a practitioner because "the family" always leads the nation in new developments. We are constantly evolving our social mores and understandings of the role families play in our lives.

In the first year of my family law career, in 2008, same-sex marriage became the law of the land, we had already begun dealing with surrogacy, in vitro fertilization (who gets the fertilized eggs after a divorce?), the increase in awareness and understanding of domestic abuse to include "coercive control" and other non-physical types of abuse. Since 2008, we have seen a development of family law in many new arenas – transgenderism, polyamorism, the entire pandemic and the isolation of children from peers that has created not only a massive online presence for our children but also lead to increasing mental health disorders, the aforementioned awareness of domestic abuse, the challenges to reproductive rights and concerns, and the rise in 3-parent children (a same sex couple with an egg or sperm donor).

A Description of the Book

I have been proud to be a family lawyer. Lawyers do not typically view family lawyers with the respect they are due – we are a "necessary evil," the "ghetto of the law," right down in the lower regions of Hades with the ambulance chasers and medical malpractice lawyers (no offense meant, people). But this area of the law is so rich with development and intrigue that it has necessitated a book-length work to help the 50% of the population of this entire country who will come into contact with the court system through the ending of their marriage.

Part I of this book is an overview of Family Law on a conceptual level so that you can understand the court's role in your divorce, should an agreement be impossible. Knowing this information will help you to negotiate with your soon-to-be ex-spouse.

Divorce is a legal Three Act Play with a beginning, middle, and end; it is much more scripted than you can imagine. I always tell my clients that their divorce is unique to them, but it is not unique to the players (their lawyer, opposing counsel and the judge) who work in family law for a living. To us, the divorce falls into a category and categories tend to have similar outcomes. I can be surprised by an outcome, but I know the vast majority of outcomes almost in the first 30 minutes of a consultation.

The book teaches what a reasonable offer is. It borrows from the academic literature of Law and Society to teach how to understand "bargaining in the Shadow of the Law" – that is, negotiating in such a way that you understand what the law says to do and what a judge will likely do if you cannot reach an agreement. It helps you to understand where your risks are if you don't reach an agreement and when you're on the cusp of making a good or bad deal for yourself. It teaches you about the Range of Normal Outcomes, the

Rule of Reasonability, and the Three Property Rules in Family Law—all as approaches to understanding reasonable settlement positions.

I also provide some techniques for deciding what things you will not surrender and what things you should be willing to negotiate away. I liken this to a white flower with a red center (I got this image from a talk given by a senior lawyer and it has stuck with me since – I cannot remember his name and I have searched for it everywhere, but I do want to give him the credit for it). The red center is what you must never trade away, and the white petals are everything else. This is an easy image to recall as you go through your divorce, and it will help you remain focused on the outcome you seek without getting sidetracked by your ex and their attorney who will try to provoke you with red herrings. Go after the red center, trade away the white petals, and drive, drive, drive to conclusion. Worth noting, you can "win" the divorce and not get taken advantage of if you get the thing(s) you want most, even if it's less than 50% (in fact, sometimes this is the easiest and most powerful "win" you can get).

I use the principal, "give a little to get a lot" to help you see that there are times when giving up a percentage or two (of your 50%) to settle a case is worth it (as long as you get the things you care about most), and I try to remind people something I have come to see repeatedly, which is:

There is a Value to Being Done, and only you know what that value is.

I am calling this point out in the introductory section of the book and will repeat it later, because it is one of the most important concepts in the book and is a corollary to the overall lesson: get your divorce done as quickly as possible without being taken advantage of. There may be a cost to you of finishing quickly (the last $10,000 in reimbursements, a fight over the $5,500 Suburban that no one drives anymore, the antique credenza that is still in the living room, etc.).

But you will be done with your case.

No more lawyers, no more court, no more cranky text messages with your ex, and no more uncertainty. Surely your peace is worth a few dollars.

In other words, there is a time to quit litigating or negotiating, no matter what your circle of confidants and champions (including your lawyer) tells you. If the price of your sanity or your life is walking away from $20,000 or the extra 12 hours a week with your children, only you can answer whether that is a deal you can live with. But do the real cost-benefit analysis to help you get to the right answer, and include into the equation the sleepless nights, the anger you hold that keeps you from forming a new romantic relationship, the toll on your children, and your performance at work. Some people are "wired" for litigation; most are not. That is why I strongly suggest that the high-earner is nearly always best-served by resolving the matter as quickly as possible even at a cost of leaving some money on the table (without giving up the red center) and especially if you have the wherewithal to make more money. The best you will do when you fight over old money is get 50 cents on every dollar. When you focus on new money, you get to keep 100 cents of every dollar.

Your lawyer will almost assuredly want you to keep pushing (as long as you are paying your bill). Your friends, parents, and siblings will want you to keep going, to "fight for your kids," or to get everything you possibly can to right some perceived wrong, or to "stick it to your ex." But your divorce is ultimately about you, and only you know the personal toll of litigation. Only you can determine whether you can keep fighting or whether it is time to call it off.

The main goal of the book is to help you stay out of court by teaching you the law so that you can negotiate from a position of strength.

I believe that every family law case can and should be settled through targeted divorce negotiation. I do not really believe in traditional divorce mediation or Collaborative Law because I believe that discussions of "fairness" or "what do you want?" fail at least one if not both of the parties and always tend to favor the more aggressive, more stubborn, and least willing to bend person in the marriage. The abuser continues to abuse. The victim continues to be victimized.

But, even with this conceit, I take advanced courses in negotiation and mediation because I believe that many people believe traditional mediation (two parties, one mediator, no lawyers), can work. And so, because at least some people reading this book will be mediators or in mediation, I do not want to alienate them. I think we can do better than traditional mediation, and I think the way we do that will emerge from better knowledge of the conceptual framework of the law. Your settlement in your divorce should not come from sheer exhaustion of resources, will, and emotional bandwidth.

Part II of the book focuses on Negotiation Strategies. Having a working knowledge of the law and demanding that your settlement negotiations center around what would happen if you went to Court (that is, "bargaining in the shadow of the law") will not only save you tens of thousands (or more) dollars in attorney's fees and in your ultimate settlement, but will also save you from a lifetime of second-guessing or feeling like you got "screwed in the divorce." I will talk about understanding your BCATNA (Best Case Alternative to a Negotiated Agreement) which is what happens if you go to court and win literally all your claims. And I discuss what I call your WCATNA (Worst Case Alternative to a Negotiated Agreement) which is what happens if you go to court and lose literally all your claims. The term "BATNA" was coined by two Harvard professors who wrote *Getting to Yes*, the seminal book on negotiations that I cannot recommend highly enough. I add the "C" which makes for a bulky acronym, because unlike the two Harvard professors, who were writing about what will happen if you don't make an agreement, I want you to see that there is a range of outcomes, from the BCATNA to the WCATNA. In *Getting to Yes*, the focus is largely on the pain of litigation as a potential outcome – that litigation itself is the punishment. Most civil cases also have only one winner and one loser – in divorce cases, both parties typically lose at trial and because divorce law across the country divides assets roughly equally, both end up with something. Traditional concepts of BATNA don't "map on" perfectly well to divorce litigation. Also, because divorce cases can be litigated in shorter trials than most of the civil litigation type environments described in their book, we are more likely to have trials, so we need to develop a range of potential outcomes so that you can see what might happen at trial.

BCATNA in any divorce negotiation is the Range of Normal Outcomes tempered by the Rule of Reasonability and the Three Property Rules in Family Law. If you know your BCATNA/WCATNA, you will always know the range within which your case will land if you fail to reach an agreement during negotiations. You should never have to take a bad deal, but you should also know when you are being unreasonable. In other words, you should be able to tell the difference between whether a deal is "bad" or just "feels bad."

Good negotiators listen.

I will tell a client before a first round of negotiation that we are on a "listening tour," simply asking questions and letting the other side disclose their bargaining positions. Once we have listened, we can almost always figure out how to come to an agreement on most issues. Listening to your soon-to-be-ex-spouse may not be your strong suit. Just hearing their bullshit may turn you off or drive you to want to walk out of the room, but if you listen, you can begin to hear what they want most of all. To the extent that they want things that you do not care about, you put yourself in a position to make deals.

The negotiations chapters have some exercises that will help you understand your red-center and your white petals. The more substantive chapters will help you understand your BCATNA-WCATNA range, and what will happen if you decide not to negotiate and instead go to trial.

Part II is also where I describe my interpretation of "mindfulness." I spent more than a decade researching the "mindful" behaviors of fighter pilots, nuclear power plant operators, air traffic controllers, and nuclear weapons scientists for my doctoral dissertation and post-doctoral graduate work. These are people of intense focus who are mindful at work because people get killed if they aren't. I want you to develop a sort of laser mindfulness as you read this book and negotiate your case.

Mindful behavior in that context has a more nuanced meaning than our popular culture vision of "mindfulness." I discuss how you can bring this level of focus to your negotiations.

················ PRO TIP ················

Here's my plug for my own daily meditation practice but don't think I come across too heavy-handed about it. I put on the binaural beats on my headphones for 20-30 minutes a day to clear my mind so that I can focus; I sit in the infrared sauna I bought myself after winning a major case; I let my brain calm down as much as possible and breathe. I do that for 20-30 minutes until the searing heat of the sauna overcomes the only peaceful time in my day. Then I put my suit on and go to work with an internal fire stoked and burning within me.

If you don't have a sauna, take a walk. It's free. It's easy. And even if you are overweight and overworked, your body can almost assuredly handle it. Find a nature preserve or a park and walk around it for 30 minutes. If you are mad, yell and stomp. If you are sad, cry. Use those 30 minutes a day to get out as much of that emotion as you can. I think you'll find that the more you walk, the less of that emotion you will feel and the more "peace" you will get. You need peace in your brain to hone your laser focus. Peace, in this context, does not mean hippie pacifism, it means: a space in your brain for quiet contemplation without the overpowering emotions: anger, sadness, shame, guilt that can cloud your judgment and lead you into making a bad deal for yourself.

By way of personal disclosure, I had 7 months between my first custody hearing and my second with my child. I spent almost every waking minute of all of those 7 months thinking about what I was going to tell the judge. I experienced a whole gamut of emotions during that time. None of them productive. My romantic relationships during that time were all short-lived failures full of clouded judgment and bad behavior. My work suffered. I didn't write anything productive and I didn't learn anything new. My diet sucked. I drank too much. In short, I was a walking damned disaster. I did not have my infrared sauna and I had no objectivity on the situation (and I did not have a lawyer). So, just, for lack of anything sharper to say about it, don't do what I did.

• •

Writing this book, representing a client in a courtroom, working on an appeal or sitting around a conference table during a settlement conference, each calls for mindful focus. I suggest in the book that you learn from the folks who must be mindful or people get killed. Skim that chapter if the concept annoys you.

Part III gives you the view from the dirt. This is where I discuss the broad strokes of the law: custody and visitation of minor children, child and spousal support, and property division. I will provide an overview of those areas of the law so you can make informed decisions. In Part III, I will also repeatedly refer back to the Range of Normal, the Rule of Reasonability, and the Three Property Rules of Family Law, and how they all correspond to your BCATNA-WCATNA and to your red center. They all fit together neatly.

Finally, Part IV gives insight into how to conduct yourself either in a negotiation or in a courtroom. It gives practical strategies for representing yourself or representing a client.

PART 1

Divorce: An Overview

CHAPTER 1

Divorce Happens in Three Acts

THERE IS A script off which the legal aspects of a divorce always play out. The legal parts of a divorce occur in three acts. Act I is the petition and the first temporary orders. Act II is the financial disclosures. Act III is the resolution through trial or settlement. These three acts, in California, take at least 6 months to play out because California has a "cooling off" period of 6 months from filing to dissolution of the marriage. But there is no reason these three acts cannot play out quickly and decisively. In really extreme cases, I have had motivated clients, with assets and children, push through all three acts in two months and they just wait for the final decree of divorce for four months. I have also, like so many divorce lawyers, had cases drag on for years (recently I helped settle a case that took 13 years from first filing to final resolution – but I was only involved in the last year or so).

The script for the three acts is essentially the same in every case. If you know that going in, you know how it needs to be done. How you choose to do it and how long each act takes is a process of negotiation between you, your soon-to-be-ex and the lawyers and judges involved. But, we can be sure that cases that don't settle take at least a year longer to resolve than the ones that do. My experience is that cases that go to trial result in almost exactly the same outcomes as a reasoned targeted divorce negotiated outcome, within a small margin of error. As one of my senior colleagues often says to me: "what do I need a judge for? I know more about the law and how it works in practice for my clients than they do. And I actually give a shit about my clients." He is very far from wrong.

Act I: The Petition and the First (Temporary) Orders

Act I is the filing of the initial Petition (sometimes called a Complaint) for divorce (in legal terms: "Petition for Dissolution of Marriage" or "Complaint for Dissolution of Marriage"). The Petition states that a person is requesting a divorce. It may also, if applicable, request spousal and child support, the division of the assets and debts, and may include a request for attorney's fees. Most people ask for support, attorney's fees and an unfair division of assets in their initial Petition. If you get served by your soon-to-be-ex and it says this, don't let this anger you. That's totally normal and it's likely nowhere near the ultimate outcome. Often, lawyers file these "winner-takes-all" Petitions for Dissolution of Marriage to make their clients feel like they are fighting for them. They know that this will never be the outcome, unless you never respond to the Petition. If you don't respond, well, if you don't respond, what your spouse asked for will be your outcome.

Act I continues with requests for temporary orders, usually filed in a separate (but often attached) "motion" or "request for order" or "notice of hearing." The temporary orders can also be called *"pendente lite"* ("pen-DEN-tay LEE-tay") orders, which is Latin for "pending litigation." These are extremely important and if you only have limited money, spending it on *pendente lite* orders is usually the wisest investment.

Act I also includes the "Response to (and Request for) Dissolution or Marriage," sometimes called an "Answer." This is the other party's response to your request for a divorce, or your response to their request for a divorce. In California, the form allows you to check a box requesting a divorce along with your response to their request. A divorce is unlike most other types of litigation, which allow you to answer a Complaint filed against you, but do not provide a way for you to sue back. In civil litigation if you want to sue back you must file your own separate Cross-Complaint, which is your way of saying, "I have my own complaints about the person suing me as well."

In a California divorce, you do not have to file a separate request for a divorce. You can simply file a response, and in your response make your own request for a divorce. Meaning that once you file a Response to (and Request for) Dissolution of Marriage in California, you have also requested that your marriage end in divorce.

If your spouse has a change of heart and decides they no longer want a divorce, they must seek your permission to dismiss the divorce filing. You can still pursue the divorce even if they decide they no longer want to. In California it only takes one person to request a divorce. At the very end of the marriage, your lawyer or the judge may ask you a series of questions to determine whether you want to be divorced. I have had people two years into a divorce believing they were ready to end their marriage only to answer, "No" to my question, "Do you wish to be divorced today and be returned to the status of a single person?" I have also had a tearful client begging the judge not to grant her husband's request for a divorce. The Judge gently pointed out (and not entirely without acknowledgment of her emotion) that in California it takes only one party to request a divorce for it to be granted. The other party does not have to "sign off on the divorce" or "sign the papers" or "agree to give a divorce" or any of the things you see in the movies.

Typically, the responding party sees the initial Petition for Dissolution of Marriage and freaks out:

"She wants what?!?! You are telling me she wants the house, the cars, the retirement, the kids full-time (sole legal and physical custody) and she wants child and spousal support too?!?! And for the pleasure of giving her everything we own or have made together she wants me to pay her lawyer's fees?!?!"

It is very easy to get lost in the first words filed in a divorce. This is normal. Both the request for everything and the response to it are completely normal. I urge you to spend 24 hours not even thinking about what is being officially "requested". Most people, including judges, never read the first filed document or "pleading" (lawyers call any filed document a "pleading") again. After the 24 hours has passed, take a deep breath, and think about it slowly. Then formulate the outcome you would like to have.

I am teaching you how to handle your divorce in a rational and sane manner to save you a boatload of attorneys' fees, and to help ensure that you leave your divorce with your assets (and your sanity for the most part) intact. You will need to work hard on being clinical about your responses to things your spouse does and not allow yourself to be swayed by the emotions that will naturally bubble to the surface. Your spouse knows your emotional buttons, and your spouse's lawyer is trained in how to push those emotional buttons in nearly everything they do.

Every divorce lawyer knows it is far easier to beat up an overly-emotional opposing party than it is to beat up a party who is calm, well-informed, and negotiating from a position of strength. They will try to rile you, attack your manhood (if you are a man) refer to you as a "deadbeat," allege violence that never occurred, threaten you with sanctions for bad behavior, demand you pay their attorney's fees, say you had an affair, say you were never there for your kids, ask the name of your kid's dentist and then when you don't know it (who does?) say that the mother is obviously the better parent. They will mock you for not making more money, and if you do earn a lot of money, ask why you are never home, etc. etc. etc. All of it is simply designed to torque you up. You get angry and see red, you say stupid things, and you appear to the judge like someone who cannot control their emotions. Find your mindfulness in Act I, particularly for the *pendente lite* orders stage of things.

Learn to blow off steam in some other manner than at your ex. My client who texted his ex that she was a "greedy bitch" saw that text blown up full-size on his first day in court. (Did it hurt him? No. The judge looked at it and said, "People say things in a divorce." Still, don't be him.)

················· PRO TIP ·················

The minute you get divorce papers, assume that the judge is the third party on every single text message you send. Speak the Queen's English to the best of your ability in each text message.

For God's sake do not post shitty things about your ex on social media, even if you block her from your postings. Chances are if you are like most of my clients you have 60+ common Facebook friends, and at least one of them will be ratting you out to her.

You can post about your personal pain, if you share that sort of thing online; you can post about how happy you are with your new girlfriend; you can post pictures of you and the kids doing insanely fun things that you could never do with your ex; you can post about all the new exercise you are doing and losing your beer belly or whatever; but running down your ex publicly is a recipe for having your ex's lawyer put it up on the overhead projector for a full courtroom of people. Maybe it won't hurt you, the way it didn't hurt my "greedy bitch" client, but then again maybe your judge won't be so forgiving.

···

I've had clients learn all sorts of ways of blowing off steam: one bought a Harley-Davidson and rode it up and down the freeway at full tilt; another bought a steel-framed road bicycle and started riding every day; one gentleman became a surfer; many others join a gym. Still more start Tinder dating and have sex with anyone who will take them. Unlike television programs like Big Little Lies, it is almost impossible that your sexual partners' faces will end up on a big screen in the courtroom, so don't unnecessarily worry about that. However, do be safe, as I have a select group of former clients who have become new fathers before their divorce was finalized. (They know who they are.).

That paragraph was geared toward men. Let this one be geared toward women. I have had women clients get new partners quickly, go on long Vegas weekends, and have wine parties. They take trips, join book clubs, work in the garden…and yes, just as much as the men, join Tinder and date and have sex and experience all of the things they were missing. They take Ozempic and join gyms. They try backpacking or go take mushrooms. They get therapy and become wicca for a little while (or forever).

I think it is harder for women who demand to have the kids full-time to get to feel "free," but even if they are only sharing the kids a little bit, they have traveled and had "divorce parties" and gone gambling and to clubs and had good experiences. Blowing of steam can come in so many ways. I love my child with all my heart. I mean, I would do anything for them, but that said, it is ok to leave the kids with Dad (or your parents or siblings) and get the f*ck out of town and do what you need to do to feel free for a few moments. Life is going to suck you back in. Take a minute and enjoy the freedom to do what you thought you were missing. I am a man and I am used to "man things" and I am a sensitive new age Berkeley man so I am very sensitive to gender generalizations and all of these examples seem so deeply gendered. In short, blow off steam, stay safe, have fun. At least for a little while until your life grabs you and drags you back in.

If you want to go to Vegas and get fall down drunk and have fun with a stranger or a (legal) sex worker or your best friend or your not-so-best-friend, go do it. Keep a low-profile for God's sake. And be the best parent you can be. The first few moments are alive with possibility. But, like I said, I have had a fair number of clients with new babies on the way not too far into their divorces. Maybe you would view that as a blessing. Maybe.

The most important thing is that whatever your outlet is, be a good parent to your children and do not put yourself in the position of having to explain why your kid busted his ribs riding an ATV at the age of 8, or why you were arrested for soliciting a prostitute, or why you blew a .26 at a DUI checkpoint. Think first. Be good to yourself.

The First Motion, Hearing, and Temporary (Pendente Lite) Orders: The First, and Most Important, Part of the Whole Divorce

Along with the initial divorce filing, you or your ex may also file an initial "motion" or "Order to Show Cause" or "Request for Orders" or "Notice of Hearing." California has changed the names of these several times in the last few years, settling most recently on Notice of Hearing, probably because it sounds more innocuous. They are all the same. A "motion," which most people have heard of, is basically a request that the Court do something—in other words "move." (In California you must wait six months to be divorced, so after you file the Petition for Dissolution of Marriage, nothing will happen other than the 6-month clock will begin to tick. Remember: the Court will do nothing unless you ask it to do something. You must "move" the Court by filing a "motion" by whatever name it is called.).

.... PRO TIP ....

Never underplay the importance of Act I. The first motion is possibly the most important motion of the whole divorce because it sets the tone for the Court's orders moving forward. If it goes against you, you will have to dig out from it. If it goes in your favor, things are yours to lose thereafter. Put everything you have into the first motion and do not hold back!

....

At the very beginning of a divorce it is not uncommon for the parties to be in chaos. Possibly one party has moved out and leased an apartment, leaving the other in the home paying a mortgage or lease payment they cannot afford on their own. There may be only a basic custody agreement where the kids are visiting the move-out parent's home. I hate the term "visitation" and will use the term I prefer ("timeshare") throughout the book whenever I can, but since California still calls it "visitation," I am forced to refer to it that way later in the book. Just know that I think "visitation" is an incredibly offensive term for what happens when the kids are with each parent.

There also may be a basic agreement regarding child support—usually if the parties are reasonable, both paychecks can go into the joint account for a couple of months with each party spending reasonably. The parties may even still live together in separate bedrooms. Sometimes they start to talk about how to divide things up. There is a little bit of conversation about what the divorce might look like. Almost always these informal "divisions" of assets, time with the children, and financial support are incorrect as a matter of law and are usually deeply unfair to one or both of the parties. Wives offer to give their husbands their pensions ("oh, I'd never take your pension that you worked so hard for"), they agree to too large or infinitesimally small timeshares with the children ("I'm the mom and they should sleep at home in their own beds every single night with me" "OK, as long as I get to see them a couple nights a week"), too large or too small support payments ("I refuse to pay spousal support, but I will give you $100 per month per kid"), etc. Both parties mean well but they are on the wrong track, and once the agreements start to fail, as they inevitably will, they seek the help of a lawyer.

•••••••••••••••• PRO TIP ••••••••••••••••

Most of the time these types of pre-lawyer, pre-divorce filing agreements try to please both parties to keep the peace rather than addressing what will or will not work. A divorce lawyer is often invaluable for teaching about the types of custody plans that work for parents, such as 2-2-5 or 2-2-3 with younger kids, alternate weeks for older kids, extended Friday-Monday weekends with a midweek overnight, alternate weekends for a busy working parent, short visits for infants or parents who have mental health or substance abuse problems, etc. Often custody plans fail because people do not understand the ramifications of the plans they make.

Example: A Google executive and her big law firm partner husband, both living in the Silicon Valley, agreed that their son would "sleep in his own bed" (at mom's house) every night, but that he would visit with dad every day for 4 hours "so that both parents were raising him together."

I pointed out to the dad that that meant seeing his ex-wife every single day. Twice, in fact!

I also pointed out that when mom inevitably got a job out of the area (which she did at Amazon in Seattle two years later) Dad would have visitation 28 hours out of 168 hours per week. Even though he was spending quality after school time with his son, it was only a 16% custody share (28/168) and he would never be able to stop a move to Seattle (or anywhere else – generally anything less than about 40% timeshare – in California, she has a statutory right to move away). Plans like this "every-day-for-4-hours" generally work for a few months and then break down as people get new paramours, or want to take trips out of town, or begin arguing about money. Divorcing couples no longer want to see each other daily. The "everyday plan" was a good one—it would allow each of the parents to be involved with the child while least disrupting the child's schedule—but it was horribly unfair for the Father in a jurisdiction that would have given him a 50-50 order that would have at least kept the son in California if Mother accepted a job out of state.

· ·

The shared bank account plan also works for a month or two before it starts to fall apart. It is best used in a case like the following: *Example: Father moves out of a rental home that Mother cannot afford on her own. There are 3 months left on their lease. The children are living in the rental house most of the time until the lease is up; while Father figures out where he is going to live longer term, the apartment property being a little too small for all of them to be there half the time. The parties share a bank account (Father's earnings are now technically separate property because they are earned after separation). Mother spends reasonably from that account, rather than immediately filing for a spousal and child support order. They share this account until the lease ends and each of them gets a new place to live and they know how much it will cost each of them to live – or sometimes, Mother is looking for a job to help provide support and Father provides additional income by sharing his paycheck until she does so.*

There are many "ifs" in that scenario, but it can work on a short-term basis and often is the smart person's way to resolve very short-term money issues. It saves an emergency motion for child and spousal support that can cost much more money and avoids needless spending on results that will almost assuredly require Husband to pay Wife the equivalent of what she is already reasonably spending out of that joint account.

Since money is a common reason for divorce, parties normally don't want to continue sharing their money. It is amicable in the first two months or so while the parties are trying to figure out how the income(s) that supported one family unit are now going to support two family units. Both parties share the same bank accounts for a short period of time so that neither panics about the mortgage or the car insurance being paid.

On the other hand, equally common is for the higher earner to open a new bank account and start depositing their paycheck into that account. Often the higher earner moves out, leaving the lower earner with the children and the bills, and no money to feed the kids or pay the bills. The higher earner tries to control the lower earner with money, doling it out in dribs and drabs, letting them know who is boss. They start demanding to have the children more because the lower earner cannot afford to buy basic things for the children (like food or paying the water bill) saying, "Well, she can't even take care of herself, much less the kids, so I guess I'll have to take them, too." The lower earner learns to fight back, usually spurred on by a friend who has been through a divorce, such as a sister, a mother, or sometimes even a crew of brothers. They drag her into the attorney's office and say, "What can be done?"

In either situation, or anything in between, the lawyer quickly drafts and files an Emergency (or Ex Parte, pronounced ex PAR-tay) Notice of Hearing (Motion), which includes a declaration with the entire tale of woe. In the motion the spouse asks for child support, spousal support, and custody and visitation orders. They may also ask for attorney's fees and to have exclusive use of certain property, like the family home. (You'd be surprised how many people move out and believe they can come and go from the house as often as they would like – and now, increasingly, they want to keep the outdoor video cameras going so they can see who comes and goes from "their" house). They may also request that one party pay one-half of the ongoing bills.

In California, unless there is an emergency (ex parte), the court will address this motion in a hearing, 30 days plus 5 for mailing, plus a few days (normally a total of 35-40 days) after the motion is filed. The motion must be served to the other party, who will have a chance to respond to it with their own tale of woe. The court will then haul both parties into court 35-40 days after the motion is filed—often after there has been a court-sanctioned mediation over custody and visitation—and hold the first hearing. In California, the court cannot make custody and visitation orders without there having been a mediation beforehand.

Custody mediation gets short shrift in this section, but I talk a little more about it later in the custody chapter. The basics are that both parties go without a lawyer. In some counties children over 6 years old go with the parents, while, in other counties, children over 12 years old go and in some counties children don't go at all. In some counties mediation is confidential (meaning if there is no agreement reached the only communication from the mediator to the court is that there was no agreement) and in other counties mediators report to the judge their observations and "recommendations" for custody and visitation.

If you are in a recommending county, mediation becomes extremely important and so you want to make sure you are calm and polite to the mediator – I cover this in much more detail in the last chapter on how to comport yourself in court, but the shortest version of that entire chapter can be summed up in a sentence: treat courthouse staff, including court mediators, judges, bailiffs, courtroom clerks, and court reporters kindly and respectfully; everything you do in court is being watched by the decision-maker (judge) and staff people talk to each other, especially about people who are rude.

After the mediation, assuming there is no agreement between the parties, there will be an initial hearing on custody, timeshare, temporary child and spousal support and attorney's fees. After this initial hearing, the court will make temporary, or *pendente lite*, orders.

These orders may be "temporary," but they play a huge role in the rest of the case. I repeat, if you have limited funds available to you and you cannot negotiate your way out of the first motion by making some temporary agreements, and you must hire a lawyer, then hire the lawyer for the first hearing. I cannot stress enough the importance of being "rational" before the first pendente lite motions are filed. Rational in this sense can mean overpaying a little, giving a little ground, making sure that you are not responding to a motion on very little time. 35-40 days is a blink of an eye and you will likely live with the orders made at that first hearing until your divorce is final and sometimes much longer than that. This is why I say to make agreements wherever possible.

By the way, I cannot stand so-called "recommending" counties on custody and visitation. I think settlement communications should be confidential; in fact the California evidence code requires that settlement communications remain confidential. In a recommending county, a mediator (often a therapist) meets you and your spouse for an hour or two and then "recommends" to the judge what the custody schedule should be if you don't agree. Because judicial resources are limited (meaning judges are very busy and there aren't enough minutes in the day for each judge to give each party their full due), judges rely on the recommending mediators to tell them what the custody schedule should be in the short-term. You might try to fight it, but fighting a recommending mediator's recommendation is an uphill battle. That is why it is supremely important that before this first mediation (if you are in a recommending county), you talk to a local divorce lawyer and get some advice or you make it a point to be calm and kind in that mediation.

The first hearing is where the judge meets you for the first time; it is where the judge reads the declarations for the first time; it is where the judge starts making determinations about who will live in the family home and who will pay the mortgage, or whether to list the home for sale. The court will make temporary orders about where and how the children will spend their time, who will pay for health insurance, and how to divide certain assets and debts. Sometimes there are domestic violence restraining orders filed in Act I (Act I is most likely time for domestic violence restraining order requests, because people are still living together and seeing each other regularly at a time when they are not getting along).

These orders are called "temporary orders," because sometimes the Judge will rule without even giving you an evidentiary hearing (an evidentiary hearing is one where the judge swears you in by raising your right hand and listens to you answer questions like a trial you see on TV), which is why it is very important that you write good declarations and portray yourself in the most reasonable manner possible. You must take all precautions in the first hearing of Act I. Oftentimes, if there is a second (or third or fourth) hearing in Act I, it is because a party is attempting to dig themselves out of a hole they dug in the first hearing.

Remember: it is vitally important that a) you learn how to write a declaration and b) that you know how to portray yourself.)

.... PRO TIP ....

Divorce winners are reasonable actors. They write reasonable (but powerful) advocacy pieces in the form of Declarations, and they carry themselves in court in such a way as to give the Court the deference and respect it deserves as the judicial branch of the government.

For example, one does not write, "He has been a terrible dad ever since he started binge drinking and failing to show up four years ago. Ezra (age 8) is still mad and doesn't want to see him."

Instead one writes, "I am cautiously optimistic that David has been in recovery from his alcoholism. He has moved out of his mother's home, where he had been for the last 4 years, and he has a girlfriend whom I like and think is good for Ezra. However, there were many years of missed pickups and late drop-offs, months of unemployment, and times when we simply could not predict whether David was going to show up drunk or sober. Ezra loves his dad and I am happy for that. But just last week, 8-year-old Ezra spent 34 minutes waiting for his dad to pick him up from school. The school called me, and I was forced to leave work early to pick him up. Then on Tuesday his girlfriend picked Ezra up for the dinner visit, and David did not make it home before she had to drop him off at 7:30 PM.

I want to believe, as I did so many times during the marriage, that David is getting his act together, but Ezra deserves to be able to trust that his dad will be there when he says he will. I think the best thing is not a 50-50 schedule, but an alternate weekend schedule from Friday at 6 PM to Sunday at 6 PM. I can get Ezra from school and get him ready for the weekend, and then his dad can call whenever he is off work and swing by and pick him up (or I can drop him off)."

What makes this declaration particularly nasty is the way in which it cautiously praises the father, lets the court know that the mother is not threatened by the new girlfriend (and in fact left Ezra with her even though the father was not home from work) and that she wants him to succeed. It also proposes an alternate plan for visitation than the plan the dad wants.

I have an opinion of every judge in front of whom I have practiced. Not all the opinions are good, but I take the view that my oath was to the Constitution and the country, and that the flags that hang behind the judicial bench represent the American legal system, not an individual in a black robe. Chances are that if your divorce has been ongoing and you find yourself staring at the flags behind the judge, your opinion of your case will not be the brightest, but I believe the American judicial system is generally fair and unbiased, and about as good a system as you will find anywhere in the world.

Note: I say the "American judicial system" and not "all courtrooms run by all judges." I also do not say "any one particular courtroom run by any one particular judge." The reality is that you are dealing with conscious or unconscious bias every time you stand in front of the judge. Since judges are people too, it is important to bear in mind that they have their own internal biases, and like anyone else they tend to favor people they like.

In a divorce the likeable person is the person who demonstrates "reasonability." Judges hate to watch former couples fight over miniscule things. When you write a declaration saying, "I want more time with my children and, if, to get it, my child support payment will not decrease, so be it," or you write a declaration saying, "I will accept any valuation between $25,000 and $35,000," or you say, "It makes the most sense for Wife to live in the family home because it is near the children's school," the Judge will listen to you. You are being reasonable and trying to solve problems. If you write "I want the children more so I can pay less support" or "I want the highest value for the property" or "Sell the house immediately no matter what the cost of living is for my ex-wife," the Judge will think you are unreasonable.

When you carry yourself in a respectful posture toward the court, acting the way lawyers should act, such as respecting what the flag stands for, never using the word "liar" (as in "Judge she is *lying!*") addressing the Judge as "your Honor," allowing the other person to finish talking even if you think they are spewing bullshit, and dressing appropriately. You do not have to wear a suit, but you should wear your cleanest work uniform, cleaned and polished cowboy boots – common where I live – or other respectfully clean and recently ironed clothing. Do not talk over your lawyer or try to address the court yourself by interrupting the Judge or the other party. You are showing the Judge that you are well-behaved and respectful, and that you can follow orders. The Judge is watching your behavior.

When it is called for, I will drop the cadence and rhythm of my voice to suggest that my client is as calm as can be. I will reserve outbursts in front of the Court for moments when I determine that too much has been said in a negative light about my client, or to show the Court that I seriously disagree with a statement or action. If you represent yourself, you should never, ever have an outburst in front of the judge. I can do it because I have almost 20 years of working with the same group of judges. They know me as a "repeat player" and understand that when I ask for something in my big boy voice there is a reason for it. You will just come off as angry, impudent, and unwilling to follow orders. Judges hate it most when their orders are violated.

You want to be the person the judge knows is reasonable and will follow orders.

Your declarations should convey this energy and emotion in them. Do not be afraid to write something nice about your ex in your declaration. All too often declarations are acid-filled, attacking the other party and featuring them in the worst light. These backfire more than they are successful. The reality is that most "other parents" are not bad people or even bad parents; they are just different from you. Acknowledge the differences and focus on what you bring to the table—why you should be in the family home; why the kids should live with you more than the other parent, why you are currently unemployed and what your approach to finding a new job will be; or why a computer-generated order for child or spousal support is necessary or unnecessary.

If you have minor children, in the first hearing ask for more time with them. My view: we should live in a 50-50 child custody world by default (unless there are drugs, crimes, abuse, mental illness, jail time, or very young or very late teenaged children). Focus on *your* parenting. Always, always, always focus on *your* parenting. Not on why the other parent is shitty, but why *you* are a good parent. You aren't defending your parenting. You are writing a letter of recommendation for yourself. Focus on the things you do well as a parent, the bonds you have with your children, your involvement in extra-curricular activities, the cooking class you took, or the things you do together. If you have 50-50 custody of your children, most of the rest of the pieces will come together.

That bears repeating. If you have 50-50 custody of your children, most of the rest of the pieces will come together.

• •

Sadly, Act I can sometimes drag on for months or even years if the parties continue fighting each other . . . or worse, fighting the court's orders.

For the high earner, the goal must always be to get out of Act I as quickly as possible (with a reasonable custody timeshare; 50-50 custody of your children if you can get it but no less than 35-65) but without making huge sacrifices. If you want your kids with you at least half the time, you must fight that out in Act I. By the time Act III rolls around—the next time you address custody and visitation—chances are you will be fighting against the power of inertia and the orders will remain from Act I.

A lot happens in Act I. But I repeat: If you only have $2,500 to spend on a lawyer, spend it on Act I.

Trying to "fix" what broke in Act I will cost you much more money in the long run. Mediocre lawyers (which most are) won't be able to fix what got broken in Act I. Great lawyers can fix it, but great lawyers are expensive and even *they* are going to have to work hard to fix broken Act I orders. Great lawyers know that – even when you lose – you may still be able to gain ground. A great lawyer will plan for a "double jump" in custody – Year 1, alternate weekends and a mid-week overnight with an admonition to the Judge that you have always sought and will continue to seek a 50-50 schedule. Year 2, after proving that Year 1 is successful (using the fact that you've never missed a single visit, that the report cards look strong, school attendance is good, your new home is close to the child's school, your mom or your girlfriend (or dad or boyfriend) are nearby and involved, etc., is the year you push for the expansion of your timeshare. Use Year 1 to gather data and then in Year 2, push for what you want. That's the double-jump strategy. Sometimes you need a "triple jump" especially when children are under-2 years old at the beginning of the divorce. Short, frequent visits with a toddler, followed by timeshare expansion in the three years post-toddling, with a 50-50 in kindergarten through high school. That's the "triple jump" approach.

I generally think that the best early agreements for timeshare have a double or triple jump approach that gives the "out-parent" hoops to jump through ("out parent" here just means the parent who wants 50-50 but does not have it). If the out-parent does so successfully, the default is that the timeshare expands. If they fail, which many unfortunately do, their timeshare does not expand. This is a way that, as a father of younger children who was perhaps not as involved in early childhood development as the mother was, you can prove that you are capable of handling the increased timeshare and parenting on your own. As a mother who may have had more of the parenting load early on, you might use this approach to keep the father from immediately making the jump to 50-50 – its an agreement that says, "you can have 50-50 after you've had a year or two of 20-80 or 35-65." Then, if he does what he says he will do, you expand his timeshare. If he does not, then you have new data you can show the court that says he did not meet his commitments to the children and you. By the way, I have had all different timeshares with my child and I think 35-65 and 50-50 are not demonstrably different.

You have to give them hope (or have to have hope) or else you run the risk of losing the children's other parent. If you cut them out of the child's life too early and too often, they eventually start new families or move away, you have a hard time collecting child support, they blame you for taking their children from them, your children hate the other parent until one day they start hating you. And if they decide later in life that you were the reason that their other parent left the scene, they may never forgive you.

This discussion may seem a bit down the road, but if you are planning to get through Act I quickly and with the goal of not going back to court umpteen times (at $3,000-$5,000 per court date), you want to get good temporary orders, which means good for you, but also not so bad for your spouse that they will not be able to accept them. In other words, you want *reasonable* temporary orders.

Act I financial orders can be tough whether there are children or not. If you are the high earner, chances are you will be paying support. Not even the most brilliant family lawyers can get you out of a computer-generated support payment. Good lawyers minimize the damage on the "Dissomaster" (the computer program that calculates support) by increasing your timeshare with the children and providing your spouse opportunities to work. That is, the more your spouse has the children, the less they can work and the less they earn, the more you pay in support.

Generally, any one of the Dissomaster input variables (and there are 30 or so of them) that increases cash to you (exemptions, mortgage interest deductions, pre-tax health insurance, pre-tax 401(k) payments, etc.) increases your support payment. Anything that decreases cash to you (mandatory retirement, health insurance premiums, new spouse income that kicks you up a tax bracket, union dues, etc.) decreases your support payment.

If you do not have children and are facing spousal support orders only, this is where making agreements is helpful. In fact, if there are no minor children consider offering to deposit your paycheck into a joint account at the earliest stages of the divorce and allow reasonable spending. (This will take some analysis, so initially just consider it.) Here's why. If you get hit with a *pendente lite* spousal support number generated by the computer, you probably won't like it. Even worse, the Court will use that number as a baseline number in Act III, and even though the Court is not permitted to use the computer to create a final Judgment-spousal support number, no judge can resist the temptation to use that number as a baseline for the calculation of spousal support after the divorce is final. I try to get a reduction of 35% from Act I support in Act III if I represent the payor spouse, and a 20% reduction from Act I support in Act III if I represent the payee spouse. In other words, we are hinging our final numbers off the computer number.

If your ex is not a huge spender, it might be cheaper to let them simply live off the bank account. On the other hand, there are many people who realize that paying a set amount of support each month will make them better off because their spouse is a spender. Do the math and consider which one works best for you.

However, in general, if you are the high earner, try to stay away from Act I orders and make a deal around them without the Judge's input – it is usually cheaper to do it that way and you do not face the possibility that a judge will make an order you do not like and are stuck with for a long time. It is imperative to learn the range of possible support numbers so that you know what the low and high ends are (BCATNA/WCATNA). If the other party has a lawyer, you will need to make an offer on the low end of (but well-within) the Range of Normal support Outcomes to stop the possibility of support being ordered on the high end of the range by a judge who sides against you.

·················· PRO TIP ··················

If you discover a range of potential spousal support numbers from $700-$1,400, you might make an offer of $900. It's a little higher than if you win all issues and get a $700 order, but it is within the Range of Normal Outcomes that the other lawyer will have to consider. And it will save you $500 per month against a possible bad outcome in which your spouse wins all issues. Plus, if you are the support payer, there is a chance that this will come with an attorney's fees order, since you outearn your spouse.

··

Act I for Men

If you are the high earner and a man, you must assume the judge is going to rule against you in Act I, and work accordingly to minimize the amount of damage caused by those orders. Men who are low-earners also often lose in Act I. In fact, it is a sad fact that, with many judges, men lose in Act I and then give up when they could gain considerable ground in Act II by faithfully following Act I orders.

For the male high-earner, this sometimes means paying a little more than you would like. For the male low-earner (which is the most difficult place to be in a divorce with children), you have to demonstrate your compliance with court orders in order to make up ground in Act II. In Act I, judges tend to rule against high earners and/or men when it comes to support. The support rules were designed for that purpose. Give it everything you've got to get that number down as low as possible, including agreeing to pay higher numbers than you want, to ensure you don't get hit with a really high number. This is called "risk management;" all of the academic studies show that humans are really bad at risk management; we tend to think we are going to win all issues. That's why people go to trial rather than settling. But judges have so much discretion in temporary order-making that you cannot, for a second, believe that you are going to get everything you want all of the time. That is why you should learn the Range of Normal Outcomes and make agreements within that range.

If you have minor children, in Act I, you should never, ever give up time that you want with your children to pacify your spouse. It is extremely difficult to get time back with your children, especially if you are a man. In fact, the very best time to get a 50-50 custody order as a father is in the very first hearing – again, judges are biased human beings – but like any person who is supposed to be unbiased, judges try to start each case out as though they do not have any biases.

After the case gets going, judges start suffering from "confirmation biases" that allow them to confirm, by your (male) behavior, the unconscious biases that are already in their heads. The best moment to take advantage of their attempts to be unbiased is immediately at the beginning of the case when they are trying very hard to not exhibit any biases. As the case moves along, they will have begun to see the "telltale signs" that you, my friend, are a jerk, the jerk they always knew you were.

Once an initial custody decision is made, judges look for reasons to confirm that their first instinct about you was correct. Always be willing to trade a little extra money in support for time with the children. It will be worth it in the long run (also your children will love you for standing up for them). Thus, there is no question that your strategy should be 50-50 with your kids from the get-go. If you cannot, because your children are too young or because you are a shift-worker or some other reason, then tell the court that your goal is 50-50 and that you are going to keep coming back until you can get to that level. But say it calmly and with due respect to the Court. "Your honor, I know that I am not in a position to request 50-50 with my children because they are only 2-years-old and even I know that is too young to have a 50-50, but I do want to state that if they were even a year older, I would be requesting 50-50. Over the long-term, it is very important to me to share equally in the raising of our children. I want to let the Court know that I do intend to come back when they are ready for 50-50."

This tells the Court what your intentions are and signals that you are a thoughtful reasonable person, the perfect type of person to have your children 50% of the time.

Act I for Women

Take into consideration what I just wrote about men. Chances are that if you are a woman, higher or lower earner, you have a special bond with your children. I do not say this to be sexist, but it is difficult to write a book on family law that does not acknowledge a mother's special role with her children. It is very common for even higher-earning mothers to have more of a role with the children than lower-earning fathers. This does not mean that a) father cannot learn and b) that you should not entrust your children to their father. There are great reasons for entrusting your children to their father.

First, you can have a life. I don't mean that you can't have a life if you have your children, but dating is difficult if you have your children all the time. It is also difficult to just relax when you have your children all the time. The first thing to assess is the effect of cutting the father to the quick on parenting time. What are the costs to you? There will be costs in your personal time and costs in your ability to work. Each of these costs exacts a toll on you and your personal development.

Second, you run the risk of angry children. Angry children tend to increase the pain of divorce by alienating you. You want a copacetic life ultimately (or most people do), where you aren't badgering your kids or fighting to explain why their father is absent or angry or what have you. And the very last thing you want are kids who get angry later in life and blame you for "keeping them away from their father," which will almost certainly be what he tells them ad nauseum if he does not get a "reasonable timeshare."

Third, dads who want shared parenting time – for the right reasons, namely to spend time with their children – will spend years fighting with you over custody, sometimes in court and sometimes outside of court. The move to a reasonable parenting timeshare (between 35-65 and 50-50) will likely free you from years of court fights and custody evaluators and lawyers' fees and the like.

When it comes to support, however, I do not ever advise my women clients to be generous in the early going. In fact, I advise my male clients to overpay support in the early stages and to do it willingly. Why? Your children are the most important thing in the world, but also money is the most important thing in the world. Having your children 90% of the time and no money is an exhausting world of relying on friends, figuring out what you can feed them, worrying about your rent. In the same way that I advise fathers to overpay support in the early going, I advise mothers to trade time for more support. Or in the case of higher-earning mothers, to trade away some timeshare with the kids for reduced support from mother to father.

You aren't "selling" your children. You are making a smart financial investment. You have to be able to live. You are going from one household to two households. Your children will be mostly fine. Again, if there are crimes, drugs, mental illness, jail, physical or emotional abuse or very young or very late teenage children, the circumstances are different. If you have school-aged children, the majority of the day is spent in school. If they play on sports teams or ballet or piano or competitive cheer, the day is stretched to include coaches and team parents and the like. Even if you have your doubts about whether your children's dad can "handle" the children more often than on weekends, remember that they are being raised by a village even if you didn't necessarily want a village to raise them. Teachers, coaches, tutors, friends' parents, doctors and therapists are all a part of your children's lives, even when they are with the other parent.

This is not meant to be the book for high-conflict co-parenting. There are other books on the subject. This book focuses on the

85-90% of cases that are "regular" people in the midst of a regular divorce. "Regular," in this context, does not mean you are not experiencing a good deal of emotional pain and suffering, worry and anxiety regarding your future and your children's future, stress about work and paying bills, extreme anxiety about court proceedings and how you are going to afford your lawyer's fees, it means that you are both human beings and are not dealing with divergent, anti-social personality disorders, violence, drugs, alcohol abuse (I don't mean perhaps being a little tipsy when the kids go to bed; I mean getting DUIs and ending up in jail or rehab), mental health problems (serious, not Prozac treated depression) and the like. We are not perfect. Your parents likely were not perfect. Your own parents already give the kids too much sugar and junk food and let them watch R-rated movies and play too many video games or have too much screen time.

I can't tell you the number of parents I have had as clients or opposing parties who assail the other parent's character over alcohol "abuse" and then post selfies with glasses of wine or shots of tequila at the club. Imagine a trial over where the children should live (already in mother's favor as father is asking for 50-50 and mother is asking for 80-20 and probably landing on 35-65) and a binder full of social media posts about what a shithead the father is and a whole gaggle of social media pictures of one alcohol-fueled extravaganza after another, profanity-laced text messages obviously written after 3/4s of a bottle of wine and the like. If you are truly a staid personality, an ascetic monk or nun eschewing the vices of the modern world and your ex-spouse is a junk food eating, weed smoking, whisky drinking ne'er do well, you are in the .0001% of the population that married someone totally opposite you. I will say that it can happen that the parents were partiers when they got together and one of the parents got sober through a 12-step program and now they have "concerns." My view is that you should air these concerns and get to an agreeable timeshare – at least at the very beginning.

Act I is Temporary

I just gave the advice that says, if you only have $2,500 for a divorce lawyer spend it in Act I because the orders from Act I are so important. While this is real advice, I also want to point out, especially to mothers who are not so sure about sharing custody of children with fathers who may not have been very present in the children's lives during the marriage, that Act I orders are temporary. Sometimes I will advise a mother client to offer "aspirational orders" to the father. These types of orders say, essentially, "I do not believe that harm will come to the children in your care (because there are no drugs, crimes, violence, jail time, or very young or late teenage children), but I am also not really sure that you want the custody and timeshare you are asking for. Let's test it out."

The test-it-out aspirational orders do not have to be 50-50 orders even if that is what the father is asking for. You can offer something that looks like a "double jump" that is more than you'd prefer and less than the father wants, but gives a path to the 50-50 he wants. This can be a way of limiting visitation, especially with a judge who is known for granting 50-50 out of the gate.

It would look like this. Father has a 60 hour a week job. He claims in his pleadings with the Court that he is in control of his work hours and can and will reduce his hours to spend more time with the children. He claims that he worked 60 hours a week because you were caring for the children and this was a way to bring in extra money for the family, but that his employer does not require him to work that much. You counter with, "that's not what you told me during the marriage. You told me that you worked that many hours because your boss made you."

Your children are old enough to go back and forth, but not such late-stage teenagers that they have their own minds made up about what they want to do. So, Father asks for 50-50. You think 20-80 is much more reasonable for him (alternate weekends from Friday to Sunday and a Wednesday dinner visit, plus all the video and text chatting he could want during the week and you live close enough that he could ask for some time on a day when he gets off work early and you say you'd be willing to do that). If you have a 50-50 judge, there is a good chance that this judge will take Father at his word and give him the 50-50 to start, under the theory that being a parent is hard and we should assume that even fathers who worked 60 hours a week can change and be more available to their children.

If this situation concerns you, then the offer could look like this: "how about Father takes 35% visitation until the end of the school year, with 50-50 over the summer vacation. Then, we can revisit the arrangement before school starts again in August?" What does this get you? First, it gives you (and the court and the father) data. Father says he will work less and spend more time with the children. There is a way to test that, which is by giving him most of what he says he wants. If Father is being rational (which many are not), he will know that if he goes to court and asks a judge, he may end up with 20% timeshare. If you are being rational, you will know that if you go to court and ask a judge, he may end up with 50% timeshare. 35% is a middle ground. It will save you each $10,000-$20,000 on a mini-trial over temporary custody and it will give you a lot of data about his work habits. Second, many times fathers in this situation realize that they are just fine with 35% timeshare. I can say from experience that there is almost no demonstrable difference between 35% timeshare and 50% timeshare, especially during the school year where the kids are mostly being raised by teachers and the majority of the time you spend with the kids is picking them up from school, moving them to soccer practice and then feeding them and putting them to bed – perhaps doing homework in between. Third, many times, mothers will realize that either fathers aren't doing such a bad job at this parenting thing or that they actually enjoy having 5 nights off every two weeks to share the parenting load. It may not mean that they turn off their mothering. I know many mothers who still make the kids' lunches and volunteer at the school or drive to soccer practice on their off days – despite me telling them that they should let the father handle it if he wants shared custody so badly "but Jude, I am not going to let my kids suffer because he does not do things." Or, "but Jude, I enjoy doing these things for the kids."

By setting this up as a double-jump from the outset, you do three different things. First, you save a trial and $10,000-$20,000 (or worse, in a recommending county you get a custody therapist who works for the court and has a bias toward 50% stating that the kids should be with each of you 50% of the time). Second, your whole family gets a chance to get comfortable with a different custodial arrangement as a result of the divorce. And third, because the orders are temporary, you preserve the ability to make a claim later that it did not work out because a) Father did not take more time off work and the kids are being raised by *his* mother instead of their own mother, or b) the kids did not do well with the arrangement.

Granted, what I said earlier still applies: it is difficult to change temporary custody orders later in the game. But it is MUCH more difficult to change temporary custody orders that are made after an evidentiary hearing (where each of you raises your right hand and takes the witness stand, even if it's not the "final trial") or after a recommendation by a custody therapist mediator with the court than it is to change an agreement you made for temporary orders. In my experience, and it also happens to be an area of law called "res judicata" (which means that it has already been decided by a court and should therefore remain), judges do not like to change orders they have previously made unless there is a very good reason to do so. But, if you buy yourself time by giving up a reasonable amount of time in an aspirational order – say 35-65 or even 30-70 – you may find that your 35% timeshare offer to Father becomes the law of the case for all eternity (or at least your children's minority). You may also find that you like it and want to expand it to 50-50.

As to support, if you are going to be receiving the support, then I suggest that you make offers that look like this: "I will give you 50-50 custody but I need you to pay support as though it was 35-65. I can't afford to live without more support." Rational men should take this deal. They don't always take the offer, but for a few hundred dollars a month in support they get their kids 50-50 without a $10,000 fight, it's a no brainer from where I sit. But many people will listen to their lawyers who will tell them that they must have a big fight over the $400 per month difference in child support. To put it in perspective, a $10,000 trial is 25 months of child support at $400 per month and if you go to trial, you might lose and end up with a 20% visitation schedule and pay an extra $800 per month. If you win, you spend 25 months of child support to get what you were already being offered.

If you are the support paying mother, I would make the following offer: "I will give you 50-50 if you agree that child support should be set at $0 and you claim the kids on your taxes." Most men, in my experience, will take this deal because, just as most women hate paying support to men, most men hate getting support from women. That said, if he declines, then you offer to pay support at 20% timeshare or cover certain (possibly tax-advantaged) costs (healthcare, private school, extra-curricular activities, school clothes, school supplies, etc.).

················ PRO TIPS ················

Higher-earning fathers can often make deals around custody by trading a higher amount of child support for more custody time.

Higher-earning mothers can often make deals around support by trading timeshare to get it.

Both of these approaches are rational and favored from a negotiation standpoint because they will save thousands of dollars of legal fees and take away the risk of losing at trial.

···

Act II: Financial Disclosures and Discovery.

Act II occurs after the Court makes temporary orders. It can also sometimes parallel and/or overlap Act I.

In California, divorce is mostly financial. In fact, California Family Code 721 has adopted the Corporations Code sections regarding the winding up of "general partnerships" (where two or more people go into business together and share expenses and profits). Act II is almost entirely the process of doing financial disclosures, and in some cases, depositions. In Act II almost all the work is done outside the court's purview on forms that are not filed with the Court.

California requires that parties disclose every material financial fact to the other spouse, whether the financial facts relate to community or separate property. Disclosures are sua sponte, meaning they do not require the other party to ask for them. In most civil cases you do "discovery" by asking for things the other party may object to. If you don't ask for them, you don't get them.

In a divorce, because spouses owe each other fiduciary duties, parties must turn this information over to one another immediately (within the first 60 days of filing for divorce) and then every time there is any change in the assets or debts, or—in most cases—their incomes. Automatic temporary restraining orders (ATROs) regarding finances restrain parties from taking loans, selling property, or cashing in stocks or IRAs or 401(k)s for almost any purpose. (Cynics will note that, because these rules were drafted by lawyers, lawyers have carved out an exception to the automatic temporary restraining orders to pay for legal fees.)

Judicial Council forms make it easier to perform these tasks. Google "California Judicial Council Form FL-142," which is a schedule of assets and debts, for a guide on how to disclose information to your spouse. FL-142 is an exhaustive form. It asks you to disclose every financial asset or debt that you own, whether community or separate property.

················ PRO TIP ················

This includes any pension that you earned either before or during marriage, or after separation. The pension value is rarely the value of the number given to you by the plan each quarter.

For California's Public Employee Retirement System (CalPERS) the number that you get on your statements is the amount you have contributed. That is the cash out number if you were to cash out your plan, something that no one in their right mind ever does, because the real value is in the annuity.

A pension valuation specialist will determine the value of the annuity based on the expected payment at an expected retirement age for an expected lifespan. (It's total voodoo, but what the hell? They tell us it is science.) Then they discount this number to an amount a reasonable person would pay to purchase the pension today.

For ex., Imagine you are 50 and you retired today with a pension worth $4,000 per month in annuity payments from CalPERS. If you are expected to live until age 80, your pension is worth $4,000 * 12 * 30 = $1,440,000. Your spouse gets half of that number, discounted by the fact that you aren't going to retire today and that he would have to wait 30 years to get it all and might not live as long as you. Chances are you will owe your spouse somewhere in the ballpark of between $450,000 and $650,000 for their share of this CalPERS annuity. Since most people do not have that much cash laying around, this is why people divide pensions rather than buying out their spouse's interest in it.

Always list your pension in the disclosures. It is virtually guaranteed that an attorney will accuse you of perjury if you fail to list your pension because you and your spouse both thought the pension belonged to the person who earned it. This is a typically California-specific rule, and many states have different ways of dividing pensions, so check with your state's rules. The Form FL-142 asks you to put a value on your pension; the proper answer at the beginning of the case is "TBD" so that you do not undervalue it and later get accused of hiding its value.

California takes disclosure rules very seriously, and there are famous cases detailing the punishments given when a spouse fails to disclose. See for example *Marriage of* Rossi, where Wife won a $1.3 million lottery payout 11 days before she filed for divorce. She never disclosed this to Husband. He found out after the parties were divorced. The Court awarded Husband the entire $1.3 million dollars for her willful and intentional failure to disclose the lottery winnings. The case does not tell us how Wife reacted to that order, but I am certain she felt as badly about giving it all to the Husband as she felt elated about winning it in the first place—perhaps much worse.

Act II costs money. In fact, I tell clients that they should expect Act II to cost between $2,500 and $5,000—even if there isn't any Act I fighting spilling over or motions demanding more thorough discovery than you have provided. Nevertheless, this is money well spent. In my office we do not spend time or money hiding assets. It would not only be unethical to do so, but it is also a bad idea. Even reasonably competent lawyers will find hidden assets, and if they do, the house of cards will come tumbling down. Failing to disclose assets is perhaps the only way for a law-abiding person to be punished in a divorce. That punishment is without mercy and not worth the risk.

Act II rarely involves going to Court. In addition to the sua sponte ("spontaneous") disclosures, each side can send "discovery" to the other side. Discovery consists, in part, of Form Interrogatories ("FROGS," in California, come on a preprinted form – you can Google "California judicial council form interrogatories, family law" and get the form), special interrogatories ("SPROGS," which are questions that you can ask your spouse in writing – these don't come on a pre-printed form), Requests for Production ("RFPs" or "RPDs" – which are documents you are requesting, such as bank statements from an account held in your ex's name only, and Requests for Admission ("Admit that you earned $137,000 from your sewing business in 2023." "Admit that you kicked in the bedroom door in a fit of rage").

Requests for Production are for documents that are outside the normal range of dates for most of the forms. The forms look back two years regarding most things, but if you want a property deed from 10 years ago that your spouse has in a lockbox in the garage, you can ask for it in your Request for Production of Documents. The same applies if you want old corporate tax returns, or copies of stock certificates inherited in 1988, or post-separation Quickbooks files, or any number of other things that may or may not have been produced in responses to Form Interrogatories.

In addition to the Requests for Production, you are entitled to send a "Request for Admissions" document. Requests for Admissions are your way of ensuring under oath that (among other things) your ex admits to the authenticity of certain documents:

- "Admit that this promissory note from my parents is authentic.
- Admit that you signed this promissory note from my parents.
- Admit that you knew about the terms of the promissory note from my parents."

These requests for admission become key pieces of testimony or evidence in Act III, particularly if there is going to be a trial. In addition, Requests for Admission ensure that you understand your ex's position with regard to certain legal claims. "Admit that we owe my parents $15,000 jointly for their loan on our home purchase." Or, "admit that you moved out of the family home on July 1, 2019." Or, "admit that you are eligible for retirement at age 58.5." Or, "admit that we separated on March 26, 2021."

Typically, these are served with Civil Form Interrogatories, which is another pre-printed form saying, "If any of your answers to the Requests for Admission was other than an unqualified admission, provide all facts supporting your contention, name all witnesses who can support your contention (and identify all documents and tangible things, along with the names and contact information of the person who has the documents or tangible things)". So if you ask, "Admit that you knew about the terms of the promissory note from my parents" and the answer is "Deny," Civil Form Interrogatory 17.1 (California) asks the other party to identify the facts as they understand them, and whether there is writing to support it. (And if so, who has this written proof). If the answer to the Request for Admissions is "Deny," the answer to Civil Form Interrogatory 17.1 might be:

"We did have a note to your parents for $15,000, but we retired the note in May 2016 when I received my accident settlement. The Bank of America account statement from May 2016 will provide proof that we paid your parents the $15,000. Your parents will attest to having received this payment since your father's signature is on the back of the check."

Requests for Admission come with a rule that says, if you do not admit to a fact and the other side proves that fact to be true, you are liable for their attorneys' fees in proving that fact. The answers are under penalty of perjury and become evidence in the case. These are powerful tools to get your ex (or you) to admit things that benefit the case.

Special Interrogatories are questions you can ask your spouse in lieu of conducting a deposition or in addition to conducting a deposition. "How much money have you received in overtime compensation in 2019?" Or "Have you sold your 2019 Tesla Model S?" Or "How many stock options have you received from Facebook since you started working there?"

Normally you can ask 35 Requests for Admission and 35 SPROGS, unless you file a declaration stating that this is a complex case and that you need to ask more.

If the other party refuses to respond or does not produce adequate responses, or makes unfounded objections in their response, your recourse is to file a Motion to Compel Production of Documents. This is usually the only the only way Act II can involve going to Court—and it can get expensive. This is where you tell the Court that you asked certain questions and your ex refused to answer them or failed to answer them, and you want an order compelling them to respond.

Motions to Compel often come with a request for attorney's fees and sanctions. You should not end up in this kind of litigation because you should be providing documents and responses to questions in the discovery time frame in Act II. Remember the goal is not only winning the divorce but getting to the end of it as quickly as possible. The chances of you successfully hiding a community property asset or devaluing it enough to make it worth the risk are slim to none. It is far more valuable and cost-effective to finish the divorce quickly and be done with it.

> *Example: In a case which I am working on as I write this book, H and W are both highly conflict-driven. Every conversation with either of them is met with a hail of "fuck yous" and "bullSHIT!s" and flat out "NO!s"—regardless of the subject. Out of the blue, W's attorney called me and said, "My client will forego the $900 per month child support payment if your client will pay the $3,000 orthodontia bill."*
>
> *This makes no sense unless W has realized that the toxicity of the relationship makes receiving $11,000 tax free per year not worth it (which is what I expect). H is balking at paying the $3,000 ortho bill, even though he has 72 months left in the children's minority. That is $64,800 in child support that he will not have to pay. The hold up? He doesn't want to make payments on a $3,000 bill because he feels like he's "getting fucked. Yet again." I asked him, "How are you getting fucked? You have two kids with her and earn double her income, and she's trading you $64,800 in support payments for a lousy $3,000 ortho bill that you were probably going to get*

stuck paying anyway." (Everyone except family law parties understands that it's not worth paying a lawyer $5,000 to fight over one-half of a $3,000 medical bill.) These two people are nickel and diming each other to death, with each of them paying lawyers upwards of $500 per hour to fight over one-half of $3,000. (My client was already on the hook for half of the $3,000 because California law requires him to pay half of the ortho bill, so he was really only fighting over $1,500 and spending $500 per hour to do it.)

Be smart.

In Act II there may be something you are not required to produce and that you refuse to produce. "Please provide a copy of your grandmother's trust." Answer: "Objection. This document is not available to me because my grandmother is still alive, and the trust may be revoked." Or "Objection, this document is subject to my grandmother's right of privacy and she is not a party to this case." Or "Objection. This document is not likely to lead to relevant evidence." The other party will determine if they believe your objections are valid and will either decide to file the Motion to Compel Production or not.

> Example: I am working on a domestic violence case. (I take those on a pro bono basis if I have the resourcing in the office—i.e., time and staff—and if they are referred by a third-party organization or person I trust.) W, my client, suffered horrific sexual abuse at the hands of H. She sought and was granted temporary restraining orders and a kick-out order from the home.
>
> H lawyered up with a decent, but extremely expensive attorney. He makes his money by being thorough, but screws his clients in the process because he forgets that 90% of divorce

work is negotiation (with the law only in the background). At any rate, she and I were scheduled to meet before the Domestic Violence Restraining Order trial, and I asked her where she was. H had been abiding by the temporary orders over the past two weeks (but had violated them previously). We did not apply for the orders based on the sexual violence committed against her, but because H found evidence of W's affair on her iPhone, had extracted all the text messages and racy photos to the cloud, and was threatening to release all of it to her boss, coworkers, family, and friends.

Her question was whether she would have to relive the sexual violence to get her restraining order, and whether the sexual text messages and photographs would come into evidence.

If opposing counsel had requested them in discovery, we would have objected by stating that they were not relevant to the claim. California is a "no fault" divorce state, which means it is irrelevant whether a party had an affair, making evidence of the affair inadmissible to prove the affair. It may be admitted into evidence for some other reason, but not for evidence of infidelity.

We decided not to produce any sexually explicit messages or photos. We objected on the basis that the sexually explicit messages and photos (both pre-divorce to the husband and to the affair partner) were not likely to lead to the discovery of admissible evidence. They were being sought only because the husband thought she would be embarrassed by them and would not want to disclose them and then he could use them to get a better settlement. We were not going to give him that power. We dared them to file a Motion to Compel their production to overcome our objection.

They did not file a Motion to Compel production but brought up her failure to produce the sexually explicit content at trial, arguing that she should not be able to pursue the claim that he had abused her because she did not produce the content. We successfully argued that the content of the messages was irrelevant to the fact that H extorted W by threatening to release content unless she caved to his sexual demands. Even if the messages were not racy, the threat of releasing the messages to get her to do something she was against doing is a crime and meets California's definition of violence.

Even while writing this book, the law changes. In the context of Domestic Violence Restraining Orders, California passed Family Code section 6309, which places major restrictions on the ability of parties to conduct discovery on domestic violence related issues. This has stirred a great deal of debate amongst legal practitioners about whether the benefits of the new law to survivors of domestic violence – by shielding them from "legal abuse" – ongoing domestic abuse through the legal system – outweighs the due process right of the accused to conduct discovery to put on a defense to domestic violence allegations. The new law took effect January 1, 2024, and already I am in a heated battle over its meaning.

In the case I am working on, Wife has a temporary DVRO against Husband, which has not yet been set for trial. Although dates are normally not relevant to my case examples, they matter here because Husband took Wife's deposition in October 2023. Husband's questions were predictably abusive – he was trying to pry into her post-separation sexual relationships, vacations and romantic liaisons, none of which would be admissible in court. The deposition got continued because Wife, on my advice, refused to answer these intrusive questions on privacy grounds. Husband filed a motion to compel her responses to the questions. The hearing was set for January 2024, after the law went into effect.

Abusive deposition questions went like this:

"Q: How many times during your marriage did your husband call you a cunt?
A: Maybe 50-60.
Q: How many times during the marriage did he call you a frigid bitch?
A: Maybe 10.
Q: How many times did he call you a bitch?
A: Including the times he called me a frigid bitch or just bitch? Probably 50-60.
Q: After separation, how many vacations have you taken?
A: 3.
Q: Who went on the vacation with you?
Me: Objection. This violates her right to privacy and won't lead to any admissible evidence."

The Husband's lawyers filed the Motion to Compel her to answer questions regarding her romantic life post-separation. First of all, in a "no fault" divorce state, evidence of romantic relationships outside the marriage, during the marriage, are irrelevant and out-of-bounds. Adultery is not actionable in a California divorce. Post-separation romantic relationships are totally off limits.

The Court agreed with us that the questions were abusive and irrelevant and denied the motion to compel on Family Code 6309. The Court also noted that the questions violated my client's right to privacy.

• •

The majority of requested information is relevant and admissible. Tax returns, life insurance policies, stock options, inherited IRAs, deeds to homes in other countries, school sign-in sheets and attendance reports, etc. are all relevant and discoverable. There are some types of documents, however, that are not, particularly ones that violate your right to privacy, that you can and should resist providing. These are, however, a very small category of documents.

Finally, in Act II either side may conduct one deposition of the other party. A deposition is an opportunity for you to ask or be asked questions under oath, in front of a court reporter only. There is no judge present. Each side raises their objections during the deposition and the party answers the questions. Later the judge will determine whether the question was within the bounds of discovery and whether a judge can consider the answer.

Family lawyers in my jurisdiction generally do not conduct many depositions, largely because they can be cost-prohibitive. Normally a deposition will cost around $2,500-$5,000, in addition to the 4-6 hours of attorney time needed to prepare for and conduct the deposition. It is worth it if you have a lot of financial documents to go through or if the answer to one or more questions may be dispositive of the entire case. I conducted a 6-question deposition recently. It took longer to set up and go through the preliminary items than it took to conduct the deposition. The 6 questions were imperative to understanding the case. I asked them. We moved on. It led to a settlement.

Act III: Trial or Agreement

As I mentioned in the previous chapter, a divorce case only ends in one of two ways: trial or agreement. A frustrated client kept calling me recently asking me why we were going to trial. "We have already made them an offer to settle. Why are we going to trial? I don't want to go to trial. Trial is going to cost me $30,000. Why are we going to trial?"

I responded to her (for the 20th time) that a divorce only ends in one of the above two ways. There is no other way for it to end (except reconciliation). We made an offer and they rejected it. They made an offer and we rejected it. The lawyers tried hard to find middle ground, but the father wanted alternate weeks visitation with a 9-month-old and the mother wanted the father to see the baby 3-4 times per week for 3 hours. We were a million miles apart. We knew the judge was going to give us the 3-4 visits per week for 3 hours with a 9-month-old. That's why we offered it. The judge was never going to give the father alternate weeks visits. The father's lawyers knew that too, but the father was unwilling to settle. He really wanted to tell the court that his ex-wife was a terrible bitch and that visitation was his red-center-of-the-white-petaled-flower issue. It was an unreasonable red center, but he really, really wanted 50-50 custody with his son, and he was willing to spend $30,000 for a chance to get it. Like my prior client who said he was "going to see a judge" if the Wife wanted to change the custody orders, this dad was not going to give up his desire for 50-50 timeshare, even though he was going to lose.

My client was definitely a "challenging" person. I was going to have to work hard to prove that she wasn't unreasonably challenging, which was tough because even my staff thought she was unreasonably challenging. (I thought she was on the very outside edge of reasonable.).

However badly my client wanted to settle, settlement takes an agreement by both parties. I told my client that she wanted everything she wanted, but that the father wanted more. She said, "I won't give him more." I said, "I don't think you should give him more, but if you want to settle the case without a trial, either you have to give him more or he has to accept less. Right now, neither of you is willing to budge. Therefore, the only option is to go to trial."

She fired me the day after I told her that and wrote a nasty Yelp! review about me "not fighting for her." She also hired another lawyer who went to trial and the judge ordered exactly what I said (and we all knew) he was going to order for the father: 3 visits per week for 3 hours each until the child reached two years old; a full Saturday visit (not overnight) every other week after 2 years old until 3 years old; Saturday overnights on alternate weekends from 3 until 4 years old; and Friday to Sunday on alternate weekends beginning at 4 years old.

Experienced family lawyers will almost always know the outcome of a case before it resolves because most cases resolve within the Range of Normal Outcomes. I have practiced for almost 20 years most Thursdays in front of the judge who decided the previous case. I know he loves the Dodgers and the local High School football team. I know that he is a big fan of SpaceX and the big rocket launches that come from the nearby Space Force Base. I know that he works on December 24th and 26th every year without fail. I know also that he is not a fan of 50-50 arrangements and how he rules generally on cases involving children of all ages—9-month-olds, 5-year-olds, teenagers, etc.—within a reasonable spread.

Sometimes the best thing to do is put your client on the stand and let them tell their story. The research consistently shows that when parties feel they have been heard by a court they are more accepting of the outcome, even if it is terribly against them. The family law system is overloaded with cases, most of which are put on by parties without lawyers. They don't know what to say or how to say it. Judges make quick decisions and do not give them a real opportunity to experience the catharsis of telling their story.

I urge anyone reading this book to make sure they tell their story to the court if it goes that far. Tell the judge that you want to have time to tell them what is important to you. When you get your chance do not clam up. Tell the story with gusto! There is one certainty at trial: if you do not use your time to say what you must, you will be unhappy with the outcome. This is also true in negotiations. I tell clients that, as they negotiate, they should only accept an outcome or agreement that they can live with. They should never be bullied into an agreement they don't like. (But they should always be reasonable, and when their spouse offers a settlement within the Range of Reasonable or Normal Outcomes they should take it—or at least give it due weight and consideration, even if it isn't perfect.)

Divorcing spouses should settle almost everything to do with money and property. The math is just math, and not necessarily even difficult math. My client today mentioned that there was a 401(k) that had $50,000 in it on the date of separation in July 2014. Five years later the parties are still not divorced. The 401(k) now has $80,000 in it (due to market growth, not additional contributions). My client understands intuitively that the math is still "divide by 2." Yet, even more difficult math, like calculating the community property ownership interest in a separate property home (so-called *"Moore/Marsden"* calculations that I discuss below) is still just math. There are even websites that will do it for free if you are willing to watch an ad.

All of the financial issues are just math so long as you know the Three Property Rules: 1) everything you get before marriage is separate property; and 2) everything you get during the marriage is community property; 3) except gifts and inheritances.

There are lawyers who will fight over math. They will do math calculations that they hope to sneak past the judge or the other lawyer to make you a few extra bucks. I would not spend $40,000 to go to trial over whether the judge knows how to use a calculator. If you agree on the value of a property—for ex., how much your house was worth on an agreed upon date—the division of the asset is simple. Real fights happen over competing property valuations. (Appraiser 1 says the house is worth $450,000 and Appraiser 2 says it is worth $500,000.) Almost always the best solution is to quickly offer to split the difference. Most times the other party will readily agree. The alternative is that you can win $25,000, for which you will spend $25,000 on attorney's fees going to trial, plus the cost of the expert testimony which might be $7,500. All together you will spend $32,500 on the chance that you will "win" $25,000. And remember the other side will also have an expert testifying. That means they will also spend $32,500 for the chance to "win" $25,000. Either of you might win, but the chance that you will win is totally out of your control and, in any event, you will have spent more to play for a chance to win than you win, if you win and, in the WCATNA (worst-case), you spend $32,500 and lose the valuation issue and you still have to pay the additional $25,000 – then it costs you $57,500 and perhaps months waiting for a trial on the issue, when you could have resolved it for $25,000. .

There are types of claims that might require going to trial, such as when the judge's orders are discretionary—typically, child custody and visitation and spousal support, but also certain types of family law reimbursements. There are categories of orders that are discretionary by law or rule, and categories of orders that are discretionary by practice. I have been negotiating with an incredibly smart engineer who is representing himself. He is always (he believes) the smartest person in any room he is in. He has read the caselaw and done the research, and he *knows* that he is entitled to certain reimbursements from my client. I keep trying to tell him that these are discretionary reimbursements and that our particular judge always exercises his discretion not to award them. But he doesn't know that and because I will never convince him of it, this case will end up in trial. There is no other lawyer he would even sit down and talk to about this. Nevertheless, he doesn't trust me and he thinks he's smarter than every lawyer in town (including me).

I hope 95%-98% of you settle your cases completely and the remaining 2-5% settle 90% of the issues before trial. Trials should be targeted only for things you cannot resolve.

Settlement Agreements Instead of Trials

The Act III agreement is sometimes called a "marital settlement agreement" ("MSA"). It will come with a "Judgment" or "Decree of Dissolution" or "Decree of Divorce" attached to it.

Preparing a MSA usually costs $2,500-$5,000 depending on the amount of negotiation needed for the parties to agree on the language in the Agreement. It is typically a simple form document that requires only certain inputs. It takes me 3-5 hours to prepare one, not because I am doing a lot of new writing, but because I have to meticulously check and recheck the financial disclosures each side provided in Act II to make sure that I am writing everything down correctly.

You should **never** have a paralegal working without a lawyer prepare this for you. You should invest in a lawyer to draft it, but if you choose not to, then draft it yourself. Your mistakes are probably correctable by claiming innocence with the court, but the document preparer's mistakes will likely not be fixable—and they almost always get the agreements wrong. In fact, although I am generally a fan of Legal Document Preparers or Independent Paralegals for many things, I think they get Marital Settlement Agreements wrong almost every time and should never do them. Period. If you hire a Legal Document Assistant and they make a major mistake, you are stuck with a terrible document that you cannot fix without spending thousands on a lawyer in the hopes they can convince the judge to fix it. More than once I have attempted to crack open these wrongly drafted agreements only to have a judge say, "Mr. Egan, your client has a lawyer now. He should have had one then." Or, "These people owned two houses, have four kids and each has a retirement and they thought they could save money by hiring a paralegal to do a lawyer's job. They saved money then, but now they are going to have to spend probably a whole lot more money trying to fix their mistakes."

I believe in properly drafted MSAs. I believe in them wholeheartedly. In fact, everything you do in your divorce case should be focused on getting an MSA in lieu of a trial. Trials are expensive and totally unpredictable in family law. You only go to trial if you absolutely must.

Memoranda of Understanding

It is very common for there to be a frenzy of settlement activity while lawyers are simultaneously preparing for trial. The reason for this is probably mostly practical. Your lawyer is pushing your case along at a slow clip while dealing with other fires all the way until it becomes clear that you are going to have a trial. With trial dates looming, your lawyer will start getting evidence binders put together, drafting briefs, talking to witnesses and experts and preparing lines of questioning for trial. As your lawyer is doing this, she is also starting to think hard about your case strengths and weaknesses and truly beginning to discover your *actual* probability of success on various issues.

A family law trial is different than virtually all civil litigation and criminal trials because there is almost never one winner and one loser; there are usually a series of issues that must be dealt with at trial. You will have "mini-trials" over each of those issues. So, you may have a custody and visitation issue, a child support issue, a spousal support issue, a separate property characterization issue (Husband and Wife bought house together, but Husband signed a quitclaim deed to Wife; or Husband used $100,000 in inheritance money as a down payment on the house, can he prove it?), a reimbursement issue and a pension division issue. That is a 6-issue trial. I think the best lawyers try to get agreements on everything, but if they can't they work on resolving 4 out of 6 issues and leave the ones that are at impasse for a 2-issue trial.

But, in the run-up to trial there start to be a lot of different moving parts, including the lawyer telling the client something like: "While I prepare for trial, I am only working on your case, and I work on your case about 1 to 2 days for every day of trial scheduled. If you have a 5-day trial scheduled, then expect that I am putting in 10-hour days for 5 to 10 days before trial. Plus, I will have a paralegal working about the same amount of time." My current billing rate is $495 per hour with paralegals billing at $225 per hour. 15 days times 10 hours per day times $720 per hour is approaching $100,000 in legal fees. Expert witnesses want $5,000 to testify as well. Because the client is looking at a cost of $120,000 for a 5-day trial (perhaps), there is great incentive to settle the case. Remember, I tell clients to put their own children through Stanford and not my child through Stanford. I also tell them, "if you have $120,000 for me for trial, you have $120,000 in settlement funds."

So, we get into a frenzied state of trial preparation and settlement at the same time. Once I smell settlement, then I can stop working on trial prep but that is a massive gamble on my part.

Example: I recently settled one of the ugliest cases I have ever worked on. It was a 4 year and 7 month marriage and a 9 year and 8 month divorce. I came in about 18 months before trial, so I did not have the long memory of the entire case, but opposing counsel had been counsel for Husband from the very beginning. She was both angry at my client and completely fried and emotionally drained by the case. During the pendency of the divorce, Wife's father died and her mom was diagnosed with end-stage pancreatic cancer, Husband's mother had Stage IV lung cancer that was found, went into remission and then came back, and opposing counsel's mother was in the hospital dying of cancer. The parties were fighting over nickels and pennies (not even dimes). It was ridiculous. And they were not paying their attorney bills and the lawyers were stuck in the case.

We were set for a three-week trial. Three fucking weeks! To fight over scraps! The parties were intractable. We could not get even the simplest of agreements on anything. Everything was the end-of-the-world for these parties. We almost lost the final deal we made because Wife wanted to claim the 17-year-old on her tax return. She was willing to have a three-week trial over a year of child exemption.

We were feverishly working trying to prepare for trial and I got into my mind a way to settle the case so I started pushing on settlement. Ultimately, we reached an agreement on the case on the Sunday before a Monday holiday and trial starting on Tuesday. It was a global settlement for the entire case. I took advantage of everyone's very real desire not to go to trial, including the lawyers, and everyone's mothers being ill. We worked in that frenzy to get the agreement and then I drafted a Memorandum of Understanding that everyone signed.

Under California law, there are agreements to agree and there are agreements. The agreement becomes the basis of the

Judgment or Decree of Divorce, but the Judgment or Decree contains a lot of important language. Agreements to agree – like a Memorandum of Understand or MOU – are enforceable if they are attached to a Judgment, but we prefer a fully fleshed out agreement in a Judgment because of the additional language.

So, I drafted what ended up being a 10-page Memorandum of Understanding, laying out, in detail, what the parties agreed to. We later had to prepare a Stipulated Judgment that contained all of the other language, but we got signatures on the MOU to save us from trial when we agreed on the deal points. It turned out that, with these parties, we could never agree on anything else ever again and the lawyers agreed to just file the MOU as the final agreement, but it is not uncommon to draft a MOU and put in language that says "this agreement is enforceable under California Code of Civil Procedure (CCP) 664.6 and if no further agreement is reached, this may be attached to a Judgment and filed with the Court." That language makes the MOU enforceable as a contract between the parties and judicially enforceable.

A short way to say what an MOU is, is to say that it is a short-form agreement between parties that is enforceable with the court. If you and your spouse are doing this on your own and you make agreements that you want to have be durable, you might consider using the CCP 664.6 language I stated above. For non-represented parties, it is not always clear that the judge will enforce an MOU as a judgment because they may think you do not understand what you are doing, but it certainly cannot hurt to try.

The Trial

After getting temporary orders and reviewing all relevant financial documents, each side will consider how to settle the case before heading toward trial. Reasonable people work toward a division of assets approximating 50-50 because they are Bargaining in the Shadow of the Law. In the family law context Bargaining in the Shadow of the Law means, "What will a Judge most likely do in this situation?"

The Range of Normal Outcomes is the Range in which settlement should be possible. If you know the boundaries of Range of Normal Outcomes, you know that if you win every single issue at trial (which is very rare), you get X (your BCATNA and your spouse's WCATNA) and if your wins every single issue at trial, they get Y (your WCATNA and your spouse's BCATNA). Knowing this, you should strongly consider any settlement offer between X and Y because this is the spectrum on which the Judge will decide the case outcome.

X	Y
Best Case for You	Worst Case for You

Any offer within the range from X to Y is an offer you should consider accepting or at least from which you should negotiate. Why? The chance that your trial outcome will be between your best and worst case outcomes is really high. You know there is a risk that you will get your worst case outcome. You also know that you will have to pay your attorney's fees to have a trial, which already reduces your best case outcome even if you get it. If you figure a trial is $10,000 per day and most trials are 4-5 days, no matter how well you do at trial, you have to reduce that by $40,000-$50,000.

There are, of course, limitations on this. If, for example, your spouse wants $50,000 from you and you want to give him $0 (but the cost of going to trial is $10,000) you might be willing to offer the $10,000 to your spouse that you would have spent on a lawyer. Your spouse may accept $40,000 (since he would have paid his lawyer $10,000) but this still leaves you $30,000 apart. Assuming neither party wants to budge, you really must assess the likelihood of your claims being successful versus his claims. Economists will tell you that if you have a 50% chance of success, you should offer to split the $30,000 difference and pay your spouse $25,000 ($10,000 for the attorney's fees you would have spent and one-half of the $30,000 difference). You can make this math work with a 33% chance of success: $10,000 (attorney's fees you would have spent) + $20,000 (67% * the $30,000 difference). However, it is not always intuitive or easy to gauge your chance of winning a particular issue, and the less ability you have to predict the outcome of the issue, the more it will cost in attorney's fees to argue it. (Research and briefing are expensive.)

In addition, even within the Range of Normal Outcomes, the Parties should always fear the "rogue judge" who makes decisions based on her "gut", or on whatever she thinks is "fair", and disregards the law altogether. After speaking to hundreds of lawyers and participating as a lawyer in more than 1,000 cases, I have learned that most judges do not like family law, do not understand family law, and do not *want* to understand family law.

Not surprisingly, there are litigated outcomes that fall outside the Range of Normal – they are rare but not rare enough to be ignored. This should scare both parties half to death and be reason enough to consider outcomes on the fringe of the Range of Normal. Even with two gifted lawyers who know a lot about family law, each of whom is able and willing to educate the judge about family law, there can be outcomes that no one expected or could predict. This is not a failing on the lawyer's part (or on your part if you are representing yourself); it is entirely on the judge who doesn't care to learn the law. Regardless, it is outside your control unless you want to consider an appeal—and even then most appellate court decisions affirm lower court decisions. (Appeals are for another book altogether.)

The reason for this is not just the fact that you cannot reasonably predict judicial behavior, or, put more academically, even when you know how a judge works in a general sense, you cannot predict that the way any judge generally behaves will translate to your specific fact-pattern and scenario. You can generalize from the specific, but you cannot specify from the general – this means even a good lawyer who understands the judge's psychology and has practiced in front of her for many years, knows that they cannot predict how any particular judge will rule on any particular day with any particular party.

I think that some judges change up their "normal" rulings sometimes, just to keep the lawyers telling their clients: "this judge is an animal. You NEVER know what he is going to do! (and therefore, you must start thinking about settlement.)." I have no evidence to make that claim other than the facts that a) judges like settlements, b) hate family law trials and c) will make, at times, wildly contradictory rulings with almost no legal basis.

This uncertainty is reason enough to settle everything possible while still being able to sleep at night/live with yourself. This is solely your decision. You should ask yourself what you can accept for your own future, and not what you can accept about what *he* or *she* got. Your spouse may have cheated on you or abused you, checked out on the marriage, quit a job and let/made you do all the work, got fat or stopped having sex with you, or any number of things that would give you very real reasons to be furious with them. But the strategy of going to war or refusing to consider reasonable settlements out of spite is one that will lead to protracted litigation that will burn up equity in your home or drain the balance of your 401(k) – you will help your lawyer buy the summer house at the lake rather than buying your own house at the lake.

In other words, you can pay me $50,000 to try the case or you can settle it, have a certain outcome and keep most of that money.

However, there are real reasons to litigate certain issues. If you are a father who believes that you will not be able to live with yourself unless you have 50-50 custody of your children, then you cannot settle for 30% even if you know that 30% is within the Range of Normal Outcomes. If your husband wants $4,000 per month in spousal support and you know that you cannot afford to pay that, then you must litigate the issue, even if his demand is within the Range of Normal Outcomes.

The goal, therefore, in Act III is to know when to "hold 'em" and know when to "fold 'em" (or as I sometimes say: "settle or push?"). But, you also need to know *what* to hold and *what* to fold. Settle all the non-thorny financial issues immediately. You know you are keeping your car and your husband is keeping his car. Agree to split the 401(k) or the IRA or the pension at the earliest opportunity. If no one wants to keep the house, list it for sale. If you moved out because you don't want it, ask your spouse to refinance you out for half the equity as soon as possible (or make an agreement that she will do so). If your spouse got a $100,000 inheritance that was the down payment on the house and you know it, don't plan on lying on the witness stand in the hopes that she won't be able to prove it. Give her the $100,000 credit and get the house sold, or get yourself refinanced off the mortgage with some cash in hand. The more you parse out issues, the more you reduce conflict. The more you settle issues that are foregone conclusions, the less time and money you spend in court. Fighting over old money of which the most you will get is $.50 of each dollar (and likely pay $.10-$.15 in attorneys fees to get it) is so much less productive than making new money while *still* getting $.50 of each dollar from that old money. Get the lawyers off the payroll as quickly as humanly possible. List out what you cannot agree on and go to trial on those issues alone.

·············· PRO TIP ··············

Remember: just because I said you should always settle within the Range of Normal Outcomes does not mean you should give up what is most important to you. In fact, if you must give up what is most important to you in order to settle, choose a trial instead—even if it means representing yourself against the baddest, meanest lawyer in town.

Only you know what the red center of the white flower is for yourself. Do not ever give up the red center (so long as it is a reasonable ask, and make sure you ask a lawyer if you are being unreasonable). If your red center is: you get to keep the house and your pension and pay no spousal support, you aren't being reasonable.

Get reasonable and determine the things you cannot live without and fight for those things. Once your spouse has said "yes," though, take yes for an answer.

··

To paraphrase Winston Churchill: "Never ever ever give up (that which is most dear to you)." If you cannot live with yourself unless you fight to keep your pension or for 50-50 (or more) timeshare with your children, then you must push to trial. You may learn that the Range of Normal Outcomes (along with your best-and-worst-case outcomes) is outside the range of what is most important to you. Yet, as long as you know that you may not get what you want and that you are walking an uphill road, you should push forward to trial. One caveat: I advise against spending $25,000 to keep your entire pension in a community property state where pensions are divided as a matter of course—unless you have a clear path to victory.

Learn from this book to help you figure out your red center and your white petals. Make sure they are reasonable for you to fight for and then, if they are, stay the course. But also, once you get into the Range of Reasonable Outcomes, start thinking very hard about settlement.

CHAPTER 2

Getting to "Reasonable" and Doing it Quickly:

How to Think about Your Case from the Beginning (and Why taking Advice from Professionals is so Important).

I HAVE BEEN practicing family law almost exclusively since 2008 in Santa Maria, a mid-sized city on the Central Coast of California. My courtrooms extend from Paso Robles, CA to San Luis Obispo, CA to Santa Barbara, CA to Ventura, CA on a north-south axis and to Bakersfield and Fresno to the East. I consult and/or act as lead counsel in high asset divorces in San Francisco, Alameda, and Marin Counties to the north and in Los Angeles to the South.

My clients are a wide range of ranchers and farmers, wine makers and wealthy retirees on the one end of the financial spectrum, and migrant and itinerant farm workers, laborers, and hospitality workers on the other end of the spectrum. I represent many blue-collar workers with union pensions, military service men and women (officers and enlisted, deployed and local) with duty station transfers and Military Retired Pay, high-tech workers with complex stock options (because SpaceX and other commercial space operators operate out of Vandenburg Space Force Base nearby, as well as numerous Department of Defense contractors), all sorts of business owners, CalPERS members, teachers, law enforcement and firefighters, nurses, and even other lawyers. I have argued Hague Convention petitions at the Federal Court and argued multiple times in front of the Appellate Court.

I have worked on probably one thousand cases since 2008 and have conducted hundreds of evidentiary hearings and trials of all sorts. I have qualified dozens of experts and elicited expert testimony.

I have been a part of countless negotiations, from formal negotiations presided over by a judge or mediator to informal, last minute "courthouse steps" negotiations.

I have represented every category of party to a divorce, including husbands divorcing wives, wives divorcing husbands, wives divorcing wives and husbands divorcing husbands, married couples dividing property purchased together, married couples dividing property where one party had most of the property before marriage or by inheritance, married couples with prenuptial agreements, married couples without prenuptial agreements, unmarried wealthy couples dividing property purchased together, unmarried couples on welfare trying to figure out custodial timeshare and child support, elderly couples divorcing for Medicare planning but do not intend to live separately and elderly couples who hate each other, elderly couples where one spouse died during the divorce, a young couple where the young husband committed "suicide by cop", a couple where the husband murdered my client and abducted the child and was, himself, killed by police officers in front of the child, couples who have reconciled, couples who get along but the grandmothers are warring, disputes over property where the couple is not planning on separating, and disputes over custody, paternity, and genetic testing. I have had several "three-parent" cases and a case in which a third-party paternity challenger was rebuffed by the Appellate Court.

•••••••••••••••• PRO TIP ••••••••••••••••

California, like most jurisdictions, has three levels of state courts. There is a trial court, which is where you will probably spend all your time. This is where the judge will hear your case. Some courthouses specialize the judge who hears family law cases; others shift judges around constantly so you may not have the same judge from hearing to hearing. Ultimately, there will be one judge who hears your trial (if you cannot settle your case reasonably). That is why this is called the "trial court." California does not have trial by jury for family law cases. All cases are heard by one judge, which is called a "bench trial," because the bench is where the judge sits. The place where the lawyers sit and stand is called "the bar."

In any case there are at least two "parties," usually the Plaintiff and Defendant. (In California divorces, they are called Petitioner and Respondent.) If any party is unhappy with the result of their trial, they have the option of "appealing" to the next highest court, which is known as the Appellate Court. Appellate Courts do not retry the facts of a case. That is the exclusive province of the trial courts. The Appellate Court only decides legal issues. In other words, they will only review the meaning of the facts as they relate to the law.

The trial court judge will decide whether the evidence supports Mother's contention that she was the child's primary caregiver. The Appellate Court will not support an appeal that asserts that Father was the primary caregiver; however, if the trial court says, "Mother is the primary caregiver and therefore can move to Washington State tomorrow," the Appellate Court will hear Father's appeal that the law requires a 30-day waiting period from the granting of an out-of-state move-away order to the date the order is effective so that the other party may appeal. Trial court judges make mistakes of law and they also regularly get presented new legal scenarios. When a case is appealed, the Appellate Court will write an opinion about why

Chapter 2 • Getting to "Reasonable" and Doing it Quickly: | 97

they rule in favor of H or W. They will give the legal reasoning and logic for their position.

These opinions interpret the law and have the effect of binding other judges who are presented with similar sets of facts. The 30-day waiting period for an out-of-state move away order is not a difficult case, because there is a statute says there will be a 30-day waiting period before any order that a parent can move out-of-state.

Conversely, there is no statute that tells us what to do when one spouse moves out of the Family Home and uses their now separate property income to pay the mortgage while their soon-to-be-ex-spouse continues to live in the home. There is, however, a law that says that income earned after separation is separate property and also a law that says, the Court must divide the marital estate equally. The trial court judge applies these two laws to the facts of the case (Wife moves out of the house but continues to pay the mortgage) and makes a ruling on what the parties must do. One of the parties appeals the ruling, and the Appellate Court determines whether the trial court's interpretation of the law is correct. The Appellate Court ruling becomes binding on other courts who will read the case and decide whether those facts analogize to their case. The thousands of case opinions written by the Appellate Court form a body of law called "the common law" or sometimes "caselaw." It is "common" because it is made on a case-by-case basis, as opposed to law made by legislatures, which is the Code or Statutes (the Family Code, the Probate Code, the Criminal Code).

There are many disagreements about how far judges should go in issuing opinions interpreting the law. Some judges go so far as to make new law in their "interpretations" of the law. For example, in 2015, the California Supreme Court issued an opinion which stated that so long as two married spouses are living together, they have not separated. This was critical to the division of certain assets and the determination of what money was community property and what was separate property. (The law says "after separation, all earnings are separate property".) The Family Law Bar (lawyers) was furious about this ruling because there were many thousands of people in very expensive homes who were separated but still living together for financial reasons. The California legislature responded by passing a new Family Code section 70 that says: "We disagree with the Court's ruling in *Marriage of Davis* and specifically override it. Parties who live together may be separated. The question of separation is based on a complete and final break in the marriage as determined by a) one party expressing this to the other and b) conduct in accordance with the complete and final break as determined by the evidence."

The third court, as I alluded to above, is the California Supreme Court. Appellate Courts must hear your appeal. It is obligatory. The Supreme Court does not. The Court decides which cases it wants to hear. It generally hears cases that are of widespread public interest, or cases where the Appellate Courts disagree with each other. Unless a case ends up at the United States Supreme Court (which is exceedingly rare) the California Supreme Court is the last word on any given subject.

··

There are many other categories of disputes in which I have been involved, but the ones above capture most of the different types of parties that can be involved in a family law matter. I have had custody orders for dogs, fights over avocado ranches, over cattle and their offspring, horses and their offspring, dogs and their offspring, surrogate parents, three parent households, one parent households, hundreds of two parent households and same sex parents. I have been a part of valuing all types of businesses, collectibles, stock options, pensions, RVs, boats, gems, crystals, dirt, property with marketable and unmarketable title, property that belonged to a Bankrupcy Trustee (oops, I got out of that one as fast as I could once I realized the pitfalls), wineries, and antiques. I have been paid in tamales and dollar store ties, assault rifles (I am not a gun guy so I never took possession but had them sold before they ever even made it to me), pink slips to vehicles, gold, work on my home (pro tip for lawyers: bad idea), and in goats and chickens (literally) and in organic, grass fed meat. I have worked on pro bono cases and cases that became pro bono cases, cases where I was paid as I billed in the hundreds of thousands of dollars and all sorts of cases in between.

I read recently that the average Los Angeles or San Francisco divorce costs $77,000 on each side. My average divorce in my city (not the expanded region in which I consult) runs about $30,000 to $45,000 on my side, plus probably the same on the other side, over the last few years. San Luis Obispo and Santa Barbara Divorces are running double that amount. Any case that I have worked on in Los Angeles or San Francisco areas has approached $100,000, which is because I only handle high asset cases or protracted custody fights in those jurisdictions.

In every single case (I am wracking my brain to think of one that does not fit), I have known the approximate outcome in the first one-hour consultation with my client, within the Range of Normal Outcomes – recall that the Range of Normal Outcomes is the range of expected outcomes in the case. The final outcome may vary a little bit within that Range, but the spread of possible, Normal Outcomes defines the range. No matter how much we spent or how we fought the case out, I could put my thumb on the scale to tip it our direction within that Range of Normal Outcomes, but almost never outside of that Range of Normal Outcomes, with the exception of a few very lucky and very unlucky "rogue" judge decisions that did not seem to fall anywhere near the law.

I've inherited cases where my client is getting pummeled by opposing counsel and the judge and tipped it back into our favor – usually through a series of strategic moves that take small advantages and exploit either desires by the other party or weaknesses we start to see through their actions – but always, always, always bringing it back within the Range of Normal Outcomes. I have also watched my clients self-destruct, snatching defeat from the jaws of victory because they got greedy and refused to consider good settlement offers within the Range of Normal Outcomes, even when I told them "Cory, it's time to say yes; this is a deal."

Through that experience, I have developed the theory of the Range of Normal Outcomes through two hypotheses, driven by my prior social scientific research on the meaning of "reasonability" in the law and my experiences as a trial litigator.

I believe that **1) the law is driven by reasonability (which means for right now: what the average person would believe to be a correct action**[1]**) and 2) Judges tend to believe that the outcome in a divorce case should be fair (which means for right now: something that looks moderately equal).** The California Family Code requires an "equal" division of assets, while many non-community property states follow an "equitable" division of assets, but in either event, "fairness" is the overwhelming odds-on-favorite outcome.

For 1) above, the law is based around the concept of reasonability – you aren't liable for someone else's injury if you acted *reasonably*, even if your actions were not perfect, but you are liable where your actions were *unreasonable*, even if accidental. "Reasonable" is normally a mashup of a) an *objective* standard: what would

---

1 Note that I did not say "the" correct action. The reason why the "range of normal" is a range is that there are a number of possible outcomes within that range that a reasonable judge could determine to be reasonable.

a normal, typical person in this situation do? (or if it is a doctor or lawyer or other professional, "what would a normal, typical doctor do in this situation?"); and b) a subjective standard: did you think what you were doing was reasonable?

For 2) above, we ask, "what is reasonable under the circumstances of this particular case?" In California, "reasonable" sounds like half, which sounds like "fairness." In equitable distribution states, "reasonable" sounds like "equity" or "fairness" – maybe not exactly half, but something that approximates half. But note, in most equitable distribution sates, most outcomes are close to half of marital assets; and in most community property states (where fairness = half), most divisions of assets are not exactly half.

Divorces in most states should divide the marital property equally between spouses (or something that looks pretty equal that is called "equitable"). For our purposes, we will treat the two as the same, since an equitable division of assets tends to look very close to an equal division of assets even though the paths to arrive there take different routes. This equation is imperfect, but the results are only marginally different.

In my consultations with new clients, I spend about 15 minutes just letting them vent about what has been happening, then I systematically—but also gently and with true compassion for them—ask them about three categories of issues that I will need to analyze their case:

> 1) **<u>Children</u>**: what are the ages of their children? Upon which parent is the burden (and supreme joy) of raising them the heaviest? For older children, what would they say if you asked them which parent they were closest to? For late teenagers, what would they like to do?
>
> 2) **<u>Support:</u>** What are the incomes of the parties? Do they have a business or W2 income? How long was the mar-

riage? Did anyone give up a career to raise children?

3) **Property:** What property do they own? How did they get it? Did they have any property before marriage, or did they inherit any property?

Those three categories cover almost everything – I certainly go into much more detail than that in my consultations with new clients, but those are the basic categories. With rare exceptions, having all that information, I can discern how the entire case will work out within that Range of Normal Outcomes, which generally means somewhere between 45% and 55% of the property items and money will end up with the person sitting across the table from me, with $X amount of support and Y% timeshare with the children.

I will also ask in that first meeting, what my client *wants* as their one-half(ish) of the property, how much they can pay in support/or need to live on and how much they think is reasonable to share the children ("If you were king or queen of the world and could dictate any outcome, what would that outcome be now that you understand the basics of the law?"). Then we drive everything in the case toward their preferred outcomes. Sometimes a party will end up with 47% of the assets but they got the assets that mattered most to them and they feel like they won – I assert that they did "win the divorce" if they got the property that mattered to them most.

So, once I have a pretty good handle on the case, the question is, why does it still cost on average $42,000 afterward? The reason, from my anecdotal and experienced perspective, is that people think it should take longer and cost more than it should. So, they pay it. They gear up for big battles. They allow their emotions to dictate their actions. They want their *Law and Order* trial or, as in a case I am working on now, they fear the *Law and Order* trial so much that they will spend tens of hours negotiating over something relatively small. And they do not listen to lawyers who genuinely try to get cases resolved efficiently and quickly. How many couples have spent $50,000-$100,000 just fighting over 12-24 hours per week of visitation with minor children or $200 per month in a 10-year spousal or child support order ($2,400 per year for ten years with no interest, payable in monthly installments versus $15,000 payable to the lawyer now with only a x% chance of success)? How many are driven by a fear-based mentality that their spouse told them they are going to "take them to the cleaners," no matter how many times I have told them that the Family Law just does not allow this to happen without a terrible agreement that I would never let them sign?

I literally just as I am typing this have been text messaging with an engineer-client who is based out of state. He has been trying to negotiate with his soon-to-be ex-wife about child support. Child support, as I discuss below, is, in almost every jurisdiction, not difficult to calculate. It is mostly done by formula. There are input variables and we do some massaging of these variables to tip the balance a little bit in one direction or another, but for the most part, the largest portion of child support payments is based on the incomes of the parties and the timeshare with the children. Most parties are W-2 wage earners and we can calculate the timeshare readily (it can be more difficult when one spouse is not working full-time or one or both spouses have trust funds or cash businesses or discretionary bonusses or stock options).

My engineer client has been running every possible set of variables to get a child support number in a negotiation. I have told him repeatedly that no matter how many different ways he can run the numbers through the computer program called "Dissomaster" to get a child support figure, the low end is $750 per month (if he wins every single argument about every single variable) and the high end is $1,100 per month (if Wife wins every single argument about every single variable), with the most likely outcome approximately

$850 ($848 per month). Being an engineer, he wants to have an "objective" outcome – a number he can count on. I tell him there is no number to count on if we ask a judge because, in order to get the low-end, we need win our interpretation of every variable (count overtime hours for the Wife, count her 20-year-old daughter from a previous marriage as a federal exemption, do not count her future health insurance payments because we do not yet know what they will be, count only my client's mortgage interest deduction from the home he lives in and not depreciation from his rental property), which is unlikely at trial. Wife gets the high-end if she wins each of these variables (no overtime, no exemption for 20-year-old, an estimated health insurance premium, and including depreciation from the rental property as income).

But the spread is not that great between $750 and $1,100 for a man who earns well over $100,000 per year – it's not nothing, but to spend $25,000 going to trial over a $4,200 per year range in child support for a child who only has 4 more years of minority, makes no sense (Quick math: the worst case outcome for my client is an additional $16,800 in interest free child support payments at $350 per month payable over 4 years; going to trial will cost $25,000 now and he still will lose at least one and may lose all of his arguments regarding the variables. For him, the optics are bad because he has a good income, lives in an inexpensive state and sees the child a few times per year on school holidays; a judge is going to want to see the support number range on the higher end of the support spectrum). You can quickly see that the only reason to go to trial over child support is spite – and that's not a good reason to do it, even if you think it might feel good.

He sent me a text message this morning to tell me that he had "checked" my numbers with a free online program and found that the most likely number was $820 per month. My number is $848.

Are we going to have a $25,000 trial over $28 per month? I hope not.[2] For purposes of completion of the story – in draft 1 of this book, we were negotiating the number. By the time I came back to editing this chapter, we had long ago settled the child support matter at $700 per month with Husband to pay for airline tickets for visits. Add in $2,000 per year for airline tickets and support looks pretty close to $848 per month ($700 x 12 months - $8,400 + $2,000 = $10,400/12 = $866 per month, but if he buys tickets in advance, he may get them a little cheaper than $2,000 per year and knock that total number down to his $820 per month).

I have taken to explaining during my new client consultations that we can draft up an agreement and resolve the entire case for $7,500 or so with a complete agreement and a judgment of dissolution, no problem; all it takes is for the other party to participate and agree. I tell them that a couple of years ago we did a divorce for a couple with $7 million in a widely diversified asset portfolio for $3,500. There weren't any minor children, so it was easier, but both parties said, "it's divide by two, right?" The math was easy: $3.5 million to each side. They took turns picking what they wanted, but it was actually pretty simple because: in my household, if I want to borrow my wife's car, I ask her and if she wants to borrow my truck, she asks me. At the end of the day, we know the truck is mine and the car is hers, even though we both pay for both. That was true in the $7 million case too. Wife wanted the commercial building in downtown Avila Beach, CA, and Husband wanted the 12 acres in

---

2   Throughout this book, I use examples from my own practice. I cut the examples to their most bare factual issues and then modify them enough that if you went to the courthouse to get all of the pleadings in all of my cases, you would not likely be able to distinguish which case I refer to. However, to dispel any worries about attorney-client privilege, all examples I use are in the public domain. If there is an attorney-client privilege issue with any example, I will have stripped the case of any identifying information so there is no way for you or the former client to distinguish; but if you went to the courthouse and read all 1,000 or so cases in which I have been involved, I am still confident that you would not be able to identify the parties in any particular case.

Arroyo Grande, CA – he liked having an ocean view and wanted to have a gentleman's farm and she liked living in the beach town where so many come to vacation and had always kept an apartment in the building unrented so she could stay in it when she felt like it. From there we started dividing investment accounts. Husband got his Jaguar and Wife got her Subaru, etc.

If you can really listen to an experienced lawyer tell you what the likeliest outcome will be (within a range), you can short-circuit a lot of the process and cost. You move quickly to the Range of Normal Outcomes and start negotiating from a position where the outcomes are most likely.

When you do this, you realize that using my prior analogy to the three-act play, most of the outcomes of your divorce are pre-scripted from the very beginning. I am not such a genius or clairvoyant because I know the likely outcome in the first hour-long consultation; I know the outcome because the outcomes are clear from the scripting. We do not have to spend hundreds of hours creating all of the conditions of a settlement agreement from scratch if you have a good handle on relevant facts from the get-go.

CHAPTER 3

A Personal Story

Of Breakfasts and Golf Games – Two Old Sayings with Real Meaning

IF YOU HAD taken a poll of the approximately 720 members of the three classes at the University of California, Berkeley Boalt Hall School of Law in the year that I graduated (2004) and asked, "Who plans on being a solo practitioner practicing family law in a mid-sized city?" zero hands would have been raised. Not only would I not have raised my hand; I would have ignored the question, since it was so far off from what I planned to do with my law degree and the Ph.D. I was earning in tandem with it. I was truly an academic who planned on working as a law professor when the law school music stopped playing. The year I graduated I was also in the throes of finishing a doctoral dissertation entitled, "The Stewardship Claim: Managing Hazardous Regulatory Environments at Los Alamos National Laboratory" (UC Berkeley Ph.D. in Jurisprudence and Social Policy, 2008).

I was not someone entertaining the idea of family law as a career field. In many respects, lawyers from the type of law school I attended think of family law as the "ghetto" of the law—until they go through a divorce themselves. A probate lawyer told me on a recent case that he wanted "nothing to do with the family law part of the action. Jude," he said, "I don't give a fuck about the family law. I don't want to know about it. And I never plan on knowing anything about it." I am continually amazed at how little probate and trust lawyers know about family law (it is important in Probate because Probate Code section 100 – the first code section – says that a person can bequeath 50% of the community property, which is a huge arena in family law). In fact, considering 50% of marriages end in divorce, I am surprised at how little anyone besides family lawyers know about family law—and that includes virtually EVERY family law judge you will meet in any courtroom. I litigated a huge trust case once against a partner in a big San Francisco firm and was shocked when reading her briefing at how little she knew about family law. Her briefing was horrifically wrong and repeatedly so. Matters became worse when the judge, whom I had then practiced in front of for more than 10 years (and thought I had educated about the family law), ruled horrifically incorrectly about the family law part of the case. I took the case on appeal and the appellate court rubber stamped the trial court judge's incorrect view of the law. You can read that case if you Google *Estate of Hanako Nelson* or *Wilkin v. Nelson* (2020) B294530. Normally I prefer to talk about cases I have won rather than lost, but I think it is instructive to learn that even when you've educated the judge and the other side has no reasonable idea of what the hell they are talking about, you can still lose. And I still believe we lost that case because the 85-year-old husband came to trial in a jacket that was 11 sizes too big for him and the trial court judge just felt badly for him.

In law school I never took a single class in family law, despite having Dean Herma Hill Kay, the greatest family law academic of the 20th Century, on our faculty. Although Family Law is a bar discipline, I went into the bar with only a thumbnail's width of knowledge. (Eddie Murphy's famous and deeply sexist line from his standup classic *Raw*: "Ed-DIE, I want HALF!" in my head.) I hoped to death there wasn't a family law question on the exam (and there wasn't). In many ways, Family Law is a "gunslinger's paradise" with few types of legal motions and a lot of emotion. The types of lawyers who gravitate to Family Law often excel above their peers from more tony law schools who expect Family Law to be purely law-driven or who stay away from the practice area out of a fear that "it's too emotional," preferring to stay in the world of antitrust or contract litigation.

The soon-to-be-birth of my now 16-year-old child was a life-changing event for me. After 4 years of looking for that perfect academic job and slogging through my career as a real estate lawyer working for others (always hoping that one day soon there would be that perfect professor job where I could leave professional lawyering behind forever), I was grounded in one place. To make matters more challenging, the developer market was falling apart as the 2008 financial crisis hit high gear and I lost my job. It was at that moment the job offer I had been waiting for came in—only it was at the Ourso Business College at Louisiana State University where I did work on disaster management. For three years after my child was born, I commuted to Baton Rouge, LA from California, and I wrote a series of disaster-themed peer-reviewed papers. (When you are bored, look them up on Google Scholar.) My Business School Dean finally offered me the Director of Research position, but only if I agreed to relocate to Baton Rouge.

My child's mom and I had already realized by then that things were not going to work out between us. Nevertheless, I knew that moving across the country without my child was not a possibility (my child has, in the intervening years, determined that they are gender nonbinary and so, if the use of pronouns seems clunky here,

I honor them and their identity by using they/them pronouns to describe them).

Right around then my ex sued me for custody of our child and child support. To say I was a devoted father is an understatement, but I will spare all the boring details. It was the most horrible time in my life. I can remember sitting on the witness stand getting cross-examined by the biggest bitch of a lawyer in town (who now, by the way, comes to dinner at my house). She asked me what my plans were, and I told her that I was going to keep working at LSU and publishing my research, and that I was going to hang a shingle in Santa Maria, CA. She asked what kind of law I was going to practice, and I said, "Family law—because I want to make sure that this will never happen to me again."

As I sat in the courtroom in front of that judge (someone whom I now—15 years later—regularly practice family law in front of), I realized truly that family court is the worst place in the entire world. You have a judge who doesn't know you making decisions about how much time you get to spend with your child—knowing nothing about him or her either—and who divides your money and tells you where you can live.

Our Judge told us we were the best parents he'd seen in his courtroom in a year. Then he told me to figure out what I was going to do with my life and told my ex that he didn't see any reason that we shouldn't have a 50-50 custody relationship as soon as our child turned two-years-old. (He also told my ex that if she were to get "hit by a bus" he would give custody to me and not think twice about it.)

After the "hit by a bus" admonition, the Judge then gave me the standard "dad" plan—every other weekend and Wednesday afternoons. He also told us he planned to review his decision in 7 months when he thought we might be able to move to 50-50. In those 7 months I went from having my child every day to sometimes not seeing them for a week. My Wednesday afternoon visits were torture. We would go to the park and I would have to take them to the park's men's room to go potty. I had four hours with them on those Wednesdays, not enough time for us to even drive home to San Luis Obispo and back to Santa Maria again.

I decided to hang a shingle in Santa Maria, CA and make a life as best as I could. It was four years since earning my law degree and I had still never practiced in a courtroom. Scared shitless, I rented an office for $150 per month with windows that rattled every time a truck rolled by. The first cases to come in the door were family law cases. I assumed wrongly that since the family lawyers were charging $350 an hour, I could charge $150 an hour and get tons of business. That is exactly how people do *not* make decisions when they hire a lawyer. They know it's going to cost a lot and they don't want to pay a lawyer willing to work for peanuts. When I raised my rates to $275, I started getting business. I am sure there are other business that work similarly.

I learned very quickly that family law is enigmatic. On the one hand there are a series of guiding legal principles and code sections that govern most cases. Knowing those few basic rules, most lawyers can practice in family court. But beyond those few basic rules, the Family Code and the caselaw interpreting it gets fractured and complex. As I went deeper into the subject, as is my custom, I began reading the cases and the code sections. I started to understand that property rules involve highly-complex accounting if your clients are willing to spend dollars litigating over pennies (it is still just math, but the math can get complicated when you don't have work arounds), pensions require precise language for division, child and spousal support numbers can be massaged, and that reimbursements and *pro tanto* property interests factor heavily in divorce cases.

The Family Code and the caselaw interpreting it—the "Rules"—are rational and reasonable and as complex as any area of the law.

I also learned that judges are enigmatic.

There are two old sayings that bear repeating in this context.

Saying 1: "The law is what the Judge ate for breakfast."

This saying derives from the fact that judges will make decisions based partially on their whims. One judge favors shared custody but higher support payments, another doesn't care a whit about custody parity but gets annoyed at support obligations. Another judge may rule based on her "feelings" about right and wrong, or even through a thinly veiled religious leaning ("I mean, he has a character letter from his minister in his evidence binder. He really can't be all that bad," an Orange County judge once said to the opposing party during a hearing I was working on).

Consequently, there are variations in rulings on nearly equivalent fact-patterns in any group of judges, which gives lawyers conniption fits.

If I write a well-researched, completely documented brief but lose in a way that has no rational relationship to one of those ways that I identified in my briefing – for example if the Court had picked a number outside the Range of Normal Outcomes – I know that the judge has ruled based on what he or she ate for breakfast. Judges normally rule within the Range of Normal Outcomes, but it's those days when they don't when I find myself walking on the beach alone questioning my life's choices.

I have peppered the book with cases I have worked on where judicial temperament mattered to judicial decision-making. If you take a reasonable approach to the outcomes you seek in your divorce, you have the highest likelihood of getting what you want, but it is only a "likelihood," no one can ever guarantee you an outcome. Because "reasonability" repeats over and over throughout the law (and across disciplines), judges are driven to look for reasonable outcomes. The person presenting the most reasonable position is the one most likely to win.

What does that mean? Great lawyers aren't the ones taking impossible-to-win positions (except to the extent they can get you to cave by threatening you with $80,000 or $800,000 attorney's fee motions). Great lawyers are the ones who although they know 50% is the most likely outcome will try and present 55% as the reasonable outcome. The good news is that in family law the law says 50%, so when you lose *an* issue you rarely lose the entire case. That said, I still remember virtually all of the times when I have butted heads with a judge over a legal issue and lost . . . and I do not like these memories one bit.

Saying 2: "A good lawyer knows the law. A great lawyer knows the judge."

The cynical part of me understands that old saying to mean, "A great lawyer plays golf with, goes to church with, is on Rotary with, or socializes with the judge." I do not, as a rule, socialize with my judges. I have worked very hard to build a reputation for honesty and assertive representation with the court. I call a judge out when I feel they are wrong and I advocate with everything I have in me. I told a new client last week, "We may not win, but I promise I will still be swinging as they drag me out of the courtroom."[3] However, I also work overtime to assist judges by settling impossible to settle cases, to reduce trial loads, to step in on difficult cases where there is no money, to represent deployed military veterans (for free), to defend parents facing petitions to terminate parental rights (for free),

---

3   That was truly hyperbole. I do not get animated in my cases unless I must, and that is very very rare. However, I do not give up. I do not accept shitty results. And I think anyone who has seen me in court knows that I will always drive my agenda until the judge sends me packing.

to represent survivors of domestic violence (for free) and to represent children in divorces (for a reduced rate).

Because I recognize that judges, even judges who are deeply wrong about the Family Law or who make no real attempts to learn it, are human beings who represent the larger legal system, I draw the line at disrespect. I refuse to disrespect any judge. Why? Number one, I think it is unbecoming of a lawyer to disrespect a judge; and number two, my allegiance is to the judicial system and not to any one judge. I am not going to be a part of undermining anyone's faith in the legal system by undermining a judge. I practice in courtrooms full of unrepresented parties and brand-new lawyers, and I refuse to be the one teaching them that disrespectful behavior is acceptable. I have had to accuse judges of bias in the past, but I have always done it in chambers with no court reporter and no citizens sitting in the gallery to watch.

Let this be the most important lesson of this book:

Do not, under any circumstances, disrespect the Court.

Not only will it do nothing for you in terms of winning your case (likely the opposite) it also dishonors the legal system in general.

Anyway, back to the second saying. A great lawyer does not "know" the judge, but a great lawyer "understands" the judge. That means, you can stand in and represent yourself, but if you do, I encourage you to go to court on a day when your case is not going to be called and listen and learn from the judge. Learn how they respond to challenges. Watch the lawyers. Listen to the amount of deference lawyers give the judge and the amount of pushback they give the judge.

My experience is that in family law virtually all judges will give nearly everyone an opportunity to speak—so speak! If you need to write it out ahead of time and read it to the court, that is not preferable, but it is fine. Apologize to the court, tell the judge you get nervous and that out of respect for the Court's time you want to read your statement so that it is clear and factual, and to make sure you do not forget anything. (If you are going to read it, keep it very short.) Remember there is a person in the front of the courtroom writing everything down, so *go slowly*. And go even more slowly than that. Look up and make eye contact. Focus on what you've learned from the judge about the way they rule. Be polite and say thank you to the Court for listening to you. Be polite to clerks, court reporters, and bailiffs. Open the door and hold it open for others coming into and out of the courtroom. This is a place for respect, but it is also a place for you to say everything need to say. Never use the word "lie" (use the word "misrepresentation" instead). Never call names. Always address the Court and never the other lawyer or party. Remember to refer to the Judge as "Your Honor," not "Ma'am" or "Mrs. Smith" or "Sir" or "Mr. Johnson." A lawyer can sometimes get away with referring to a judge directly as "Judge" as in "Judge, this case has the following facts in it...," but you should not. There is one way to address a judge as far as you are concerned and that is as "Your Honor."

Make no mistake, the two "old sayings" should strike fear in your heart. I practice regularly in front of a dozen judges, know their psychology very well, and I still do not like to base my clients' outcomes on what the judge ate for breakfast or on their basic psychology. For you it is worse because you are a "one-shotter" for whom this court experience will be your one and only. It is why trying to settle is so critical. Most of the time keeping the ball out of the judge's hands is the first, smartest move you can make whenever possible.

Remember that Family Law, like the law in general, seeks to find reasonable outcomes. Be yourself in court, but be your most likable and *reasonable* self. Acid-dripping declarations that list every time your soon-to-be-ex-wife cheated on you with the baseball coach and how she did it in front of the nanny cam to make sure you would see the footage, can backfire on you. Remember the example declaration I gave previously: be filthy by playing clean. "I am hopeful that he will improve on his parenting in the time to come and I will absolutely encourage the children to spend more time with him as he grounds himself." Do not argue with the Judge and, by all means, DO follow their orders.

And as I have said repeatedly, do not make deals that you cannot live with.

Remember that this is not only your origin story (how you became a single mom and had to learn how to do all sorts of things or how you became a single dad and learned to be more present for your kids) but it is your children's origin story (how their happy and contented single-family lives became fragmented and broken into two homes, and how their parents rose to the occasion and were, daresay, better parents for it). I cannot tell you how much pride I take in standing to do battle for someone who has taken the high road and can be proud of following the approach they set out to follow.

PART II

The View from the Clouds (50,000 Feet)

CHAPTER 4

The Rule of Reasonability and The Range of Normal

Why No One Should Get "Screwed in the Divorce" and How Those Threats of "Taking Everything" Aren't Real

The Rule of Reasonability

PREPARATION FOR THE bar exam begins with two stacks of books three feet tall. My law school classmates with whom I studied for the exam had those photographic minds that can memorize 6 feet of bar review books in 6 weeks. I tried it. I have a great memory and am a great test taker. In fact, I joke that taking tests is my gift; everyone gets at least one gift from their DNA or their god and mine was the gift of taking standardized tests. But memorizing that much information in that short of a time wasn't going to work for me.

I had to come up with a better way than rote memorization to get through the bar exam.

For the first time in my legal education, I lined up all the legal subjects next to each other and learned or re-learned each of them. I had developed a theory that the law is guided by a single principal, and from that principal almost anyone can reason their way to the right outcome. Let me say this: this is not my original theory; there is plenty of writing on this subject, by very famous law school professors, but professors tend to be stovepiped into their areas of expertise, and I had not come across any academic writer who was writing about how the American Law (writ large) might be reduced to a single principal.

That principal saved me on the Bar Exam. Anytime I did not know the answer to a specific question I went back to this general rule and reasoned my way to what the outcome of a case should be. There are times of course when the actual legal rule does not intuitively track this General Rule, but by thinking through it you can still usually find your way to the solution.

This general rule is the "Rule of Reasonability."

The Legal Role and Rule of Reasonability

Reasonability has other names in the law: Rationality, Equity, Fairness, Justice, and Negligence, in particular. The Range of Normal Outcomes fits in here as well because although "Normal" is not a legal word per se, what is "normal" is usually "reasonable."

The Rule of Reasonability asks, "Did the person think their action was reasonable? Would another person—similarly situated—think the action was reasonable?" This is subjective-objective in its application – would any particular but nonexistent "normal" person do this? (Objective). Did the actual person who did it, think it was reasonable when they did it? (Subjective).

Although the law is famously littered with exceptions to general rules, it turns out that reasonability applies across all sorts of areas of the law. For ex., minority shareholders' rights in a corporation are reasonable (examine books and records; demand equal and fair distributions as majority shareholders; not pay more in taxes than they are obligated to pay, etc.); innkeepers owe their guests higher duties of care than I owe you on the street (because people are sleeping in rooms designed to be rented to them for that purpose); doctors have to treat you at the standard of care for other doctors situated similarly as they are (but not more than that); and police officers and firefighters are immune from prosecution for making mistakes while doing their jobs (because they do them under high pressure and the nature of the tasks is such that it is not always clear that anyone will always make the right decision in the field). However, they are not immune from prosecution when they do things outside their jobs. (Sexual violence or biased police work are, for example, still things for which police officers can be held liable).

What I learned while studying for (and passing!) the bar exam is that even the exceptions are really just the Rule of Reasonability pushed a little harder. In the next section, I give a few examples about exceptions to the general rule of reasonability to illustrate the point.

Reasonability matters more than anything else in the law. Since most legal rules are Rules of Reasonability, most of how you approach Family Law (or any legal issue you face) should begin with reasonability as your focus.

This is why I can determine Range of Normal Outcomes in the first hour of meeting a potential new client. If you know the facts, you know what a Reasonable outcome looks like. Community property states, like California, say 50% of the marital property goes to each party while "equitable distribution" states say property should be distributed equitably to each party. Knowing this, plus the basic facts of a case, should be enough information to form a Range of Normal (Reasonable) Outcomes. This is generally true in both community property and equitable distribution states.

PRO TIP

In a legal sense "equity" means "fairness." Fairness almost always means "reasonability". We cannot be 100% sure that "reasonable" always means "fair," but we can be sure that "fair" always means "reasonable." Thus, "equitable distribution" is "reasonable distribution" under the particular circumstances of a given case. Normally that also means a type of "fair distribution." This is not meant to sound like gobbledygook, but rather to show you that there are a number of legal-sounding words that are repeated over and over again, and although you can split hairs over their definitions, in many senses they mean the same thing or something very similar.

My overall point is that "equal," "equitable," "fair," and "reasonable" (and you can probably add the words "just" or "justice") all have similar meanings, but are used differently in different contexts. I use the word "reasonable" to suggest an outcome that would include "equal" (which would be exactly 50-50) and "equitable" (which would be near 50-50 but may include specific circumstances limited to each of the parties).

Let's look at this in practice:

Example 1: Reasonability in Child Custody Determinations

Increasingly throughout the country—assuming each parent is emotionally and mentally well—courts are leaning toward larger shared custodial timeshares and more joint custody of the children. I suspect this is because of the increasing role fathers are playing in the day-to-day child rearing activities and because mothers are increasingly high-earners with careers that they care deeply about.

The California Family Code sets forth that "reasonable visitation" means "continuing care and contact." This means that a judge has wide-latitude in making almost any custody determination she sees fit to make, but in no event should custody be shared "unreasonably."

You could almost start with the idea that "continuing care and contact" is the reasonable outcome of any child custody determination. And, for parents who do not have much timeshare, any deviation from "continuing care and contact" is "reasonable" based on other factors (usually: drugs, crimes, violence, or mental health issues).

For California courts, the most reasonable custodial orders are those that look something like the status quo. California (like many states that have moved to a "continuing custody" framework for the children's "primary caregiver" when deciding future custody orders) takes a sort of "reasonable" approach. These state statutes regarding custody orders reflect the legislatures' beliefs that it is reasonable for the parent who carries the heaviest burden of raising the children to continue to do so – or stated more positively, the children have a right to not have their lives disrupted by divorce and, as a result, the parent upon whom they most rely for their daily needs is likely to be the parent upon whom they will continue to be able to rely.

This is the definition of a *status quo* finding – we do everything we can to keep the status quo for children even though their world is being turned upside down by their parents' divorce. "*Status quo*" is usually viewed as reasonable in a divorce, since that is what the parties were doing prior to the divorce. For the other parent, who presumably carries the heaviest burden of providing financial support for the children, the *status quo* is maintained for that role as well. This tends to mean that the parent who was doing more of the day-to-day activities with the children will be responsible to continue doing that and the person who was doing more of the earning and financial provision for the family will continue to do that. Courts call the day-to-day caregiver, "the primary caregiver." The other parent who is tasked with providing financial support and does less day-to-day post-divorce parenting is the "supporting" parent or the "support-paying parent." Many state legislatures (and judges) believe it is unreasonable to assume that these roles would flip-flop in a divorce.

This is typically why the stay-at-home or part-time-employed parent tends to be awarded custody of the children with "visitation" to the other parent. It is not because the stay-at-home or part-time employed parent is "better" or "more parental," but because reasonability requires that each parent continues the role they were in before the divorce—in part at least to minimize the impact of divorce on children by not upending their parental caregiving and in part because typically families will already have determined that it makes more sense for the one parent to be the primary caregiver and the other to be the supporting parent. This is conventional wisdom—although lawyers like me (a divorced dad) have worked very hard to push back on this type of judicial thinking.

We found in 2008-2010 as the country sank into recession (and when men, employed in the trades, were out of work, but women who worked in the helping professions—teachers and nurses in particular—continued working) that the gender-neutral logic of the law was not reality. The judges were still awarding custody to working mothers and telling out-of-work fathers to get a job. If you are like me and you seek to create greater parity between the sexes when it comes to parenting time, you will understand my basic position that we should always begin with a default 50-50 order for custody and then reduce that for one side or the other depending on whether there are drugs, crimes, violence, mental illness, or, perhaps, where a parent's work schedule does not allow for extended time (such as certain types of shift workers). I believe that ultimately this is better for mothers too, because it gives them more time to work on careers and their own lives. This is one area of the law where "reasonability" is very hard to predict (unless you follow the conventional wisdom that "primary caregivers" should have primary custody with the other parent resigned to paying for things, which I do not). I will discuss this more later in the book in the custody and visitation chapter.

The chapter on child custody and visitation later in the book also describes how we work in my practice to overcome the notion that the "reasonable" approach to parenting is more of the same pre-divorce parenting. On the other hand, we are seeing a newer and younger and more diverse group of judges recognizing that it is very common for two parent households to share the laboring oar of child rearing in relatively new ways – mom starts work early so dad drops off at school; mom gets off work earlier, so she picks up from school. Dad takes daughter to dance; mom takes son to soccer. Someone is stopping at the store for dinner and they take turns getting the kids through the shower and into bed. These can be pretty equal parenting responsibilities, even if one parent is resentful that the other does not "do enough" parenting, which happens in many relationships that are ending up in divorce.

By way of foreshadowing, I argue that the part-time or stay-at-home parent should be given the opportunity to self-actualize in the work force – that is, long-term, better not only for the kids but for the parent as well. I also argue that that full-time working parent should be given an opportunity to grow into their role as parent – it is not uncommon at all for the division of family labor to be based on historical family decisions. If dad, for example, has a higher hourly rate as a union shop construction foreman, mom may not take additional shifts as a dental hygienist. When the kids are home sick, mom takes the day off. When we were stuck in pandemic hell, mom was home doing the homeschooling. This may not be what anyone *wants*, but financial pressures have created these incentive structures in the home. This does not mean that in a custody context, we cannot aspire to different parenting structures – including the use of childcare (familial and free or paid and structured) – to give both parents more parenting time and provide that the part-time employed parent has an opportunity to provide for themselves and the children financially. The data seem to suggest that parents who become full-time caregivers after divorce have a harder time financially, are less likely to remarry, and feel more bogged down by parental duties, while the (very) part-time parent feels alienated from the children, does better financially (even if paying a large support amount) and eventually starts a new family to make up for the loneliness of not having their children around. This type of approach is lose-lose.

Again, the parenting timeshare section has much more detail on this, but the feminist literature is mixed on parenting responsibilities for mothers. On the one had, there is a the general feeling that women do the heavy lifting in child rearing so when you give 50-50 out of the gate to dads, moms lose (because less child support). On the other hand, there is a body of literature that says that there is nothing to say that parenting is "women's work" and that more parenting time tends to harm women financially. All situations are unique but my general take (as a CIS-gendered white man with a nonbinary kid in an interracial marriage – so take my position with a "knowledgeable grain of salt") is that the best outcome for entire families (moms, dads, and kids) is for dads to pick up half of the parenting load, support moms via spousal support (to make up for child support losses from the 50-50 shared custody) for a period of time to let moms get trained and look for good paying jobs. As with anything in the law, there are as many exceptions to this as rules (crimes, drugs, violence and mental health, of course, ages of children, availability of child care – it makes no sense to pay a child-care provider to watch children if that will cost more than mom's income – special needs children and etc.)

Although custody decisions are perhaps the most challenging decisions to predict ahead of time, the Range of Normal Outcomes for most judges is readily predictable—provided the parents are mostly reasonable. We know that it will be no less than "objectively reasonable visitation" for either parent (in the absence of drugs, crimes, violence, or mental health problems. And even then we can argue that limited visitation is reasonable for people suffering those maladies).

In my courthouses in front of my judges, the Range of Normal Outcomes on a 14-day schedule is between 4-10 nights with each parent. In other words, unless I know I am in front of a 50-50 judge—or unless there are drugs, crimes, jail time, abuse, or mental health issues, or one of the children is very young, or has special needs or one parent works far away or works odd hours—I can be sure that a judge will rule that one parent will have 4 nights out of 14 on the low-end and 10 nights out of 14 on the high end, with 7 nights out of 14 as the most likely result (5 nights is every other extended weekend: Friday after school to Monday school drop-off plus a mid-week overnight). The other factors are where most litigation occurs.

················· PRO TIP ·················

Almost all my highest litigation expenditure cases have involved fighting within the Range of Normal: one parent (usually the Father) has 5 nights out of 14 but wants a true 50-50 (7 nights out of 14) and spends $50,000 - $100,000 to try to get it. I wanted 50-50 with my daughter too, so I fully understand this. But you must always ask yourself if it is worth litigating for it when you are already within the Range of Normal Outcomes?

In my own circumstance we made the initial agreement for 5 nights out of 14. Then I asked my ex, "When is it going to be time for 50%?" She told me when she thought it would be appropriate. I held her to it and to her credit (and I always try to give her credit whenever I can because we have mostly gotten along) she kept her word—even though I know that she did not want to.

My overall philosophy is to stop fighting once you get within the Range of Normal Outcomes. I will not tell you that accepting less than 50-50 is a reasonable and acceptable outcome because it is "in the children's best interests." I hear that phrase being strewn about particularly by mothers who use it as some sort of justification for cutting fathers out of children's lives.

Hear me now, loud, and clear...

...I do not for a moment believe that it is in your child's best interest to spend less than half the time with either parent, unless there are one of several factors at play: drugs, criminality, violence, long distances, very young or special needs children, children who are very close to 18, or serious mental health problems. "Best interests" arguments made by parents are usually just emotional arguments appealing subjectively to an "objective standard." It is a debate fallacy and one that should be rejected.

That said, I absolutely do think there are great reasons to settle your custody dispute within the Range of Normal Outcomes even if it is not a true 50-50. First, 36% (5 nights out of 14) is actually a lot of time, and (most importantly) it ensures the other parent does not have a legal or statutory right to move-away with your children. Second, as a backup position from 50-50 it feels like you are giving up a lot of ground, but 2 nights out of 14 (especially school nights) is not as big a deal as you might think. Third, this is where you can get sucked into spending your entire 401(k) in attorney's fees, fighting with lawyers and judges over what seems to any reasonable judge as a reasonable timeshare. I DO believe it is in the children's "best interests" for you to spend less money on lawyers and less time fighting in the courtroom, especially with all its attendant stresses and sleepless nights.

By now you should know my mantra by rote: Get to the Range of Normal Outcomes and make an agreement—UNLESS it is something that you absolutely cannot accept.

....

Example 2: The Mental State of Reasonability: Keeping Reasonable Outcomes on the Front Burner of Your Mind

Keep Reasonability in your mind as you negotiate what you want from your spouse or the Court. This second type of Reasonability is a state of mind; the former is the state of the law. The law seeks a Reasonable outcome. It is being reasonable when it develops a Range of Normal Outcomes as a framework within which you should be negotiating. Within this range, visitation offers to either parent will not be unreasonable. You are being reasonable when you accept the Range of Normal Outcomes as the most likely outcome, and shoot for outcomes within that range.

If you try to negotiate outside the Range of Normal Outcomes, or if your spouse tries to jam you into an agreement outside the Range of Normal Outcomes, you will (or should) end up litigating (having trials and being in court repeatedly). As a rule, good parents get reasonably good visitation schedules. If you are a good parent who does not have a reasonably good visitation schedule, I would want to know what happened to put you there. Did you have a lawyer and a contested hearing? Did you make an agreement that you later wanted to change but could not? Were you rude or obnoxious to the court (be honest here)? Were there true cultural or gender-based biases at work in the courtroom? An example of this is the conceit of the "tender years doctrine," which says that younger children should be with their mothers. This doctrine is long-dead in California, but that does not mean that, at a fundamental level, some judges still believe that young children should be with their mothers.

Also, you have to truly ask yourself with an honest heart about whether you are an involved, good parent. I assume that, if you have bought this book, you are an involved, good parent, or that you want to be. I do not believe that most judges are biased and it is rare for a judge to be biased against a party, per se. It is much more likely that the judge who gave you less than "reasonable" parenting time saw something in you during testimony that gave them pause or cause for concern. I just finished, as I write this, a long-cause multi-day hearing over whether my client (a mother) could have her boyfriend around the children she had with the father. We argued that mother was a fit mother and that she should be able to make decisions about who is around her children. Father argued that the boyfriend had just had a 6-day contested hearing regarding his own custody schedule and was awarded professionally supervised visitation once a week at his own expense (which is patently objectively "unreasonable" visitation – except, as I said in the case of drugs, crimes, violence or mental health issues). My view going into trial was a larger picture view. No one claimed that my client was unfit as a mother. The father did not want to change their 50-50 schedule; he just didn't want the boyfriend around the children. I have to say that the boyfriend is one of the most unlikeable people I have ever met – I have no idea why she would date him given that she is educated, young, smart, has a good job and has a great personality. The Court heard testimony but read the ruling from the boyfriend's judge and said "I read [the boyfriend's Judge's] words very carefully. He did not say many words but the ones he did say were impactful.

He said: '[mom's boyfriend] is living in a different reality than the rest of us. His testimony is rarely credible and although I do not believe there was actual violence, I believe he has abused his children in the past." The judge ruled against my client regarding the boyfriend (but left the 50-50 schedule in place.

Now, I was aware of the boyfriend's situation – both cases were proceeding in tandem, so I read the boyfriend's judge's words only a day before my client's trial started, but I took a fundamental view that fit parents should be permitted to decide what is healthy for their children and that judges should not substitute their views (in the absence of drugs, crimes, mental health issues or violence) for a parent's decision about how to raise their children (well, "detriment" factors in as well, but that's a conversation for later in the book). So, then, why didn't I talk her out of going to trial, if I knew that her judge would read the decision by the boyfriend's judge? I tried. I tried and tried. I told her that there was a good chance the judge would rule this way. I did believe (incorrectly) that the judge would make an order for a period of time – say, one year – and then would review the situation to see if boyfriend either a) was still in the picture or b) had rehabilitated himself. But she did not. She made a permanent order. I think she made the order permanent because, like me (and like the ex-husband and the ex-husband's lawyer), everyone likes my client – she is fundamentally likable and caring and everyone believes she is a good mother to her children. The father and the father's new wife both said on the witness stand that the children are thriving and that they did not want to change the schedule. I told my client that I thought it would turn out this way and that she could manage that by not having a trial and making an agreement to keep the boyfriend away for a period of time. She refused. I do fundamentally believe that good parents should make decisions about their children without the court being involved –

and I believe this judge, who I think is one of the best judges I have ever worked with, holds the same belief. But the boyfriend's judge's words and his deep unlikability (including numerous episodes of him trying to control my client in front of me – telling her to "shush," dominating our conversations with his own disagreement about his own case, telling me the law, etc. – led me to conclude the same as did her judge, the father and the father's lawyer that she was in a toxic, controlling relationship). Her judge was likely trying to make having a relationship with this boyfriend so difficult that she would break up with him and find someone more healthy for her and the children. I don't know that for a fact, of course, but that's my hunch. I also think that I am correct that healthy, good parents should make associational decisions for their children without the input of the court – the court should say, "no derogatory comments permitted within earshot of the children," but then trust the parent to ensure that does not happen, not determine that children are not to be permitted around even a controlling jerk of a boyfriend.

Examples of a Reasonable Mental State: Reasonability in the Law – The Repeating Pattern

Let me give you a few examples of reasonability as a state of the law. A couple are from the law in general, and a couple are specifically from family law. I will also provide "Pro Tips" to help you grasp the issue of reasonability as a state of mind.

I am launching into this part of the discussion quickly because I develop my own rules of reasonability in this book and throughout the *Better Divorce* series. I believe that if you understand how the rules work on a conceptual basis, you can almost always reason your way to a correct conclusion and action. Again, "a" correct outcome, not *"the"* correct outcome, because within the Range of Normal Outcomes there are many possible correct outcomes.

Locking yourself into a belief that there is only one correct outcome will almost guarantee litigation or in you selling yourself short.

················ PRO TIP ················

In a divorce there are only two options: make an agreement (where both parties agree) or litigate. If you litigate, the Range of Possible Outcomes is generally somewhere between you-get-everything-you-ask-for and your-spouse-gets-everything-they-ask-for; in fact, it is almost impossible for a "one winner" outcome in a divorce because the law provides for 50-50 or equitable division. The Range of Normal Outcomes cuts away at the things that neither of you will ever get. You want "no visitation" to the other parent? Highly unlikely and unreasonable in all but a limited number of cases (even the "bad boyfriend" got professionally supervised visitation in the case example above). You want the house and all its equity without giving your spouse anything in exchange? Highly unlikely and unreasonable in all but a limited number of cases (I had it happen where the Husband had moved into assisted living for dementia and the wife, my client, had severe mental health and physical health problems and could not move – because if they sold the home, Wife would be much worse off and because Husband, if he was awarded cash from the sale of the property would likely end up paying it all for his care, the Court gave the wife the home).

You can go to trial with unreasonable expectations or requests because they are possible outcomes. However, understand that they are highly unlikely and (because they are unreasonable) will sometimes backfire into rulings that work against your requests. If you bring your requests into the Range of Normal (Reasonable) Outcomes, you are more likely to be successful. Thus, you may pay your spouse for the equity in the home, but you will bring a reasonable expert to court who says that the equity value is lower than your spouse says it is. Only in family law – when you buy out your spouse's equity in the home – do people want their property to be worth less.

Our question is, "How would a judge likely rule?" You can look at what the law requires to narrow the Range of *Possible* Outcomes down to the Range of *Normal* Outcomes. Possible outcomes gives us the entire range of reasonable and unreasonable outcomes, including those that a judge who flat out ignores the law could make, but almost certainly won't, like not dividing the pension or not awarding any visitation or refusing to sell the house until the 6-year-old turns 18. "Normal outcomes" are "reasonable outcomes." The range of normal outcomes is a range of potential outcomes that are most likely to occur – we focus here because we can analyze law and fact, and to some extent, judicial psychology (don't punish parties, divide assets in half, have reasonable timeshare to each parent, order sustainable support payments) to get to the most likely outcome with regard to any issue.

By focusing on the range of normal outcomes, we focus our attention on the range of outcomes with the highest likelihood or probability of being ordered. If we know that the range of normal custody timeshares is between 35% and 65% with 50% the most likely outcome, we can focus our attention on developing a settlement range from Best Case and Worst Case Outcomes. I usually say, "If we win every issue that we raise, we will get x; if they win every issue they raise, they will get y. The range is the spread between x and y."

If you use the "bad boyfriend" example above as a way of doing a non-monetary analysis, you can say, the most likely outcome (in my mind) was a 6-month restraining order against bad boyfriend being around the children with a review of the situation in 6 months. I told my client this. She wanted to litigate because she really did not want her ex-husband to control her post-dissolution romantic life by using her bad boyfriend against her. I don't like it either.

From my perspective, if we think a parent is good enough to have custody of the children, we should trust their choices. I told this client (the truth) that the law is unsettled on whether a judge has the power to exclude a bad boyfriend who has done nothing bad to the girlfriend's children of her prior marriage; because our judge is a strong feminist, she might say that she was not going to tie mother's hands – in fact, that was the strategy we employed – we did not call the bad boyfriend as a witness and made the case about the good parenting everyone agreed my client was doing and that we should trust good parents not to place their children in harm's way.

My client (and the bad boyfriend) wanted me to relitigate the bad boyfriend's own custody case, and show that his ex-wife and her lawyers were liars and that his judge and her lawyer should be brought up on ethics charges and the like – all of which would have been a loser for us. Our best bet was to hang our hats on "well, his judge may have found him to be a bad guy, but there is no allegation that he has done anything to my client's children, and you think my client is a good parent who makes good enough decisions to have the children 50-50. So, unless something untoward happens, the Court should not get involved."

I still think that argument should have been a winner – but we lost because a) the boyfriend's judge's comments about the boyfriend's version of reality being different than everyone else's, b) the finding of some non-physical abuse and c) the deep and abiding unlikability of the boyfriend – even though he did not testify and I excluded him from the courtroom because a potential witness is excluded from hearing other testimony, the other judge's written comments about him made clear that he was utterly unlikeable. My client sent me a letter written by the bad boyfriend but signed by her after trial blaming me because I did not call him as a witness. I am certain that if I had called him as a witness, she would have lost custody of the children and I did not call him because I could not take that risk on her behalf. Lawyers control strategy and clients control settlement agreements – I decided not to call him as a witness because I knew that no good could have come of it.

In order to develop an accurate Range of Normal (Reasonable) Outcomes you need to know what is and what isn't a "reasonable" claim. Some claims are not real threats because they will never happen. You don't want to get caught negotiating a midway point between your reasonable position and your spouse's completely unreasonable position. One of my important roles as a divorce lawyer is to be able to counsel my client on the difference between what is a very scary (to them) but entirely impossible threat by their soon-to-be-ex-spouse and what is a reasonable request. The threats to "clean them out" or "take the children away," or to "close the business and work at Taco Bell," or to "never pay a dime in support" are all incredibly scary to someone who isn't knowledgeable about divorce outcomes. But those are ZERO threats to experienced divorce counsel (and hopefully now to readers of this book, too).

I am still amazed when opposing counsel sends me a "settlement offer" that ignores the law. "My client will keep her pension and your client will waive alimony." I often just ignore these letters, not wanting to waste my client's money on a response. But lawyers get in trouble for not communicating – because judges don't like it – so I have taken to responding by saying: "Please treat me like I know what I am doing. Your client could never get that at trial. Let's follow the law. Let's divide " the pension in half, figure out reasonable alimony and decide what to do with the house. If your client does not want to pay alimony, let's see if we can trade for something else."

In determining that Range of Normal Outcomes, you must also always account for two separate "x-factors":

1) If you have a lawyer, you will pay attorney's fees. If you don't have a lawyer, you will have immense stress and perhaps put on a

bad case and lose issues you did not expect to lose or issues you may not have even thought about. Bad boyfriend did not have a lawyer in his case and he got demolished – he likely would have gotten demolished anyway, but his personality is such that he thinks he's the smartest person in any room including lawyers and judges who do this for a living and that they were colluding to take his kids away from him.

2) You may get a rogue judge who could care less about family law and who makes any ruling she sees fit.

As a quick aside: even if you are a brilliant engineer or a successful teacher, contractor, or accountant, thinking you are smarter than the lawyers and judges in the room is always a bad bet. Even the dumbest lawyer knows more about his or her trade than you do. Just as I would not attempt to do structural dynamic load calculations for a bridge build or teach a second grade class, even though I am smart and have a PhD from Berkeley, because I am not trained to do such things, you should not fail to hire a lawyer because you are smarter than all the lawyers you meet. That may well be true, but once you start making your case and get walloped with evidentiary objection after evidentiary objection and cannot get any evidence in front of the court, you will see why the job is more than just "being smart."

Keep the two "x-factors" in mind as you develop best-and-worst case normal outcome ranges for your case.

For example, "If I do not take the agreement being offered to me, I will go to trial and pay $10,000 for attorney's fees. If I win everything I ask for, I pay $10,000 in attorney's fees plus $0. If I lose everything I ask for, I pay $10,000 in attorney's fees and pay $60,000. No matter what I am going to pay $10,000 in attorney's fees. And there is a miniscule but not 0% chance that if I lose I will have to pay $100,000 because judges can sometimes be completely out of their minds."

• •

If you do this type of Range of Normal Outcomes from best to worst case, and including the "x-factors" calculus, really taking seriously the chance that you will lose issues you think you will definitely win, you are then "bargaining in the shadow of the law."

In other words, the legal system, the costs of counsel, the risks of winning and losing, and the costs of the transactions. Economists tell us that every transaction has a cost, and yours are attorney's fees, stress, sleepless nights, your friends and family called as witnesses, your children angry or upset, and being present yourself in the courtroom. You want to negotiate using the reasonable and rational Family Code and the judicial decisions interpreting it, and not with the whims and flights of fancy of judges eating bagels or pancakes for breakfast. You want to know when your ex's offers to settle are bunk and when they are reasonable.

Ideally you will push to get the most you can within the Range of Normal Outcomes and accept outcomes that are within that Range. Sometimes I will tell a client when we have a trial date approaching and a settlement offer within the Range of Normal Outcomes that I want to try to negotiate "just a little more." The argument I make is that once the offer has been made within the Range of Reasonable Outcomes, we are already "playing with house money." If they have made a reasonable offer and we are getting close to trial, there is a chance I can squeeze just a little more "reasonability" out of them. This happens, usually, when I think the other side has miscalculated their own Range of Normal Outcomes. I routinely make all my attorney's fees from the negotiation back for my client in these last-minute negotiations.

•••••••••••••••••• PRO TIP ••••••••••••••••••

In a recent case we hired a farm equipment broker as an expert witness who was willing to testify that a piece of farm equipment was worth close to $80,000. My client had thought its value was closer to $5,000. The other party thought it was closer to $5,000. They made stink about wanting $2,500 for it. We had initially offered to just sell it and split it. Instead, when I discovered this information, I made a deal that my client would "buy it" for $2,500. She then sold it a week later for $80,000. Because my attorney's fees in this hard-fought case were approaching $40,000, she was able in that day-of-trial negotiation to make back everything she had paid me. Before you castigate me for "failure to disclose" the information to the other party, once we had learned it, I did ask the other side if they wanted to value any of the equipment. They did not want to. What they wanted was a set price for all of the farm equipment and in that set price valuation, I could extrapolate that they valued it at $5,000. I learned that one piece of the equipment (some metal irrigation piping) was worth more as scrap metal because of what it was made out of, than as farm equipment. I gave them every reasonable opportunity to value the equipment and they declined.

There were several ways that we took advantage of this mistake by the other side, but the biggest one was taking the time to value this piece of equipment – when they relied on Husband's self-valuation. We were also able to exploit the other side's misunderstanding of the value of a large arena fence that we believed to have less value than the cost of its removal. My client was not a horse trainer, but her husband was, so she wanted the arena removed for farming. The Husband thought it was worth $17,000. We agreed to split the cost of removal and the sale price. In the end, because we were right, the Husband ended up contributing to the cost removal above the sale price, but it nearly offset. My client made money on the farm equipment and the removal of the arena fencing.

••

Therefore, it is imperative that we talk early about how the law tends to fit together, particularly because from the perspective of a layperson or a lawyer new to family law, family law might seem confusing and complicated.

The Unreasonable Negotiator Or Why, in General, I am Opposed to Traditional Divorce Mediation and Collaborative Law

Traditional divorce mediation involves two parties without lawyers meeting with a third party who sometimes, but not always, is a divorce lawyer. Collaborative law is a process by which each party has a lawyer who they have all agreed cannot represent them in litigation. The process often involves long-term settlement negotiations, the result of which is that the parties never see a courtroom. Negotiations are less legal-based and more focused on perceived fairness by the parties.

The negotiations aspect of mediation and collaborative law mean they focus on emotional outcomes where neither party knows the law and can simply walk away from bad settlement offers. One party may end up way outside the Range of Normal, using the same tactics (anger, shaming, tears, threats, rage) that led to divorce, to push the other party into a bad agreement.

Remember that if one party takes a position outside the Range of Normal and you take a position inside the Range of Normal, you are negotiating between an unreasonable outcome and a reasonable outcome. The reason, for example, so many custody cases resolve with 5 nights out of 14 is that one parent wants 2 nights out of 14 and the other wants 7 nights out of 14 and 4-5 nights approaches the midway point. The proper response to an unreasonable settlement offer is to reject the outside-Normal-Outcome positions and not negotiate with them – to basically say, "Please try again and treat us like we understand family law."

Divorce mediation and collaborative law approaches, in my estimation, give too much credence to outside-the-norm positions. If High-Earner Husband in a 30-year marriage says, "I don't want to pay spousal support" in a mediation or collaborative law context, the negotiator has to take that position seriously in the negotiation. In a negotiation and settlement conference where both sides have counsel, I would reject that position out of the box (whether I represented Husband or Wife) and say "we aren't doing that. If that is what you want, tell it to the judge." I may also force the other side to negotiate with themselves by saying "that won't do, please make a better offer," without providing a counteroffer.

You don't counter a bullshit position with a negotiation. You say no to bullshit positions and wait for another offer. Or you make your own offer within the Range of Reasonable Outcomes.[4]

I have heard stories of collaborative or mediation-based negotiations lasting for months based on completely unreasonable offers— such as no spousal support, or keeping the community property pension, or an agreed upon move-away with children—that would

---

[4] Clients who read books like "Never Split the Difference" and other negotiations books ask me why we don't make unreasonable offers to get the other side negotiating between our unreasonable offer and whatever they will offer. They basically ask me why we do not "anchor" (the negotiation term for setting the floor or ceiling on a negotiation by making the first offer) the negotiations to an unreasonable offer. The basic reason is that, in my experience, the most likely response to an unreasonable offer is an unreasonable offer. Then, both sides are unreasonable, running the risk of offending the other side so they will not negotiate with us. To be sure, you can lead with an unreasonable offer and attempt to anchor the negotiations to your position. But, this book takes as its fundamental premise that the best financial and emotional value is in settling your case quickly within the Range of Normal Outcomes, not spending tens of thousands of extra dollars trying to put one over on your spouse. I have represented clients who were expert negotiators in their businesses who, frankly, used negotiation tactics to get their spouse to agree to an outside-the-norm settlement. This is a possible strategy, but I do not believe that the cost of the negotiation (including co-parenting children for another decade) was worth the outside-the-norm settlement.

have ended in 3 minutes as a non-starter had both parties retained experienced counsel.

Proponents of mediation and collaborative law respond to that by saying that it does not matter whether the outcome is within or outside the Range of Normal so long as the parties agree to it and think it is fair.[5] I disagree strongly.

In the interest of full disclosure, during the process of writing this book, I got divorced. We used a mediator for our divorce. The mediator was a married couple – wife an accomplished family lawyer and husband a therapist. They are based in Montecito, CA and they were amazing in the way they kept us negotiating when my ex-wife was really mad and challenging. We used a mediator because of our privacy concerns. My ex-wife was mad at me, but she also understood that our fortunes were tied together. There were lawyers willing to represent her, who hate me, and wanted to prey on her anger, but they wanted $50,000 retainers and told her it would cost $200,000 to litigate our divorce. They would attempt to embarrass me in court and they would open our finances for the entire county to see. I'd have to get divorced publicly in my workplace. My ex-wife also knew that, fundamentally, I am a fair person. The mediators kept us mediating and helped us get an agreement. It was quiet, private and ultimately fair.

If you have concerns about your privacy, private mediation and/or collaborative law is a good alternative process, but take heed to what I write below.

First, I think that mediation and collaborative law reward bullies.

---

5   Two concepts that pervade family law. 1) People tend to keep agreements that they make, rather than orders that are made and 2) fair agreements are durable agreements. So, a collaborative law practitioner would say: our clients satisfy these two check boxes – they make an agreement that they think is fair. My response is: what happens when they realize later that it was deeply unfair to one party or the other? The aggrieved party comes to me to undo the damage and they end up litigating anyway.

·················· PRO TIP ··················

Both men and women can be bullies. Usually, it's the tactics that are different.

For men, they tend toward a false charm that thinly masks an underlying aggression. They will talk too much or too quickly. They will tend toward "pat" answers to questions, to try to demonstrate that they are being overly generous in the divorce, or that they are losing hours at work, or that they just lost a large account causing a drop in income. Outside of mediation there is a threat of anger (possibly violence) and of not getting along in the future. There may be alcoholism or pill popping, or affairs, or hidden money. Mediation for them is a way of not fully disclosing assets and of hiding sexual affairs – mediation is confidential and private and these men-bullies do not want the court to shine light on their behaviors. Mediation is a place where there is no judicial power to order documents produced; lawyers still have subpoena power, but to issue a subpoena in a mediation is an act of war, disrupting an otherwise peaceful-ish process.

For women bullies the tactics are different. They use tears or self-righteous anger to drive negotiations. They threaten to take the children away or say they are going to move cities. They dominate passive men with loud yelling and comments such as, "You know you can't take care of the children," or "You know that what I am asking for is fair." Another popular one is "Do what's in the children's 'best interests' and stop thinking about yourself for once." Passive men get bullied in these deals when wives spend $15,000 on a family law attorney retainer during the mediation "so that they have someone to talk to about the mediation." In reality, it is the threat of litigation that underlies the process.

The dominated spouse in the marriage continues to get speed-rapped or be subjected to terroristic threats in the mediation. He or she tends to give up far too much in the process, and there is almost nothing the mediator can do except to say, "Well, Marie, do you think this is fair? If you don't think it's fair, what do you think is fair? He won't agree to that. Is there anything you can get to make you feel better about his most recent proposal?"

Eventually, Marie just caves. She caves to save the process, to hope that she can get through years of soccer practices and teacher conferences, and (eventually) weddings and graduations and family events. She agrees just to keep the peace and avoid the anger she expects to receive from pushing back. She does it because she knows he will quit his job or take a pay cut or stop doing good work, or drink too much around the children, or any number of other things the aggressive husband did to her during the marriage. She knows he will do it because he has always done it. She caves and walks away with so much less than she is entitled to.

Men cave to their bully ex-wives as well for all of the same reasons, but perhaps also more. Men cave because in their hearts they believe that the mother of their children is sacred and that their children are better off with their mother. These men will often continue to refer to mom's house as "home" and dad's house as "dad's house" for a decade, even with a 50-50. They cave because when the mom-bully attacks their parenting, at some level, they believe it. It's low self-esteem and it may be that the low-self-esteem is what kept them in the marriage where they were being bullied.

In either case, if you are getting bullied in your marriage, mediation is where the bully gets to continue bullying. Judges, by and large, hate bullies and do not put up with bullying behavior. Mediators don't like it either (no one does) but they have little power to stop it.

• •

Second, I think once a party realizes that their mediated or collaborative law agreement is outside the Range of Normal

Outcomes they get angry and do not want to abide by it any longer. This speaks to the footnote above that describes fair agreements as durable agreements.

People who realize that their agreement is outside the Range of Normal Outcomes try to go back to Court to change their agreements. They stop making their payments or stop following the orders. They say they "got screwed" in the divorce and they are angry. And you know what? They did get screwed, and in the worst possible way . . . they *agreed* to it! The biggest problem was that their ex was a bully during the process ("No spousal support"; "I'll let you take the kids if I don't have to pay child support"; "I worked for my damned retirement, no deal if I don't get to keep it"; "I keep my business or we don't go forward", etc.)

Third, another problem is that they do not know the law. If they only understood that spousal and child support are a given (almost all the time) like death and taxes, or that retirements and businesses are valued and split, and that 1,000 out of 1,000 judges will make these orders in favor of the most unrepresented party against the meanest, baddest lawyer in the state, they would not agree to get screwed. If they only understood that spending $5,000 now can save $100,000 or more later. Repeatedly, the people who get screwed the worst are those who fear litigation so much that they are willing to agree to whatever their bully ex-husband or ex-wife demands of them—oftentimes in a mediation.

Taking it a step further, in 2006 a California court decided *Marriage of Kieturakis* (2006) 41 Cal.Rptr.3d 119, which said that mediation agreements—even god-awful, terrible agreements—are binding on the parties, including agreements where one spouse bullied the hell out of the other spouse. The spouse could not claim duress because a mediator was present when they made the agreement, and the court said that mediators will make sure that one party is not under duress. Plus, the Court said, the signed Agreement stipulates that "neither party is under duress." The Court further restated the mediation privilege, which holds that:

> **"Unless all parties to the mediation expressly agree otherwise, no 'report, assessment, evaluation, recommendation, or finding of any kind by the mediator' concerning the mediation can be submitted to, or considered by, a court (§ 1121), and section 703.5 provides, with certain exceptions, that mediators are not 'competent to testify, in any subsequent civil proceeding, as to any statement, conduct, decision, or ruling, occurring at or in conjunction with' the mediation." At pp. 121-122.**

This means that people who attend mediation not only cannot claim that they were bullied and under duress during the mediation, but they also cannot bring the mediator in to testify that they were bullied during the mediation.

Good agreements are durable agreements that allow both parties to get what they want as much as possible, avoid litigation, and work together in the future to avoid additional litigation. I believe mediation agreements made under duress or with bullying (whether that bullying is overt or implicit) are not durable and lead to litigation in the areas of the agreement that can be reopened to the Court, such as custody and support.

What this book aims to do is solve a fundamental problem with mediation and collaborative law: the Parties do not know the law, so they get bullied and make bad agreements.

When parties in a lawsuit do not know the law, the advantage shifts to whichever party has the most physical, verbal, or emotional power. Every marriage has one party who has the power. The law is supposed to be the great equalizer. If you take the law out of the equation, the dominant partner in the marriage becomes the dominant partner in the divorce.

This is not to say that lawyers cannot screw things up. We absolutely can. Sometimes the way we screw it up is by forgetting that a divorce negotiation is a business negotiation. What I mean by that is that we forget to tell our clients that it makes sense to settle cases to reduce their attorney's fees; a better way of saying it is not that we "forget" to explain that, but rather, we allow clients' emotions to dictate how hard we fight over things where the cost-benefit analysis does not make sense. You should always be asking your lawyer what the potential benefits are (how likely are you to win what you are asking for? What will you get by winning what you are asking for?) as against the known costs (How much will it cost to ask for this thing? How likely are you to have to pay the other side's attorney's fees?).

Reasonable is Reasonable (Mostly) Wherever You Are

Although I am a California lawyer practicing in a community property state, many of the tools and logic I provide cross over to non-community property states also.

I remember having one of the leading torts (personal injury) professors in the world teaching a seminar in advanced torts tell our law school class that his research indicated that no matter the legal system, the results of the legal process were almost always so similar as to be indistinguishable from each other. In particular he compared the American system to the European system. He argued, although not in these exact terms, that Reasonability is the same across cultures and languages, no matter how you derive it. If that is true for different legal systems, it is also true for different legal terminology.

To be fair, he said Americans will never litigate aesthetics but will litigate morals, while the Europeans will never litigate morals but will litigate aesthetics. Americans would litigate over a brothel in the neighborhood; the Europeans would only litigate if the building is hideous. That is probably stretching the point, but I tend to agree that what is reasonable in Sacramento is probably reasonable in Duluth—and is almost assuredly also reasonable in Raleigh.

I have had divorce cases that touch on family law in India, Singapore, Israel, Yeman and several European countries (including England and Ireland, as well as Netherlands, Spain and Germany) and even though every system has its quirky differences (return of the gold in India to the families from which it came, to 3-year separation periods in Singapore, etc.), in generally the principles of equitable or "fair" distribution work in virtually all such countries.

The 9 states that use Community Property as the basis for dividing marital assets are: Arizona, California, Idaho, Louisiana, Nevada, New Mexico, Texas, Washington and Wisconsin, and Alaska (if the parties elect).

In the community property states, parties are assumed to equally share all income, property, and debts accumulated during the marriage. In theory this means a strict 50-50 distribution of community property assets and debts—but only community property assets and debts, because separate property remains separate.

The "equitable distribution" states (all others) theoretically give the judge more leeway, but in the end, they go through a very similar analysis of separate and "marital," rather than "community," property. An attempt is then made to equitably distribute the marital property, which often looks like 50-50 but is not required to be. A full analysis of how outcomes differ between "equitable distribution" states and "equal division" states (the community property states) is outside the scope of this book. However, I have read law review articles, including empirical studies, on the subject and find that many of the rules and exceptions to the rules in equitable division states are similar to the rules and exceptions in equal division states.

••••••••••• FOR EXAMPLE •••••••••••

California requires an equal division of a community property home. If Wife (W) owned the home before marriage and had $200,000 in equity in the home on the date of marriage, and changes title in the home to community property on the date of marriage, under Family Code section 2640, W receives her $200,000 back and the parties split any remaining equity in the home.

This is not an "equal split" of the community property asset—it is an equitable split. And it is also reasonable. W gets her $200,000 back (because she put it in out of her own separate money before marriage) and the parties split the remaining equity. If W owns the home before marriage but does not add H to title during the marriage, but the parties use community property income to pay down the mortgage, then the community "buys" an interest in the home in proportion to the paydown of the mortgage principal. Complicated, but also reasonable, because it would not really be fair for Wife to use community property income to pay down her separate property mortgage without the community getting something in return.

Equitable division states treat the entire home as part of the marital estate, but they ask whether someone owned it before marriage or received an inheritance to buy it. Many states begin with the presumption that the marital estate should be split equally, and then allow either spouse to attempt to rebut that presumption with evidence of unequal contributions. Non-monetary contributions, such as raising children, also count as contributions.

••••••••••••••••••••••••••••••••••••

In either case the law is complicated, but from my review, most cases in both jurisdictions follow similar Ranges of Normal. The community property system begins with the rule that marital assets should be divided equally and then creates a host of exceptions to the rule. The equitable division system considers the entire marital estate to determine a "fair" division based, in part, on separate contributions such as inheritances and contributions before the marriage. Fairness can depend on a variety of factors, including contribution to raising children, the use of inherited funds or funds from before marriage, the length of the marriage, the health of the parties, and the ages of the children and (if applicable) who will raise them. While the equitable distribution states take these factors into account as part of "equity" or "fairness" in the distribution of assets, the community property states build them in as exceptions to the basic rules.

Since community property states build equitable distribution into the statutes, the judge should divide property 50-50; however, she has discretion to decide which 50% to distribute to whom, as well as discretion to let equitable factors determine outcomes and always has the power to change division of assets "in the interests of justice."

Returning to the beginning of the chapter, "equity" (as in "equitable distribution") is just another word for "fairness." The fairest outcome is usually one-half, but there are times in which the 50-50 outcome is not the fair outcome, such as in the pre-marital home ownership example above.[6] A 50-50 outcome is the default position and is viewed as "equitable" or "fair" because of its similarity to Reasonability or Rationality. "How would a reasonable person divide some stuff that was purchased by two people in a partnership when those two people sought to divide the stuff?" California even adopts the Corporations Code regarding general partnerships as part of the Family Code. Although we call it community property, in practice we are equitably dividing assets and debts between two "business" partners who are dissolving their partnership.

My experience is that the discussion of differences between the systems is more-or-less a distinction without a difference. This book is written with California cases and examples because I am a California lawyer and Family Law Specialist Certified by the State Bar of California Board of Legal Specialization. (The State Bar makes me say that whole mouthful.) So that is where most of my background knowledge comes from. Also, I have been practicing in three litigation-heavy counties in California and have a Ph.D. in Jurisprudence and Social Policy (a "Law and Society" program in which researchers bring empirical, observational, and measuring methods to various areas of the law). Thus, I have both theoretical and practical knowledge.

---

6   There is a concept that should be further explored by researchers and academics that 50-50 is an inherently unfair distribution of assets, because the higher-earner will leave the marriage with an ability to continue to earn more income than the lower-earner. This creates an immediate equity problem that child and spousal support are supposed to rectify but, as most support recipients will say, does not really rectify. Higher-earners tend to be upwardly mobile (meaning they get raises more often and for larger amounts than lower-earners) and they tend to marry upwardly mobile new spouses, increasing their wealth. Even when they have the children half the time, they tend to be able to afford child care so they can work, and this allows the income inequality between higher- and lower-earning spouses to continue to spread. By dividing assets 50-50, there is a fundamental equity problem. It might make sense for courts to divide assets unequally to make up for this problem. This is just theoretical thinking because in practice assets are split close to 50-50.

Plus, two of the three more important states for legal rule creation—California and Texas (from which we get both very liberal and very conservative statutes from legislatures and opinions from Appellate Court judges and State Supreme Court Justices)—are community property states. One of the three (New York) is an equitable distribution state. These three states are continually influencing each other as family law develops across the nation. I don't know if we will ever get to a standardized system for family law on a national basis, but that is irrelevant to this book because of the common thread running through it.

This book uses the term "community property," but its basic argument is that regardless of the jurisdiction there are only minimal differences in the outcomes mandated by the courts. Therefore, if you follow the basic principles of Reasonability, you will almost always be able to reason your way to the proper legal outcomes of virtually any case.

CHAPTER 5

Reasonability in Action

LEGAL "REASONABILITY" FACTORS heavily into virtually every legal rule and legal exception. Some historians of the law have argued that the law, particularly what is called Common Law (law made by judges) developed around "conventional wisdom" or "reason." Common Law decisions are rules that develop in cases that are then applied to other cases by analogy: *"Do the facts of this case look more like the facts of case A or case B?"*

Much of Family or Matrimonial Law is based on these types of decisions. They are how courts interpret rules made by legislatures. It is difficult even for a family lawyer who has been in practice for many years to truly grasp all the statutes and common law rules that apply to every situation. Experts are people who recognize patterns and who understand the basic play within the law. Thus, when you describe your case, as a woman was doing to me earlier today, I can say, "Your case is uniquely yours and it is (hopefully) the only time you will have to go through this. But to an experienced family lawyer your story fits into different categories or types of stories we hear very regularly. Your case is normal, and with this particular judge here is how I think it will play out."

What I did was apply my experiential knowledge of various cases that sound like hers to the Rule of Reasonability as applied by our judges. That is why, with a few pieces of information, I can predict the outcome with some certainty. Below I give two examples of Reasonability in Action to illustrate my point. One example is more general and the third is family law specific.

Example 1: The General Duty of Care and Special Relationships

We owe each other a general duty of care, meaning, for example, that when I see you on the street, I owe you a duty not to drive my car into you. More generally, I must obey basic rules of the road and treat pedestrians with special precaution.

This general duty of care is the duty not to create unwarranted risks to others who might not be expecting those risks. This is a neutral position. I do not have to take extra special care for someone on the street, but I do have to make sure that I do not do things (turn left on a red light, speed through an intersection, flail my arms around in line at the bank, etc.) that increase the risk that I will harm you through my actions.

This duty of care exists for every relationship I have, from people who trespass onto my land to my own beloved child. But what is considered "reasonable" changes with each relationship.

To a trespasser I owe a certain duty not to set traps and not to create "attractive nuisances" (i.e., ultra-deep "swimming pools" from which there is no escape except drowning; rock quarries that fill with water; "pit traps" covered with dry branches with spikes to impale unwitting walkers; or shotguns wired to fire if someone steps on my property). For trespassers my duty of care is below the general duty of care, but I am not permitted to create secret hazards they might walk into or create attractive conditions that invite them into danger.

In the middle is the general duty of care described above: the neutral position. "Do not to create unwarranted risks to others who might not be expecting those risks."

To a person I invite into my home I owe a duty to warn them of hazards: "Hey, that step is a little loose," or "Be careful. The water over there freezes on cold nights and it gets a little slippery." This duty is higher than the general duty of care where my duty is limited to not putting other people at risk with my actions. Under the general duty of care, I don't have to walk down the street telling people about an icy patch I slipped on a block back or flash my high beams at cars going in the other direction to warn them of a rocks on the road ahead. Conversely, if I invite a person into my home, I am a little more intimate with them, a little closer. Therefore, I have a duty to give them a *little more* care, such as maybe warn them of a hazard but not actually *fix* the hazard. I do not owe social invitees into my home a duty to fix my wobbly step; I just have a duty to warn them that the step is wobbly.

To people I invite into my law office or the café I used own with my ex-wife, I owe a duty to affirmatively fix hazards on the property. It isn't enough to just put up a yellow sign that says, "Wet Floor." We must dry the floor. It isn't enough to point out the broken step or the broken chair; I must *fix* the step or the chair. This is higher than the duty I owe people who come to my home, even though they are invited, because in my store I am expecting people (or "inviting" them, to use the legal parlance) to spend money in my establishment, as opposed to a social gathering in which I am not making a profit. I have never participated in any MLM or "Tupperware parties", but if I did it would be arguable as to whether I would owe the increased duty of care expected when I invite someone into my business. This invitation to come and spend money does increase the obligation I owe to another.

Then there are "special relationships"—those relationships are where we owe an *even higher* duty of care. Or rather we owe a higher duty of care because the relationship is special. Spouses, parents and children, innkeepers and their guests, commercial carriers (buses, trains, and planes) and their passengers—all owe a higher duty of care to each other than the general public owes each other. We categorize special duties of care as duties owed by one who enjoys a relationship of trust and confidence with another; alternatively, you might state the special duty of care as "he or she in whom another has entrusted their life, money, or love and affection owes a higher duty of care to the one who entrusted it."

Fiduciaries – people who control your money – also owe this higher duty of care. These special relationships are relationships of trust and confidence that apply specifically to entrusting money.

Spouses have both a confidential and a fiduciary relationship. This is really important. In fact, fiduciary duties and duties of trust and confidence are the most important area of development in family law over the last two decades (aside from possibly the issues relating to same-sex parents and three-parent households). It is the area where all the major action is in the appellate courts, and the area in which doing it wrong can really cost you a lot of money. I will discuss fiduciary duties later in the book, particularly when discussing financial disclosures and the possible waste of marital assets.

(Lower) <-------------------- {Duty of Care} -------------------- > (Higher)				
Trespassers	General Duty of Care	Home Invitee	Business Invitee	Special Relationships: Spouses, Kids

The general rule of Reasonability stated in terms of a duty that I owe another is the General Duty of Reasonable Care. I owe you a duty not to ram you with my car by driving on the wrong side of the road—generally stated as my duty not to increase your risk of something bad happening to you. Most "accident" cases are just accidents in which someone fails to live up to the General Duty of Care. They take a corner too fast in their car, they squeeze their coffee cup too tightly and spill the contents on another person, they aren't able to stop well on their skis, etc.

We could think of lower duties of care owed to trespassers or higher duties of care owed to spouses as exceptions to the General Duty of Care, or we could simply think of these as reasonable extensions of it – I prefer the latter (and this is how I got through the bar exam, as I mentioned above). By thinking of them as reasonable extensions of the same rule, we can make sense of the exceptions and reason to the right conclusion. It would not surprise anyone that I do not have a duty to warn trespassers about icy patches on my land, but that if there is a spill in my café, I have to clean it up. This is all just following an axis running from a (reasonable) lower duty of care owed to people who unlawfully (and without permission) come onto my land, all the way through the highest (reasonable) duty of care owed to someone who has entrusted their money and placed their confidence in me.

Seeing reasonability as an axis-based on relationship rather than a bunch of exceptions to a general rule helps us make sense of the law more generally, but can also help you understand that the family law, like virtually every area of the law, is based on reasonable action. If the General Duty is that I owe strangers I pass on the street a duty not to create hazards for them, it is completely reasonable that the care I should take in dealing with others who I know and socialize with, who I invite into my business to spend money, and who have entrusted me with their love and affection, money, or life would all expect (and therefore make the law require) a higher level of precautionary behavior on my part.

Example 2: Family Law Fiduciary Duties

The Family Law specific example says that spouses owe each other fiduciary duties. "Fiduciary duty" essentially means "financial duty." Basically, a fiduciary is someone to whom you give your money to hold for you, to invest for you, to make financial decisions for you, to operate in your best financial interest . They have different obligations to you than someone who doesn't have your money. Because, in California, both spouses hold all of one another's money for one another (meaning that one spouse can go to the bank and withdraw 100% of the money at any time), they are fiduciaries of each other.

In a California divorce, the California Family Code sections 720-721, 1100-1101, and 2100-2107, all talk about how spouses are obligated to disclose everything about their finances during the litigation—even if they are living separate and apart (and even if they've been separate for a long time). The rule is that spouses' finances are so tied together that they have a right to know the status, so that they know what to ask for. This means not only divulging details about your pension plan, but also details about a small inheritance left to you by Uncle Ernie after you separated but before you filed for divorce; all the details about the 401(k) you began before you got married; whether you won the lottery; and even property that any reasonable person would agree is your separate property because you got it before you were married or by inheritance or gift.

The fiduciary duties extend all the way until the last assets are divided, so DO NOT let the actual entry of judgment of divorce fool you as it has too many people in the past. Let me qualify that. After your divorce is final you have continued fiduciary duties for whatever asset has not been divided, not for all the assets. For example, if you get a raise after the divorce papers are filed but before there is a judgment of divorce, you must tell your spouse about it. Conversely, if you already agreed to give your spouse $100,000 for their share of the equity in the home, you do not have to consult them before undertaking to put on a new roof, even though you may still owe your spouse $10,000 for their half of a stock account you haven't yet liquidated.

In equitable jurisdiction states, there are fiduciary duties not specifically enshrined in the law. I argue that these are basically the same thing as the California fiduciary statutes, but just by a different name. To find a breach of fiduciary duty in California that occurs during a marriage, the breaching spouse would have to commit an egregious act. For example, if Husband sells the community property home to a third party without telling Wife, or if Wife won the lottery before separation but did not tell Husband she had won it (*Marriage of Rossi*). In equitable distribution states, even ones that specifically reject fiduciary duties, the Courts will look to "marital waste" or "dissipation of assets" to find fault. In most states the remedy is something called "constructive trust," which essentially gives the injured spouse their part of the property plus damages: interest, attorney's fees, sanctions, or some method of making the other spouse whole.

Fiduciary duties between spouses are simply more Rules of Reasonability. Spouses are like business partners in most, if not all, jurisdictions. They have a right to know what the partnership produced and to confirm that one partner has not taken all the assets belonging to the partnership without sharing them. It is reasonable to require each spouse to share with the other spouse all information about all the assets, and then to promise not to do things with the community or marital property that would damage the other's interest for their own benefit. In other words, you have a right to be free from your spouse's sneaky behavior. If they are sneaky then you can ask the Court for sanctions, usually an award of the property (or half the property and your attorney's fees). It is a big deal, and it is increasingly common for parties to ask Courts to analyze whether the other spouse breached their fiduciary duties.

Both of hypotheticals demonstrate a way in which Reasonability finds its way into the law. It is not meant to be an exhaustive list by any means, and I do not expect these three examples to convince lawyers or law professors that we can reason to the correct legal conclusion in all cases if we just use the Rule of Reasonability. However, I do hope to convince you that the law craves reasonability so much that every legal rule has reasonability as its baseline. When you start from this position, the Range of Normal becomes the target of your negotiations.

Tying your case to the Three Property Rules of Family Law, the Rules of Reasonability, and the Range of Normal is a way to resolve your case more quickly and with reduced pain—financial, emotional, and physical. If both sides can recognize the Range of Normal as applied to the Three Property Rules and to the basics of child custody and visitation, there is little more that needs to be done to bring the case to resolution. Let us now address the Three Property Rules of Family Law.

CHAPTER 6

The Three Property Rules of Family Law

OK, SO IF the basic rule of law is reasonability, then how does that apply to family law? If there is a Range of Normal, how do I find it?

This chapter will help you reason your way to the correct legal outcome without needing to know the finer points of the law. With the Three Property Rules of Family Law, you can, with reasonable certainty, know what the proper division of assets is in your case.

Leaving aside custody, visitation, and support for now and just talking about property, the Three Property Rules of Family Law (I'm going to use the term the "Three Property Rules" from here on out) make a lot of sense. They derive from the basic Rule of Reasonability and feed into the Range of Normal. These same rules apply to equitable distribution jurisdictions as much as they do to community property jurisdictions because they are rules of reasonability. Although they are part of the Family Code in California, specifically sections 760, 770 and 2550, this is an example of a legislature codifying (making into law) a Rule of Reasonability.

Family Code section 760 says:

"Except as otherwise provided by statute, all property, real or personal, wherever situated, acquired by a married person during the marriage while domiciled in this state is community property."

This means, if you get property during the marriage, no matter how you take title, it is presumed to be community property.

Family Code section 770 says:

"(a) Separate property of a married person includes all of the following:

(1) All property owned by the person before marriage.

(2) All property acquired by the person after marriage by gift, bequest, devise, or descent.

(3) The rents, issues, and profits of the property described in this section."

This means (a)(1) any property you got before you married or (a)(2) by gift or inheritance during the marriage, is your separate property and (a)(3) any income or profit you got from that property is your separate property.

Family Code section 2550 says:

"Except upon the written agreement of the parties, or on oral stipulation of the parties in open court, or as otherwise provided in this division, in a proceeding for dissolution of marriage or for legal separation of the parties, the court shall, either in its judgment of dissolution of the marriage, in its judgment of legal separation of the parties, or at a later time if it expressly reserves jurisdiction to make such a property division, **divide the community estate of the parties equally**."

This means, unless you agree otherwise, the court shall divide *community property* equally. Note: it says divide *community* property equally. It does not require the court to divide your *separate* property at all. So, that is one reason I know in the first 30 minutes of any consultation how your case is going to resolve.

It is going to resolve with an equal division (one-half – because "equal" does not mean "fair" or "equitable", "equal" means "half") of community property. I also know that any gift or inheritance is separate property and separate property is never divided by the court, because separate property is yours.

This takes me back for a moment to the discussion of mediation agreements and other types of agreements. If you make an agreement to divide your community property any way less than exactly half, you are going outside the bounds of the law. But, the law allows you to do that: "Except upon the written agreement of the parties, or on oral stipulation of the parties in open court...."

Similarly, if you agree to divide any property that was acquired with separate property (gift or inheritance), you are going outside the bounds of the law. This is very common: mom and dad give you $50,000 as a down payment for your first home. That's a gift. Mom and dad leave you the cabin by the lake in their will. That's inheritance. This can get complicated quickly, as when mom and dad leave you a lot by the lake and you and your spouse build a house on the lot with community property money, but that can be handled with "reasonability" too: you get the value of the lot when you inherited it and the community shares in the value of the house you built on the lot.

Finally, Family Code 760 creates a community property *presumption*, which means that the law *presumes* that anything you got during the marriage is community property. This means that if you have separate property that you acquired during the marriage, such as any gift or inheritance, you have to prove it. And proof means proof.

In one of my current cases, Wife received a $75,000 gift from her wealthy mother to buy the first house in 1994. In the divorce almost 30 years later, Wife wants to prove the gift. She has a gift letter signed in 1994. But, the parties have bought and sold 3 houses and have had 4 cash out refinances during that 30 years. Wife must prove that the $75,000 existed through each transaction, which is, itself, a large undertaking over almost 30 years of transactions, including up real estate markets and down real estate markets. This was something she was able to do, by God, and it annoyed my client to no end that she could do it. However, I had to tell him "Dave, listen, most people don't have the goods from 30 years ago, but she does. We are going to lose this issue at trial so let's stop fighting over it and work on the issues we are going to win."

One of my basic arguments in all my legal scholarship is that the law typically derives from the Rule of Reasonability. That is, law can be made by judges—where rules and norms are established over time in a series of judicial opinions which are then followed based on the principal of *stare decisis* or "precedent" (the idea that the legal rules existed before are the legal rules that should exist after, because we want to be able to plan our lives based on a set of laws that do not change on a whim)—or it can be made by legislatures who pass laws in the form of codes (which are basically, the laws as you think of "the law'" because it is what is written down in the form of rules).

In California, although the Family Code controls family law decisions, there are a number of judicial interpretations of the Family Code that extend the law and apply it to particular situations. Thus, when this book refers to a case name like *Marriage of Moore*, it refers to the way a court interpreted the Family Code. When the book refers to a code section such as Family Code section 760, the legislature has made it a rule. A case like *Marriage of Moore* interprets the family law rule that community property is divided by 2 during a divorce.

We always want to ask the question, "What is community property?" Community property is anything obtained by the community during the marriage. Separate property is anything that one spouse obtains before marriage or after separation with separate property funds. *Marriage of Moore* resolves the question, "What do we do when the home is owned by Wife from before marriage, subject to a mortgage, but the community pays the mortgage?" *Marriage of Moore* provides a formula to pay the community back for paying down the mortgage on Wife's separate property home.

Oftentimes the cases help us interpret the intersection between the Family Code and actual situations. For example, Family Code section 770 tells us all property obtained before marriage is the separate property of the spouse who obtained it. That is great, but what do we do when the spouse who had separate property transmutes it into community property? What happens to the separate property interest? The caselaw tells us what to do in that specific situation. But before dealing with that, let's set forth the Three Property Rules.

The Three Property Rules are:

1. Whatever you obtain before marriage or after separation is your separate property (Family Code section 770).
2. Whatever you obtained during the marriage, however you get it, so long as it was not a gift or inheritance to you or your spouse directly, belongs to the community (Family Code 760).
3. Gifts and inheritances belong to the party who received them, including gifts given by the husband to the wife or the wife to the husband (Family Code 770).

I often shorten these rules to: "1) Anything you got before marriage or after separation with your separate funds is *yours*, 2) anything you got during the marriage is *ours, except* 3) gifts and inheritances."

These rules give us guidance in every family law property issues. The specific situation can create complexities, but the complexities are solely in the form of technical and execution questions. If family law property issues were a *Jeopardy!* answer, the answer is 50%. The Question is "50% of what?" The "of what" question is where having a lawyer, or this book, is beneficial because many times people have no idea where to begin with the "of what?" question.

The short answer to the "of what?" question is, "of everything!" "Everything" being defined as "anything of value" – positive value such as assets and negative value such as debts. But the "of what?" question is still subject to the Three Property Rules of family law: half of everything earned or received during the marriage (not before the marriage or after the separation) that was not a gift or inheritance.

This can get really complicated and can hit you where you least want it. As some of the hypotheticals show, the Rules can include unvested pensions, unvested stock options, retirement accounts, equity in houses, vehicles, motorized toys, the camping gear, the Cutco knives, the beach house, the timeshare, the RV, the Victoria's Secret credit card, the money someone owes the casino, the money you borrowed from your mom with no written document memorializing it, the money you borrowed from his mom that was recorded as a second deed of trust, money borrowed for breast augmentation ("But Jude, I never even got to see them!") . . . Basically, it covers just about anything you can think of.

The largest assets are usually the following: the house and the equity in the house, the defined benefit pension plan such as PERS or FERS, or a DoD/DFAS plan ("You're going after my pension?!?!" "Uhm...Yes, I am taking my half of *our* pension. Why do you ask?"), the deferred compensation plan, and even the military retired pay.

I live in a military town where we don't have a lot of stock options (except increasingly SpaceX and some of the other commercial space operators), but we do have a lot of military retirements. There are clear and specific rules for how to divide a military retirement plan.

Getting the pension divided once and for all is important. If it's supposed to be divided (which it is unless you have an agreement not to divide it for some reason), then get it divided, because for so many people the retirement plan is the most valuable asset in the family—often more valuable than the house. If you have an agreement not to divide it, then get the darned thing in writing.

Right now, I am representing a fire captain who got divorced (final) five years ago. He hired a paralegal to do the divorce for him since it was "uncontested."

················· **PRO TIP** ·················

PLEASE don't hire a paralegal to do your divorce for you if you have assets or debts. They are perfectly fine in cases where there are no assets or debts, but if things get complicated you should at the very least hire a lawyer to make sure the disclosures are properly done and to draft the Marital Settlement Agreement.

···

The fire captain did not list his California Public employees' Retirements System pension in his disclosures and the paralegal did not award it to him in the Judgment of Dissolution. It was probably worth $1 million when the couple divorced. No one listed it in the Judgment because he and his wife made an oral agreement that he would put her through nursing school and she would waive her interest in the pension. Had this worked it would have been brilliant for him. He would have gotten $500,000 in value and she would have gotten a higher paying job. Win-Win for him. Not bad for her either. Although I am not pretending it was a perfect outcome, it wasn't a horrible outcome either since nurses where she lives command salaries in excess of $100,000.

She told him she was going to nursing school, so for three years he reimbursed her for payments she made for nursing school. At some point there were miscommunications so he wrote a check directly to the nursing school. Guess what? Right! She had not been going to nursing school at all.

Now he has a lawyer in court screaming that he committed perjury and a violation of his fiduciary duties because he did not list or divide the PERS pension in the divorce papers. He says, "Wait, we had an agreement." The judge says, "Well, let me see it." He responds, "Well, judge, it's like this...." Not good for him at this point. I am going to do everything in my power to show that there was an agreement, but this is downright unfair. I can show $100,000 in payments made in three years--in cash. But the problem is that half a 20-year PERS pension is worth a lot more than nursing school tuition. People make agreements and then they get stuck with them. We are probably going to get the $100,000 back against the pension, but we are also likely going to have to divide it because he didn't have the agreement in writing.

Two lessons from the fire captain: 1) get all agreements in writing and 2) don't let someone else tell you that you don't need to file a pension disclosure, even if both parties are well aware of the pension. In my experience pension earners—whether firefighters, law enforcement, military officers or enlisted, union drywallers, Federal Bureau of Investigation agents, schoolteachers, etc.—and their spouses are very well-aware of the pension. They may not know how to properly value it, or even that they are required (at least in California) to divide it, but they know it is there. It is not perjury, at least not true perjury, to not list your pension in the disclosures, but it is improper and it allows your spouse 10 years later to come screaming into court about what a liar you are. It is not good for the professional reputation of a fire captain to have a lawyer screaming in open court about what a liar he is.

If you have property—positive or negative (assets or debts)—you must properly disclose all of it to your spouse. If the property is worth anything, hire an attorney to do your disclosures for you or read a NOLO press book to make sure you disclose correctly. If you have an agreement, put every single term of your agreement in writing. Email probably won't suffice, but if that's all you can do then send it in an email. You don't have an agreement unless your spouse tells you he agrees to it. Even then, there is nothing like a single document with both of your signatures on it (and including the CCP 664.4 language I mentioned above). If you save yourself $50,000 in attorney's fees by negotiating without an attorney, spend $3,500 to have an attorney draft up your agreement properly. Get it done right.

Avoid the fate of a restaurateur former client of mine who is paying his ex-wife $50,000 because the agreement prepared by a paralegal 10 years ago omitted important terms, such as the repayment term for a promissory note he was paying his wife. With no repayment term the Court said, "Well, if you don't have a repayment term, I'm going to have to write one for you and that will include 10% interest back ten years." This couple had well over $2 million in assets and an income of $500,000 a year. Both were smart. Why didn't they just hire lawyers back then and have the lawyers write up the agreement? Simply to save a few thousand dollars. If you have an agreement, get it in writing and disclose all your property to your spouse. Pay a lawyer a few grand to draft your agreement properly. Don't rely on paraprofessionals, amateurs, or your own legal brilliance.

Back to the Three Property Rules.

Here are some hypotheticals (different from my real-life examples). I use these hypotheticals to give some context to the Three Property Rules and help you see that those rules are really just derived from the Rule of Reasonability and, once you know them, you can very readily discern what the Range of Normal is in your case. I also use these examples to demonstrate the complexity of trying to figure out what must be divided in half (the "community interest" or "marital interest" and what remains separate property).

Hypothetical 1: The Inheritance and the Bathroom Remodel Problem

Husband and Wife had a 35-year marriage. When they got married, they were both 19 and neither had any money or property. Husband avers that he had a 1977 Firebird but sold it a long time ago to get Wife a station wagon for the kids, which they started having only a couple of years after they were married. Husband was going to join the military but ended up being an electrician's apprentice instead because it paid a little better. Husband joined the union, became a journeyman, and spent the entire 35-year marriage working for various defense contractors at a military base in California. He contributed to three separate electrician's pensions. He retired with pensions valued at more than $1.5 million.

Wife had mostly been a stay-at-home mom, but when the youngest child reached high school age, she started a house cleaning business. She said, "Mostly I did it to drink wine with my friends during the day, but I ended up making more than full-time minimum wage working fewer than 20 hours per week."

During the marriage, Husband's father died. Since his mother had died long before the marriage, and since Husband had no siblings, he inherited his father's estate. The estate consisted of two relevant things: $100,000 in cash and a decedent IRA containing $150,000.

The Parties received the $100,000 into their joint bank account—the only account they had. Husband rolled the decedent IRA into his name and they never touched it.

Husband bought himself a Chevy Pickup Truck with some of the money in the account – paid cash. A manly man's truck. A big ass Chevy truck. That was the only major purchase for a couple of years. Then they decided to remodel the bathrooms in their home. The bathroom remodel cost $15,000. Not much else was done with the money—some vacations, the purchase of a Jeep for their son, and a few other things that frittered the money away.

The couple decided to divorce, and it was not amicable. Husband's attorney said, "Hey, you can pop champagne now that this thing is over." Husband said, "I'd never drink to her." Wife responded, "Yeah but you'd drink to everything else."

That aside, there was a problem with the Three Property Rules. The rules are that you get whatever you brought into the marriage, while everything else is community property—except gifts and inheritances. Husband inherited $250,000. How should the money be divided at divorce?

In theory, we should have given Husband his $100,000 back and given him the decedent IRA, but this was more difficult than it would have seemed. The decedent IRA was easy—everyone agreed that the IRA was Husband's. He got it as part of his father's estate and he never touched it during the marriage. He got the Decedent IRA.

The $100,000 was more difficult. It went into a community property bank account. Some good old-fashioned family law cases tell us that the character of money can never be changed. Certain types of property can be "transmuted," which means that the character of the property can be changed. This can be done a couple of different ways, the most common of which is when Wife puts Husband on the Title to Wife's house she owned before marriage. When she does that, she changes the character of the house from separate to community property. Another way is through an agreement called a Transmutation Agreement, in which the parties clearly state their intention to transmute separate property into community property.

In the absence of a Transmutation or a Transmutation Agreement, the character of community property money remains community property no matter which account it is in, and the character of separate property money remains separate no matter which account it is in.[7] So when Husband put the $100,000 into a community property bank account, it was still separate property. There was $10,000 in the community property bank account when the $100,000 went into it. Now there was $110,000 in that account, $10,000 of which was community property and $100,000 of which was separate property.

Husband was left in a bind because even though the law provides for a method to determine the character of funds, and even though $100,000 of the $110,000 in the bank was separate property at the time Husband bought "his" truck, we could not be sure whether he used only separate property funds to buy it; in fact, the rule is that married couples always use community property funds first if the funds are mixed community and separate property. He wanted to prove that the bathroom remodel several years later was done with separate property funds also (and get those funds back). The only way for him to do it was to prove that the money spent on the truck and on the bathroom came from his father's estate. In theory this could have been simple, but in practice it involved bank records from 25 years earlier.

---

7   For those who want to read the cases that say so: *See v. See* and *Marriage of Mix* (both somewhat appropriately named cases for proving the character of assets and determining the character of mixed assets).

The Three Property Rules clearly give him the Decedent IRA. We didn't fight a losing battle over that. My client would have given him his beloved truck anyway; there really wasn't a fight there. She got her car; he got his truck (her car was community property; his truck was separate property but, despite the animosity, he really wasn't a jerk). The bathroom remodel money was dead in the water because there was no proof of how much they spent, when they spent it, or how exactly they spent it.

We settled on the issue with Husband keeping the Decedent IRA and his truck, Wife getting her vehicle and selling the house with the proceeds split equally. Wife got one-half of each of the three pensions. Son got to keep his Jeep, even though it was in Husband's name. Husband had to keep it insured until Son registered it in his own name or insured it himself.

This hypothetical brings up an important point: if you are going to use the Three Property Rules, you need to be prepared to provide proof. It is not enough to say, "I got an inheritance." You must say, "I got an inheritance, and this is what we did with the money," and provide proof. Or you have to say, "I got an inheritance, and the money is still in an account in my name alone." A third way of "tracing" the money from your inheritance is, "I got an inheritance, it went into a joint account, and the money we spent afterward was more than was in the joint account." This is called "exhaustion" accounting or "indirect tracing." Husband did a sort of exhaustion accounting with the truck by saying, "We had $110,000 in the account when I bought my truck. Only $10,000 of that was community property. So my truck was at least separate property with only a $10,000 community property investment." We didn't have to do that in the end because my client, Wife, was happy with keeping her car in exchange for his truck.

Hypothetical 2: The Dueling Mother's Gifts

In another case, I represent Husband. Husband is a naturalized US citizen from Japan. Wife is a naturalized US citizen from Russia.

Husband was in the United States for his work with a Japanese firm. Wife came to the United States from Russia. It is not clear to me how they met. Husband owned a home in the U.S. state of Georgia where he was working. Wife moved in with her daughter from a previous marriage. The Georgia house remained his separate property, but the community paid the mortgage from earnings and income.

He was transferred to Kentucky. They moved to Kentucky and purchased a home in Kentucky together. They did not sell the Georgia house, but rented it out at a break-even amount. They had a child together in Kentucky. They lived in Kentucky for 10 years and Wife one day put the children in the car and drove them to California and did not tell Husband where she was going. He figured it out when he received divorce papers. Although Husband could have fought jurisdiction in California, he decided to allow the divorce to proceed here.

During the marriage, Husband's mother had given him $120,000. The amounts were documented in transfers from a Japanese bank to his bank. They went into a joint account. The funds were commingled, but they were used to do things like remodel the Georgia and Kentucky houses, and they allowed Husband to make larger contributions to his 401(k).

Wife's mother gave them $10,000 when they purchased the Kentucky house as a down payment. This was easily traceable as it went directly into the escrow account. In Wife's mother's case, she had to write a "gift letter" to both of them to satisfy the lender. In

Husband's case, there was no "gift letter" because these gifts were portions of his inheritance.

At dissolution we were left with some problems. Husband was especially adept at record-keeping, so he was able to show every transaction during the entire marriage. I have a banker's box of bank statements in my office. We could easily show that the money came in and went out, but other than the remodels on the houses, the money was used for things like private school for his Wife's daughter and their son, and various hobbies, over a ten-year period.

Wife could easily trace receipt of and use of her mother's gift, but Husband, who had the much larger gift, could not—other than the money used for the remodeling of the houses, which was not close to the amount he received. We would need to use the "exhaustion" method of accounting to show that the 401(k) contributions could never have occurred if the family did not have use of the separate property money. Then the Husband would at least keep his 401(k).

The Georgia house was his separate property because he owned it before they were married, except for a small amount of time when they lived there (that's *Marriage of Moore* that I referred to earlier). There was a separate property lease on the home, because passive income on separate property is separate property according to Family Code 770 (also reasonable). Wife was going to get her mother's $10,000 gift back from the down payment on the Kentucky home, but we were stuck on how to get Husband's gift back.

We argued that Husband had no obligation to pay for his step-daughter's private school, and that he should get $800 per month back for 10 years. That was probably going to be a reasonable argument for some of the money, but not all of it (and also, it was a very "lose-able" argument because it could be seen as a gift). We also had the argument with the 401(k). The problem was that the Range of Normal was smacking us in the face. Normal outcome there is that Wife and Husband get the gifts they can prove were spent on assets that they still have. Wife could easily prove hers, but Husband could not.

Finally, I told Husband we could put on a 4-5 day trial over this money, and that we could prove somewhere in the neighborhood of $60,000 to $80,000 of the funds between the remodels, private school, and the 401(k). He called his ex-wife and played on her emotions ("shouldn't each of us get our mother's gift?"), accepted part of his fate (he couldn't prove where all of his mother's gift went), and settled the case for about $30,000 in cash.

The Three Property Rules give us some basic ideas of how to handle property issues, but you can see that the issues can get complicated. The biggest issue is proof. It is not enough to *say* that it happened; you need to be able to *prove* that it happened. Both examples above show what can happen if you cannot prove it. On the other hand, both examples show how the Three Property Rules work in practice.

The Husband's negotiation with the Wife in both cases provide a segue in thinking about how to negotiate cases even when you have a deficit of proof. Just because you cannot prove every little thing does not mean that there is no way to win in a negotiation. At the same time, emotions can run very hot and even when you can prove it, it is not always clear that you can settle the issues with your spouse.

Although there are a number of important family law cases in California that deal with particular situations, a basic understanding of the Three Rules of Property helps you reason to a correct conclusion in nearly all cases. I mentioned *Marriage of Moore* several times, which is normally coupled with another case called *Marriage of Marsden*. In fact, the rule of how to calculate the amount of interest the community has purchased in a separate property home is called *"Moore/Marsden."*

There is also Family Code section 2640, which describes the way a spouse who owns a house before marriage but puts their spouse on the title, gets their money back. Family Code 2640 says each spouse gets back any separate property money they used to acquire community property, meaning that you get back your separate property investment (the amount of equity in the home when you add your spouse to the title or the amount of separate property down payment—such as a gift from your parents—you use to buy a house with your spouse). There is caselaw for how to divide pensions and whether spousal survivor benefits are a divisible value; how to divide military retired pay (and not VA benefits); reimbursements for installing drip irrigation systems, etc.

The Three Property Rules, however, provide a guide for a type of reasonability analysis. While each of these rules and cases provide a specific method of analysis, we never stray far from reasonability, which is why it is not difficult to see the following:

Hypothetical Number 3: The Rancher's Son

Some years ago, I had the opportunity to represent the eldest son to one of the area's wealthiest ranch families. He was a world-famous rodeo cowboy and horse trainer, and as handsome as the handsome-ist cowboy you ever saw. His wife had a horse breeding business (my office referred to her as "Cowgirl Barbie" because she was about as gorgeous a woman we had ever seen and was always decked out in fringe-covered cowgirl gear. They were one good-looking couple and they had good-looking kids to boot). As I came to learn, it is not unusual for ranch family children to not have any real money or land of their own until their parents hit retirement age. I was surprised at how little rodeo paid him, and also at how little horse training and breeding paid. They were almost entirely reliant on his family for money.

He owned a home that his parents helped him buy several years before marriage. The house was in dismal shape and needed repair in almost every facet of the home. He would borrow money from his parents to make repairs on the home.

Husband never added Wife to the title of the home, largely because he bought it in 2004 when the market was low, took out a huge refinance loan in 2006 at the height of the market, and then watched the market collapse around him in 2008. Wife did not want to be on title to a toxic asset. By the time they divorced, the house still had less equity than his separate property (because premarital) down payment.

At their divorce trial—Wife hired a lawyer who as far as I can tell, never ever settles any cases—Wife argued that Husband should give her one-half of the equity in the home under *Moore/Marsden,* while Husband argued that under Family Code 2640, he was entitled to be reimbursed for his down payment into the home. We argued that the Family Code trumps the caselaw that in any event, he should recover money that he was owed from the beginning of the marriage before Wife could make any claim to money that was paid during the marriage.

There was another, hotter, issue that played a part in this case—bankruptcy court. (Wife had filed bankruptcy and the Bankruptcy Trustees were attempting to use *Moore/Marsden* to support a finding that the home was community property so they could seize and sell the home.)

We fought them off on this issue, and the Court agreed that the community had taken an interest in the home by paying down the mortgage and that Husband's separate property interest was first in priority and amount. Therefore, the community property interest was 0% and $0.

The numbers in Hypothetical #3 were smaller than would have justified the expenditure in attorney's fees in the case, but the big problem was the presence of the Bankruptcy Trustee lurking in the wings, trying to take and sell the home. My client was unwilling to lose his home over his Wife's bankruptcy (particularly because she had filed a bankruptcy on loans given by his parents to him and not to her).

In the end, the parties spent more on litigation than the estate was worth—each was playing for a chance. Our dice roll worked out in our favor because the law was on our side (I would not have rolled the dice without a strong leaning that we were in the one-up position, but no outcome was guaranteed). We could not settle the case because the other lawyer would not even sit down with us to talk about settlement – remember your case only resolves with a settlement or a trial – so we had to put on a roll-the-dice kind of trial, which means we would "win" if we could convince the judge of our position on the law and if we did not convince him, we would "lose." It's tough, because my client probably spent $40,000 fighting over $90,000 (which is not a good bet), but if he "lost," he was not only going to lose the $90,000, plus $40,000 in attorney's fees, but also lose his home, and he could not be convinced to walk away from the house.

CHAPTER 7

Dispute Resolution

Mediation, Collaboration, Negotiation

7-1 Showing Mercy: Or Recognizing that Litigation must End Sometime

REMEMBER THAT THE goal of this book is to put you in a position to negotiate a good outcome in your case, whether that happens in a settlement meeting with lawyers, a mediation with no lawyers, a collaborative law setting with no mediator, or in a party-to-party negotiation.

If you know what the law allows you to have, you can make certain concessions (show mercy) and receive concessions in exchange. Good family lawyering should multiply value for the family wherever possible. If we can find ways of creating money from no money, we should do it whenever possible. For example, instead of requiring a small business owner to purchase external health insurance for the children because she earns more income, you shift the responsibility to provide health insurance for the children to the low earner, who might qualify for some assistance or a reduction in premium price. The benefit will be that the high earner will pay more child support because health insurance premiums—no matter on whose behalf they are paid—impact child support by increasing the support payment of the person who is not paying for it or reducing child support for the person who is paying for it.

Even better, sometimes a spouse can get coverage through their employer for a child cheaply or at no cost. When I was a professor I had great benefits for my whole family, but when I resigned to be a lawyer and author, suddenly I did not have low-cost insurance available. I continued to cover my daughter, but the premium was enormous. I had a discussion with my daughter's mom, and we agreed that she would add my daughter to the insurance she received as a teacher in the school district. It so happened that the district had changed the rules to allow for one-dependent coverage for no additional charge. Since her husband also works for the district, they were able to cover my daughter and his son from another marriage at no additional cost. We saved perhaps $1,500 per month in health insurance premiums, and the coverage is better than I could get for her on the health insurance exchange. End result? I voluntarily increased her child support and now she gets more support for relieving me of a burden at no cost to her. We negotiated a good outcome for all of us.

Another example of creating money from nothing is regarding capital gains taxes on rental property. In a recent case, Husband and Wife owned a large family home in a tony neighborhood in my community and a beach house rental property. Wife moved in with her boyfriend to the beach house shortly after separation. Husband did not need the 4,000 square foot family home and wanted to sell it. It was easy enough to sell the family home because they had lived there for more than 20 years and raised their adult children in that home. No tax consequences. The beach home, however, was more complicated. Neither of them had ever lived in the beach home and they had a capital gains tax on any sale of that home, unless Wife lived in it for two years. Wife did not want to be forced to live in it for two years, but also did not want to pay the capital gains on a sale. Husband did not want to pay capital gains taxes on a sale of the home, but was willing to do so to resolve the divorce. The equity in the beach house was actually greater than the equity in the family home, but there was a value to each of them for Wife to take the beach house.

We had a careful negotiation over the potential capital gains taxes. The law says that you cannot charge a spouse for transaction costs that you have not incurred (in the case of real estate, this means costs of sale – realtor's fees, closing costs, etc. or capital gains taxes). On the other hand, 35% is real money and it would save Husband a lot of money for Wife to keep the house – considerable value to him. And, because people often just want to cut ties with their former spouse, Husband did not want to wonder for the next two years whether Wife would live in the house or sell it and have a capital gains tax sneak up on him.

Husband came up with a plan to give Wife a little more of the equity in the beach house in exchange for indemnification from capital gains liability. This additional equity was not close to half of the capital gains liability, but it was enough incentive for Wife to take the beach house and the potential tax liability. If she stays in the house for 2 years, she makes about $30,000 on the deal. If she sells the beach house, she takes all of the capital gains liability. Both are very savvy businesspeople and I would be deeply surprised if the $30,000 divorce profit was not enough incentive to have her live in the beach house for the next two years, obviating any capital gains liability altogether.

By carefully negotiating, we got the outcome that my client (Husband) wanted – to not give up more than half of the assets and also be completely free of Wife – and the outcome Wife wanted, which was to minimize her tax liability and have a place to live.

Both parties came out ahead and each party felt like they had "won" that issue. Wife felt she had won because she got more equity in the house than she was entitled to and Husband felt he had won because he was not responsible for any part of a potential of a 35% capital gains tax.

Sometimes a client's ego gets wrapped up in a case, and driven by their desire to win, they try to grab everything they can get. Generally speaking, I believe in my clients getting 50% of every dollar available to them. However, there are times that call for mercy. When I use the word mercy in this situation, I do not think of it as just giving away something for nothing because you feel bad. I mean standing in a position of power and trading something you own legally for something else you want. My ex showed me some mercy by agreeing to shift the health insurance from my private, market-based insurance to her employer-based insurance. I gave her more support in exchange. We both were better off for it. Failure to show mercy can also have reverse consequences.

Example 1: Failing to Show Mercy Sends the Business into Bankruptcy and, with that, Everything Falls Apart.

A lawyer I've known since we were both family law beginners and who I think is perhaps the best family lawyer in our city and one of the best in the state, told me something that I thought showed massive growth on his part. I will reveal it after the following three "mercy" examples. In my first family law case, which happened to have this lawyer on the other side, my client was a Husband who owned a business with his Wife. It was a union drywall subcontracting company that required a contractor's license that Wife did not have, so my client was the "in-spouse"—the one who was going to keep the business.

The business had done well and was making around $700,000 per year in profits. The parties had lived the American dream, coming to the U.S. legally from Mexico speaking only Spanish, and carrying all their belongings in a couple of duffel bags. They had built this empire through a mix of aptitude, sacrifice, hard work, and some luck. My client had a little bit of arrogance (actually a lot of arrogance), but he was lovable because he loved his kids and his ex-wife a lot. The judge had really taken to beating him up in court before he ever came to me, partly because he was disrespectful to the Judge in Court repeatedly. Hilariously so, but also inappropriately so. This other lawyer was taking him to task repeatedly.

By the time I got him, he was hurting pretty badly. I remember telling the other lawyer: "we have to settle this soon because I can see my client is unraveling and the whole thing is going to hell." I probably didn't say it word for word like that, but basically there were signs that the business was falling apart because my client's mental health was deteriorating. The empire depended on him to run it, and he was being dragged into court three times a month and threatened with jail for contempt and fines and for all sorts of things. He was running ragged, and I could see the entire thing happening. My client was wearing the stress all over his face and body.

The other lawyer had created a series of hoops for him to jump through to accurately report to his wife what was happening in the business. The hoops would have been bordering on impossible for anyone to jump through even with help, and he had no help because his wife used to handle reporting and compliance. And like many small-business people I have known in my practice, they probably did not accurately report everything they earned—a potentially acceptable risk when you are married, but not when you are in a divorce and must report everything to your spouse.

Each time he failed to report or to give access to an account, the other lawyer would file a contempt motion. The Judge referred to opposing counsel in a hearing on a contempt motion as "the King of Contempts!" Finally, after 7 or 8 contempt motions with the judge never ruling on any of them, we lost a very small issue. My client was supposed to give the Wife a Quickbooks password so she could access the business records, and he was a few days late in getting it to her. Out of the blue, and despite so many more egregious violations, the Judge said, "I find you in contempt and remand you to custody of the Sheriff." He was handcuffed and taken out of the courtroom, yelling, "I will appeal you." The Wife sobbed in open court. The judge took both lawyers into his chambers and said, "I'm going to bring him right back. I just want him to see the inside of the jail so maybe he will start doing what I tell him." He also admitted, "I learned a lot by sending him down to the jail. Look, his wife has been screaming at me for a year to put him in jail, then I finally do it, and she is in there bawling her eyes out."

The other lawyer and the wife refused to make any deal with us.

A couple of months later my client filed for bankruptcy protection, merely to get a break from what had become constant harassment from the other lawyer. This move turned a $4,000 per month support order and a $1,500 per month attorney's fee award into an $800 per month support order and no attorney's fees award. The wife ended up losing her house in the foreclosure crisis and everyone was the worse for it.

Ten years later, I am still friends with this former client. He is a little worse for wear, but in general, he has risen like a phoenix from the ashes. He has another business doing something similar to what he did before. He remarried. He has a young daughter. He is generally happy. And he is my friend (which, let's be honest, is not all that normal for a divorce lawyer and a former client). He still sends me clients. He has used his trade to do work on my home and business. And I think, despite filing for bankruptcy protection in that particular business, he emerged bloodied and bruised, but better off.

The wife did not. When she lost the support payment and then lost the home, things unraveled for her. I did not wish this on her. She behaved very badly in the divorce, but most importantly, she let her (then, young) lawyer lead her down a path of "total victory," but my client still had the bankruptcy card to play. She tried to get everything, and then get more than everything, and in so doing, she crushed my client's spirit. By not showing any mercy at all, she ended up killing the goose that was laying the golden eggs for her.

Example 2: Failing to Show Mercy Leads to a Padlocked Gate.

Later, that same lawyer and I had another family law case together, which was, at the time, probably the most epic case of my career. I again represented the husband who was the "in spouse." His business was average in terms of profits, unlike the other client's business, but it did well enough that he and his wife owned a house and some other property, and each drove newer American cars.

The other lawyer did what he always did before he became a great family lawyer, which is nitpick everything and make a huge deal out of it. My client, also a touch arrogant, was losing his mind over the details of the case, while also trying to get up for work every day for his business. He couldn't eat or sleep. I got a call from him one night around midnight. He was out jogging 8 miles from his house and wanted to stop by and chat with me. I came out to the front yard, and we chatted for an hour, my client jogging in place much of the time. I sensed he was just burning energy. I finally offered him a ride home, but he said he wouldn't be able to sleep if he didn't run for another couple of hours.

I kept telling this other lawyer that there is a balance. Some lawyers think it's fun to pin someone down and make them squirm. They feel a sense of power when they do it. I am not saying this lawyer felt that way, but he was (is) damned good at being a punisher. In fact, many years later, I saw him in court representing a husband against one of the worst people I have ever met in Santa Maria and I had had business dealings with her and hated her (and I don't hate that many people, but she is on the short list) and I told this lawyer "give her the Murial Jackson treatment" after a different client of mine that he had punished for years (not her real name). But I have often thought his early fixation on punishment was also his, perhaps only, weakness.

One day my client simply closed the business. It was a violation of the Automatic Temporary Restraining Orders that are issued in a divorce case as soon as the divorce is filed and served, but there was little anyone could do about it. He sold all his inventory and padlocked the entry gate to the business's sales yard, figuring that he would rather let the Court punish him than undergo the constant punishment he was taking in his own mind. Ultimately, there was little the court could do. Both of my two business owner clients in these last two examples went back to work as wage earners, earning substantially less than they had when they ran their businesses, and I was successfully able to argue that the businesses were no longer viable.

In both cases my clients closed the business and the wife ended up with a more normal support order: $800 or so per month, having lost thousands of dollars per month in spousal support when the business closed. Not unlike one of the first examples in this book, where the motivational speaker offered his wife half of the publishing empire that ended up being worth more than $100 million in order to get a one-time $9 million payout, the use of punishment as a tool can backfire for the client, and in both of these cases it did.

Example 3: We Show Mercy and My Client Continues to Enjoy a Huge Support Award

This other lawyer and I also had a case together in which the roles were reversed; he represented the in-spouse husband and I had the out-spouse wife. The husband threatened to close his business because of a chronic health condition (Crohn's Disease) that, although mostly manageable with medication, still required a strong work ethic to suffer through. My client called it the "shitting disease," but I am not one to judge about these things. I understand it can be debilitating. The business had his name on it, and he was driven enough by his ego to work through his sickness. If we took away his ability to lead the business, my client believed he would succumb to his illness and let the business collapse.

The business, a large construction engineering firm, had posted a profit of over $10 million the year before, which would have meant my client was entitled to $40,000 per month in support. She knew the numbers were skewed, however, because of the crushing debt the company had taken on during the market crash of 2008, and that if we got a number like $40,000 per month in child and spousal support from a judge, the Husband would just close the business. The couple also owed almost a million dollars in taxes, which my client did not want to pay. So we reverse-engineered how much she needed to live comfortably, and we asked the husband to tell us what he thought he could afford to pay while accepting the entire tax debt. He told us that he could pay around $9,000 per month plus health insurance (and he accepted all the tax debt). We would have accepted $6,500.

I think the other lawyer was so shocked that we didn't crush this guy's *huevos* when we had the chance that they negotiated from their top number. It was so much more than we were willing to accept that we did not even counter-offer—although we did take half an hour in the other room to ask for certain non-monetary concessions. But we were tactical about it. There was no point in getting a $40,000 a month order that the husband would never pay and that would lead to my client facing the thing she feared most: getting stuck with joint and several liability on $1 million in tax debt. My client told me recently that, six years later, she has gotten every payment from him—not always on time, but with very minimal arrears. We let the husband keep persevering with the support payment he offered, knowing that when a party makes a deal that is their deal, they are more likely to uphold their end of the bargain.

Anyway, earlier I mentioned the massive growth shown by the other lawyer in the last three examples. Here it is. Recently he said to me, "I've almost always represented the out-spouse on division of the business. I finally know what you are talking about for the in-spouse. I have another case where I have the in-spouse and this divorce is just killing him. I can see it in his eyes that he is going to snap. I don't know if he will be able to make it through the divorce and keep running the business on a day-to-day level."

Business division and support are perhaps the area where (particularly men) get screwed the most in a divorce. In fact, the only time I believe the law allows for a party to get "cleaned out in the divorce," besides when they agree to it, is when there is a business. In Example 1 above, the business had been valued at between $1 million and $1.3 million, meaning the husband was going to have to give the wife between $500,000 and $650,000 in other assets.

As my client pointed out, fully half the value was intangible (or as he described it "my good name"). So, when we were dividing the business, he pointed out that his wife was getting all the trucks, equipment, real property, and assets, and he was getting all the debt and his "good name." Plus, he was being ordered to pay her $4,000 per month in support—something some family lawyers believe is a "double-dip," where the business is treated as an asset and as an income source. Ultimately, the Bankruptcy was a potent weapon in reducing all of this to next to nothing; except, however, that in filing for Bankruptcy protection he also lost his business.

If this other lawyer learns the skill of knowing when to stop pushing someone (there is a place for mercy in the family court), he will be unstoppable. As I have said, he is already the best family law litigator in the area, perhaps the state; if he also becomes the best family law negotiator, phew, he's going to be very difficult to beat.

But you can neutralize exceptionally strong litigator-negotiators in a few important ways:

1) **You take the competition for assets and debts out of their hands by looking for ways to multiply assets.** Instead of dividing a business, you have the parties remain partners with the out-spouse remaining a silent partner. We did that recently in a $65 million business/real estate case in which extracting $32.5 million in cash was an unlikely possibility, and the wife (my client) was in no position to run any of the businesses; she was in her 80s and did not need $32.5 million and was mostly focused on "having enough money to buy my grandchildren gifts from Target" and keeping her house. There were 14 separate LLCs and Corporations. If she had received them, she would have had to sell them or immediately gift them to her children and deal with substantial gift tax penalties.

In downtick real estate markets, sometimes we will make deals where one party will live in the home for a specified period of years (tied to the youngest child reaching the age of majority) and then the house will be sold with the out-spouse (my client in both cases) getting half the equity. The advantage of this type of deal in a downturned real estate market that is normally very hot is that rather than sell the house to the spouse below typical market value, the out-spouse remains an investor in real estate, something they probably could not afford otherwise. If neither spouse could qualify for a mortgage on their own at this time, almost all the current equity in the home will be lost in the transaction fees, leaving both spouses with nothing. Looking to multiply value wherever we could, we might negotiate to let the parties remain partners, rather than separating everything.

2) **You use emotion to get a party to make agreements**. Going back to the Dueling Mother's Gifts Example, both parties wanted their gift back. My client was willing to give his wife the gift she got from her parents and keep the one he got from his. The wife, however, wanted her gift and half of his. The best tool we had for negotiation is not what the law says to do (gifts are separate property) but instead making the emotional argument that the gifts are gifts from parents (inheritances) and that those belong to the party who received them. It took a lot to get Wife to see this, and because his gift was so much larger than hers, he had to grease the wheels with some cash, but ultimately, Wife agreed because she fundamentally agreed emotionally, that gifts from parents should be gifts from parents to their child.

3) **Figure out early what is most important to the other side and give that to them in exchange for things you want**. In Example 3 above, the most important thing to the husband was keeping his business. He had built it. He wanted it so badly that he agreed to pay $1 million in tax debt and pay his wife $9,000 per month (plus other significant concessions) to keep his business. My client was not an

engineer and never could have or would have wanted the business. This was a logical and reasonable outcome which resulted in multiplying wealth and assets. We traded away an order we would never have been able to enforce ($40,000 per month in child and spousal support) to get a livable (for my client) $9,000 per month with significant concessions.

Example 4: Where Showing Mercy Failed and My Client Got Murdered

Showing mercy doesn't always work. In August 2017, I had the most emotionally difficult case of my career. The short version is that my client and her husband were both Russian immigrants. The husband was very controlling. The wife, my client, told me early on that she was afraid of him, but we knew she could not get a domestic violence restraining order on the facts she had. He had been rough with her a few times, and was very controlling of her, but he had not *hurt* her physically. The law in this arena has changed in the last few years in California and California now recognizes "coercive control" as a basis for domestic violence restraining orders, which means that we do not need actual violence to get a DV restraining order. The big problem is not the law – I thought we had facts enough for domestic violence restraining orders in 2017 even without actual physical violence, but it was a close call, and we had a judge who was old and set in his ways. He punishes parties for asking for DV restraining orders if there is no physical violence and I believed that at least a part of what ensued was a result of his strong belief that domestic violence can only mean physical violence. I will never win a "coercive control" case in front of him, and I know that. I think so highly of this judge in all other respects that it overcomes my anger at him for this singular issue, but he has finally retired, and

I believe that our clients will be safer because of that in the long run.

We tried to pacify Husband by giving him something we knew was important to him early on in our negotiation—shared custody of his son. I knew we could get the custody orders we wanted, but she wanted their son to know his dad (which I believe is almost always the right thing to do) and she needed money, which he controlled.

We believed he was mentally unstable, so the first thing we told him in our settlement conference was, "You are going to share custody of your son. We would never take that away from you." The problem is that he wanted custody of his wife, and she had already found another boyfriend. We got the monetary settlement we wanted, but there were tragic and disastrous results.

I got a call at 2 A.M. one night from opposing counsel with whom I am friends. She was hysterically crying and sobbing. She told me: "My client murdered your client and abducted the child. He is on the run. Please protect yourself." With five bullets, the husband had murdered my client in her apartment while the child sat in the car downstairs. A nationwide Amber Alert was issued, and for two days we watched the news and social media updates as he went through a series of planned vehicle exchanges, ditching one car for another and keeping ahead of authorities. We assumed he was going to try to get on an airplane for Russia. Finally, he was found in Tarzana, several hours away. LAPD shot and killed him when he pulled out a gun to greet them. His 9-year-old son, even more tragically, watched out the window as his father was shot. The child ended up losing two parents in the span of 48 hours. I later represented the mother's boyfriend in his attempt to get guardianship of the child, a case we settled in 2019 with the child staying with the boyfriend.

That is only the second time I've written anything about that case and it's all I am ready to write at the moment. If you want to know more, you can look the story up under my name and the city I practice in with key word, "Russian." She meant a lot to our office and so does her son. We were deeply affected and remain so.

Although I have said I do not believe in traditional mediation and collaborative law on their own, I do believe in negotiated settlements. I believe every case can lead to negotiated settlement and that every case should have a negotiated settlement. However, you should know what the rules are so that when you sit down to negotiate you are not basing it on "fairness" or "equity," but on a strong understanding of the law.

I also believe you should have other negotiation skills at the ready. I believe you can show mercy and that at times you should, but I also believe that mercy comes from a place of personal and legal power. You do not give your spouse the business or waive your interest in her pension because they are trying to convince you it is fair or equitable to do so. If you are going to grant her wish, do it because you know exactly what you are entitled to and that you are giving it up either to get something you want in return or because there is another intangible reason to do so.

Mercy derives from strength. In most traditional mediations without lawyers present, you do not come from a place of strength. You come from a place of guilt or shame or embarrassment or anger or sadness. If you do happen to come from a place of strength in a divorce mediation, the mediator is trained to take your spouse's position to balance the bargaining positions. None of those options put you in a strong negotiating position.

7-2 What I don't like About Collaborative Law or Mediation (But I do Like Divorce Settlements).

I will not win any points with a branch of the judiciary or a large number of lawyers for saying this, but I am not a fan of traditional mediation . . . and I dislike "collaborative law" even more. I hope my reasons are noble; otherwise, the American Academy of Matrimonial Lawyers will never offer me membership.

I grew up as a civil litigator, where mediation is par for the course in just about every case. In fact, most civil litigation cases will not even see a settlement offer until mediation (or if there are pre-mediation offers, they are only there to expose weaknesses on the other side— "Let's see if they will take a handful of wooden nickels and a buy-one-get-one-free coupon"). In most cases, the first non-mediation offers are not strong offers; they just get made to see what the other side is thinking.

In a divorce, mediation seems like an obvious choice since, in almost every case, the outcome is a foregone conclusion. I have already mentioned the Three Property Rules:

Whatever you had before marriage or after separation is your separate property.

Whatever you get during the marriage, however you get it, so long as it was not a gift (or inheritance, which is just a form of giving) to you or your spouse directly, belongs to the community.

Gifts belong to the party who received it, including gifts given by the husband to the wife or the wife to the husband, or from deceased people in the form of inheritance.

The Three Property Rules backed by the Rule of Reasonability allow us to know before we even file the Petition for Dissolution of Marriage exactly how the case is going to turn out (or near-exactly). With that in mind, every divorce case should settle with an agreement—and most do. So, divorce, then, is the perfect candidate for mediation, right?

Not exactly.

Let's discuss mediation beforehand so that we have defined our terms. I do not want to bash divorce mediation until you understand what I mean by divorce mediation.

A typical divorce mediation involves one lawyer who has agreed not to represent either party and instead acts as the mediator. The parties arrive at mediation with all their concerns about the case outcome, seeking to achieve their own goals. Effective mediators listen to both sides. Typically, they meet with each party individually to understand their perspectives and then aim to bring the parties together to reach agreements on what they are willing to offer each other. In emotionless divorces (which never happen), mediators simply assist each side in articulating their desires, while each party hopes to persuade the other to meet their needs without conceding important priorities. During mediation training, mediators learn to remain unbiased regarding the outcomes and focus on ensuring the process is effective.

In fact, mediation focuses more on the process than on the outcomes. There's a reason for this: a fundamental legal principle I have mentioned before states, "Good agreements are durable agreements." We don't just want *any* agreement; we want one that is built to last. Durable agreements typically arise when the process is strong. Both parties feel heard, understand each other, and collaborate to achieve the best outcome for both, recognizing that each has hopes, dreams, and aspirations. Therefore, the process can often be more significant than the substance of the outcome.

The mediator succeeds when both parties sign the Marital Settlement Agreement. The outcome for the parties themselves is irrelevant; each may feel as if they have won or lost, yet they are unaware of what the outcome should look like under the law. The mediator's role doesn't necessarily involve bringing the law into the equation. Generally, mediators tend to avoid challenging topics such as spousal support and child custody if they believe it could jeopardize the likelihood of reaching an agreement. Worse still, they might spend significant time indulging the Husband's belief that he shouldn't have to pay any spousal support. "Now, Francine, we must allow Edward to explain why he believes he shouldn't pay spousal support. It's against his conscience. I understand Edward's perspective when he claims he shouldn't have to pay."

If Edward is a doctor and Francine financed his medical school while working as a nurse, and now he has moved on to another nurse who is 25 years younger than she is, she is getting spousal support. I believe a lot of time is wasted in mediation considering outcomes that would never occur in a court trial. While I think settlement agreements offer many options not available in court, we should also stop deceiving ourselves and wasting time. We ought to agree on a number that Edward can manage, provide a larger support payment in the short term, and let Francine know that she needs to start figuring out her plans for the future because the support will eventually dry up. Inform Edward that he will be paying support for a few years, but the understanding is that there will be an end date... so he needs to "deal with it." In other words, we can consider reasonable settlement positions, but mediators often entertain unrealistic ones because they focus more on the process than the outcomes. The mediator "wins" when both parties sign the agreement, regardless of whether one or both parties has "won" or "lost."

I think matters can and should settle in mediation. If someone isn't being honest about their income or they are hiding assets, then mediation is not the best place to be anyway. If someone is dead-set against paying spousal support in a spousal support case – like the cliché doctor/nurse case above – then mediation is not likely to be the best place either (even though a productive mediation should still resolve all of the rest of the issues).

Mediation agreements are also often vague when it comes to the most difficult issues. It's easier for either side to feel like they won when they read a vague term in a mediation agreement, sort of like why "bipartisan" legislation often reads much more vaguely than the politicians' descriptions to their constituents of what the bipartisan legislation means. Or if the mediation agreements are not vague, they are precise to a fault and cannot be expanded to analogous situations; this can be because each party is so untrusting of the other that the agreements they make are hyper-specific, precisely so that they cannot be analogized to additional circumstances (for example, "The parties agree that Father will pay the 2024 team fees for Son's football season." What happens is Son decides not to play football but has team fees for the soccer team instead? Or what happens in 2025?).

Mediators are not really supposed to tell the parties what the law says. They may interject about the law (if the mediator knows family law, which civil mediators will not and non-lawyers definitely will not) from time to time to get the parties closer to an agreement, but it's not really their goal. Instead, they work toward processing issues and getting agreements, which means their final agreements may look nothing like a court might rule in the same situation.

Sometimes parties give up many issues just to "be done" with the divorce. There is no way to quantify the relief that comes with being "done" with a divorce. There is a huge value in being "done" with a divorce. It feels like such an enormous relief to be "done" with the divorce. However, only you know what the value of being "done" is for yourself. I say that because you may really be suffering emotionally and that may make you willing to leave money on the table in order to be "done" – i.e., accepting your spouse's crappy offer on one of the issues in order to be free of him. In fact, most people who make agreements ultimately leave something on the table to get the deal done. They get back their peace of mind, get me off their payroll (savings on attorney's can often overcome waiving certain financial claims), get to focus on living rather than litigating, and most of the time, get a financial concession they really want in exchange. But there are reasonable concessions and there is outright theft. And the worst kind of outright theft is the kind you agree to. The mediator will not tell you in most instances that the other party has bullied you into permitting outright theft. As a lawyer, I let my clients "drive the bus" when it comes to agreements, but I always tell them when they are giving things up within the realm of reason and when they are getting punked.

In the mediation I dislike, neither party has a lawyer, and the mediator tries to help them agree about what is "fair." Both parties try to convince each other of what is "fair;" except that one party usually uses their superior bargaining power—charm and gregariousness, willingness to fight to the metaphorical and financial death, threats of taking the children, threats of quitting work, angry outbursts, tears, screaming, character attacks, all different versions of extortion, etc.—to convince the other party that what they want is not only fair but *better* for the other party.

Many divorce mediators are divorce lawyers who believe they can change their practices from litigation to the kinder, gentler art of mediation. But divorce lawyers-turned-mediators are usually not particularly good at mediation because they are trained to litigate. They will often pick an outcome they would like to see and then work to drive the parties toward that outcome. This might not be the worst thing in the world, since the outcome will bear a resemblance to legal reality; however, divorce litigators turned mediators often lose the most important element of mediation—the process itself.

So, now I have complained that some divorce mediation is overly process-oriented, and some divorce mediation loses the process altogether. These are both key problems in divorce mediation. In a commercial mediation normally there is almost no process. Both sides talk to the mediator and the mediator tries to get either side to throw out a number to negotiate from. In a divorce mediation, there are normally so many issues with the divisions of assets and liabilities, plus custody and support, that a good mediator should be trying to figure out what is most important to either side, placing the most wanted item(s) in the desiring party's column and seeing what the outcome would look like when that is done. In fact, when I am working on a divorce settlement proposal, I often start with giving my client every single asset that they want

Good divorce negotiations should have some process-focused and some outcome-focused goals. We want soon-to-be-former spouses to talk through issues – good discussions, even if difficult, can set the tone for compliance with agreements later. Remember that people tend to follow agreements much more than if there were orders foisted upon them against their will (and they tend to hate "agreements" foisted upon them against their will). We also want to be realistic about what the law says to do – this is why I really like 4-way settlement negotiations where each side has a lawyer to advocate for them and understand the law, but where the goal is resolution and not posturing or puffing.

My biggest problem with divorce mediation is that there is a guaranteed cost with no guaranteed outcome. If you do not resolve the matter in mediation, then the only other option is litigation, where the costs continue, and the work begins again.

A few years ago, I had a case where H was a Chief Financial Officer and W was a stay-at-home mom and homemaker, who eventually built a small (very small) multi-level marketing business, once the youngest of the kids went off to college. They had two paid-off houses (they lived in the California house while the Idaho house sat empty for their vacations) and $1 million in an IRA. A total estate of around $2.5 million.

H, in recent years, had taken to being a fractional CFO for hire, making perhaps $80,000 per year, but loving his life helping small businesses, which is his true passion. When H worked for a venture capital firm, he could earn $300,000 per year, plus stock options. The venture capital firm where he had last worked was based in Dallas, but they would or could send him anywhere in the country. After moving the family to California's central coast, he took a local but nationally-known company public, funded the IRA and paid off the California house. The next gig was in Minneapolis. W and the daughter did not want to move, so for three years he commuted to Minneapolis from California's Central Coast. Eventually, they agreed that he could work to build a financial life and career in the local area in California. He started a management consulting company with the fractional CFO business, and when I met him, he was doing the consultant/fractional CFO thing for little, but enough, salary to cover the day-to-day.

W announced that she was filing for divorce, and he consulted with me. Pretty easy divorce from my standpoint. They had three main assets: two houses and the IRA. All were acquired entirely during marriage. Since one of them would have had to give the other cash for one-half the equity in the California house and neither one wanted it, they sold it in California's hot housing market and pocketed $300,000 apiece. Each kept their own car. The kids were off to college. Dividing the IRA and the Idaho house would be simple enough. Spousal support was a sticking point because he could earn $300,000 as a CFO but was earning less than 1/3rd of that with his new business.

Mediation seemed like a reasonable option for them. However, Wife hired a lawyer to "guide her through the process." She not only hired a lawyer; she hired a big, bad asshole of a lawyer from a neighboring town. They paid $7,500 for the mediator, and she paid another $8,000 for the lawyer. The lawyer has a reputation for being a tough guy, but really it is just a willingness to argue stupid things and argue hard for them—despite knowing he will lose. He seems like a tough negotiator, but the end results are always similar to those you would get if you gave the whole thing to a judge (meaning no value-add for the money, unless the goal is just to make your ex feel small, which is this lawyer's specialty). .

The parties saw a very well-respected divorce lawyer who also acts as a mediator. They agreed on how to divide their property, but Wife wanted Husband to go back to work making $300,000 per year, so she could get spousal support; Husband, who had left his work at the private equity fund two years before, did not want to do it. In the meantime, Husband, even against my advice, went out and got a $150,000 CFO job in the local area, meaning he was no longer making $80,000 per year and now actually had spousal support liability. Even though I had advised against leaving what he loved, I thought this was a pretty good compromise – H was 59 and had severely high blood pressure. He had not worked as a venture capital CFO in several years and had been earning $80,000 per year for the last 3 years. Using his income at $150,000 per year seemed very reasonable to me – what I would have offered would have been support derived from the $150,000 income and a percentage of everything else above $150,000 but below $300,000 (which is how the case settled several years later).

Wife spoke with her lawyer and left mediation in a storm of curse words. They had spent six months mediating their case, nearly reaching a resolution, when she walked away (incurring about $15,000 in the process), prompting Husband to hire me at what was no longer the end of the case, but the beginning once again. And this was a straightforward case. Ultimately, Wife hired another costly lawyer, and each party ended up spending about $50,000, only for Husband to achieve a better outcome at trial than he was willing to settle for during mediation. Two years later, Wife brought him back to court over a minor issue, resulting in *another* $15,000 in fees for each side, and once more, Husband prevailed because Wife persisted in her quest for moral victory.

In a case like this, where Husband made all the money, there was a likelihood that he would be responsible for all of the attorney's fees. So, for Wife, there was no obvious harm in pulling the plug on the mediation and restarting the matter in litigation. Plus, the mediation privilege is absolute, meaning nothing you discuss in mediation is permitted to be brought into the court. The one saving grace is that all the discovery and disclosure documents prepared for mediation are permitted to be used in litigation.

But by pulling the plug on mediation, the wife ultimately sacrificed the best deal she could have had. Why? Because in mediation, without lawyers, she could leverage the husband's emotions to persuade him to agree to terms he never should have accepted. He was willing to comply because he didn't want to go through litigation with her and because she tapped into his natural urge to care for her, to the extent that he closed his business and took a higher-paying job so he could afford to pay her alimony, in addition to offering her the Idaho house and part of the IRA.

In this case, the issue discussed in mediation was one that could be easily resolved by the law. If they had understood the law, they could have resolved it themselves. The divorce mediator could have helped in that situation, but he did not, and ultimately, the Wife walked away from the table after investing so much time and money into the mediation. Once the Husband hired me, I taught him the Three Property Rules, and we managed to secure about $500,000 more than he was initially willing to give her. The Wife was so angry that she kept taking him back to court... and losing.

Mediation could be much more successful and fairer if the mediator told the parties the law on any particular issue. Then, the parties could "bargain in the shadow of the law"—that is, they could bargain with each other knowing exactly what the law gives them, so they would know what they are getting and what they are giving up.

The law allows parties to reach any agreement they desire, but if the case goes to court, the judge is bound by legal requirements – such as "equal division of community property assets." Informing the parties about the state of the law and likely judicial outcomes, while also explaining the costs and risks of trial, would empower them to negotiate around these trial-related risks. For instance, if a judge is known for implementing a "week on/week off" custody arrangement, and the parties want a different custodial setup, they could negotiate accordingly. Mom may prefer that Dad has less than a 50-50 split, but the mediator could indicate, "Dad is almost certain to receive 50-50 with alternating weeks." Mom might understand that 50-50 is forthcoming but may not want to go a week without seeing the children; thus, the mediator suggests alternative schedules that still maintain a 50-50 division. Each parent achieves their objectives by "bargaining in the shadow of the law," rather than engaging in a series of mediation sessions where Mom insists that Dad should "act in the kids' best interests" by allowing them to live full-time with her, while Dad remains focused on an alternating weeks custody plan instead of exploring gentler arrangements for the kids.

7-3 What I Don't Like about Collaborative Law

Collaborative law is another type of mediative method for resolving divorce disputes. Both parties get lawyers—but both parties (and the lawyers) agree in writing before they sit down that if negotiations break down, neither party will be permitted to retain the lawyer they have engaged for litigation. There is no neutral third party or mediator in the room. This is essentially an even more costly version of "guaranteed cost with no guaranteed outcome."

In the collaborative law method, the parties and the lawyers work together to reach an outcome that will work for everyone. They bring in experts as needed: CPAs, financial planners, educators, counselors, whoever is needed to help the parties reach an agreement. There is a "restorative" quality to the collaborative process. Two people at odds with each other engage in a process of conciliation to reach a good outcome. The process not only often yields agreements, but it also is touted to help heal wounds and allow the parties to go forward as co-parents for the future.

I had a course in law school where the professor was a collaborative practitioner. Before I had ever practiced a single minute of law, it seemed like an incredible idea to me. Here we were, budding litigators, ready to take part in the legal system while at the same time questioning how it worked and whom it benefitted. Collaborative law was a way of taking the decision out of judges' hands and putting it into a process that would yield good results for everyone. Rather than wounding one another, the parties would leave the collaborative process almost better than they had ever been.

This professor touted Collaborative Law as a way of handling not only family law cases, but also construction defects, contract law cases, and others. Its practitioners noted that it was "catching on." It was the brainchild of a former lawyer turned counselor, who saw the legal process as broken for so many people who encountered it. It all made sense.

However, after several years of practicing law and forgetting all about the collaborative process, it reemerged in my life when a friend of mine described her divorce using the collaborative process. The more I heard about her case, the more I realized that she had gotten completely bowled over during the collaborative process.

She was married to a lawyer and had twins with him. It was a quick romance followed by a quick wedding and a quick pregnancy (not necessarily in that order, if I recall correctly). He left her for another woman shortly after the kids were born. She was in shock, of course, but she also was trying to be a single mother and finish her teaching credential. She had Ivy League undergraduate degree and a Berkeley master's degree. She was not an inconsequential person. When I met her, we were studying for our Ph.Ds. together at UC Berkeley. She took some time off from the program to have her babies and follow her husband to the Central Valley in California. He was a recent graduate of UC Berkeley's Boalt Hall School of Law, as was I, who had landed a job in the Central Valley where her parents lived. He worked for a big firm making $180,000 per year when he left her.

Since she was trying to complete her teaching credential and was raising the twins full-time, while he was earning $180,000 annually, she would have expected a substantial support payment each month. It wasn't a long-term marriage (maybe three years), so she would have anticipated spousal support for at least half the duration of the marriage. If I had been her lawyer during litigation, I would likely have requested spousal support for as long as it would take her to finish her credential program and complete her student teaching, allowing her to be self-supporting. I would base this request on the notion that she gave up her chosen career to support him and rely on his promise to provide for her through his job. That would have likely been a close call, but I believe she could have expected around $5,000 to $6,000 per month for child and spousal support for two to three years, along with ongoing child support of $3,500 per month thereafter.

Here are a few "facts" to help understand my concerns with both traditional divorce mediation (one neutral/mediator, no lawyers) and collaborative law (two lawyers, no neutral/mediator).

Fact 1: Bad Decision-Making at a Tough Time in Your Life: Bullies Tend to Win

Husband asked her to engage the collaborative process. She, being more of a lover than a fighter, thought it was a good idea to skip the court system if she could. She also rightfully feared representing herself and facing off against a big firm litigator, although even a decent lawyer could have gotten Husband to pay her attorney's fees. On the 5th day of the collaborative process (more than $30,000 into the process), Husband told her he was quitting his job at the firm to have more time with the kids and to start his own practice, so he would not have income for a few years. (A few years?!?!) He would not pay support, but he would take the two toddlers with him 35% of the time so she could go to school. Now, to be clear, in most courts this would not fly. A judge would not tell him that he had to stay employed at a big firm, but would likely tell him that he would pay her support as though he was working at the big firm for at least a couple of years. With toddlers, the timeshare was probably a little higher than most judges would grant right out of the gate, but I would have expected a 35%-50% timeshare within a couple of years.

The collaborative process allowed him to follow his heart and his dreams of being his own boss, even with no clients and little experience. Because there was no authority figure (judge) to keep him in check and little threat of actual litigation, he was able to make decisions to her detriment that a judge would almost certainly never allow. The collaborative process meant that she had to basically accept that this was his chosen path and that she could do very little (or nothing) to oppose it.

Each of the lawyers who represented them was a solo practitioner, so they could empathize with his desire to leave the big firm life and go out on his own, even though it was highly unlikely that a judge would have supported this type of decision with twin toddlers. In the end, through a mix of emotional arguments and twisted logic, he was able to convince my friend to accept unreasonably bad positions for herself.

Where was her collaborative lawyer during all this? With no ability to file a single court motion to stop him from taking these actions, there was nothing my friend could do except throw in the towel on the process and start over with an attack dog lawyer charging a $10,000 retainer. She did not do this, because he had already quit his job and she had no money.

She, with her two Ivy League college degrees and the twins, moved into her childhood bedroom at her parents' house. He practiced law out of his garage and gave her no spousal or child support. A couple of years later he took her to court seeking "full custody" of the twins and he was self-represented. She hired experienced local counsel, who finally had the opportunity to crush him in court. He lost time with the twins and ended up having to get a job to pay child support.

I was emotional about this case because she was my friend and I saw the case only from her point of view. However, I have been a big firm lawyer and know how alienating it can be. I also know the suffering of the long hours of working and what it's like to be a father missing his child, so I could empathize with him as well. But what I could not understand was how or why he would not agree to give her some support so she could finish her teaching credential and get a job. Instead of supporting his children, actually instead of supporting his ex-wife for a couple of years so that *she* could support their children, he passed the responsibility to her parents. They accepted that responsibility happily, but they should not have had to.

Fact 2: Mediation and Collaborative Law are a Guaranteed Cost Without a Guaranteed Ending

From a conceptual point of view, I am also concerned about cost. Collaborative lawyers say the cost is about the same as litigation, but the threat of litigation still exists. Instead of paying one mediator, the parties each pay a lawyer. A day of collaborative law is about the same cost as a day of trial. If each lawyer charges $400 per hour, and a day of collaborative law takes 8 hours, the cost for the day is $6,400. If a case goes to trial, it may be the same amount of cost, but when the trial is over, the judge rules on the requests. In other words, a trial is a guaranteed cost with a guaranteed outcome.

Collaborative law is yet another guaranteed cost without a guaranteed outcome, except the parties are paying for *two* lawyers who are trying to help them reach a fair outcome with zero threat of actual litigation—no "range of best-and-worst case outcomes in the trial court" nor any "bargaining in the shadow of the law." This leads to $180,000 per year lawyers not paying any child support for 9-month-old twins or spousal support to wives who left graduate school in Berkeley to follow them to the Central Valley.

And like mediation, collaborative law is non-binding. If you fail at collaborative law, you must start all over again. In fact, that is the biggest hammer in the collaborative law process: "Do you really want to walk out of here and have to spend all that money again?" And since collaborative lawyers make an agreement with their clients that they will not represent them in court if the process fails, parties must find "litigators" to see the case through court, forcing them to spend even more money.

Collaborative participants will often accept a poor agreement just to avoid going to court, admitting, "I just finally gave in to him because he would not stop about it; I had to be done. I just couldn't take another second of him grandstanding and bullshitting us all." Collaborative law, like mediation, benefits the "stubborn one" more than the "dealmakers." The threat of having to hire a "litigator" for another $10,000 beyond the $30,000 my friend's parents had already loaned her from their retirement accounts because she "failed" at collaborative law, created an additional layer of guilt to her already (unjustly) guilty conscience.

At the end of the collaborative process, she was in a far worse-off position than she ever would have been if she had just hired a "litigator" from the get-go. It not only cost her probably the same amount of money litigation would have cost her (or negotiating from a wartime posture), it also likely cost her between $100,000 and $200,000 in child and spousal support, and however you quantify the ignominy of moving back into your childhood bedroom at 32 years old with twins under a year old and two Ivy League degrees. I do not want to put too heavy a spin on this. I know her well and I know that, although the process beat her up, she also recovered incredibly elegantly (because that's the type of person she is).

Fact 3: The Restorative Process is a Stretch: Why Would Two People Who Can't Stay Married Sit Down and Go Through a Restorative Process?

The collaborative process asks two people who already do not fundamentally get along (although they may still love each other in some way) to sit in the same room repeatedly and reach a resolution on their matter. I inherited a case that had been languishing in the collaborative process for 6 years. My client was upset that his wife had pulled out of the process and hired a different lawyer. He hired me and we took the case to trial in 8 months. He spent $35,000 on me and she spent $57,000 on her lawyer (plus she is sending him a check for another $10,000 in attorney's fees this week). They spent another $35,000 on the collaborative process between them.

I mention the money to point out not how egregious the costs are to go to trial (although they are) but to say that they were never ever going to make an agreement in their case. They had assets that were questionable and both were extremely stubborn, and no two lawyers were ever going to get them to agree. Rather than continue to beat the collaborative process to death, they both should have pulled out early, hired counsel, and gotten the divorce done. At least half of the wife's cost in the case was trying to sort out the finances of what was, by the time it was all resolved, a seven-year separation. Good collaborative lawyers (or a mediator if they had gone that direction) should have told them they were never going to reach an agreement on the specific issues plaguing them and that they should go to court. The only way to sort the matter out by agreement would have been for both sides to step back, analyze the cost of litigation and come to an agreement that seemed reasonable. But neither was reasonable when it came to the other and no amount of sitting together was going to change that.

Fact 4: You Need the Shadow of the Law to Understand Your Range of Normal Outcomes

Most of the issues in a divorce have been raised before and ruled on in appellate or Supreme Court decisions, so family lawyers are pretty clear on the outcome before we even walk into court. We always try to settle those issues. However, there are issues that we will never agree on, even with two Certified Family Law Specialists trying to reach an agreement.

Those are issues where neither the facts nor the law is clear. In the 7-year divorce case I mentioned above, the issue was the value of a community property business at the date of the parties' separation compared to the value at the date of trial. The California Family Code says to value assets at the date of trial unless there is good cause to value the assets at an earlier date (at or after the date of separation). Because this was a 7-year separation, and because the business was a fledgling start-up with a 50-50 partnership with a third party, we argued that it should be valued at separation. The Wife, not surprisingly, thought it should be valued at the date of the trial, even though Husband had done essentially all the work on the business after separation.

The Family Code in California provides for valuation for "good cause" on an earlier date than separation, but there is also case law the Court could have relied on to award Husband his post-separation contributions to growing a community property business (*Marriage of Imperato*). This is where the interplay between the Family Code and the caselaw that interprets it can get very complex.

The question is, "What is the asset being valued?" We only wanted the community property asset. Remember what the three property rules say: Anything you got before marriage or after separation is your separate property. And anything you got during the marriage is community property, except gifts and inheritances. Great, but what about those complicated assets that have a "mixed character"? Add in the problem of fiduciary duties (Rule 1: you cannot personally benefit at the expense of the community, and Rule 2: the community cannot benefit at the expense of either individual) and the issue grows even more complicated.

In the case of a business owned by a spouse before marriage, the business is the separate property of the spouse who owned it. But all energy, work, and effort of either spouse during the marriage is community property. Thus, the minute you get married, everything you do is community property. What happens when you use your community property industry to build a separate property business? You could ask this question about a separate property home with a mortgage. After you get married, ALL your income is community property. If you pay down a separate property mortgage with your community property income, you are benefitting yourself at the expense of the community. So, too, with a business. If you put your effort into increasing the value of a separate property business during the marriage, you are using community property efforts to "feather your own nest." The fiduciary duty statutes don't like that for either separate property businesses or separate property homes.

On the flip side, if you have a community property business or home, everything you do or earn after separation is your separate property. If you put your separate property industry or income into a community property business or home, shouldn't you also get the benefit of that effort or industry as your separate property?

This is where caselaw helps us decipher the outcome. Lawyers spend many tens, if not hundreds, of thousands of dollars fighting over these "credits" and "reimbursements." We are taught to argue issues by analogizing their specific facts to the facts in a previously decided case in which a judge ruled in one direction or another.

I'll spare you the gory details of the caselaw, but suffice to say that we end up with cases dealing with the separate property business/community property effort/growth (*Marriage of Perreira* and *Marriage of Van Camp*) and separate property home/community property paydown of mortgage (*Marriage of Moore* and *Marriage of Marsden* (*Moore/Marsden* mentioned earlier) and later cases (*Marriage of Bono* and *Marriage of Branco*). Each of these instructs us how to find the correct outcome whenever one spouse benefits personally at the expense of the community. The solution always is to determine how much the spouse's separate property benefitted and to reimburse the community for that benefit.

This is relatively easy in the case of a mortgage paydown because you can figure out the amount of a mortgage principal on the date of marriage and on the date of separation, the percentage of the total amount of the value of the home, and then even award some growth in value on those numbers.

Determining value becomes more complex with separate property businesses, where you must assess whether the spouse received a reasonable salary from the business or reinvested community property income into it. In either scenario, there are formulas we can use to reach these conclusions. Often, they are readily available for you to plug into a calculator—the *Moore/Marsden* calculation is recognized by family lawyers everywhere. A Google search can help you find CPAs who will handle it for you. Additionally, there's a free downloadable *Moore/Marsden* Excel spreadsheet you can use—though, like any spreadsheet, it's subject to GIGO (garbage in, garbage out). Furthermore, in any family law context involving numbers, disputes almost never center on the formula itself, but on which numbers should be plugged into that formula. The only time you want your home value to decrease is when you're purchasing it from your spouse. Your spouse, who will not keep the house, hopes for a higher valuation. Consequently, we find real estate brokers, appraisers, financial analysts, and CPAs in the courtroom testifying about values, which can cause your case expenses to soar from $10,000 to $50,000.

This explains why I always advocate a process-based agreement. In the case of a separate property home to be valued on the date of a 2002 marriage and a 2019 separation, the process-based agreement could look like this:

"1) We agree that we don't agree on the value of the home on the date of marriage in 2002 and we don't agree on its value at divorce in 2019, but we do agree that Jill Smith is a fair and unbiased appraiser who neither of us knows in any context, except professionally.

2) We agree that she can give a fair value for the home on both dates and that it will cost us $750, of which each of us will pay one-half to get those values.

3) We agree that neither of our lawyers, nor either of us, will speak to her *ex parte* (without the other present).

4) We agree that whatever the numbers are that she gives, those numbers will be admissible to the court.

5) Finally, we agree that once we have those numbers, all we need to do is use the *Moore/Marsden* formula to determine community and separate property ownership in the home."

This is a process-based agreement in which we agree to a fair process to determine a value and save probably $20,000 apiece in fees and expert costs. The process is to hire appraiser, Jill Smith, to appraise the property in 2002 and 2019 and to use the *Moore/Marsden* formula to give us the number. We both agree that we can make Jill Smith testify and attack her credibility, but essentially, only if she does something egregious. Otherwise, her numbers are *the* numbers. We save $20,000 apiece by not having her testify, not bringing in new experts, and not having lawyers prepare cross-examinations and the like.

In the case of the 7-year separation languishing in the collaborative process, the business was community property, but Husband had been working it for 7 years after separation and less than one year before separation. The case law said to value it on the date of trial. But there is little fairness in forcing Husband to pay Wife for 7 years of his own industry in developing the business after he was no longer in the marriage.

The parties started the business during the marriage. And when I say, "the parties," I mean the Husband, because Wife had no interest or involvement. Husband viewed this as a hobby business, not unlike selling Arbonne or Amway. He wasn't making any money at it and wasn't really doing much for it. But after separation, he got very sick and had to quit his main job. Having no other source of income, he began building this business. Wife was long gone at that point. For 7 years, he worked on the business full-time all with post-separation efforts. As we tried to settle the case, Wife was convinced that we should follow the Family Code, which says to value the business at trial. Husband thought there was good cause to value it at separation. Husband also thought that even if we did not value it at separation, we would have *Marriage of Imperato* to tell the Court that it should award him post-separation contributions to the growth of a hobby business into a going concern.

In any event, the stubbornness of the parties (and, I admit, the lawyers) made settling this case very difficult. Husband thought the Wife should get $0 or something close to it. Wife was convinced that this was a business worth $1 million or more and that she should get half of it. I tried to give her side all the documentation so they would know the business was not worth $1 million, and I gave them the case law and the code sections that showed that even if it was (which it wasn't), she would not get more than its value at separation. Wife did not care. We asked the court to split that issue off from the main trial (bifurcate) so that it would be easier to settle the case. But because the case had been pending for 7 years, we had four different judges handling it. Ultimately, we had to go to trial over it.

For the record, even though I was stubborn in the case also, I did point out that Wife's worst case Range of Normal Outcomes was $0 and her best case was around $100,000. It was $0 if the judge valued the business at the date of separation. It was a $200,000 valuation if the judge valued the business on the date of the trial (of which Wife would get 50%). We also pointed out and proved in Court that on the date of separation, Husband had a 50% partner whom he later bought out after separation, which meant that Wife could only take a 25% ownership interest in the business if its value was ruled at separation.

Because you can NEVER predict with precision any judge's decision-making in a particular case, our judge did what we expected: in other words, something totally unexpected. He gave my client his request to value the business at separation. Then he found the value to be $80,000 worth of inventory a year after separation. He gave him no credit for the cost to sell $80,000 in inventory (which he proved was about 60% of the value of the inventory), but because my client had a 50-50 partner at separation, Wife was awarded 25% of $80,000 ($20,000). End result? Wife spent almost $60,000 in attorney's fees to get $20,000. My client had offered her $25,000 two months before trial. Yet, to get my stubborn-ass client to agree to offer $25,000, I had to beg and twist his arm and cajole him (and even take him out for drinks) and tour the place where the business was based (without billing him). She still rejected our offer.

Not to mention that my client paid me $40,000 to take the matter to trial, meaning he spent $60,000 on his side of the equation as well.

All this and we KNEW the law before the trial started.

The Parties were in Collaborative Law for 7 years to fight over whether to value the business at the date of separation or the date of trial. They spent money on lawyers during that time and got nowhere. They were never ever going to agree on the date of separation or the date of trial as the date to value the business. They could easily have just agreed on a process-based fairness approach or done very rational calculations of value at both times to determine the Range of Normal Outcomes and then agreed that the Range of Normal Outcomes was between $0 and $100,000. They could have agreed that the likelihood of a $0 valuation was just as slim as the likelihood of a $200,000 valuation and said "the most likely outcome is between $25,000 and $75,000 with $50,000 being the very most likely outcome." If Husband had paid $50,000 7 years earlier, he would have saved the $40,000 he paid me, plus whatever he paid his collaborative lawyer (call it $20,000 just to pick a number), plus the $20,000 he paid and 7 years of anguish. He would have saved $30,000 and 7 years of his life that he can never get back. Wife would have done MUCH better than the negative $40,000 result she got (plus at least $20,000 spent on the collaborative lawyer).

They were never going to agree on the date of valuation. They never *could have* agreed on that point. So, their other option was to get the hell out of the collaborative process, make a process-based agreement like I described above in the house example, and ask the judge to pick a date for valuation. They would know their Range of Normal Outcomes depending on the upside and downside risk to them. They would spend the $5,000 to get the business valued and then they would have resolved their case.

Sometimes it makes sense to give it your best effort, settle everything you can (including a process-based agreement) and put the tough issues in front of the court (in this case, ask the court to pick the date of valuation of the business).

And sometimes, in fact almost always, the threat of trial is a purifying fire that forces people to make hard decisions and come up with decent outcomes. In fact, I like trial dates for that reason. Nothing makes people work hard to get an agreement like a looming trial date where things can go completely haywire, with judges making whatever the hell decision they feel like making, based on whether they had bagels or pancakes for breakfast. In the 7-year separation case, either side could have appealed the fact that the Judge's decision was not likely grounded in any law that the lawyers could discern, but the reality was that all the parties really needed was someone to just make an order. Once the order was made, everyone was mad for a couple of weeks and then Husband refinanced the home to give her the $20,000 and both went on with their lives.

Fact 5: Trials on All Issues are for Suckers. If You Litigate, Don't Take All Issues to Trial: Use Your Range of Normal Outcomes to Pare Issues Down as Much as Possible, and Only Then Try What You Absolutely Can Never Agree On

I've told you why I don't like mediation or collaborative law. Does that mean you should take everything to trial? Hell no. Not just Hell no, but really REALLY Hell no.

You should only take to trial things that legitimately cannot be resolved by sitting down and negotiating. But to know your Range of Normal Outcomes you should be negotiating in the "shadow of the law". This means you must know both the facts of your case and the law that will apply to them. I am a huge fan of negotiation. I am also a huge fan of knowing the facts and the law.

Good negotiators use what I've mentioned earlier, the Best and Worst Case Alternative to a Negotiated Agreement when they negotiate.

This is a complex way of saying, "What happens if we don't get an agreement?" The authors of *Getting to Yes*, when they write about BATNA, use a win-lose world as the negotiation arena. That is, "what are your chances of winning in court (minus the cost of going to Court)?" And "what are your chances of losing in court (minus the cost of going to Court)?" In family law, as I've mentioned, it's not really a winner/loser scenario – normally, you win some issues and lose some issues. So, I describe this as a BCATNA and WCATNA (Best Case and Worst Case) because that anticipates what will happen if you win all issues and lose all issues to develop a range of outcomes.

In family law, BCATNA and WCATNA are close to the two extremes of the Range of Normal Outcomes. They are what you get when you "run the table" at trial and get everything you ask for, and what you receive if your spouse "runs the table" at trial and gets everything they ask for.

If you enter a negotiation without knowing the law or the relevant facts, you cannot determine your best-case or worst-case outcomes if you decide to walk away from the bargaining table. In a divorce context, it's important to recognize that if you do not reach an agreement, you will end up going to trial. You must consider the cost of going to trial, which can be 4 to 10 times the initial retainer for many lawyers. Additionally, you should understand whether going to trial makes you liable not only for your own attorney's fees (which you will incur) but also for your spouse's attorney's fees. In California, the Family Code requires the higher earner to contribute to the lower earner's attorney's fees (Fam. Code 2030). Attorney's fees can also be awarded when one spouse possesses more property—whether separate or community—than the other spouse (Fam. Code 2032).

So what happens at a trial? The judge is going to hear facts (and a little law) and make some decisions about what to do. Good judges will tell you they prefer agreements, but if you cannot agree on who gets the house, the Judge will pick one or neither of you (by ordering it sold) to get it. Just like the 7-year Separation case, the judge may make orders that neither party asked for and neither party likes because they know that there is little likelihood you will file an appeal. And even if you do file an appeal there is even less likelihood that you will actually win a reversal of their decision.

CHAPTER 8

Outcomes and Resolutions

Default Judgments

WHEN PEOPLE SAY, "My wife cleaned me out in the divorce," they most likely reached an *agreement* that *allowed* them to be cleaned out. The reason is that family law is primarily self-executing. Even a default judgment—where one party does not show up—must list all assets and liabilities and propose a fair and legal division. If assets are omitted, the defaulting party can return to court and argue, "Even though I was defaulted in this case, my ex forgot to include three of our most valuable assets, which is why this resulted in a totally unfair division of assets and liabilities." Houses, cars, 401K plans, pensions, and Visa bills have objective values that must be divided equally. This is true even if you never respond to the original divorce petition. If you do not participate, you won't have a say in which assets get assigned to whom, but you will still receive roughly approximate justice.

This is important because when dealing with facts and law in the "shadow of the law," a strategy of non-participation in a divorce may not necessarily lead to disaster. The law mandates an "equal division." If there is $1,000 in a bank account, a default judgment should indicate that the account holds $1,000 and recommend that each party receives $500. This is straightforward with money (bank accounts, 401(k) plans, IRAs, even, Defined Benefit retirement plans like pensions, where one-half means one-half). However, it becomes more challenging when assessing items with an indeterminate value, such as houses, vehicles, RVs, timeshares, businesses, and so on.

I frame it out for clients by saying, "If the other side takes your default, you are still going to get half, but they are going to decide which half." And not only are they going to decide which half, they will also decide the values of things for which there is no predetermined value. For example, we know that if you want to buy the house from your spouse you want it to be worth less and your spouse wants it to be worth more. We also know that some appraisers (like refinance appraisers who work for banks) are only appraising the property with the goal of ensuring that the bank has proper collateral for the loan they are going to make; thus, if you want to borrow $50,000 on your home, even if you have $250,000 in equity, the refinance appraiser is mostly checking to ensure that there is adequate equity in the home to support the $50,000 loan. They may give you a full appraisal of value, but the goal is not to determine the best price you could get for the home. The goal is for a reasonable amount of collateral for the loan amount you are trying to get.

Therefore, most family lawyers know that if they are representing the spouse who is going to be buying the home, they want the "in spouse" to use a refinance appraiser to give the value of the home, because refinance appraisers typically give the lowest valuation you can get for a home. This is not a hard, fast rule, but it is where the smallest numbers typically come from.

On the other hand, a hot real estate broker who outsells the competition or who is trying to get your business, may value the home 10-20% higher than a refinance appraiser. Online tools like Zillow and Redfin make checking the range of values easy. I sometimes check Zillow on my first consultation with a potential client, but it's typically a sucker's bet to rely on the online programs for final value, because they base their values on what the site considers comparable homes. There is no way to add or subtract value for the condition of the home.

Conversely, an appraiser for hire costs money (maybe $500) and will give you a range of values based on their understanding of the market and on which neighborhoods are comparable. I have had trials with appraisers giving expert testimony on the one hand and real estate agents or brokers giving 10-20% different values for the same parcel of real property. One of the jobs of a judge as "finder of fact" is to determine which witness is more credible – 90% of the time an experienced appraiser will be the more "credible" witness, but I have seen judges make findings that a real estate broker, who is predicting the market over the next 60-90 days is a better arbiter of value than an appraiser, who is looking backwards 180 days.

So, in the default context there is a wide range of potential numbers your spouse can give the home. If your spouse is the only participant in the divorce, i.e., you are letting them take your default, you will be stuck with their value.

In a case I took on some years ago there were 5 properties. Wife, who later became my client, was having some substance abuse problems and did not respond to Husband's initial Petition for divorce. Husband was a shark, as was his lawyer. Husband listed the values of the 5 properties as follows: Properties 1-4 at the absolute lowest defensible value—refinance appraisal minus 20% (later in that case I argued it was flat out perjury). For Property 5 he listed the value at its highest plus 20%. The way he finessed the numbers, he was positioned to take Properties 1-4 and leave Wife with Property 5, which was a toxic asset for a number of reasons beyond the scope of this example.

I got the case after he had taken her default. His actions were beyond shady. He sub-served her, which means instead of serving her, he served someone else whom he said was living in her home—which was untrue. Nevertheless, California law allows a default judgment to be set aside, almost by rule, meaning you need only ask for it within 6 months. A default divorce judgment can be set aside within 1 year under certain circumstances (2 years in still additional circumstances). In this case, we set aside the default judgment and in the end the parties split Properties 1-4 in half. Property 5 was so toxic that both parties let it go for property taxes (and it remains undeveloped to this day).

The point is that even when Husband was trying to take Wife's default, he still had to give her something to equal the division of assets. He had to maintain that his proposal was equal, so he stretched his numbers beyond what I believed to be a reasonable amount under the circumstances—especially with the toxicity of Property 5. However, the judge in a default judgment case has no facts to go on other than what is presented to him or her. That means in most default situations, the court will simply accept the representations made under penalty of perjury and assume that the other party will raise a fuss (seek to set aside the default judgment) if they disagree.

The Court, properly, allowed me to set aside (or cancel) the default judgment against my client, and to do a proper division of the assets. However, one of my early mentors taught me that, as a lawyer, it is always a good idea to start with the following question, "What happens if I do nothing?" In the divorce context usually the answer is, "Well, it's not too good for me, although it probably could be worse." Still, it makes sense to start with that question in any case.

Default with Agreement

The flip side of the Default Judgment is the "Default Judgment with Agreement," which, in my mind, is the very best outcome of any divorce case. In this judgment, only one side filed (and paid the $435 filing fee), but the two parties worked out an agreement and attached their agreement to a default judgment with the Court approving it. They paid one filing fee, never went to court for any reason, and made an agreement. That is both effective and efficient.

In California the Petition for Dissolution costs $435 (as of this writing). A Response to and Request for Dissolution also costs $435. Someone must pay the initial $435 to get the case started, but after that, the only reason to spend the second $435 is if there is a problem with the proposed division of assets and debts (or child custody, child support, spousal support), or you cannot reach an agreement.

Assuming your spouse is honest about the values of property (or uses numbers that you can live with), one possible strategy is not to respond and let your spouse default you. If, for example, all you have are two credit cards with a $10,000 total balance and a bank account worth $10,000, and your spouse proposes that they keep all the cash and take all the debt, that might be a fine outcome for you. However, maybe you'd rather have $5,000 in debt and $5,000 in cash and decide for yourself when to pay the debt and what to do with your half of the cash. If you do not accept your spouse's proposed division, you need to either pay your $435 and answer the Petition, or you need to negotiate.

In California your spouse may, but does not have to, accept your default if you do not answer the Petition within 30 days of it being served on you. If I have a new client who has had a Petition served on them but they are negotiating with their spouse, or if there is a lawyer with whom I have a strong track record of settling cases (or if we file the Petition for a client and the other spouse wants to negotiate), the first thing I will do is request that we make an agreement that no one file a default judgment in the case until 30 days after we stop negotiating. I try to get this in writing. The best is a stipulation that both parties sign, but often an email agreement will suffice. Or I will write a letter saying, "So long as we are still negotiating, we won't take your default." This signals to the other side (hopefully) that we want to negotiate an agreement with a default judgment, which is again, the most efficient and cost-effective outcome in a divorce. I tell the other party when we have filed the Petition that there will be no surprises and that my letter will serve as my promise not to move forward with a secret default judgment. Then we negotiate. Sometimes these negotiations break down and I will inform the other party in a letter:

> "Per my promise, today is August 5. I promised you that if we stopped negotiating, I would give you 30 days to respond to the Petition for Dissolution. That means that on approximately September 5, I will file the Default Judgment in the case. The default judgment is going to contain the following terms: Wife gets the $10,000 in debt and the $10,000 in the bank. If you would like a different outcome than that, I suggest that you file your Response to and Request for Dissolution before September 5. We will call you on or around September 1 to be sure of your intentions if you have not filed and served your response."

I am not required to do this, but I do it because I think it is proper to honor my word as a lawyer and member of the state bar. There is also strategic value; if we take the default after warning them about taking their default, the Court may not set the default aside. I could certainly just drop an email to the other party saying,

"Today, negotiations broke down. You have until September 5 to file your answer or we will take your default." However, me honoring my word not only engenders trust from the other side (and from the Court), it also leaves open the possibility that on September 4—the day before we file the default judgment—I will get a phone call with a reasonable proposal, and we will transform our disagreement into an agreement that both sides can live with.

I want to get default judgments with an agreement whenever possible because it saves the client a ton of money—and usually yields the types of outcomes that are durable and agreeable to both sides. I will leave open the door to settlement all the way through my opening statement at trial.

The Standard Process for Getting an Agreement

As I said in more detail above in Chapter 1, a divorce proceeds in 3 acts. Act 1 is the initial filing for divorce, the filing of the answer, and the seeking of temporary orders. Temporary orders usually involve some sort of hearing. The hearing may be a full evidentiary hearing in which each party brings and calls witnesses, the parties testify and get cross-examined, and the Court may even meet with a child or children (usually over the age of 11 or 12, and certainly if they are over the age of 14) or appoint a lawyer for children. That is where we get orders about temporary support, where the kids will live in the short term, whether the parties want to sell the house, whether one party will live in the house exclusively, what items the "out spouse" (the one who moves out) can take with them, etc.

It is not uncommon that Act 1 is highly litigated. Why? The parties have "new money" on retainer with the lawyer, they are still very emotional about the divorce (sometimes angry, sometimes sad) and they are always trying to jockey for position in the short-term.

The lawyers want to litigate; the parties want to litigate. Everyone is fired up for Act 1.

Act II is the exchange of financial information. Sometimes Act II and Act I are happening at the same time. In my office, Act II means that the client is working with my paralegal and associate attorneys to get all the financial documents to be transmitted to the other party. Act I means litigation, an impending court date, family members who are going to come out to support the parties, friends of the parties "trash talking", etc.

Act I is usually a bloodletting for everyone. Most judges will use Act I as a way of letting each of the parties know that they better tone down their litigiousness or they will be sorry at trial. Costs exceed the retainer, and the client must write a second check. Usually, because divorce is a 50-50 affair, there are things that both parties think they "lost," and as a result, both parties are miserable and exhausted when Act I ends. Sometimes Act I does not end. The judge makes a temporary order and then says she wants to review it in 3 months. The judge tells the parties to take an action, such as listing the home for sale, or that she wants to review the children's report cards at the end of the Fall semester or that she wants to meet with the children again, or that one party has 60 days to move out, or anything that requires the lawyers to go back to court and inform the judge about the progress of the orders. Act I misery continues. Sometimes, parties are still bitter and angry, and they want to wage a second round of Act I warfare, and they continue to gear up. They write the lawyer a third check.

Usually, after two or three appearances in court, the parties begin to show fatigue. They question whether it is "worth it." They have paid the lawyer double the initial $5,000 or $10,000 retainer. They have half the time with the kids, not enough support (or they are paying too much support) and are making due with less. They discover it is unsustainable paying a lawyer $495 per hour while paying a mortgage, child support, spousal support, and private school tuition. They are tapping into retirement funds or borrowing from their parents.

They come in and ask: "How do we end this?"

I want to be clear that I will have told them the Range of Normal Outcomes and their BCATNA/WCATNA in almost every conversation commencing with the first consultation. I will tell them before Act I what I think the outcome of Act I is going to be within a range. If we are within that range after Act I, I will tell them that we are within that range and point out that we end it by agreeing to stay within that range, but by trying to improve their position in the range. I will remind them of the white petals and the red center and work with them to define the red center. From the beginning, I will know what my client absolutely cannot live with/without, and I will tell them whether that is within the Range of Normal Outcomes. If it is not, I will tell them that too. I will give them the odds of success on things outside the Range of Normal Outcomes, and the likelihood that something bad will happen in Court.

Once Act II (the exchange of financial information) is completed, I propose a settlement offer to my client that I can also propose to the other party's lawyer. Almost always (in fact, on the order of 95% of the time) that proposal is very close to what I told them I thought the outcome would be in the initial consultation. Then, if my client agrees, I make that proposal to the other side. If they are as bloody and beaten up as we are, I would expect them to be willing to discuss. Many times, we reach an agreement at that point. Other than reaching an agreement in the first 30 days of a case, the next most likely time for us to reach an agreement to settle the whole case is immediately after the first hearing of Act I.

Act III is where we spend our time in serious negotiations for a final agreement. If we did not know how the case would turn out with certainty at the beginning, we are approaching 95% certainty by the time we get to Act III, unless we have the kind of question that a judge is going to need to answer (such as whether to value the business on the date of separation or 7 years later at the date of trial). Once we have Act I temporary orders and Act II financials all done, Act III is where we start working hard to put the two together into one agreement.

Going back to the Toxic Properties Case with the 5 properties above, we spent a lot of money on attorneys' fees not because the property was difficult to divide, but because my client was using methamphetamines and there were three minor children. Dividing the property was not all that difficult. You should be able to readily discern your BCATNA and WCATNA, and therefore the Range of Normal Outcomes, and not have to spend $57,000 even in a hotly contested divorce.

Even if you can't agree on most things, like the case of the collaborative couple with the 7-year separation, you can agree on a process and a conceptual outcome. For example, for the 7-year couple, they should have agreed on what to do if the judge decided to value the business on the date of separation and what to do if the judge decided to value the business on the date of trial.

In the Toxic Properties case, they spent probably $140,000 in attorneys' fees between them, but the fight was over custodial time with the kids—Father was controlling to a fault, and Mother was using meth. The teenagers all loved and wanted to be with their mother, but she was in and out of jail, and the court could not give her any ongoing and continual timeshare, even though at one point the judge told my client, to my surprise: "I want you to take 4 drug tests over the next four months. Meth stays in your system for

90 days. I am leaving the children with you 50% of the time and I expect your first three tests to be dirty. If the fourth test is dirty, however, I am going to take the kids away from you." This was an unexpected and outside the Range of Normal Outcomes result. She blew it anyway by being arrested for methamphetamine possession and being under the influence with the three boys at home with her.

CHAPTER 9

Dealing with Difficult Questions in a Negotiation

THERE ARE SOME complex family law issues based on the Three Rules I outlined above that can be lost if you don't make the arguments to the trial court. However, the basic division of property is mostly self-executing. That is one of the reasons I am writing this book, so that you can see that it's complicated but not impossibly so.

The rules in a divorce are relatively simple and straightforward. If you know just the Three Rules you can have a negotiation in a divorce—at least about property issues. You can reason to the right conclusion about a pension. For example, Husband works for 15 years for the State before marriage, and 15 years during the marriage. How much of the pension is community property? 15/30 or one-half. One-half to Husband as Separate Property and one-half to the community. Husband gets 75% and Wife gets 25% of the pension.

You can reason that Wife's inheritance belongs to her. So long as Wife can show where the money went, anything bought with Wife's inheritance belongs to her.

Credit card balances on the date of separation are community property (so long as there was a $0 balance on the date of marriage) even if Husband didn't know about Wife's credit card spending—

unless it was spent on having an affair. (More on that later.) But the short version is that you aren't allowed to give anything away during the marriage without telling the other spouse, because it breaches the fiduciary duty you owe the other spouse. Thus, the community has a right to be repaid.

We have developed shorthand rules for what to do in certain situations. There are so many situations that it creates a whole body of rules, but they are all simply ways of making calculations using the Three Property Rules. For example, if Husband has unvested stock options before marriage and then gets more unvested stock options during the marriage, and some of those options begin to vest before separation, we can rely on the *Marriage of Nelson/Marriage of Hug* formulas to tell us how to best deal with them. *Pereira* and *Van Camp* formulas show us what to do with separate property businesses, and *Moore/Marsden* with separate property real estate. But all of them derive from the Three Property Rules. They are dense, but if you hold onto the Three Property Rules, you can make sense of them at least conceptually.

Example: The Ranch Kids

The basic issue was this: Husband and Wife borrowed money from Husband's ranch-owning family. It is not uncommon for the children of the local ranch-owning families to work the ranch into their adult years, making very little money. The parents "loan" the children money when the children are young adults, and when the parents die, the kids inherit the ranch and the debts are wiped out. The ranch was worth about $25 million and the couple had borrowed about $250,000. Husband had not really sought to force Wife to pay half the debt in the divorce – it was really "income" that he earned working the ranch and would be forgiven when his parents died. We half-heartedly requested a contribution to this loan, but mostly as an offset to other claims the Wife was making to Husband's house. Husband owned the house prior to marriage. They paid some of the mortgage down while married, but not a lot. They weathered the utter destruction of the California real estate market in 2008, and the house only became right side up at the tail end of the divorce.

Wife filed a strategic bankruptcy. She bankrupted all the parental debt and figured out that one of the debts she bankrupted was a community property loan from my client's parents to put a new roof on the house and remodel a bathroom. The loan was community property. It was an asset of the bankruptcy estate. That made a portion of the house an asset of the bankruptcy estate. She was bankrupting on a loan from husband's parents that had been used to improve Husband's house and was then claiming ownership in Husband's house because the loan they took was community property—even though they never paid a dime on the loan and would never have had to pay a dime on the loan.

It was a gross injustice, but no matter how I read the law, I could not figure out how to say that the debt did not give her some claim to the house. The other lawyer and the bankruptcy estate lawyer argued that the debt gave the wife a property interest in the home, which would allow the bankruptcy trustee to sell it. We argued that, at best, it conferred a reimbursement right to the Wife from the Husband but not a property right.

This was not a distinction without difference. If it was a property right, the Trustee could sell the house. If it was a reimbursement right, the Trustee could not sell the house. The irony was that if the Trustee had sold the house to pay the debt, the Trustee would have been displacing the Husband to pay a debt to Husband's parents, who would never have attempted to collect the debt from their son.

We won the finely-detailed point that this was a reimbursement right and not a property right, but we lost our arguments that there was no reimbursement right at all. As per usual, you take a matter to trial and you win some issues and lose others.

Negotiations, particularly over challenging and difficult questions, give us an opportunity to be creative. Creativity, however, only works well when you understand the boundaries within which you are working. In the Ranch Kids case we made reasonable settlement offers based on the potential that my client could lose his house in a sham bankruptcy proceeding that was overpaying uncollectable debt to my client's family, who was never going to try to collect it. The opposing side, in this case the Bankruptcy Trustee, refused any reasonable settlement, which left everyone in a worse off position.

This case was similar in certain ways to the 7-year Separation Case because everything hinged on one difficult legal question. In this case the question was, "Did the loan from my client's parents create a property interest or a right of reimbursement?" Since the entire case depended on that answer and no one could agree, we ended up in litigation. I think this was also in large part because there was never going to be any money changing hands. If Wife had been negotiating, rather than the Bankruptcy Trustee, we might have gotten a reasonable deal.

Getting a reasonable deal in a case with difficult questions is possible, but you must understand the Range of Normal Outcomes and communicate it to the other side.

For example, understanding that a pension not only has a value, but that the value is both a present and a future value, allows you to make sure that when you negotiate, you are negotiating apples and apples rather than apples and oranges. How? Here is an example from the California Public Employees Retirement Systems (CalPERS).

The CalPERS plan is a defined benefit plan (a pension) with a cash contribution. Every month you make a mandatory contribution to PERS in the amount of X% of your earnings. Usually the employer matches this (or contributes more than X%). This means that for every month you work for a California PERS employer, you are making a cash contribution to your plan. However, you are also getting service credits. The credits themselves have a value that far exceeds the X% + employer cash contribution because the service credits are a defined benefit based on your rate of pay and the number of years you have worked. When you are valuing a PERS plan (or any other defined benefit plan) it is tempting to say "My PERS plan is worth $120,000 because that is how much cash my employer and I have contributed to the plan." However, that is not the whole story. If you have worked for 12 years, then you also have 12 years of service credits, which may be worth $300 per month per credit, from retirement age until your death. $3,600 per month from age 65 to age 90 at death is $1,080,000!

At the same time, if you have a house that has $200,000 in equity at the time of the divorce and a pension plan with 12 years of service credit and $120,000 in cash contributions, it would be an unfair trade to say, "You get the house and all its equity (you owe me $100,000 for the equity I am giving you) but I will keep my PERS Defined Benefits Plan worth $120,000 (and I will give you back $60,000); therefore, you owe me $40,000." The 12 years' service credits are worth so much more than the cash contribution. On the other hand, the PERS Defined Benefits Plan is also not worth $1,080,000 right now because that value depends entirely on the length of the employee's life after retirement.

What do we do? We can engage an actuary who will use actuarial tables and they will give you a *present value* of the community property interest. This value is discounted for the length of time the employee is expected to live after retirement, the number of service credits now, and the number of credits at the expected age of retirement. There are a number of variables entered into the equation and certain discounting is done if the non-employee spouse chooses a survivor's benefit, which means the payout will continue on the defined benefit until the death of the non-employee spouse, in effect measuring two lives instead of one and lowering the payout. The present value creates an apple (today's cash value of the defined benefit) to measure against an apple (the cash equity value in the home).

Understanding this allows you to make trades of today's cash against today's cash, instead of today's cash against tomorrow's cash—and you are using the correct measures of what cash we are talking about.

Also, if your spouse lets you trade pension or 401(k) dollars (future dollars) against something that has present value (like a house), do it.

The present value is always a "fiction" because it assumes the price someone would pay to buy your pension from you today, something for which there is no market. Also, when the non-employee spouse wants to buy the house, it assumes an imaginary amount of equity in the home based on our "best guess" value. Moreover, there is a rule in family law that says you cannot include fees or costs that were not actually incurred; therefore, the spouse who buys the house, buys it without factoring in the cost of the transaction. The "in-spouse" buys the house for full value and would sell the house, presumably, for full value minus real estate commissions.

Nevertheless, despite all that, we CAN do what many people want to do: trade equity in the house for cash value in the pension if we make an agreement.

If all else fails and we cannot reach reasonable agreements, then lawyers must make every legal argument they can. They do their homework on both facts and law, and then press the Court for outcomes that they seek. That said, I will take a good negotiation 100 times out of 100 against going to court. Why? Judges are complete wild cards, some people call them "jokers", but that probably carries the playing card analogy too far. Even under the best of circumstances with good law and good facts, there is still a chance you will lose. One senior lawyer with 43 years of experience in family law told me: you face a 30% chance of losing, even when you have the right argument and right facts. You also have a 30% chance of winning if you have the wrong argument and the wrong facts. This is the nature of litigation.

Taking a case to trial is an ugly thing. That a person making all the decisions may doze off in a just-too-warm-courtroom after a big meal, or may be feeling "hangry" leading up to the lunch break, or may bring her various prejudices with her to the bench, should SCARE you in a big way. There are judges who don't like stay-at-home moms: "Get a job! I did!" And judges who don't like contractors: "You should see the botched job on my bathroom remodel." There are judges who don't like people talking a lot about God in the courtroom, and, conversely judges who don't like it when people don't talk about God in the courtroom. All, and many more, are possible. And if what a recent study suggests, is true: that the difference in favorable decisions to unfavorable is 65% based on how close to the last meal break it was when the decision was made? We should all be very afraid of going into Court with unresolved issues.

And so it is that a firm like mine, that prides itself on thorough, aggressive representation in the courtroom, can take "sure things" to the Court and still lose. That's why you should never, ever, believe any lawyer who says that something is a "slam dunk." It's never a slam dunk in a courtroom, even when a judge telegraphs how they are going to rule in similar situations repeatedly.

What makes a good negotiation?

I believe a good divorce is one where both parties leave the negotiating table feeling like they've won. How do we achieve that? We work diligently early in a case to understand what is most important to each individual. Almost 100% of the time (but not quite), we find that Husband and Wife each value a specific item of property more than any other, and that item differs for each spouse, like a pension or a home. Once we identify those priorities, we can steer the negotiation toward that outcome. I strongly advocate for transparency in negotiations, but I also support the idea of slow-playing to ensure we don't reveal our crucial item too early—even if we already know the other side's most significant issue. We aim to keep emotions out of the negotiation for as long as possible to better position ourselves to achieve our goals.

There are steps to accomplish this:

We always work on the least emotional issues first because "small yesses lead to bigger yesses." For example, often we begin with the vehicles. There are times when they might trade cars, but they clarify it first with each other. And it is always by agreement. We virtually always know whose car is who's.

This is true in essentially 100% of couples I have helped in a divorce. Everyone knows whose car is whose, regardless of the age or make of the car, so negotiating over cars is simple. We assign each person their car and the equity value of each car in their "column."

After the vehicles are divided, it is easy to divide other things like bank accounts, 401K accounts, and credit card debts. Most people realize very quickly that it is not cost effective to have their lawyers wasting time dividing the knives or the pots and pans. We make sure to discuss the basic rules—if Mom gave Wife her armoire before she died, Wife gets it at dissolution.

The next most emotional subject (but still not very emotional) is the "man" vs. "woman" items. Most households intuitively know "what is whose." Husband has a garage full of tools or a shed with yard tools, or even a boat or a camping trailer. Wife has household items ranging from the Dyson vacuum to nonvaluable artwork (and so on). Is this super stereotypical and gender biased? Yes, which is why I say it is the next most emotional issue. Husbands are smart to give Wives tools and yard equipment, and Wives are smart to give Husbands some of the interior stuff. Sometimes it doesn't break along gender lines. I know it is gender-biased to use these examples, but when the same examples play out in the same way 95% of the time, flipping the script in the writing of the book just to say "Wife gets the air compressor and Snap-on tools and Husband gets the Kitchen Aide mixer" even though that is rarely the division anyone wants, doesn't make sense. Suffice it to say, we have entered a very new era in which Wives want Snap-on tools and Husbands want Kitchen Aide mixers – I have collected kitchen items and meat smokers and grills and small appliances for years, for example. I just finished a divorce where the auto shop in the garage was Wife's domain.

Guns and collections are usually easy too. Once, opposing counsel and I spent three hours going through a gem collection only to find that the $2,000 we spent doing so was only offset by the gem collection's total value of around $1,000. The Parties then invited us to go through a coin collection and a stamp collection. We declined. My opposing counsel, "I'm not spending another three hours going through fake samurai swords and bags of pennies."

Oddly, guns are usually divided by gun owners in a very fair manner. I say oddly because I really know nothing about guns and don't want to know about them, no matter how many Apple TV spy thrillers I watch. I used to think that gun owners were these "others" who were not like me. I have never tried to learn about guns. My only gun experience was shooting skeet in Louisiana on a balmy post-hurricane afternoon. Good times; bad shots. Gun owners, however, are serious about gun ownership and they, likewise, are typically deeply fair about gun division. I think that is because guns are registered to individuals under Federal law, so couples knows whose guns belong to whom.

Only once did I ever come across a situation in which Wife asked for a gun that Husband would not give her. It was a "lady grip" pistol. She eventually got the "lady grip" pistol by giving the Husband something he wanted. I think it was an ice chest; not even one of the fancy new ones. Bad use of lawyer time, but they were both quite spiteful.

Otherwise, it has never been an issue with gun owners. I must admit that gun owners (of the lawful variety, which most are) have educated me a whole lot about gun ownership. After all I've been through, I still don't like guns, but I quite like gun owners. Is that gun ownership or some other thing talking? I don't know. One day I will write another book about what I've learned about people in divorces, but I will encourage someone else to do all the extra social science research for me. At the end of the day if we could divide all our things the way gun owners divide their guns, the divorce world would be a more peaceful place. Though the Berkeley-hippie-liberal in me is probably never going to give in on my feelings about guns.

After dividing the easy things, we approach some of the more emotional issues. I usually try to talk about the house first, which gives me a chance to size up how attached to the house both parties are. Next is the pension/retirement. Most of the time the house and the pension are the two largest assets and the only things that can be traded for one another. If the relationship between the parties is deeply strained, for example, if there was an affair or some sort of abuse, I let both parties know quickly that we are going to try to get each of them what they want most.

I firmly believe in the concept of Speed Mediation when we are negotiating over "stuff." In fact, if each side comes prepared, we can negotiate all the "stuff" in two hours or less. Any longer and we are dealing with spite and negativity. Spite and negativity may be a divorce lawyer's stock and trade, but they are completely unnecessary and usually just add to the divorce expenses (Beware attorneys who stoke your rage, there is little surer way to run up your fees than you being really mad). Follow the Three Property Rules and know that your spouse is going to get half of everything you got during the marriage that wasn't a gift or inheritance, no matter whose "name it is in." Don't fight it unless you have good reason, and the good reason should be a great reason.

For example, you may well have used your inheritance to buy a riding lawnmower and a dining room table. You may have spent $7,500 on both things. If you get both, you get something worth considerably less than $7,500 because now they are used. Let's say they are worth now, generously, $5,000. You get $2,500 in stuff. The lawyers are billing at $400 per hour apiece to sit there with you. Yes, you are entitled to it, but is it worth spending $800 per hour to try to get it? It might be worth 5 minutes. "C'mon, you *know* we bought that with my dad's inheritance money. I should take both." "Well, I need a dining room table when the kids are at my house. You need a riding mower at the family home. Why can't I take the table and you keep the riding mower?" Indeed. Think hard about this type of thing before you let your lawyers take over and spend the entire value in attorney's fees. Or say, "Look, the dining table means a lot to me and you don't need a riding mower at your new condo. How about I give you a grand or $1,500 for them both?" "OK, when can I get the cash?" "If you want it today, I'll write you

Chapter 9 • Dealing with Difficult Questions in a Negotiation | 243

a check for $1,000; otherwise I'll give you $1,500 when I get the refinance done." "OK, deal." Moving on.

Support, child custody, and visitation are by far the most emotional of all issues. Depending on our success in the property division, I may ask to bracket those two issues for resolution later, under the theory that getting a bunch of "yesses" should not be undone by wildly angry "nos" that derail the partial deal we have already put together.

For wage earners, the temporary support is a relatively straightforward calculation using a computer program. For self-employed people it can be more of a challenge. Almost everyone understands the importance of child support and most people will take a quick deep breath and say they are willing to pay it—whatever the computer tells them. In California, people understand that child support is entirely dependent on the difference in earnings and in the timeshare each parent has with the children. This can turn a relatively congenial discussion of how to share the kids into an all-out war. I have a lot to say about negotiating child custody and child support a little later in the book, including my views on "no fault" child support that might make some of our most horrific custody battles a little less nasty.

Suffice it to say the following: people fight a little over money, but once that has been sorted out, they mostly live with it. Virtually all my $100,000 divorces have been custody battles. People spend years and their 401(k)s fighting over custody of their children.

My experience is that, generally speaking, kids do just fine with shared parenting. In fact, I have a more general theory that kids do better with shared parenting. It is not based on voluminous scientific research on shared parenting (and non-shared parenting) but rather on the following observation.

Typically, dads walk into my office and say, "I'd never take my children away from their mom. I just want 50-50 [parenting]." Moms often (although the world is ever-evolving on this front) say, "I am the primary parent. They should visit their dad, of course, but only every other weekend." We end up negotiating between 20% and 50%, landing around a 35% timeshare for Dad. It is almost understood that the kids will primarily live with their mom from the start of the negotiation. Why? Dad asks for 50%. Mom asks for 80%, and we end up right in the middle.

I believe that more timeshare for Dad is better for Mom, Dad and the children. I have developed this belief from experience in my practice.

1. Dad ends up with 20% timeshare (every other weekend Friday after school until Sunday at 6 pm, and Wednesday afternoon/evening dinners).
2. Mom stays in the home because it makes more sense for Mom to be in the home if the kids are with her more.
3. Dad pays support at a level where he can still afford, maybe, a two-bedroom apartment. All the kids' stuff—books, games, computer, videos, beds, bedding (and even friends) are still at what is now "mom's house," which is often referred to as "home" by both Mom and Dad.
4. The kids come to Dad's house for the weekend, and (let's call it what it is) an awful, boring, and uncomfortable time. Dad does his best to make it fun, so they spend time going places—amusement parks, pizzerias for lunch, video games, grandma's house, etc. Dad becomes the "Disneyland Dad" so often referred to pejoratively by moms and the media. He has no choice. He has nothing and nowhere to go and money is tight.

In the beginning, I spent many horrible afternoons at the same damned park with my two-year-old daughter. Taking her into the men's park bathroom when she had to go, playing on the same slides, and feeding the same ducks. I did my very best, but it was awful.

5. Dads spend 80% of their time without the kids. They go from being regular, involved members of the family (maybe slightly less involved with child-rearing and slightly more involved with work, but functioning members of the family unit, nevertheless) to being alone 80% of the time.

6. Dads continue to go to work and because all they do is work and maybe exercise, they have nothing but time. After a few months of suffering through depression, they meet someone at work or online (both sides usually go online looking for sex partners immediately, but actually settling on a partner takes some time). She will also, almost by definition, have a job. Often, she has her own kids (whom she also has 80% of the time).

7. Now Dad starts filling his time with this other woman and her kids, while still trying to play "Disneyland Dad" to his own kids, whose feelings are hurt and getting more hurt by the day because he is making a new life separate from them. The kids want to come less and less, and the new girlfriend, even if she is completely awesome and totally loves the kids, feels the pressure from her boyfriend's kids. Pressure often put there by Mom's distrust and dislike of Dad and certainly by the worry that the children will replace her with a "new mommy."

8. The kids hear that Mom is unhappy, but they know that Dad is no longer depressed because of the new woman in his life. Often, they worry about the new kids in his life supplanting them.

9. It begins a downward spiral lasting into the teenage years when the kids become old enough to say they don't want to go to Dad's house anymore.

Truly, after working with so many dads going through this and experiencing my own Dark Nights of the Soul, sitting alone in an empty house staring at my little girl's bed and feeling that tremendous sense of loss at not having her there, I can state definitively that there is no pain like not having your children. No matter what any mom thinks about dad's involvement in their children's lives, not having your kids leaves a cavernous gaping hole in your chest. It is an unfillable void.

When dads start checking out on their kids and support obligations it is often because *they* have already been "checked out" by the lack of time with the kids, a lack of money, and guilt. I believe lack of *real* time is the major reason why dads don't pay their child support. It's easier to love and feel connected to someone you see all the time. The more distant they grow, the harder it is to feel like paying money to the ex, whom he (usually) perceives to be keeping the children away. This is a very gendered conversation because I cannot remember a time in the last decade where a mom wanted custody, did not get it, and had to pay child support, although upon reading this, my law partner reminded me that we have one such case at the time of writing this.

The surest way to keep dads involved and paying their support is to give them regular time with the kids. Keep Dad involved in the kids' lives from the start. Yes, there is a little less child support, but you'd be surprised how little the timeshare truly matters in the support calculation. Perhaps you can negotiate with Dad that he pays child support as though he only has them 30% of the time, but you give him more timeshare in return. Most dads will take this deal. Moms say, "That's gross, I'm not selling my kids." I point out that there is no "selling" going on. The parents are making a deal that splits the support from the timeshare, which I argue in favor of anyway.

If you give dads time with the kids—real time, actual time, time when they can be parents with all the cuts and scrapes that go along with it—they stop being "Disneyland Dads" and become regular, involved parents. That means figuring out dinners and school lunches, shuttling kids to dance and soccer practice, scheduling play dates, and feeling that same exhaustion that moms, no doubt, feel every day. The flip side is that moms have more time available to date, to spend time alone, to spend time with girlfriends, to work and earn more money, etc. It is more of a win-win than most people recognize.

I also believe in shared parenting because every child has an inalienable right to know both of their parents, warts and all. The world is filled with too many "deadbeat" dad stories and too few stories of redemption and of fatherhood-by-the-shoestrings. Some dads have no idea what they are doing with their kids. They were the moneymakers who came home to a half bottle of bourbon and zoned out on their phone until bedtime every day, while mom ran herself ragged trying to keep up with everything else. Does that disqualify the dad from sharing parenting? Not at all. In fact, many more times than we acknowledge, uninvolved dads become great fathers without the mother doing everything for them.

I would venture to say that moms jump to their child's rescue or attend to their needs a few minutes before dads would do it. They do it so often that dads never think of taking care of a need or of anticipating an issue with their children before the mother does. She *always* ends up doing it. She thinks he doesn't care, but in reality, he isn't sure how to be more involved. It's not that he couldn't or wouldn't if given the chance. It is that she does it first. She does it ten minutes before he would do it. Maybe that's his laziness and maybe that's her hypervigilance, but regardless of the reason why, my feeling is that dads who let moms do most of the child rearing can step up after separation and do a perfectly acceptable job of parenting the children when Mom isn't around.

But I also believe this benefits moms. Moms have a right to experience joy in their lives too. That joy can come from the identity as a mother, but they also have more identity than just motherhood. They may want to work and dedicate time to a career or hobbies, or exercise or friendships. They may want to travel or write or paint or find new interests, partners or friendships. An 80-20 custodial timeshare reduces moms' abilities to do those things. They become completely dominated by taking care of children and end up not reaping the benefits of not having to parent all of the time. I understand that as parents we are "on" 100% of the time for our children, even when they are not with us. That said, getting breaks can make parents more available for their children when they are the responsible parent and can make them have more to give to their children when the children are with them. If you were not exhausted all of the time, think of how much more you'd have to offer your children.

Hence, as you negotiate consider how to best ensure long-term success. Know where the trigger points are. A dad who gets a 20% visitation and custody order will likely either check out or continue to fight for more custody. Both are terrible options for the children and the mom. A dad who gets a midway 36% visitation order will find that this is really a ton of time with his kids. I have had many dads who have taken the 36% timeshare (5 nights out of 14) with a "step-up" plan to move to 50% after two years who when the time came said, "Jude, the 5 nights plan is working for everyone and I'm not going to change it."

Good negotiating is an art form. Doing it right involves a number of important things.

First, you have to **know your best-and-worst case scenarios**. It is important to read books like this one, to consult with a lawyer who knows family law (ideally a specialist who understands not only what the law says but also how the local judges will react to specific situations). Experts understand that under the best-case scenario you will receive Outcome A and under the worst-case scenario you will receive Outcome B. When you understand your best and worst cases, you understand the Range of Normal or Reasonable Outcomes and can reasonably negotiate a settlement that puts you closer to the best case. You will also understand that even outcomes you don't love may be within the Range of Normal Outcomes. Negotiating in that way takes you out of the blind and into the open. You can share your thoughts on how to best divide assets to help you get what you want most.

The second major step is to **negotiate interests and not positions**. This is a fine and delicate art. It means understanding not only what you hope to accomplish, but also taking the time to listen to what the other person hopes to accomplish.

Despite the attorney-client privilege, most lawyers do not take any time to actually listen to their clients. We have no idea what our clients truly want from life. We do not hear about clients' hopes or dreams. We do not hear about why they want the retirement or the house or why they fear the children spending too much time with the other parent. Even if we do hear about it, most lawyers spend little time comprehending why it is important. Sometimes housing security is important for reasons we don't understand—so, if we know, then if the house is too expensive for our client to keep, we can negotiate another outcome that creates stability.

Instead of becoming rooted in your position ("I want this or that," or, "it has to be 50% or nothing") become open to understanding interests. I often spend the first half hour or so of a negotiation just listening. I let the other lawyer control the meeting even if it's at my office. In fact, especially if it's at my office.

I tell my client, "Today, we are on a listening tour. We will get much more out of this negotiation if we spend time listening first." I use humor and self-deprecation to loosen the atmosphere. I let people know that they are free to speak candidly in my office, that negotiations are sacrosanct and confidential. We work on putting people at ease. Then we leave them to sit in a silence that they fill with puffery and bravado, ultimately, letting them negotiate with themselves. We are listening and learning.

My client will usually tell me what they are interested in. I spend time asking them. I ask them several times over several months before the negotiation. I want to know what moves them. How are they going to be happiest after this is all over? I ask them what they believe their spouse will care most about. They often know better than anyone except their spouse. They will understand what makes their spouse tick. I tell them that we want to be consequentialist about things. That we are working toward a resolution that lets my client leave with what they came for.

Recently, I hosted a negotiation with another lawyer I know very well. We are a small bar, so I am very familiar with everyone I practice with. They are my colleagues rather than just adversaries. This lawyer has been practicing for 30 years in this town and she is well known for her courtroom antics, although not particularly detail-oriented about the law. She is a kind of gunslinger, preferring to do her work in the courtroom. She has her own style of manipulation. In this case my client is handsome and very wealthy, and he owns a restaurant chain that is wildly popular. Everyone goes there. This was a negotiation over timeshare with the kids. They have been divorced for 10 years and the kids are approaching high school. The ex-wife is still bitter because my client had an affair ten years ago (with his now wife) and left her. He took care of her financially, but she has always controlled him with the kids. A meeting in the hallway outside of court led my client to use his charm on this lawyer. He told her,

"I haven't had a complete weekend with my kids in ten years." He said it nicely, but the lawyer got it.

We had a strategy going into the negotiation. I told him that this lawyer will do almost anything for you if you just give her attention. You listen to her endless (and repeated) stories, you praise her for whatever bullshit she is slinging, you let her talk. When you do this, she becomes your advocate. Sure enough, we put out a royal (OK, not "royal" but still "nice") spread for her and her client at my office. Coffee, fresh berries, donuts, and orange juice. We told her it was because she came to our office for the negotiation. She went on and on about how the judges had been begging her to join them on the bench. She talked about how many houses she owns. She talked about how she does her finances much like my client. When my client said he needed more vehicle insurance coverage for the soon to be 16-year-old, she agreed that she had the same problem. Once we had won her over to our point of view, we had to do very little to modify the parenting plan to almost exactly what my client wanted. After his ex-wife left, my client gave the other lawyer a hug and told her she could have her favorite Chef's Salad on the house. She smiled.

I walked him out to his car after the meeting and he said, "We got everything we wanted. I couldn't be happier." We played the player. She worked her client over. To be fair my client had his child support double in a previous hearing, but as he told me when we rejected a settlement offer lower than the amount eventually ordered, "I don't care about the money. I'd rather give her less for sure, but I do not want [my ex-wife] to ever be able to feel like she was taking less than she was entitled to because she would hold that over my head. And this way, she has to share the costs of cleats, car insurance, medical bills and school stuff." He was finally free. It was expensive, no question, but we saved him probably $5,000 per month in support in the process.

The point is that you should be negotiating from interests rather than positions. You should be focused on what it is you want to accomplish from the negotiation. What do YOU want to get from it? How important is it to you to get that? What are you willing to give up to get that? Would you, for example, pay twice your current child support obligation to have your kids with you twice as much? Would you give up the dining room table for the riding mower?

You should also understand the law and your judge if you can. This is where lawyers who practice regularly in your community are helpful and worth the money. Don't spend more than two hours' worth of time and money on negotiating the "stuff," but you should spend some time understanding how your judge is likely to rule on custody, visitation, and support issues. These are areas where the judge has lots of discretion to decide what is best for the children. Negotiate in the shadow of the law.

The third negotiating step is to **always negotiate with mutual gain in mind**; that is, to the extent possible **work toward an outcome that will benefit the other party as much as possible without injuring your own interests**. If you get what you want, show restraint and mercy. When you do that you will be surprised at how you also get other things by agreement that you never considered.

I have a very smart client who was in the middle of an ugly and acrimonious divorce. He literally caught his wife in his bed with another man, a man he knows and hated well-before he found her *in flagrante dilecto*. His wife needed a good car and his employer had been paying for his car—a newer model Chevy Suburban. The Wife coveted that car. He bought it from his employer and gave it to her early in the divorce without any difficulty and completely on his own. The Wife, in exchange for a $15,000 car, did not request spousal support for 18 months, a savings to him of probably $50,000. He did right by her early on, at little cost to himself, and ended up putting himself at a tremendous advantage. I wish I could take credit for that, but he did it on his own.

Another client, an owner of a very successful professional practice in town was in the middle of a similar type of divorce. The wife was having an affair. He was angry and bitter. The Wife had the right to value his professional practice and take half of it. I told him that I would not be surprised if the value was well over $1 million. I asked him what she wanted. He said she wanted her car paid off and no credit card debt. I asked how much was left on the car loan ($4,000) and on the credit card ($1,000). I said, "what am I missing here?" He said, "If she wants to have a little boyfriend, he can pay all of that." I said, "We've become friends over the years, and so I'm not going to pull any punches with your legal liability the way you don't pull any punches with my tax liability. What the fuck is wrong with you? Pay the debts and sign the deal! You don't need her valuing your tax practice and owing her $500,000 because you wouldn't pay $5,000." He left my office in a huff and called me two hours later to tell me he'd paid the $5,000. He said he went to his men's group and asked them, and to a man, everyone agreed with me. He apologized for his anger, which I told him, and I tell everyone, never to do. I tell them to channel the anger into my office and let me be as objective as possible. We wrote up a deal right afterward. Wife got what she wanted, which was no debt on the car or the credit card; Husband kept his professional practice worth over $1 million.

The fourth negotiating step is that whenever things get really difficult, **work from objective criteria**. Back off the emotional arguments and start with "facts" as much as possible. In the above Restaurateur negotiation about the kids, the mom's objections were that the kids didn't want to change their long-time schedule. When we talked about it, she admitted that the oldest child really did want to change the schedule (he was almost 16). The younger ones (14 and 12) did not want to change the schedule. Once she admitted that, we discussed splitting their schedules apart and allowing the older one to have the week on/week off schedule that he wanted, while leaving the younger ones on the existing schedule—except that we gave each parent 2 full weekends per month. (They had been splitting weekends, exchanging on Saturday afternoons, for 10 years.) We also came up with a plan if the younger ones wanted to follow the older child once they got a taste of it.

The objective criterion in that case was "what do the children want?" We only asked that of the children because of their ages and experience with the situation and because we were not planning to change the 50-50 schedule but rather tweak it to fit their needs. Mom and Dad agreed finally (a HUGE step for them) that the children tell them different things. We put both parents in a room for the first time in ten years. They agreed that the oldest was clear on what he wanted, and that the other two weren't against it, but were not sure about it, either. We came up with plans for what to do in Situation A and in Situation B. Objective criteria. No one can argue with objective criteria unless they have a completely different view of the world. If that's the case, *guess what?* You can bring in information that will help everyone get to objectivity. And even if we can't figure out objective factual criteria, I say, "We can all agree that if each of you gets what's most important to you that it will be a good deal for everyone, right?" Or "If we understand what the kids want, we can work toward making it happen, correct?" We can even use humor, "They are teenagers. They don't want to spend time with either of you, right?" As long as Mom understood that she would still get her child support, a major factor in that particular negotiation, we could get almost anywhere. Especially with moms who have (at least in their own minds) been doing everything for years and years. You offer them a break.

Finally, here's one other thing you can do that may seem like the most foreign idea you've ever heard. Offer a compliment. Mark Twain said, "I could live two weeks on a good compliment." Compliments are both inexpensive (from a negotiation standpoint) and valuable. In another hotly contentious case that was ready to explode in perhaps the bloodiest trial I have been involved in in many months, my client and I talked beforehand and decided to make one last attempt to settle. She said to me, "I'm actually impressed at how hard he's been working to be a good dad. I wish he'd been like this when we were together. But I've been really happy the last few months." I asked my client if I could relay this to the other lawyer and she said yes. The other lawyer told his client.

This small olive branch, she did not even need to tell him herself, settled the case quickly and cleanly, getting both parties exactly what they wanted. All the father wanted was to be acknowledged for his efforts to clean up his life. The two of them once had genuine care for each other. The small acknowledgment led the father to say something nice about my client and we made an agreement before they torched their relationship for years to come.

This last point is important when dealing with any emotions. Fisher and Shapiro in their book *Beyond Reason: Using Emotions as You Negotiate* (2005), suggest using a number of tools to respond to emotions. The first one, "express appreciation," is exactly what my client did intuitively just before the bloody battle of trial was about to destroy their ability to co-parent effectively for many years to come. She expressed her appreciation that the father had worked so hard to make himself a better father. She wished he had done it during the relationship, but in the absence of that she knew that he had the same interests as she did at heart, a better life for their 2-year-old son.

The latter point also intuitively turned him from being an adversary with different interests into a colleague working on solving the same problem. That was not unlike my Restaurateur negotiation with the attorney who craved attention. We turned her from adversary into a colleague, and in the process did what Fisher and Shapiro call "Building Affiliation."

I love both books, *Getting to Yes* and *Beyond Reason*, because they translate the intuitive actions of good negotiators into concrete terms. *Getting to Yes* teaches you how to listen, while *Beyond Reason* shows you how to disarm negative emotions without revealing too much in the process. Intuitive negotiators and well-liked people are naturally capable of these skills, which is why they can appear "charming" or "likeable" right from the start. Too often, we enter a negotiation firmly fixed in our position—we know what we want, and we are determined to demand it. If we don't get it, we walk away. In doing so, we overlook all the potential solutions available at the bargaining table that aren't accessible to us in the courtroom. We forfeit the chance to achieve much better than our BATNA by simply taking a few minutes to listen to what the other side has to say, even if they're throwing verbal bombs your way. If you can set aside your pride for 15-20 minutes and allow the other person to speak, you can usually glean everything you need to know to reach an outcome that fulfills your desires.

Being a Consequentialist

In a divorce there is usually one pie that gets divided in two pieces. Every possible outcome leads to less than you started with. Everyone (or almost everyone) knows this before they start to negotiate in a divorce. Being a consequentialist in a divorce means being outcome focused. If you give in to your own negative emotions, you can lead yourself astray.

Many lawyers are willing to take your money to fight for things they can never get you.

I break the last sentence out as a separate paragraph because it is really important. Let it sink in. **Many lawyers will be willing to take your money to fight for things they can never get you.** Although this book may not reduce the cost of your divorce to the $35 cost of the book, it may save you $50,000 or more on attorney's fees. Do not let your lawyer talk you into spending tens of thousands of dollars fighting over things that you will never (or probably will never) get.

If you are a consequentialist, you accept certain things about your fate. You will end up with about half of everything you own. There are some chances you may get more or less, but not a whole lot more or less; think, on the order of 48%-52%, not on the order of 95%-5%. If you are the high earner, you will probably pay some support. As much as you think it hurts to write that check, the low earner thinks it is not close to sufficient. Both are correct. It will be high enough to be a punch in the stomach to the payor, and not enough for the payee to live the same lifestyle. Everyone hurts.

If you distance yourself from your emotions about the process and everything your spouse did to you during the marriage and after the separation, you become a consequentialist about the negotiations. If you get what you want, what importance is it to you that your ex got what he or she also wanted? I have said repeatedly that good agreements are *durable* agreements. Durable agreements come from both sides feeling like they were heard and getting something they wanted. If you reach a good agreement, I believe you are more likely to receive your support on time, get necessary documents signed in a timely manner, and ultimately end up with an opportunity to reboot your life more quickly and with less pain than if you extract something out of your spouse.

Settling Issues – Litigating Others

Finally, and I will keep this short. Settle whatever you can. Anything you agree on is worth agreeing to. "Global" settlements are great. We all want perfect agreements. **But if you cannot get a perfect agreement, get a sufficient agreement. Resolve everything you can to reduce the issues for trial.** This will save you not only immense heartache, but a lot of money as well.

You should always include the cost of litigation in your Range of Normal Outcomes. Sometimes a savings of $10,000 in attorney's fees is a deal maker. Most good attorneys will tell you that—if not while sitting at the negotiating table, then at least when you take a break.

However, by agreeing to what you can, I don't mean accepting table scraps. Most cases have 10-15 issues, of which 8-14 can be easily worked out in a negotiation. The difference between a 15-issue trial and a 2-issue trial is three days of 10-12 hours of billable time. (Some lawyers charge two hours of prep for every one hour of trial). Regardless, a 12-hour trial day is about $7,500. Three trial days is $22,500—for each side. Most of the time when trials occur over 12-15 issues, it's because the lawyers did not make a concerted effort to resolve the easy stuff. Lawyers who try to milk your money will try the easy issues last, when everyone is mad, and the judge is too exhausted to have worked the issues out earlier. **Always, always,**

always, work on the easy issues first. Agree to whatever you can. Don't hold easy items over the other side's head for hard items—don't tell your spouse you won't deal on the vehicles (even though you already know whose vehicle is whose) unless they agree on spousal support or child custody. This is just a waste of money. Divide the vehicles and then fight over spousal support. The vehicle division is a foregone conclusion.

CHAPTER 10

Mindfulness Negotiation and Strategy

MINDFULNESS SHOULD BE a meaningful concept, but it has been used so broadly in recent years that its definition is unclear. Therefore, I must define what I mean by mindfulness if I am going to use the term. The concept itself is very helpful in the divorce context and can be applied to both negotiations and litigation.

I begin with the organizational management literature on managing high-risk operations, and then move on to the more familiar self-actualization literature on being aware of one's own self. I have a long personal history with both literatures, including a Berkeley Ph.D. on the organizational management side of this, so bear with me as I develop the reasons for using the literature on mindfulness in organizational management.

Mindfulness Part I: Strategies of Fighter Pilots, Air Traffic Controllers, and Nuclear Power Plant Operators for "Locking In" to Work Practice

Karl Weick and Kathleen Sutcliffe in *Managing the Unexpected* describe mindfulness as "a rich awareness of discriminatory detail." They explain that "when people act, they are aware of context, of ways in which details differ, and of deviations from their expectations. Mindful people have the big picture, but it is a big picture of the moment." (p. 32).

This type of mindfulness is diametrically opposed to the "focus on the breath" mindfulness surrounding us in popular culture (although that can be very helpful, too). My own doctoral work before I became a family lawyer was in the field of organizational behavior and governance. Specifically, I spent four years at the Los Alamos National Laboratory studying the ways in which the laboratory workers—nuclear weapons researchers—respond to safety and security rules. Much of my work was focused on High Reliability Organizations. These types of organizations successfully manage high-risk, high-hazard types of technologies—aircraft carrier captains, fighter pilots, air traffic controllers, nuclear power plant operators, surgical response teams, emergency managers, and first responders. We studied how they manage to be effective while facing great odds.

Weick and Sutcliffe's enunciation of the importance of this specific type of mindfulness has been very helpful in understanding how it is that organizations achieve success in high-stakes environments. I want to take their understanding of mindfulness and apply it to the divorce context, not because there is a real risk of tens of thousands of people dying if you fail, but because I think the type of vigilance it teaches will help you ensure that you are approaching your negotiations and your litigation with the right concepts in mind. Then I want to take the more popular culture idea of mindfulness and give some thoughts on how that will help as well.

First off, most organizations – and people – learn through trial and error. You do something for a while and then determine whether it works. If it does, you tinker with it to make it better, and if it doesn't, you tinker with it or change it and see if the results improve. Most of the research on organizational learning says that failure isn't so bad, so long as you are learning from your failures. High Reliability Organizations (HRO) have little room for trial-and-error learning. Your first error is your last trial. Why? Because things blow up or crash if you make mistakes.

Your divorce is something like an HRO in that way. You only do it once (hopefully) and when you do it, you must get things right because you can't fix them later. You don't do much tinkering. Well, you can tinker with a custodial schedule over the long-term if it isn't working, but most of the other issues need resolution correctly the first time. This book is a way of hopefully guiding you toward that right outcome at the outset, while also helping you get through the process without losing your mind entirely.

"Mindfulness" in the Weick and Sutcliffe model means understanding the big picture before you sit down to negotiate or head to trial. It is an understanding of not only your Range of Normal Outcomes, but also what exactly you have to divide, where you and your soon to be ex-spouse are each headed in terms of career and earnings, what your kids need from you, a sense of the feelings and emotions that are driving the friction in the case, and an understanding of your own and your soon to be ex-spouse's interests. This is having "rich awareness of discriminatory detail."

When you do that, you act in accordance with context. Too often women play the short game—they try to get everything they can as quickly as possible, which leads to a front-loading of support, property, and timeshare with the kids. It also leaves them short down the road. Remember the motivational speaker with the $100 million publishing empire that he offered to give Wife half of and she turned it down for $9 million immediately? She also spent a million dollars on attorneys' fees to get it.

Men often play such a long game that they are well-outside what is reasonable. They sacrifice their home now for their pension later;

they take the view that Mom is more equipped to raise the kids because she does it more than they do; they give up timeshare now that affects their relationships with their children for the rest of their children's lives; they agree to pay more support on the front-end in exchange for less support later—which is a good thing for many families, but it also means that in the short-term they have little access to the cash they'll need to set up a home.

In other words, both sides act without paying close attention to context. The Wife who seeks to extract everything she can from the community property business operated by Husband risks destroying the goose that lays the golden egg – as the examples I gave earlier with the Bankrupt Drywall Subcontractor and the Padlocked Gate can attest to. This lack of contextual awareness can be disastrous in a family law setting. Every family lawyer knows, or should know, that there is a "sweet spot" within which the support payor will make regular and recurring payments and divide property, and outside of which she will rebel by refusing to follow orders and by "losing her job."

Contextual awareness in family law is a bit like a wrist lock in martial arts – it means understanding where the break points are and applying enough leverage to them to make sure you get what you need while backing off before breaking the bone. Once it is broken, the party ordered to pay will realize that compliance is almost completely optional (even at the risk of a 5-day jail sentence for contempt of court, particularly since most judges will not put a contemnor in jail).

Situations where there is no control over the party lead to outcomes that no one can predict. Men will stop paying support and disappear, moving out of state or filing bankruptcy. Women will take up with bad boyfriends or alienate the children. And alternatively, women will return to court repeatedly to argue over narcissism and diaper rashes on the babies' bottoms; men will shack up with women half their age. Or vice-versa on all the gender roles.

Once parties realize that the Judge can only threaten them with 5 days in jail (for which very very few Sheriffs are willing to actually put someone in jail) for violating an order, and judges are deeply reticent to do this, they will simply do whatever they please...and disaster often results from this. For those of you watching at home, don't think that this is support for breaking orders at your whim. That is a costly undertaking as well.

Weick and Sutcliffe talk about the "big picture," but they also note the importance of understanding the "big picture of the moment." Thus, you are unfailingly aware of the totality of the global circumstances and context in which you are operating, but you must also be aware of the totality of the circumstances *in each moment* and in each particular circumstance. Momentary awareness is a recognition that things are constantly in flux. Your life happens in real-time while court-time is much slower. What was important to you three weeks ago can sometimes be so far gone that the motion we filed to get it is totally moot (without need). You should be paying attention to the situation. Did you or your spouse get a new job? Did the kids start school? Did your ex-spouse's boyfriend or girlfriend break up with them? Did a grandparent die? Is there an inheritance coming to anyone? Did the stock in the company go up or down?

More common than those things is the level of exhaustion that forms—an exhaustion that only goes away when court issues are resolved. People who start out with piss-and-vinegar in their blood usually start to fade after a couple of rounds of fighting.

In family law, everyone leaves a hearing with cuts and scrapes, broken bones, and puncture wounds. I am constantly doing "gut checks" with my clients, not unlike my varsity basketball coach who would look us in the eye to decide who had that little bit of energy to push through to the end. As matters drag on, I find that most (rational) people start to burn out. The purifying fire of litigation burns away the chaff and leaves the wheat. People stop caring as much about small things and start caring more about getting things resolved.

"Give me victory, but if you cannot give me victory, at least give me peace." Peace has a value. It's an intangible value that only you know, but it is a real value, and one for which you must name your own price. Are you willing to give up the furniture, the extra overnight visit, $500 per month in support, the tax obligations, your inheritance contribution to the down payment on the second home? What are you willing to walk away from now because of exhaustion that seemed so important to you before? What is your spouse willing to walk away from?

In my own story, my ex and I had a 18-month-old daughter when we separated. She had the lawyer whom I mentioned above (the attention seeker), and I hired the baddest lawyer I thought I could find. They set our matter for a full day trial. My ex's father had just died, and she was very close to him. She knew how important I was to our daughter, and I knew how important she was to our daughter. We realized we were going to spend $12,000 on this one-day trial and that neither of us had the money to spend.

We agreed to sit down at Starbucks and talk it over. Our song came on the piped in music and we both relaxed. She teared up. We made our "Historic Starbucks Accord" that day and have been making agreements ever since then. We were geared up for an ugly battle, but we stepped back from the brink and made an agreement that we have been expanding on ever since. I voluntarily increase my child support as I earn more. She doesn't ask for increases. We share time more and more, almost eliminating the need for a schedule where changes are requested. We work together.

I don't expect everyone else, or anyone else for that matter, to have the same experience. This one works for us. We both had contextual awareness in our case. Her father had just died, and I had been there when he had his lung transplant. Our lawyers were gearing up for a fight neither of us wanted. We were both sad to share our daughter, but we both believed the other was a good parent. We realized that things had changed from when we first started our separation.

Having contextual awareness, including both the Big Picture and "today's picture," is the key to getting the outcomes you want.

The other thing mindful organizations do is have a preoccupation with failure. They seek to avoid failure above all else, which is relevant to the divorce context. Rather than focusing on being successful, the organizations focus on not failing. This preoccupation with failure leads them to take conservative actions, something that cannot be overstated in this context. We should take actions that do not destroy our ability to problem-solve. Mindfulness means not only being aware, but also using that awareness to work toward an outcome that will work for everyone.

You should also be thinking about how your emotions will impact your ability to reach resolutions. If you understand your emotions and you have a good understanding of your ex's emotions on the matter, you are being mindful. But being aware is not enough. You must work toward resolution. You are playing not only so that you do not fail, but also so that the entire process does not end up involving litigation (which is its own sort of failure).

This type of mindfulness is a type of vigilance—a dedication to being aware of the context in which you are working. Litigation is hell on everyone. Divorce litigation is hell on steroids. There are the emotions that come from getting divorced; plus, the emotions that come from litigation. It ruins people for years, scarring them, and leaving lasting damage. You say and hear things said that cannot be unsaid or unheard: infidelities, carefree spending, temper tantrums, etc. . . . And as you listen to those things, your lawyer instructs you to make a laundry list of everything your ex-spouse has done to you. "Fighting fire with fire!!" You write down every grudge, every hurt, and reopen every wound.

If you choose to go through this process alone, I understand. Lawyers are unbelievably expensive, and in a divorce, there is a tendency to get into a spending frenzy. However, if you go it alone, you must be your own passionate/dispassionate advocate. There is no person on earth who is better equipped to explain your relationship with your children. Your spouse may try to minimize your role or overstate their own role in child rearing and caretaking, but only you know the truth and how to best advocate for yourself. But there are times you will need to step back from the emotional depths and provide the judge with a dispassionate declaration regarding custody and visitation. The same is true concerning the financial and property issues. You will really need to stay dispassionate. There is little to be gained using passionate advocacy regarding the property issues, except to the extent that you are aware of your spouse's preferences and can clearly state your own.

That means mindfulness. Know when you are getting upset. Know when you are losing track of the things you want and those you cannot live without. Know when you are veering off course.

Staying mindful in the Weick and Sutcliffe model means to keep situational awareness in the face of extreme pressure. This is no easy feat. And Weick and Sutcliffe, and the other academics who work on these issues, will tell you that having and keeping situational awareness in the "fog of war" is "damned difficult" (that's my dissertation advisor, Todd La Porte commenting on High Reliability Organizational work). The way to do this is to develop your best and worst case alternatives and think through your end-game. Where do you want to be when this is over, knowing that you will be giving up half of everything, including time with your children? What matters most to your ex? How can you multiply benefits to everyone, including your children, in the middle of a "zero sum game" where whatever one person gets reduces what the other gets?

The process of developing contextual mindfulness means going through your assets and liabilities, looking at your work schedule, thinking about having a new partner and what they might need (even if you don't have one yet), thinking about what your spouse needs to keep or create a new home your children will love, thinking about how much money you need or can give each month, and balancing your stress, fears, loneliness, resentment, pain and the cost of lawyers litigating for you, and deciding what it will take to get through all of this living nightmare. Staying dispassionate and objective in every way that you can is a tall order. But you must attempt to do this as much as possible.

Mindfulness Part II: Self-Actualization and Mindfulness

The other kind of mindfulness is the one prevalent in popular culture. The mindfulness that asks you to be still and contemplate the moment you are in. The here and now. From Eckhart Tolle to Deepak Chopra and many other celebrity doctors and gurus whose work I am not familiar with, to the yoginis and corporate CEOs, there is an immense amount of focus on mindfulness in popular culture.

I meditate every day. It's my thing. I also have a heavy punching bag in my garage so I can wail away when things get particularly stressful. You go through this divorce stuff only once; I live in a perpetual *Groundhog Day*, reliving divorce over and over again. Obviously, it's not with the same emotional taxation as my clients, but I am constantly pressured to be a high-performer. A lawyer can have an incredible track record, but for each client he is only as good as the results he brings in their specific case. For every client, I am their therapist, coach, counselor, champion and gladiator.

For me, meditation is a way of relieving the accumulating stress and processing the emotions that are always present—from anxiety and worry to self-doubt and sadness. The immense sadness of being around people who are suffering in the worst possible way. Divorce lawyers are a type of legal counselor (very high-priced) who are not trained to be counselors/therapists. I consult sometimes with clients in an almost therapy-type setting where they come to me solely to be heard. To have me understand them and their concerns, and to sit with them and provide answers when I have them. Because lawyers have no training in how to care for the caregiver, and because divorce litigation is so counseling-heavy, I am under tremendous pressure. And yes, I know that nobody cries for lawyers.

A combination of sitting meditation, hitting the heavy bag, throwing the ball for the dogs, and painting in the studio (plus writing books like this one) gets me through it.

I urge everyone going through a divorce to find a method of processing their emotions, whether it is meditation, music, something physical like dance, anything. I am no guru or yogini, so I don't purport to speak for what they mean by mindfulness, but I have been fortunate to have had "peak experiences." Sometimes athletes call it "being in the zone." I've had that great rush of endorphins known as a "runner's high," and the experience of feeling time fall away so that nothing in the world exists but what I am doing at that moment. And I am not alone.

One client takes his Harley out and revs the engine on long drives; another goes to the shooting range with his AR-15s; another goes swimming and does Tabata workouts; still others surf, play with their dog, or go to church. The choices are endless.

I think of that falling away of time and space as the feeling of mindfulness. If you can find that place for 15-30 minutes a day, it will help you navigate the divorce process and give you greater control over your emotions and a sharper focus on getting the outcomes you want.

If you are going to represent yourself, I do have a two additional suggestions.

1) I was a lawyer for four years before I ever appeared in Court. At the big firms, young lawyers are not given many opportunities to appear in Court. When I went to Court the first time for a client (who was with me), I wanted to puke right there in the courtroom. I was so anxious about what was going to happen, what I was going to say, and how I was going to say it that I could barely breathe. I had learned a trick/technique some years before for calming my racing heart and reducing the intensity of my anxiety. I touch my middle and ring fingers to my thumbs on both hands, like a Buddha statue at my sides or even in my pockets, and take three deep breaths. By the third deep breath, my heart rate is noticeably slower. Once I see that I can control my heart rate, I know that I am in control and can more calmly view the task at hand.

2) Do not be afraid to write things down. In fact, I suggest that you do write things down. Worst-case scenario, you read it to the judge. Best-case scenario, you can enunciate each of your points succinctly and clearly to the court. Either way, you will say everything you came to say, even if you cannot quite deliver it in the manner you most hoped for. If you read a statement, read it slowly and dramatically so it sounds like you are saying it. There is a court reporter writing everything down, so if you speak too quickly the judge will stop you. Go slowly.

CHAPTER 11

Fiduciary Duties

FIDUCIARY DUTIES ARE a hotbed of activity in the family law. If I had to hazard a guess why, I think it's because many lawyers who get involved in family law think family law is a dirty business full of people fighting over children and child support. They don't like the messiness of that type of work. So, they tell themselves that, even though they are family lawyers, they don't do "that" kind of work. Then there are organizations like the California Family Law Specialists (of which I am one) and the American Academy of Matrimonial Lawyers (which this book will probably ensure I will not be one) that pride themselves on being above the emotional fray and focus on the financial aspects of high asset divorce.

You will see "high asset" divorce on a lot of family law websites, mine included. Why? We figure that we can make our living doing discovery and acting like civil litigators in the family law context. That way, when we see our friends from law school at bar events and dinner parties and they ask us what type of law we are doing, we don't have to feel ashamed of saying we are family lawyers.

A typical exchange might go like this: "Hey Earl, what kind of law are you practicing?" "Family law," Earl says back. "Oh wow. My hat's off to you. I could never do that kind of emotional work." "Oh, don't worry, I only do high-asset cases. I leave the custody stuff to other lawyers."

I hate to break it to Earl and all the other "high-asset" divorce lawyers out there, but high-asset divorce is every bit as emotional as custody cases. All divorce cases are fraught with emotion. That's part of the point of this book – to get you to back off the high-intensity emotional stuff and try to be as cool and calm as you can be. All of this stuff can be as emotional as you let it be or as emotional as you let your lawyer get about it.

No one rants and raves over a contract dispute or a personal injury case. Civil litigation discovery is pretty dry stuff. Family law discovery is like a new battleground every time you communicate with the other side. I was just accused in open court of being "disingenuous," "nefarious" and "subterfuge" by another member of the state bar – me, personally. Wow. We get routinely accused of being liars and thieves and posturing and bluffing. And that's on the financial issues. And that's the lawyers. The case where I was accused of disingenuousness and subterfuge is a financial case only. No kids.

So, don't believe the hype when a lawyer tells you they only do high-asset divorce, as though that somehow makes them less dirty than the riff-raff who represent moms and dads trying to get more custody of their children or reduce their child support payment from $1,400 to $1,100 per month. Family law is messy business because it involves high emotional intensity whether fighting over children or money. Every motion is painful. Every trip to court creates a sucking feeling in your chest. Every minute spent litigating is another opportunity for anxiety and exhaustion. And your lawyer is in business. And the business model is to enflame your anger so that you will spend more money on billable hours.

California is a "no fault" divorce state. The idea is that we have divorce because you want to be divorced. No allegations of adultery or cruelty or abandonment needed. But, there are some statutes that are fault-based in the Family Code. For example, commit domestic violence and lose your right to get spousal support. Drink and drive with the children in the car and lose your kids (maybe not forever, but certainly you can expect a punishment). The other area of the law where we have fault is in the breach of the fiduciary duties owed between spouses.

What are Fiduciary Duties?

Fiduciary duties are a heightened duty that is owed by a person who holds your money in trust for you. Bankers, real estate brokers, CPAs and lawyers are all fiduciaries. We hold your money in our bank accounts and cannot spend it or pay ourselves unless you say it's ok. When someone is a fiduciary for you, they are in a position of trust and confidence with you. They are expected to treat your money with the same care and diligence that they would treat their own money. This is a heightened duty of care.

Remember earlier in the book, I talked about "duties of care"? We have a reasonable duty of care to people we see on the street not to increase their risk of harm due to our actions. We have a duty to trespassers not to create attractive nuisances on our property that might get them hurt or killed. We owe people who come to our business a higher duty of care than we owe people on the street and we owe people who entrust us with their lives, safety, security, etc. with an even higher duty of care. We owe our children and spouses the highest duty of care because we have relationships of trust and confidence with them; they trust us and should be permitted to trust us – we would never act in any interest but their best interest. This is why spouses have a privilege against testifying against one another. There is an old notion – that isn't really so old – that our spouse is and should be the one person, besides perhaps our priest, our therapist, our doctor and our lawyer, who we should be able to tell anything to at any time without fear that they will share (by compulsion or anger) what we have said with another. The law refers to this as a "confidential" relationship.

In addition to trust and confidence, the Family Code also enshrines "fiduciary" duties between spouses. We have an obligation not to benefit ourselves financially at the expense of our spouse – even by accident! We are allowed to transact with our spouse, but we cannot take advantage of our spouse. In any transaction in which we benefit at our spouse's expense, the law always examines the transaction "with a jealous eye."

Therefore, a spouse can add their spouse to title of their separate property real estate without consideration – meaning without getting anything in return (except love and affection). At separation, however, the Court will examine this to determine whether the adding party knew what they were doing. That's because marriage only ends in one of two ways: death or divorce. If death, we assume Spouse 1 wanted Spouse 2 to get the house (because trust and confidence); if divorce, we assume Spouse 1 did not mean to give Spouse 2 the house in its entirety (because fiduciary relationship).

The community may also make an investment in one spouse's separate property by paying down the mortgage or adding a second story on the home or contributing $100,000 to a 401(k). Parties may transmute the character of property (change its ownership from community to separate or separate to community) and they may give each other gifts, expensive gifts at that (like Porsches and diamonds), but they must do so with full knowledge of what they are doing, or the fiduciary duty laws will kick in and ask the question: was there any "undue influence" in the transaction? Did everyone involved know what they were giving up and getting? Did one spouse breach their fiduciary duties by taking advantage of their spouse?

Undue influence is a funky term, just like *breach of fiduciary duty*. Both sound like nefarious plots to undermine the other's financial status. They sound like fraud or duress (holding a gun to the other's head) or other acts of, well, subterfuge. But most of the time, they are not. Undue influence *can* mean "fraud, perjury or duress," but it can also just mean that one party did not understand the impact of the transaction.

> 'Generally, a fiduciary obtains an advantage if his position is improved, he obtains a favorable opportunity, or he otherwise gains, benefits, or profits.' [Citation.] The spouse advantaged by the transaction has the burden of dispelling the presumption of undue influence. [Citation.] The presumption can be dispelled by evidence that the disadvantaged spouse entered into the transaction 'freely and voluntarily . . . **with a full knowledge of all the facts and with a complete understanding of the effect of the [transaction].**' " (*In re Marriage of Kieturakis* (2006) 138 Cal.App.4th 56, 84 (*Kieturakis*).) "Thus, ' "[i]f one spouse secures an advantage from the transaction, a statutory presumption arises under [Family Code] section 721 that the advantaged spouse exercised undue influence and the transaction will be set aside." ' " (*Lintz v. Lintz* (2014) 222 Cal.App.4th 1346, 1353; see also *In re Marriage of Mathews* (2005) 133 Cal.App.4th 624, 628-629.)

This means that the law presumes that the advantaged spouse took advantage of the disadvantaged spouse, whether they did so intentionally or not. The word "presumption" shifts the burden to the advantaged spouse to prove that there was a free and voluntary transaction with full knowledge of all the facts and a complete understanding of the effect of the transaction. That means that, if your spouse signed a quitclaim deed in 2012 during your marriage, giving you the house that you bought with community property money for whatever reason, you have to prove that the transaction was valid and that she understood its significance.

·············· **PRO TIP:** ··············

Just because you have a deed does not mean you win the deed.

···

Imagine that you have been operating for years under the assumption (shared by your spouse) that you have been given the family home because your wife signed off on a quitclaim deed giving it to you – for whatever reason. Then, at trial, she says she did not understand quitclaim deeds when she signed and now after all these years of operating as though the property was yours, you find out that the Court is setting the agreement aside because Wife says she did not understand it when she signed it.

This happened in real life in the unpublished *Vanherweg v. Vanherweg* case in which the parties were married for almost 40 years and raised 7 children together. Wife got some worthless dirt as an inheritance. Husband was industrious and good with land. First, he farmed the dirt and then he began working on developing the dirt. Wife went to an attorney and drafted a "transmutation agreement," actually using all of the "magic words" associated with changing the title and character of this worthless inherited property. For 17 years, they operated as though the transmutation was good between them. Husband, with his industry and skill, turned the worthless dirt pile into a $5 million piece of property. At divorce, 17 years later, Wife said she did not understand the meaning of the document she signed giving him equal ownership of the property. She had hired her own lawyer to explain it to her. 17 years of Husband's energy and drive going into the property. Husband testified that he did not save for retirement and instead put 7 children through college, while Wife did not work outside the home because they had the $5 million in assets for retirement. The Court ruled that the agreement was invalid because Wife did not understand it when she signed it.

The Appellate Court affirmed. In other words, there is no way to guarantee that agreements you make with your spouse will be binding at trial. The Court determined that there was "undue influence," not because Husband intentionally harmed Wife, but because she simply did not understand the meaning of the document she signed.

In other words, "undue influence" is a hot term that normally has a banal meaning to it. Most people do not mean to harm their spouse in their business dealings with their spouse. It is true that there are a host of transactions between spouses that spouses do not understand and do not think they need lawyers to help them with. Every one of those transactions will at least involve a question of whether there was undue influence – i.e., whether both spouses understood what they were doing.

One of my chief complaints about the undue influence interpretation requiring spouses to fully and completely understand the implications of a transaction with their spouse is that the family law rules can be deeply esoteric. We hold spouses to the standard of knowing the esoterica of the rules that, frankly, not even very good family lawyers know offhand – and surely no one else. How can we expect spouses operating in real time to understand?

The doctrine of "waiver" – where one party waives a legal right – requires that the party waiving that right understand the right in its entirety and specifically waive that right. But "understand" is a very nuanced term. Wife in *VanHerweg* understood that separate property meant "inheritance" and she understood that she was giving her inheritance to the community. She also understood that Husband had mixed his labor with the land to give it value, a value that would never have been there if Husband had not done so. Still, the Court set it aside because she did not seem to understand the meaning of the word "transmutation" or that she could never get it back, once given.

Let me give another example from a case that I lost at trial and then appealed and also lost on appeal. This was a probate case rather than a family law case per se, but the Probate Code 100(a) (which means the first entry in the code) permits a party to devise (will away) one-half of the community property. This means Probate Code 100(a) implicates the entire family law apparatus regarding community property. As I have mentioned previously, probate lawyers very rarely understand community property and do not want to understand it.

My clients' mother died. She left a trust that was defined as a separate property trust that included a home in Santa Barbara. She also left a will that said "all my property to my trust." She did not understand the esoterica of community property and neither did the lawyer who wrote her trust and will. We argued that "all" means "all." Husband had a house in the Bay Area from before marriage. During the marriage, Wife kept her separate property home in Santa Barbara completely separate from the community. It was always rented out and always covered more than its costs and therefore provided cashflow to the community. Husband, however, during the community, refinanced the Bay Area home three times (using Wife's credit and income to qualify for the refinance loan) and then paid the mortgage off using a mixture of his own income from employment (community property) and Wife's separate property rental income. The house always remained titled in Husband's name. We had a four-day trial in which the Court determined that the Santa Barbara home was clearly 100% Wife's separate property and that the Bay Area house was clearly 100% community property, even though it was in Husband's name, because the parties had refinanced it several times and retired the mortgage together.

Wife made a will that said: "all my property to my trust." We argued that Wife was permitted to will away her one-half interest in the community property and did so with her will. But the trial court ordered that the will did not include community property even though it said "all my property" because no one explained to her that the Bay Area home had a community property component to it, which ended up being 100%. The Appellate Court (and trial court) stated that unless a party has the full extent of their community property and separate property rights explained to them, any will or trust might be reformed because they did not know what they were giving up or devising to their children and at who's expense.

But what do we make of the fact that few trust and probate lawyers know what is or isn't community property? We had to have a *four-day trial* to determine whether the Bay Area home was community or separate property. Wife surely could not have known that the home, titled always in Husband's name, was community property on her own. And the Appellate Court stated that the trust drafting lawyer (not me) had committed malpractice in drafting the will because he did not explain community property "well enough" to her. I hope that all 400+ pages of this book are proof enough that "explaining community property" to someone is not a simple task.

The Appellate Court did an act of legal contortion, going so far as to accuse the original trust drafting attorney of malpractice in the Appellate Court's decision, rather than simply follow the clean, clear dictates of the will that said "all my property." It is esoteric, but it is well-established that a will that says "all my property" or "the residue of my estate" means every single thing that you own whether you know you own it or you don't. Even Husband's expert admitted this under cross-examination.

The *Wilkin v. Nelson* Court established that probate lawyers better get on their "A game" if they are not going to get sued for malpractice and that second marriages should have clear delineations between community and separate property. In fact, when people are engaging in estate planning in second marriages, I advise that they meet with a family law specialist to help them understand community and separate property concerns before they go out and simply sign a document drafted by an estate planning lawyer who does not understand family law.

What this did was show that, even though not even lawyers really understand community property all that well, parties making wills and trusts as well as parties transacting with one another during marriage, must understand the intricacies of family law property issues for their agreements to be binding, or else the court will set them aside. Don't just skim over this paragraph. It matters not only in the context of your estate plan, but also if this is your second marriage or your spouse's second marriage. *Vanherweg v. Vanherweg* set aside a very clear agreement between the parties because the trial court found that the Wife did not understand it 17 years earlier when she signed it (despite the fact that she had counsel and admitted she knew what it meant) and *Wilkin v. Nelson* set aside very clear language ("all my property") because the probate lawyer, they said, did not explain esoteric concepts in family law to her before she signed. In both cases, the Court decided, with no evidence, that the Wife did not understand what she signed when she signed it.

There is a lot more to *Wilkin v Nelson* than I just described, but this part is instructive about how we must think about "undue influence" and breach of fiduciary duties. It is too easy to get emotionally enflamed about these issues because it sounds like you are being accused of fraud, when in reality, you are doing what many people do, which is act in a common-sense manner with your spouse. The Wife in the *Wilkin v. Nelson* case had no idea that she had ownership in a home owned by Husband and titled in Husband's name during their 34-year marriage. So, arguably, she did not know, when she created her trust, that she had any interest in the home. On the other hand, she clearly stated in her will that she wanted "all my property" to go to her trust. Our position at trial and the admission of the trial expert on the other side, was that "all means all." It would include oil wells willed to her by an uncle she never knew and property she did not know she had.

Further, in that case, Husband began transferring community property to his separate property trust while she was suffering from Alzheimer's Disease. This is a clear breach of fiduciary duty – in fact, arguably, these transfers constituted a clear breach of duty with intent to harm the community. And still the trial court, feeling bad for the Husband, sanitized these transfers because he did not know it was a breach of his fiduciary duty (knowledge of which, by the way, is not required). The Appellate Court in one of the most disgusting opinions I've ever read (they knew it because they depublished the family law portion of the opinion because it was so terrible and they are smart and knew it was terrible, sanitized this part of the decision as well) made up some very bullshit excuse for why what was a clear breach of fiduciary duty by Husband in stealing Wife's assets while she suffered from Alzheimer's Disease was not a breach of his fiduciary duties.

OK, enough of my soapbox. Breaches of fiduciary duty happen any time a spouse benefits at the expense of the other spouse unless each spouse was fully informed of their rights and obligations in the transaction. In California, the punishments are severe. The Court must award 50% of the transferred asset and order attorney's fees for recovering the asset. Or the Court may award, in the case of actual fraud, 100% of the asset. Actual fraud is very rare, but it does happen. I think most judges do not attempt to make actual fraud rulings on purpose. Actual fraud rulings are punishment rulings. Judges don't like to punish people in family law proceedings.

Be Careful of Breach of Fiduciary Duty Claims: They are Usually more Valuable to the Lawyer's Attorney's Fees Bill than they are to You.

OK, all of the above having been said, family lawyers really really like these breach of fiduciary duty arguments. It makes them a lot of money. It enflames clients into spending needless money. And judges will do circus-level contortions not to grant them.

Family law is extremely lucrative. So, the lawyers who pursue breaches of fiduciary duty are especially very smart lawyers who like to tell people at dinner parties that they only deal with *high-asset divorces*. There is almost never a high-asset divorce that does not involve lawyers on both sides screaming that one or the other party violated their fiduciary duties. This is just a spinning cash register for the lawyers. Both clients get worked up into a frenzy and being worked up into a frenzy means spending money on attorneys' blindly and without a goal in mind, when the most likely outcome of any breach of fiduciary duty filing is to divide the community property part of the asst 50-50 (and ignore the attorney's fees portion of the law). The worst thing you can do is spend money on attorney's fees in hopes of getting attorney's fees later.

If you find an asset that was probably transferred in breach of fiduciary duties, you should work to divide that asset. If you have to spend some money on attorney's fees, do it, but be focused on dividing the asset, not trying to prove that your soon-to-be ex-husband is an asshole who should pay $100,000 in fees for stealing your property – even when he is an asshole and did steal your property. The Court already knows you feel that way and proving it in court will only a) tell the Court that he is an asshole and b) by extension, make the court think you are an asshole.

There is a legal truism: "associates of people who stink like shit, stink like shit." That means if your ex stinks like shit, you will stink like shit by extension. Focus on outcomes, not proving that the smell in the room comes from your ex.

Nobody wins. And you lose ultimately, because even when you get attorney's fees awarded to you, you only get money owed to your lawyer; it is not money in your pocket.

Just divide the asset. If Husband is being ridiculous in his arguments, then prove it, but do not spend a lot of time trying to prove fraud unless there is actual fraud and you can show it. Otherwise, get the asset divided and send the bill for how much it cost to have the actual asset divided.

In my view, breach of fiduciary duty arguments are the "spinning cash register" in family law. You want to do it because you are mad. Your lawyer wants to do it because a) it makes them feel like they are a real civil litigator fighting over money rather than children and b) because it is a tremendous money maker for the lawyer's law firm. You will be mad and let them do whatever the lawyer wants to do so you can be vindicated and tell your friends and kids "that asshole stole money from me, but I have the best lawyer in the world because he found it." Yes, he did find it. But it took him 3 years and $200,000 to do it. And your life was on hold for three years and you took money out of your 401(k) or borrowed from your parents or spent your entire paycheck and maxed out your credit cards to accuse your husband of fraud, when you could have done this in less than a year for $30,000 if you had just offered to split it when you found it.

Just remember what I say right now when you are at your maddest. The only person who benefits when you get mad during your divorce is your lawyer. If you must get mad then get mad at the walls, at your therapist, at the ocean; build a massive bonfire and throw old photos in it (not of the children); take the $30,000 you'd have spent on lawyer's fees and buy a Harley-Davidson and even if you can't ride, learn how to start it up and rev the living shit out of it; take a kickboxing class and wail on the heavy bag; go on tinder and fuck the first 7 people who will fuck you (safely please and with full consent: #yesmeansyes for fuck's sake). But do anything but let your lawyer talk you into spending $200,000 trying to prove that your husband defrauded you. Find the asset and ask to divide it. Send the bill for the cost of division.

That's all fine and good in 99.75% of cases. There are the occasional cases where there really is pervasive fraud and there are millions of dollars worth of it. The above advice is relative. You should go after it, but you should still engage in a cost-benefit analysis when you do it. You should still analyze your WCATNA and BCATNA. You should still ask what your chances of winning the motion are and what the cost will be. You should still make your lawyer explain to you what she is filing and why. Even pervasive fraud may not be worth the effort if it will take weeks of trial time and countless experts to prove at trial and delays you moving on with your life for years as breach of fiduciary duty cases often do.

Do not get caught in the "he's going to get away with it" trap. Men who steal from their wives are usually unabashedly self-absorbed (I refuse to use the word "narcissist" because of overuse and underspecification, but you know what I mean). They will fight you forever. It is a game to them. They will always "get away with" things. The best you can do is get free of them. Do not walk away from your life's fortune. If it's the only asset or some other case-specific fact, then you must stand in there and fight. But generally speaking, you find the diverted asset, offer to divide it in half, and send the bill for locating and dividing it.

Fiduciary Duty Parting Shots

I do not mean to understate the value of fiduciary duties. We do owe our spouses the duties of loyalty and the highest good faith. We have trusting and confidential relationships with them. Only complete jerks use their position of trust and confidence to steal or hide money from the person who trusts them. The law provides specific punishments for people who do this, and Dante has a level of Hell for them to reside in forever after.

But, I am concerned about *you*. I am concerned about *you* not spending foolish money to chase after the dream of having the judge pronounce that your ex-husband is an evil bastard deserving of an even worse level of Hell than Dante would have placed him. Getting judges to say things like this is damned near impossible. In a recent case, tangentially related to my own (I was not involved but the Husband in that case was my client's new boyfriend), the Judge said of the Husband, very simply "He is living in his own reality; a reality unrecognizable to the court." For that, Husband's ex-Wife probably paid $100,000 in fees. Well, her parents paid it. I am certain it felt vindicating to read that. But…uhm….that's IT!?!? $100,000 for one sentence in a judicial finding.

Breaches of fiduciary duty are worth pursuing for the sake of recovering the asset. But, you will read the fantastical outlier case of *Marriage of Rossi*, no doubt in your late-night internet crawling. I've already mentioned it. To recap: Wife won $1,336,000 in the lottery before the date of separation. She deliberately did not tell Husband. She filed for divorce and had the checks sent to her parents' home. The Court found that she fraudulently concealed the lottery winnings and awarded 100% of the winnings to Husband.

This case is just tantalizing enough for any would be litigant to think that courts routinely find fraud and award 100% of the asset. Plenty of inexperienced and experienced lawyers alike will read *Rossi* and convince you that if all she did was hide the money and he got 100% of it, surely what happened in your own case is way worse. I am here to say that it is exceedingly rare for judges to find fraud and order 100% of the asset. Much more likely, on a scale that is orders of magnitude more likely, is that the court will divide the asset in half and order payment of some attorney's fees. If you find a hidden asset, offer to divide it and send the bill for finding and dividing it.

Family Code 1101(g) requires that the Court making a finding of breach of fiduciary duty divide the asset in equally and order attorney's fees. Family Code 1101 (h) requires that, if the Court finds "oppression, fraud or malice" in the breach of fiduciary duty, it award 100% of the hidden asset. Courts are just loathe to find a real breach of fiduciary duty in the first place. They don't like it because it sounds like "fault" and "punishment" and the family court is a court of "equity" and "fairness" and is not a place for "winners" and "losers." We see this throughout the Family Code. Judges don't like punishing family law litigants. I have never been to judge school, but I have heard from judges who have been to judge school that they are taught not to punish family law litigants unless they absolutely must.

You may have a family law judge get upset, sometimes pushing back on litigants who have their hair constantly on fire or overzealous family law attorneys screaming at each other in the courtroom (or more probably in the hallway). They may even make admonitions about following their orders or over-litigating the case, but rarely do judges punish litigants and even more rarely do they make an unflattering pronouncement about them. "He is living in his own reality; a reality unrecognizable to the court." $100,000. That is two years of tuition at Stanford. For one f*cking sentence.

In a recent case that took 14 years for resolution, both sides asked for more than $300,000 in attorney's fees. Both sides behaved like jerks; that's why the case took 14 years. Each blamed the other. There were some, but not substantial assets. $300,000 was more than either of them had. Both lawyers took "haircuts" on their fees (they were angry at each other, and it showed). At the fee hearing, when the entire thing was over, the judge said: "Both sides behaved badly, Wife worse than Husband, but not enough worse to justify me making a big fee award as a sanction. The truth is I thought they were both liars and I thought they both created their own mess. They deserved each other." Then, the judge did not award *any* attorneys fees. Well, I represented Wife's parents and we weren't getting any fees (yes, Husband sued Wife's elderly parents, one of whom died during the litigation), but I told Wife and both lawyers that there was no way the judge was going to award fees. Wife did not like that. She persisted in spending another $25,000 on her attorney to try to get the fees. Husband did the same. Both lost and, honestly, the judge excoriated them both.

You have heard why I think going down the rabbit hole in pursuit of a judicial finding of breach of fiduciary duty is a sucker bet that, if you have even the most reasonable nest egg, some lawyer will be destined to pursue. If you have an asset that you have hidden (nefariously or not), disclose it and offer to divide it pursuant to the Three Property Rules that I talk about in great detail throughout this book. If you think it is your separate property, disclose it and say so. If it has a mixed character – part separate, part community – it will come out. I am not saying you won't have to work to prove the community and separate property interest, but I am saying get it divided quickly and save yourself fees and aggravation and time and being called lots of names by a lawyer on the other side trying to make a cool $100,000 by enflaming your ex. You will have to read declarations that say you are a thief and a liar and a mastermind and a crook. And no matter how stolid your resolve, they will hurt.

If you overlooked something or got caught trying to hide something, apologize and disclose it and get on to the business of dividing it. And if you are on the other side, hear me well please, I did not say "walk away from the asset." I said offer to divide the asset in half and send the attorneys' bill for finding and dividing it. Walk away from trying to get the judge to proclaim that your spouse is a fraudster, liar or thief. Chances of that happening are so minute and the pleasure of hearing it when you are exhausted and broke and anxiety prone and filled with rage will almost never make the pursuit worth the cost. The only time is when your ex simply refuses to divide the asset and continues to engage in fraud, oppression or malice and you have no choice.

This is the end of Part II of this book wherein I have tried to provide a mid-level overview of Family Law concepts with tips and techniques. The next section drops down another level and finds us in the weeds. These are California-centric rules, but I believe, as I have said earlier, that these rules apply more generally and often whole cloth in other states. Fundamentally the rules focus on the push and pull of the law in specific areas. Part III covers child and spousal support, child custody, and property division. None of the chapters attempts to be exhaustive in its coverage of the law. What I am trying to do is teach you how to think about the law. To understand that your support will increase as your taxes decrease; that dividing property follows fundamental concepts that can be applied broadly depending on the circumstances and that the Rule of Reasonability applies in almost every context.

PART III

The View From the Weeds (Trudging through the Dust)

CHAPTER 12

Child Custody and Visitation

UNFORTUNATELY, USUALLY THE most important part of the divorce (at least from an emotional standpoint) is, in many ways, a wild west that follows no rules. That is child custody and visitation.

Custody is divided into two types: Legal and Physical. In some ways these names are oddities peculiar to Family Law, with some people feeling they are meaningless designations and others feeling they have real value. I probably lean toward meaningless designations with my focus being placed on "timeshare" or "visitation."

Legal Custody

Legal custody is the right to share in decision-making about important issues: education, religion, and health care. However, there are other issues that people consider important: extracurricular activities and bedtimes, how much TV to watch versus how many chores to do, etc. It only takes the smallest examination to realize something important: if the two deciders (parents) could agree on every type of important thing, chances are they would not be in divorce court. Jews and Catholics get married all the time. When they get divorced, besides the shared feelings of guilt, they do not have much in common. Does the child go to Temple on Fridays and Mass on Sundays? Bar Mitzvah at 13 and

Confirmation at 14? Do they just live the *Life of Pi*?

Religion and custody is an area of the family law that I think is dead wrong. Basically, the Courts have said "we won't abridge a parent's right to raise children in the religion of their choice. Unless it's detrimental to the child." Proving detriment is next to impossible. So impossible that you might give it a shot, but you will lose.

I had the following exchange with a Judge recently. My client and his now ex-wife were evangelical Christians together. My client, Husband, was the kind of handsome that most of us can only dream of (pun: it was his cross to bear). To top it off, he was a fire captain who taught CrossFit on his days off. I kid you not—handsome, studly, brave, and one of the nicest, best guys I've ever met in my business to boot. Anyway, he had an affair. I've stopped judging affairs. I would not like it if it happened to me, but when people come to me—the cheaters and the cheated on—I can almost always recognize that people have their reasons for the things they do, and often it takes two to tango. California is a "no-fault" state, so his affair was irrelevant to the divorce proceedings; however, it was relevant to the Evangelical Church they attended, so he left the Church (probably under a hail of threats of excommunication) and his wife stayed in the Church. Wife then started taking the kids to church 4 times per week. She also took the kids to a Christian counselor who told them that their dad was being possessed by evil and that "they should pray" that he would come around before he died and went straight to Hell. I brought this up to the Judge. The exchange went like this:

> **Me: "Your Honor, let me be blunt about it. Say that Wife tells the kids 'your dad doesn't go to church, so he is going to Hell.' Would you consider that derogatory language and alienation?"**

Judge: "That is derogatory, and I would tell the Wife she could not do that."

Me: "OK, how about this? Wife tells the kids, 'People who don't go to church go to Hell.' The kids respond, 'Daddy doesn't go to church. I hope he's not going to Hell.' Is that derogatory?"

Judge: "No, that's not derogatory. Look I'm not here to sit on the bench and tell someone what they can believe. They have a First Amendment right to believe as they do."

Me: "So the fundamentalists win? In other words, if she is more fervent than he is, doesn't she win the long-term battle with the kids? Isn't that spiritual abuse?"

Judge: "It's her First Amendment right."

I do not believe that it is her First Amendment right to indoctrinate her kids into her religion at the expense of the Father who does not have the same degree of what my old friend who is a minister in Berkeley used to call "Hell-ology."

In another scenario, a child who needs immediate medical attention always gets it, regardless of the joint legal custody designation. A child who needs long-term care always gets that too. I had a Jehovah's Witness blood transfusion case that required Child Welfare Services to get a juvenile court order every time the child needed a transfusion because the religion did not allow for the parents to make that decision. The parents were devout.

> "Jehovah's Witnesses believe that a human must not sustain his life with another creature's blood, and they recognize no distinction "between taking blood into the mouth and taking it into the blood vessels. It is their deep-seated

religious conviction that Jehovah will turn his back on anyone who receives blood transfusions. Thus, Jehovah's Witnesses regularly refuse transfusions for themselves and their children because they believe the procedure creates a risk of losing eternal salvation. Legally, such refusals are based on the constitutional grounds that the transfusion is an invasion of the right of privacy and a violation of the individual's freedom of religious practice." (Thompson HA. Blood transfusions and Jehovah's Witnesses. Tex Med. 1989 Apr;85(4):57-9. PMID: 2727941.)

Ultimately, medical decisions are shared decisions (or decisions not made at all). The Court can step in. These parents, like all parents, wanted their daughter to live, but they were forbidden from making the decision to allow blood transfusions for their daughter. The Court understood this. The Church also understood this. So, a guardian was appointed for the child regarding transfusions, and each time she needed a transfusion, because Jehovah's Witnesses recognize the power of the Courts to make orders, the guardian would ask the Court to order a transfusion and the Court obliged. Also, neither the parents nor the Church objected.

Education has some degree of cooperation needed, but a parent can always block parochial education (but not religion—go figure). Generally speaking, joint legal custody means both parents are on the child's emergency card. That is important, but it is mainly emotionally important and not critical to the child's upbringing. I tell my clients that if there is a disagreement, the tie-breaking vote goes to the parent with more physical custody (or the parent in whose custody the child is at the time the decision is made) – this is truly a rule of thumb and not an actual rule, but when one parent avoids or stymies the other by not responding to messages or making decisions, the parent with more custodial timeshare will likely be the one to make the decision. Many men, in particular, try to use joint legal custody as a weapon of control – they insist on their say but then they don't say anything. The Courts increasingly recognize this type of control. I tell my clients to write messages and document time to response – putting things in writing helps document the non-responsiveness of the other parent or the elements of control. I have a case now where the Father refuses orthodontic treatment, well, he does not refuse it, he refuses to discuss it. The Mother will probably be allowed to move from California to Hawaii with the children because the court has caught on that his behavior around the orthodontia is a symptom of his larger behavior patterns.

Please communicate about your children.

Almost every judge in the state awards joint legal custody as a matter of course. It is only in cases of drug or physical abuse, domestic violence (where a criminal conviction creates a presumption against joint custody) mental illness, or prison time when joint legal custody will be taken away from the get-go. But, if you are a real jerk, you can lose it.

Physical Custody

Physical custody—*Kramer v. Kramer* style—is where the day-to-day action occurs in family court. California Family Code 3020 states that it is the public policy of the State of California that each parent should have "frequent and continuing contact with both parents." This is vague and very difficult to spell out in any practical sense.

In the old "Dad plan," "frequent and continuing contact" meant alternate weekends from Friday after school to Sunday at 6 pm, and every Wednesday for dinner. That is a 20% timeshare for child support purposes. It's a new world today with dads who not only wear Baby Bjorns around Target, but who also stay at home (*Mr.*

Mom). Dads are getting much more custody, but it is still a highly discretionary area of the law. And discretion means that Judges have almost unlimited power. This is a crucial issue. In fact, for many people it is the reason you bought this book. So here is an in-depth explanation.

The Family Code is designed to disrupt children's lives as little as possible, so the "primary caregiver" is given preference for the majority of the timeshare. Tying it to "reasonability" for a moment, the law presumes it is reasonable to have continuity of care for the children. The parent who does most of the caregiving is considered the primary caregiver, so the Court attempts to continue giving the primary caregiver most of the custodial time.

It is sometimes difficult to determine who the primary caregiver is. I have had hearings in which the line of questioning went like this:

"Who is the child's doctor?

Who is the child's teacher?

Who is the child's best friend?

Who is the child's dentist?

Who is the child's day care provider?

Who is the child's favorite TV character?

Although the child does both gymnastic and dance, which one is her favorite?

How many times has Mother/Father taken the child to the doctor without you?

How many play dates have you set up?"

My blood pressure soars even writing this. The primary focus of parenting is creating love in the family and raising strong, well-educated, well-adjusted kids. Or at least that is what I think it is. The above questions are throwaway questions meant to insinuate that one parent is more involved in the kids' lives. Typically, one parent tends to dominate these things and the other steps back. It doesn't mean they are less of a "primary caregiver." Indeed, it is entirely common (in fact way more common than not) that one parent has permitted the dominating parent control these types of activities because either they have much more investment in certain areas of the children's lives (medical in particular) or because the dominating parent is so dominant that pushing back comes with a lot of pain.

Moms, who are more likely to baby their kids, will take them to the doctor for every sniffle; Dads, who are more likely to want their kids to toughen up and get used to suffering a few bruises and scratches, will pump the kids full of Dayquil and send them to school. No judgment here. I represent moms and dads and I see value (or anti-value) in each position. Both are probably right. Both are probably wrong. There is a reason all our children are going to spend 10 years on a therapist's couch in their 30s. At least we all agree now that beating kids is bad—except some judges (one of ours) who seemingly believe in the old Rule of Thumb: so long as the switch isn't thicker than your thumb it is OK. Back to the religious issues, some religions believe that a father has the right to beat his child—or his wife—if she doesn't behave and some judges (fewer now than 20 years ago, agree). And you shouldn't co-sleep with your child either (once you are in a divorce situation) because it gives the other parent fodder for all sorts of disgusting and untrue claims. Don't do it. And make an agreement that your spouse won't do it either.

In the modern two-income family, a typical dynamic is like the following:

Mom rushes off to work at 6:45 AM to her job. Dad packs lunches and gets the kids to school at 8:30 AM, having worked things out with his boss that he will work until 6 PM and not take a lunch so that he can make sure the kids get dropped off at the elementary and middle schools. Mom gets off at 3:30 PM and picks everyone up from school, makes them a snack, runs through homework, gets their soccer cleats and tutus on, and rushes them to two different practices. (Some people go back for a second shift or flip open their computer after the kids go to bed, like I did most of my daughter's young life.) Dad, leaving work at 5:53 PM, arrives at dance rehearsal just in time to pick up Daughter 1, and then grabs a rotisserie chicken at Costco (or a large pizza) for dinner, while Mom hurries to soccer to pick up Daughter 2. Both are too exhausted to cook anything fancy, so the kids shower and finish homework while one parent warms up something simple to go with the chicken or the pizza. Out of a last feeling of guilt, the parent will throw some "greens" in a bowl (for something healthy) with a bottle of ranch dressing nearby. A quick dinner. An hour of TV. And the kids are off to bed.

Who is the primary caregiver in that situation?

Both parents think they are the primary caregiver. Wait, let me check that. Mom and Dad both think *Mom* is the primary caregiver, a view that I think is sexist and demeaning to women and patronizing to men. The short explanation is that it essentializes women into being child caregivers who should raise their kids first and put their jobs second. It also demeans dads into unimportant afterthoughts.

Still, even dads with 50-50 custody still refer to mom's house as "Home"—as in "I take the kids home on Fridays"—and Dad's house as "my house." The sexism is endemic, and it lives in parents of both sexes. My view is that we are only going to get real equality when women and men share child rearing responsibilities equally, and both learn that although children are an absolute joy, both parents need alone time to date, to work, to take care of themselves, and to have time off. Many of my half-time parents admit to me later that they are much better parents on a 50-50 schedule. I know that I certainly am. And I do not believe, in a very general sense, that the 80-20 plan works for anyone (moms, dads or kids). In fact, I am convinced that 80-20 plans lead to harried moms who have severe difficulty getting their financial, emotional and relationship lives on track, although they may have great relationships with the children who are going to leave them in just a few short years, and to alienated and distant dads, who find new partners, end up much stronger financially and feel the burning pain of having deteriorating relationships with their children. For kids, the 80-20 plan leads to a lot of questions, anger at Dad, and ultimately, often, anger at Mom.

I hold dads to a very high standard as a father because I am a devoted dad. I tell them that if they want more time to spend with their kids, I will fight until my last breath to get it for them, but if they want more time with their kids just so they can reduce their child support payment, then I have a Rolodex full of my competitors' business cards that I can give them. I have no patience for people who don't pay child support.

I do believe however in an analogizing to something Mitt Romney said while running for President. When asked about his taxes he said, "I believe we should pay all of the taxes we owe. And not a penny more." I believe that is true about child and spousal support as well, except with the following caveat: the payor spouse should recognize the importance of creating stability for the payee spouse. If the high-earning Father does not pay adequate support to the lower earning Mother (for example), she will figure out how to get stable. Usually that's when she moves a boyfriend in that you (and maybe the kids) hate, who thinks he gets a say in how to raise your kids because, after all, *he's supporting them.* Or your ex files a motion to move in with her parents in Stockton, 4 hours away.

Child support is decided based on two main factors (although there are many smaller input variables): the amount of time the children spend with each parent, and the difference in income. When people realize this, child custody battles become proxy battles over support. Judges hate support battles, so savvy lawyers make the fight over custody and then say, "Judge, now that we have done this, I suppose we should modify support as well." Or they simply file a second motion for support modification when the timeshare changes. Like it or not those are the tactics. No one wants to be perceived as asking for more time to pay less support.

•••••••••••••••••• PRO TIP ••••••••••••••••••

File your motion to modify custody and visitation without moving to modify support. If you get your custody modification, then go modify support afterward. Much more on this in the next chapters.

••

The law goes through various movements regarding physical custody, normally based on perceived shifts in the psychological literature regarding what is best for children regarding living in one home or two versus having lots of contact with one parent or half time with each parent. When I started family law in 2008, it was an uphill battle to get a 50-50 order for physical custody or visitation, but now it is pretty standard across courtrooms.

Schedules

There are many ways to do schedules and to calculate timeshare. The easiest is the alternating weeks schedule, ideally where parents exchange through school on Fridays. Mom drops off on Friday and Dad picks up on Friday. That really means two sets of everything – one for each home. Some parents get nitpicky about the clothes the kids wear, so, if that is the case, the kids go to school on Friday with whatever they were wearing the previous Friday (ideally washed and cleaned). This is a good way to make sure Mom gets those fancy jeans back from Dad. I do not prefer this type of nitpickiness. With my own child, we just agreed that anything they owned was theirs and could be wherever. It did get annoying to me sometimes that everything would end up at Mom's house, including shoes and dolls and jackets and umbrellas and lunch boxes. But every now and then, we would just gather a bunch of things up from Mom's house and I'd pick them up and we would start the process of slowly moving everything back over to Mom's house over the next few months. It only ever got annoying when I would say "Hey kiddo, let's go for a walk" and my kiddo would say "I would, but all my shoes are at Mom's and all I have is this pair of sandals."

If you are going to do a 50-50 schedule, you need one of everything at each house. That doesn't mean the exact same things – like the same blue jacket – but it does mean a jacket at each house. There should be toothbrushes and facewash and hair dryers and make up (for teens) and a bed and complete bedding, school clothes and pajamas. Each house should be completely set up for your kids to come to your house and have it function perfectly. If you have to take your older kids shopping to make sure they have everything in their bathroom they need, then do it. Sports uniforms are tougher because they are often only issued one uniform, so it is worth it to make sure you develop a system. Cleats, shin guards, baseball gloves, hats, volleyball knee pads, the clarinet or tuba, or amplifiers or horseback riding tack, or anything else your kids need, either needs duplicating or you need a good system for transporting the items back and forth, otherwise you will be doing a fair amount of driving to the other parent's house to retrieve items. Schoolbooks are more and more online, but there will be days when you find yourself driving to the other parent's home after dinner on a school night because the homework is over there.

This is much simpler on different versions of the alternating weeks schedule that remain 50-50. I use overnights as a rule of thumb for counting the days with the kids. Therefore, timeshare operates on a 14-day schedule because we frequently have a Week 1 and a Week 2 schedule. Utilizing a 14-day schedule gives us a clear way to understand timeshare.

Classic "live nearby" schedules look like this:

1. **The Old Dad Plan:** Every other weekend from Friday after school until Sunday at 6 PM with a Wednesday dinner visit (after school until an hour before bedtime). That is 2 overnights out of 14 with another 6 hours. If you add in half of all holidays and holiday breaks, that is usually described as 20% timeshare.
2. **The Extended Dad Plan:** Every other weekend from Friday pickup at school until Monday morning drop-off at school plus Wednesday dinners and half of all holidays and alternating weeks during the summer. This is 3 nights out of 14 plus a little bit of extra time. I call this about a 28% timeshare.
3. **Extended Weekends with Wednesday overnight.** This is the Friday to Monday alternate weekend plan with Wednesday visits being pickup at school Wednesday and return to school Thursday. This is 5 nights out of 14 and is about 36% timeshare. This is the first schedule that is within the Range of Normal Outcomes and it is a great step back from 50-50 for very recalcitrant mothers. Mom may not want to go to 50-50, but this is a baby step toward it, and as one who has had both this schedule and a true 50-50 schedule, there is no discernible difference between having an extra night each week for homework and school drop-off.
4. There aren't many plans that are 4 or 6 nights out of 14. This would be asymmetrical weeks. It happens when a

parent does Wednesday overnight and every other weekend from Friday to Sunday so that the kids can get ready for school at one house or the other on Sunday nights or where on the "off week" Wednesday is an overnight and on the "on week: (defined by the weekend), Wednesday is a dinner visit. You also see it with certain shift worker schedules where it makes sense for the kids to spend 6 nights with one parent because the other parent starts the work week with a graveyard or swing shift. In any event, neither schedule is very common.

5. The 50-50 schedules run a gamut from 2-2-3 to 2-2-5 to 7-7.
    a. **2-2-5 Schedule.** The very best schedule, in my opinion, is the 2-2-5 schedule. Mom has Mondays and Tuesdays. Dad has Wednesdays and Thursdays. The parties alternate weekends from Friday to Monday. That means that one week, Mom has the kids from Friday after school until Wednesday morning and the next week Dad has them from Wednesday morning until Monday morning. But the kids get used to the idea that if it is Monday, "it's Mom's day" and if it is Wednesday, "it's Dad's day." This is also an "every other weekend schedule," which makes planning easier. This one is harder to conceptualize in your mind's eye than it is on paper. It's actually a really simple schedule.
    b. **2-2-3 Schedule.** This one is better for younger kids on a 50-50, so that they do not go even 5 days without seeing each parent. But it requires a good deal of concentration by both parents = on a two-week schedule. Week One: Mom has Monday and Tuesday, Dad has Wednesday and Thursday, Mom has Friday through Monday, Week Two:

Dad has Monday and Tuesday, Mom has Wednesday and Thursday and Dad has Friday through Monday. No one can really remember the days very well. The kids don't think about the "if it's Monday it's Mom's day and if it's Wednesday it's Dad's day" because it rotates. This requires a lot of calendar checking. Calendar checking leads to confusion. Confusion leads to arguments. Arguments lead to court dates.

c. **7-7.** In some ways this is the easiest schedule of all. You just exchange the kids through school on an alternating weeks basis. It's just that it is a long time in between seeing your kids and them seeing you. Some parents modify the 7-7 schedule with a Wednesday overnight (or dinner) visit for the other parent during that week.

d. **In general.** With any of these schedules there is a balance between "calendar checking" (like the 2-2-3) and "coordinating children's items" – this means, the more back and forth, the less dire it is that the child forgot something at the other parent's home, because they can always get it tomorrow. On the other hand, this can mean a lot of checking the calendar and planning ahead for your days. The flip side is the 7-7 schedule where you really have to be good about ensuring the children have the things they need because otherwise there will be a lot of back and forth to pick things up. 2-2-5 is my favorite schedule for these reasons as well – it balances the ease of managing children's property with calendar checking (you always know that Mondays and Tuesday are Mom's days and Wednesdays and Thursdays are Dad's days).

Move Away Requests

Some judges have said that "move-away requests" are the very worst decisions they have to make. A "move-away" is when one parent wants to move with the children to another town. Usually, depending on where you live, you can make a 30-minute or maybe even an hour-long commute work for regular timeshare, but an hour is getting to be a bit long to get the children to school every day. It may be that if you live in Encino and Mom wants to move to Woodland Hills, a distance of only 7.3 miles, you may add an additional 30 minutes to the commute at peak commute times. Where I live, the distance from Nipomo to Santa Maria is more than 7 miles but at freeway speed, they are about a minute per mile apart. The question about whether something is a "move-away" or not may be a factual one based on particular circumstances.

There is an important move-away case that described a 40-minute move as a move-away because the children would attend different schools, making it very difficult for the non-moving parent to get them to school each day, even though children living in rural areas might take a bus for an hour each way to school.

I put the Move Away section after the custodial timeshare or physical custody section because of the importance of physical custody in making move-away determinations. In California, a parent with Physical Custody of a minor child has a presumptive, statutory right to move with the child. See, Fam. Code, § 7501, subd. (a); *In re Marriage of LaMusga* (2004) 32 Cal.4th 1072, 1078.) (*LaMusga*, pronounced La Mu-SHAY). Where parents have joint custody, custody may be modified if in the child's best interests. (§ 3087; *In re Marriage of Burgess* (1996) 13 Cal.4th 25, 40, fn. 12 (Burgess).

Determining whether a parent has sole or joint physical custody can depend on the parties' actual practice. In one case, for example, where the father saw his son as frequently as four or five days a week (notwithstanding the formal arrangement), the court said that the parties had joint physical custody. (*Brody v. Kroll* (1996) 45 Cal.App.4th 1732, 1735-1736.) In the *LaMusga* case, the mother had primary physical custody and the father had visitation for a few hours two nights per week and overnight visits every other weekend. The court treated this arrangement as mother having sole physical custody.

In other words, the way you designate custody as Sole Physical or Joint Physical custody probably does not matter in the move-away context. What matters more is the actual practice of the parties. In *Brody v. Knoll* Father had the child overnight on Tuesdays and Fridays and all day on every Saturday. Timeshare percentage was about 3 days out of 7 (even if it did not include Saturday overnights). This looks like about 35%-42% depending on how you count hours (168 hours in a week, Father gets "credit" for when the child is in school on his days, it's close but something like 2.75-3 days per week and that is why I use a 35%-42% range).

In cases where there is clearly one parent who has physical custody (regardless of designation), they have the presumptive right to move away with the child. Recall an example I gave earlier in the book about the Google executive divorcing the Amazon executive in the Silicon Valley. Father (Google) and Mother (Amazon), initially agreed that the child should "sleep in his own bed" every night at Mother's home. Father would see him every day after preschool for a few hours. Father felt he was doing the right thing by the minor child by having him keep all of his routines tied to the place they had lived together in his first few years of life. However, as I pointed out to Father, this would give him between 15 and 20 hours out of 168 hours of parenting time per week or between 8% and 11% custodial time. While we are not told by the law what timeshare percentage counts as true "joint physical custody," we know that the "every other weekend with one or two dinner visits per week" plans (20-ish%) are not joint custodial time (*LaMusga* and *Burgess*) and we know that the every Tuesday and Friday overnight plus all day on Saturday (what I am calling between 35% and 42% timeshare) is true joint physical custody.

In other words, the Google dad was, by making this agreement, allowing the Amazon mom to move to Seattle as soon as her employer snapped its fingers and asked her to move, and there would be almost nothing he could do to stop her because she would have a "presumptive right to move" based on her having *de facto* sole physical custody of the minor child. By doing the "right thing" in his mind for the minor child, he was doing exactly the wrong thing for himself if he wanted to keep the Amazon mom from moving to Seattle later on (and perhaps, the wrong thing for the child).

Move away law is highly detailed and precise and more than this book can cover in a short chapter on child custody, but there are some lessons to be taken away from the case law that you should think about in the context of making custody agreements.

1. Most judges are 50-50 judges in most counties. That is not to say all judges are 50-50 judges and some counties are more conservative about child rearing than others. The old "tender years" doctrine (that said, "kids under 5 should be with their mothers" has been dead for 50 years, but that does not mean I do not practice in front of an old judge who still says things like "well, the child is of tender years…." If you take your case to court and ask a judge to decide on custody and you are a dad, you are likely to do better than you would do if you make an agreement with the child's mother extolling you to "do what's in the children's best interests." You may find yourself like Goo-

gle Dad, being convinced that the child should "sleep in his own bed" every night and put yourself in an 8%-11% timeshare bind in one of the most liberal jurisdictions in the state where 50-50 timeshare is the norm.

2. The parent who has 70% (or so) timeshare, has a presumptive right to move away with the child. You can still stop such a move away but it is really hard and really expensive. You have to show that there would be detriment to the child in moving away, and that showing cannot just be that it would be hurtful or harmful to the child that they do not get to see you regularly. This is why it is so important to get yourself to at least a 36% timeshare (5 overnights out of 14) from the very beginning. This is also why I say, if you only have enough money for a lawyer to complete part of your case, spend the money at the beginning of the case. The judge will make temporary child custody orders at the beginning of your case and those orders will almost assuredly look like permanent orders later in the case (except where the children are very young or where you ask for changes in the orders as the children get older).

3. Proving "detriment" to stop a move away is a very bad position to be in, just as it is near impossible in the context of religion. The Amazon Mom was not necessarily going to get a job transfer to Seattle (although she did two years later) and your ex-spouse may not even be contemplating a move away when you separate. But, you put yourself in the best position to defend against a move away if you lock down something like 5 nights out of 14 and I would prefer it if you had 6 nights out of 14 (or better yet 7 out of 14) to ensure against a move.

4. Even if you have true joint physical custody (35%-50% ish), you can still lose a move-away request. At that point, the moving party who wants to take the children with them, can still move with the children by proving to the Court that it is in the children's "best interests."

I was involved in a case in 2021 that went on appeal and the Appellate Court made one of the worst decisions I have ever been a part of in affirming the trial court's decision to allow the minor child to move to St. Louis, MO with her mother. The case had actually been in the trial court for four years before the court granted the final move away request. *Ramsden v. Peterson*, 76 Cal.App.5th 339 (Cal. Ct. App. 2022). I had been Tyson Ramsden's counsel from the first time the child's mother had sought to move away to another state with a then-boyfriend. She left town for about 3 months, leaving the minor child with her father. Then, she came back into town, picked the child up from school and took the child to another state where the boyfriend was. She sent Tyson a text and said "it's in the minor child's best interest that she move out of that shithole of a town [Lompoc, CA]."

We filed a motion to bring the child back. The trial court granted that motion and after a full trial on the issue of her moving away, the Court denied her request, but allowed her to keep joint physical custody on a 50-50 basis if she did not move.

Then, about 12 months later, she filed another motion to move away, this time with a new husband (different than the first boyfriend). We had a fully litigated multi-day trial and the Court, again, denied her request to move away with the minor child and again stated that she could keep her 50-50 timeshare if she did not move. She did not move.

Then, about 3 years after that, the little girl reported to her mother that her father had been drinking beer at a BBQ on a Sunday and drove her home. He bumped a curb. He then got into an argument with his girlfriend while the little girl was present. She texted her mother to come pick her up and her mother did come pick her up. There was no violence and no proof that the father had been drunk when he drove her home. He admitted that he had had some beer while BBQing at the party. Mother filed an emergency motion to change custody of the minor child despite 9 years of stable 50-50 parenting.

The Court granted the motion on a temporary basis and gave father a 20% timeshare schedule. I objected and stated that the court could not change custody without a hearing. The Court disagreed. Then the Court appointed a lawyer for the child. That lawyer said that she would support a move away, even though the mother had not requested a move away. So, the Court permitted a third move away trial to occur. At that hearing, because the mother still had 50-50 custody of the minor child, the Court determined that it would be in the child's best interests to move away with her mother.

We appealed and the Appellate Court affirmed, stating that the test for whether a parent could move away with a true joint custody schedule was whether it was in the children's best interests, even though the Court had already twice found that it was not in the child's best interests to move away. Now *Ramsden v. Peterson* is the law of the land. I think it was a bad decision and it has had statewide implications for Minor's Counsel (Family Code 3150-3151) who are empowered to make recommendations on custody (when they/we – because I do 3150 counsel appointments as well) are not qualified as custody experts to make such recommendations. This is an area of the law that has considerable confusion.

That being said, we understand that if you have less than 35% timeshare, you likely cannot prevent a request to relocate, as you must demonstrate detriment to the minor child, and you cannot use the detriment from the child not seeing you as the basis to stop the move. If you have over 35% timeshare, the inquiry shifts to whether it is in the child's best interests to remain or to move. This standard is quite different from proving detriment. In a "best interests" assessment, you might argue that the child has connections to family, friends, school, sports, church, etc., and that removing the child from those connections would be more harmful than remaining in place. You would also assert that you have been a joint physical custodian of the child and that there is no indication of primary parenting – that neither you nor the other parent can claim to be the one the child most heavily depends on.

Vacations and Holidays

There are standard vacation and holiday schedules that should be relatively easy to figure out. Most jurisdictions have a form that states what normal holiday and vacation calendars look like.

Generally, Mom gets Thanksgiving Week in Odd years and Dad gets it in even years. Winter Break is divided in half with Dad getting the first half including Christmas in Odd years and Mom getting it in even years. Spring Break goes with Thanksgiving Break. And then summers are split on a 7-7 schedule, each side getting a little longer for a noticed vacation. You can add in a notice provision that Mom gets first choice in odd years, as long as she notifies the other parent by May 1, and Dad gets first choice in even years so long as he notifies the other parent by May 1.

Mother's Day and Father's Day to the Mother or Father. Parents' birthdays with the children. Children's birthdays on the day they fall. I don't give a rip about Halloween, but some people care about it so alternate the holidays you care about. This is easy and standard stuff. Don't spend a lot of time arguing about it.

A personal note: my child's mom is a schoolteacher and I am a practicing trial lawyer. The schoolteacher gets summers off; so does our child. I do not. So, even though a 7-7 schedule would make sense for most parents in the summers, we do not follow that because she's off work and I am not. But we do share more liberally in the summer so that when I can get a real vacation our child can go with me. Last year I turned 50 and my child was in Europe with their mom, by agreement. Things happen. We just work with it.

The more you can work with things the better. Holidays and vacations do not have to be difficult. People make them difficult because they are fraught, emotional times. Learn to celebrate Thanksgiving on Friday with prime rib if you live near enough by to have second Thanksgiving meal with your children or have Christmas morning on December 26th, or an Easter egg hunt on Saturday if these things matter to you. After a couple of years, it gets much easier.

Fighting Custody Battles in Court

There are some very basic rules to custody battles that I will go over here and then leave the nitty gritty to later work.

1. **Say more things about what you have to offer than what the other parent does not offer.** The custody battle should be about how good you are and not how bad the other parent is. Focus on your strengths, what you have to offer, how involved your parents are, how involved you are in school and extracurriculars, the things you do with your kids and what they love about you and you love about them.
2. **Compliment the other parent on their parenting and aim for 50-50 unless there are drugs, crimes, violence or mental health issues in the other parent (or in yourself and you**

know it). Let the court know that you are not going to be one of those parents who tries to withhold the children from the other parent or alienate the other parent. Your focus is on you. If you have to say something about the other parent, say something nice. Remember my example declaration above:

"I really appreciate the way that Dad is making strides to reduce his alcohol use and be more involved with the kids. I see marked improvement in him and I know he can be a good father to the boys when he is sober. I would ask that the Court go slowly with his newfound sobriety and keep a watch on him. I propose that the children spend the rest of this school year with me during the week and every other weekend and he have weekends and mid-week visits, and that we check in at the beginning of the summer to see how he is doing. If he keeps his sobriety, then I would be willing to move to alternate weeks visitation."

3. **Be respectful to the Court above all else.** If you are a jerk in Court, but tell the judge that you are such a great parent, they will believe the person they see in court and not the one you have written about on paper. Be your best self.

4. **Write yourself a letter of recommendation, but avoid pure self-aggrandizement.** It's a balance. Be your authentic self, but also put yourself in your best realistic light. If you have a Berkeley PhD say so. If you have a job where you work long hours, say so, but say "I have talked to my boss and I can work from home in the afternoons to pick the kids up on my days." Or, "my mom, the kids' grandma is very involved in the children's lives. She only lives a few minutes away and will do the afterschool care until I get

home from work."

5. **Stay strong.** Your children are better off with you in their lives somewhere between 36% and 64% of the time. You should have them somewhere between 5 and 8 nights out of 14. More than that and your ex better have drugs, crimes, violence or mental health problems. Less than that and you either have drugs, crimes, violence or mental health problems (be honest) or you are giving up too much. You should not make an agreement that gives you less than 36% timeshare for anything. Joint physical custody is worth fighting in court over.

6. **Find the balance.** Fighting for 12 extra hours a week to be exactly 50-50 is not worth going to court over. Get to joint physical custody as your goal. I prefer 50-50. It's the best place to be. But if you cannot get there, get to 6 nights out of 14 – give a little bit to get what you want and stop a future move away and you will find out that the one extra night every two weeks gives you additional peace. Or take the extra night and have 8 out of 14 and give your ex a little peace. Spending $100,000 or years of your life fighting over a few hours per week with your kids, most of which they will be either in school or sleeping (or you will be working) makes no logical sense. You spend $100,000 just to try to figure out what's for dinner on Tuesday nights? Stop it. Spend 5 nights out of 14 with your kids for a year and see if you actually feel like you are missing anything. I am willing to bet that you will not feel like you are missing anything at all. 5 nights out of 14 (which I have had with my own kid) feels very little different than 7 nights out of 14; in fact, maybe it's a relief. True story, I actually had 6 nights out of 14 with my kid

for about a year because they wanted to spend Monday night with their mom when it was my weekend, so we made that a thing. I actually relished having Monday and Tuesday nights two weeks a month to work and focus on other things and it did not feel like I missed a single second with my kiddo. When they decided they wanted to spend that Monday night with me again, I was elated, but it did not feel like I had gained more time. It was another day to rush to their school at 3:30, come home and work remotely, and then figure out what was for dinner and get them to bed. Every one of those things will one day be in the nostalgia box, and I will be glad I did it, but we should not pretend that that extra night every two weeks changed either of our lives.

7. **Show up.** My most favorite and least favorite judge (all in one fun-loving asshole of a guy who is both a neighbor and congenial, mostly, colleague on the bench) says that "your kids know you love them because you show up." Show up one day per month if that is all you can show up. Show up 50-50 if you can do that. But show up, for God's sake. If you are fighting for time with your kids out of spite for your ex, then look at yourself in the mirror for a full five minutes. Ask if you are doing right by your kids. I have been a part of numerous aspirational orders. We help the other parent (or my client) aspire to be a good parent. They haven't been the "bath-to-bed" routine person every night for their children before, but they aspire to be that person. Sometimes they succeed – in fact most of the time they succeed. Sometimes they fail. If the other parent succeeds even when you thought they couldn't, then celebrate and honor that. Your children

have two happy, healthy parents. What more could you ask for? If they fail, be gracious and tell them you will give them another chance in the future. You aren't just giving the other parent a chance, you are giving your children a chance at having two happy, healthy parents in their lives. You should want that for your children. You should want that for yourself. If you fail, ask for help. Don't be shy about it. These are your children. Ask for help and say "I am trying but I can't run a business at the high level I am doing it and have the kids 50-50. I want them all the time. I want them 100% of the time, but I cannot do it even 50-50. Can you help? I'll pay a little more in support. Let me continue to work on it." Reduce the conflict whenever you can. Be reasonable. Be the caring parent you would have wanted when you were 6, 7 or 11 years old. Don't put your kids in the middle; don't ask them to choose; don't talk shit about the other parent. Be better than the other parent whenever you can, even if that means admitting that it's more than you can handle. But, for God's sake, learn to handle it. Balance work. Balance your new partner and their children. Balance your alcohol intake. Do whatever you can to help yourself succeed. And believe in yourself.

8. **Believe in yourself.** Yes, I know I ended the last bullet point with that same phrase but it deserves repeating. You are likely a much better parent than you give yourself credit for. In fact, most parents that go around touting how good of a parent are, aren't. Mom is not a better parent because she is the mom or because your teenage boys back her ferociously. Dad is not a better parent because the little girls adore him. These things are supposed

to happen. I tell dads that when the teenage boys back and defend mom, they have done a good job of raising boys to protect and defend women. I tell moms that when 10-year-old girls back their dad, it's not because he is alienating them but because the moms have done a great job modeling good behavior, so the girls identify with their dads in those tween years. Show up for your kids and believe in yourself. You are doing more and better than you think you are.

A whole book can and should be written on child custody issues. I can't cover it all here in an already too-long chapter. Like in every part of your divorce, try to live by principles rather than counting minutes. Get as much time with your kids as you can possibly live up to. Recognize your children's relationships with the other parent and be supportive of that. The last thing you want is to be like my mom client who recently said to me: "why do they think I am alienating my 16-year-old from seeing her father? Do they think I don't want to have my own life? Do they think I really want her here every single night of her entire teenage years? This is exhausting." Support their relationships with the other parent. When my kiddo came out as nonbinary, initially their mom was mad at them. They told me they didn't want to see mom. I said, "Bullshit. You are going to mom's today as planned." And what happened? They are closer than ever. And they love me too. They have enough love to love both of us. I trust that their good relationship with their mom (and stepdad – which makes me jealous sometimes) makes their relationship with me even better too.

CHAPTER 13

Child Support

THIS IS THE first chapter that no one will like . . . but we gotta do the hard work. We also must make sure you understand how child support is calculated and how to make sure you pay what you owe—and not a penny more. Or, on the flip side, that you get every penny you are entitled to…and how to get a little extra if you play it right.

I'll just tell it to you straight: the high earner is going to pay child support to the low earner. Even John Cryer from *Two and Half Men*, who had 96% custody of the child, was still ordered to give his ex-wife $10,000 per month in child support so that she could get herself a house if she ever got her act together. *In re Marriage of Cryer*, 198 Cal.App.4th 1039 (Cal. Ct. App. 2011).

California child support is calculated by computer, using a complex formula that includes a variety of input variables to arrive at a monthly support number. There are many variables, but the two most important—by far—are percentage timeshare with the children and the difference in incomes.

Many divorces start out calmly, with low conflict, but heat up into intense battles when people start to understand child support. Most of our custody battles are fought not over who is the primary caregiver of the children—that is excepting those parents who want the other parent to see the children very little—but over what the timeshare percentage will be for support purposes. We say we are fighting over the great glory of parenting and the sheer joy of watching our children sleep at night in our homes while we watch TV, but what we are fighting over really is the "visitation" or "timeshare" percentage that will be slotted into the computer calculation.

The reason is that (for the most part) W2 wage earners' salaries are set. Aside from annual cost of living raises or promotions, wage earners can usually be relatively certain of their incomes for support purposes, which means that of the two most important support variables, only "timeshare" – the percentage time you spend with your children that I talked so much about in the last chapter – is changeable. Timeshare is originally set by (and modified by) a Judge who is already hearing your case and naturally assumes that the timeshare for each parent is at issue. It is relatively easy to ask a judge to make custody and visitation orders in the process of the divorce. However, although asking is easy, going through with a custody and visitation hearing can be financially devastating and emotionally demeaning to the point where it is worth reviewing what is being offered against what you are really trying to get.

Most parents who walk into my office know there is either some support coming to them or some liability to pay support. You would be surprised at the number of people, however, who believe that the man always pays child support—even when the woman is the higher earner or when the man is more responsible for the kids. Even judges fall prey to this basic sexism. Child support was created at a time when the law put forward the basic societal belief that women should stay home with the kids, that they were weaker, and that their virtue had been destroyed by the predatory man who put babies into them and now wants to shirk his responsibilities. As a result, the woman's capacity to earn money or to find a man to take care of her and her children (because she is now, according to the old conventional wisdom "damaged goods") was so diminished that she now had to receive maintenance and support to survive. Child support basically had a gendered and sexist past.

In today's world, women greatly outpace men in college and graduate degrees and are increasingly out-earning them. This means that there are many more households where, as in the case of my recent terrible LDS Church Hippie negotiation, the woman believes that the man's job is so menial and minimal that he should take time off to care for the kids, but that she is –, somehow, the primary caregiver. This sounds familiar—from the stone ages of American sexism.

With two-income families, the lower earner often does care for the children (especially, for example, if the kids are sick and home from school) while the higher earner goes to work. It is simple economics. If the higher earner misses a day of work, the family may lose $400. If the low earner misses a day, the family may only lose $200. It is a rational decision for the family to choose to have the lower earner take the day off work.

Child support is supposed to be about children sharing the lifestyle of the higher earner, and the only way to do that is via wealth transference from the higher earner to the lower earner. I hope that books like this one will help encourage people of both genders to accept that the higher earner should pay child support to the lower earner, rather than an outdated belief that the man should pay the woman child support. Often it makes logical sense to do so. For example, if a mother with three kids would have to pay $1,500 per month in additional childcare to have the children most of the time, but would only have to pay her ex-husband $900 per month in child support to keep the kids during that time, would it not make more sense to pay the ex-husband? Typically, but not always, when both parents work at their maximum, more money stays inside each individual parent's family unit and there is more money overall for the family.

In this and the upcoming chapters, I will provide more case citations than explanations so you can get a flavor for the Court's reasoning on some of these issues. With some of these judicial decisions you will also encounter footnotes—don't be shocked, that's how all legal writers do things. Nevertheless, you can safely ignore footnotes for the most part, unless it is something you really want to know about in more detail. There is a fine balance writing a book like this. I want it to be entertaining, but I also want to give you some "red meat" to sink your teeth into.[8]

---

8   As an aside, you may or may not know about the relationship between statutes and case law. The brief summation is as follows: the legislature passes a series of laws (called the Family Code in this context) that set forth a variety of legal rules. These rules can sometimes be vague. (I think they do this because it's difficult to write specifics when you have two parties fighting over every word; they also may do it because vagueness gives the trial courts some leeway in how they interpret the rules.) Case law comes about when trial court judges make rulings in cases that parties do not like. They then file an appeal to the next court up—the Appellate Court. The Appellate Courts are the first line of appeals. They must take any appeal that is given to them. They review the case file and decide whether the judge did things correctly or not. They usually give a reasoned response to their analysis of the trial court's decision and reasoning. They will then write an opinion about what they think is correct or incorrect about the opinion, and then set forth what the rules are. These opinions become binding on the trial courts below them and set forth understandings of rules. So, for example, a statute says each parent has to support the children according to their station in life. Then one parent quits their job as a stockbroker to work at Taco Bell because they don't want to support their children. The trial court says, "That's fine but we are going to impute income to you as though you are a stockbroker." The Taco Bell worker appeals and the Appellate Court decides whether a stockbroker can reasonably quit their high-paying job to work at Taco Bell without having to pay more support than their current "station in life" allows for. The Appellate Court is not a place to hear new facts or new legal arguments. They are restricted to deciding whether the trial court judge did it correctly based on the record in front of them. It may not surprise you to know that the Appellate Court does everything in its power to try to support the trial court's findings and orders. There is a lot more to this, but that is the basic course. I will sometimes refer to the Family Code (or "Fam. Code") and sometimes give you a full case citation. If you want to look up a case that I cite, just go to your favorite search engine and type in the name of the case. You'll usually find a couple of websites that have the case online for your reading pleasure. Many people don't like reading cases; I really do. The court starts with the facts and the history of the case, and then discusses the ruling and what the rule should be. It can be entertaining if you are into that kind of thing.

What follows is an excerpt from the *Marriage of Cryer* case I referenced above in which the Court sets forth some of the statutory grounds for the payment of child support and (in particular) the importance of using the statewide uniform guideline.

"The amount of child support normally payable is calculated based on a complicated algebraic formula found at Family Code section 4055. Although we call this formula "the statewide uniform guideline" (§4055), "guideline" is really a misleading term. (*In re Marriage of Hubner* (2001) 94 Cal. App.4th 175, 183.) The formula support amount is "presumptively correct" in all cases (see §§4057, subd. (a), 4053, subd. (k)), but "may be rebutted by admissible evidence showing that application of the formula would be unjust or inappropriate in the particular case, consistent with the principles set forth in Section 4053. (§4055, subd. (b).)." *Marriage of Cryer* (2011) 198 Cal.App.4th 1039.

Here the *Cryer* court states that you should expect the computer program that runs the child support algebraic formula to be presumptively correct. Only in rare instances will the Court deviate from this formulaic approach to child support. I've seen it done, but it's truly a rarity. You must show that it would be a true hardship to pay the full amount. Everyone says it's a hardship because you simply don't have an extra $784 per month to shell out to your ex to take care of the kids for you.

But that's not the standard for hardship.

You *might* get a hardship when you are placed on furlough from work due to no fault of your own, or when you are experiencing a major health crisis, or when you have to report for active-duty military, or (maybe) when you have additional children in your home from a new marriage. The first thing you will need to do if you want to make the argument that you are paying an unjust or inappropriate amount of support is to figure out how you fit into the types of "hardship" categories set forth above. (The likelihood of that is slim). Your time will be better spent analyzing the other factors that go into calculating "guideline" support.

> "Section 4053 sets forth a number of principles, foremost among them being the protection of the child's best interest: "The guideline seeks to place the interests of children as the state's top priority." (§4053, subd. (e).) Among other principles, section 4053 also provides, " (a) [a] parent's first and principal obligation is to support his or her minor children according to the parent's circumstances and station in life"; "(d) [e]ach parent should pay for the support of the children according to his or her ability"; and "(f) [c]hildren should share in the standard of living of both parents. Child support may therefore appropriately improve the standard of living of the custodial household to improve the lives of the children."
> *Marriage of Cryer* (2011) 198 Cal.App.4th 1039.

The main reason it is difficult to prove injustice or inappropriateness in paying guidelines for child support is that the children's interests are placed first and foremost. The Court will want to ensure that both parents have a place to live and both parents can feed the kids.

If you are in a somewhat standard situation in which Father makes $60,000 per year as a construction worker and Mother makes $30,000 per year as a part-time office worker and you have two kids (and you're on a 25% timeshare) the possibility of paying $1,036 per month in child support is enough to give you nightmares. You already only take home $3,900 per month, so an extra $1,036 means that you are going to have to pay all your bills on less than $3,000 per month. Be grateful that the Mother is working though because if she wasn't, your payment would jump to $1,365—and that's with her claiming both children on her taxes. Plus, you don't get a tax benefit from paying child support.

"In light of these principles, departure from the standard child support formula may be appropriate when application of the formula "would be unjust or inappropriate due to special circumstances in the particular case" (§ 4057, subd. (b)(5)), so long as the variance is consistent with section 4053." *Marriage of Cryer* (2011) 198 Cal.App.4th 1039.

The "consistency with section 4053" issue is the big one for *Marriage of Cryer* and for most cases where the payor argues it is unjust or inappropriate for him to pay child support at the guideline amount.

Marriage of Cryer is a great case not only because the numbers make you bug-eyed, but also because it is such an outlier that it gives you reason to pause. John and Sarah were both actors. John's career took off, while Sarah's career went nowhere fast. John and Sarah agreed to a $10,000 per month child support order when John was earning over $300,000 per month. (This is WAY below guideline support by the way.) John had a 35% timeshare. When Sarah fell upon hard times, the Court awarded John physical custody of their child and monitored Sarah's visits. John asked (reasonably) to modify the child support order since he had the child 96% of the time. The Court denied the request under Section 4053 of the Family Code, stating that it was in the child's best interests for Sarah to have a home for the child to visit once she was in a position to have the child over.

Injustice? Maybe. Since John was earning at least $327,000 per month, this was just 3% of his earnings. The Court felt like no injustice was being worked on him for having to pay. Guideline support should have dropped to $858 per month. But that would have made the Mother homeless and a whole bunch of other bad things would have begun to happen to her. In short, it is not easy or simple to get out of paying child support.

For child support, timeshare is the variable that is most likely to change, although there are a variety of other variables that make a reasonably large difference in the support calculation. This chapter walks through some of the input variables so that you can understand them. It also discusses the concept of "earning potential"—which is how much any party should be earning even if they choose not to earn income.

A Brief Aside About How To Report Income to the Court

California has a set of mandatory forms that it uses for divorces. Good attorneys and paralegals not only know how to fill out the forms, but also which forms to fill out. All forms are freely available on the Judicial Council website. (Google: "California Judicial Council Forms" to find it.) For Income purposes the most important form is the Income and Expense Declaration. It is four pages, and it cuts to the heart of each party's income and expenses.

It is also one of the first forms completed in a divorce. I tell clients they can save a few bucks by filling it out themselves—which they like—but that I can help if needed. I give the following little speech every time I hand someone the form:

"Go home, put the form on the table, and pour yourself a glass of wine. Drink that glass and then pour yourself another, and then start looking at the form...." It takes an hour or so to fill out if you are getting all the information together as you go. It asks for two months' paystubs and all your income information. On the third page it asks for all your monthly expenses. Always check the "estimated expenses" and round off. You don't have to be a hero and pull out every gas bill or cell phone bill and list exact amount—just estimate.

The other major way of exchanging information is through what is likely to be a local rule for each county. In Santa Barbara County it is called Local Rule 1419. In San Luis Obispo County, it is called: "Policies and Procedures 2.8:2." In Marin County, "Local Rule 6.13." These local rules require you to provide two years' tax returns, four months' paystubs, and 12 months' bank statements for any account on which you are a signatory. Ventura County doesn't have a similar rule, but you must bring a tax return to a support hearing.

It is especially annoying to people when they must produce the same half ream of paper that their spouse already produced because they are essentially still sharing a bank account and tax returns. But produce them, you must. And update them. These are called "financial disclosures." These financial disclosures are very important to an analysis of each party's account deposits. Often, when we analyze financial disclosures, we find out about rental income, recurring gifts from a new boyfriend or girlfriend, or other types of income or potential income. If I have a party who owns their own business and claims to make less than minimum wage, yet deposits $7,600 into their account each month, I try to show that they are understating their income. It's not easy to prove, as I talk about below, but that's one method of doing so.

This Income and Expense Declaration and your paystub go together in demonstrating to the Court what your income is. The Court uses gross numbers—pre-tax, pre-withholdings, pre-health insurance, pre-wage garnishments, pre-everything. Each of the withholdings is a factor in the computer support-calculating program, but not in the calculation of your earnings.

The Basic Child Support Rules

As a basic rule, each of the variables below impacts your support in the following way. (This is not unlike the Three Property Rules above or the Rule of Reasonability):

Basic Child (and Spousal) Support Rule: Anything that tends to reduce your tax liability or increase your refund tends to require that you pay more child support (or receive less if you are the child support recipient).

There are some additional rules along with this basic rule, such as your new spouse is never obligated to support your children (but you don't get to claim that you support their children to reduce support either). There are some add-ons that are dollar-for-dollar add-ons—for example, you pay one-half of all the unreimbursed medical expenses and one-half of all the childcare costs so your ex-spouse can work.

Child support continues until the child turns 18 and graduates from high school or turns 19. Questions that emerge about this are as follows: What happens if we have an 18-year-old who is a part-time high school student? What happens if the child is 17 but has already left for college? What happens if we have a disabled adult? None of these is easy to answer and is why people litigate these types of questions.

A note about the Child Support Calculation formula. No one really knows or understands the formula. We understand that there are additions to or subtractions from the calculations, but as far as anyone (including the judge) knows, there is no way of ensuring that the guideline recommended is the actual "Guideline"—even though California touts the formula as the perfect way to set support. The reality is that the Court is taking your money (or giving you money) based on a black box that none of us can see into. That should worry everyone. It is a system that keeps almost everyone out. In fact, I believe part of the reason we don't reform it is because most of us don't understand it. But don't take my word for it, listen to some judicial comments:

"[W]e are left with a process for determining child support not understood by the legislators who enacted it [citation], judges not regularly handling family law cases who are assigned one and do not understand the formula and who may not have the computer resources or the computer know-how to compute it, and parties with child support orders imposed upon them by a formula which no one can explain to them. Even Lewis Carroll, when writing *Alice in Wonderland*, could not have contemplated such a bizarre situation. Historically, although California has been in the forefront of the development of family law, no other state uses California's approach to child support. It is truly a sad state of affairs, when one considers that child support is a critically important financial issue affecting the lives of hundreds of thousands of parents and children in California." (*In re Marriage of Carter* (1994) 26 Cal.App. 4th 1024, 1029 fn. 5.

"These are proceedings where emotions and the level of conflict are already running high. A bad situation becomes more inflamed when an order for child support is calculated in a manner which the parties do not understand…Indeed, the entire statutory scheme appears to be an unprecedented effort by the Legislature to micromanage child support hearings and determinations in a manner which was neither contemplated nor required by federal law. The result is a process of determining child support which is complex and unduly costly, which requires the use of a computer and which is not understood by anyone, least of all the affected parties. There is no way that either the payor or the recipient of child support, even if represented by counsel, can comprehend how the court determined the amount ordered. As the trial court stated during the course of one of the seven separate hearings in this case: "I guess you're pointing up the absurdity of the legislative efforts in this area, aren't you? How do we get to these guys? Maybe somebody [who] authored this bill should explain it." *Marriage of Carter*, supra.

"What was once a short, simple, inexpensive process, easily understood and accepted by the participants, has become an increasingly costly and confusing nightmare. This process previously occupied little court time, but it is now so complicated, especially for the increasing number of parties representing themselves, that it now occupies considerable amounts of court time in an already overburdened court system. We pride ourselves on a system of justice, especially in family law cases. In a just system, parents being ordered to pay or receive child support deserve to know how the amount of the support was arrived at and that the process used is one that is fair and reasonable to both the payor and the payee. This would not only make it more likely that the order will be complied with, but it would also eliminate the amount ordered for child support as a source of ongoing conflict between the parents, the fallout from which is clearly harmful to the child.

It is indeed unfortunate that the Legislature, in its efforts to micromanage child support, lost sight of how important it is that the parents understand and accept the fairness of the calculation. Without this, the payor always believes the amount ordered is inappropriately high, and the payee believes it is too low, leaving the parents with unnecessary ongoing conflict indisputably detrimental to the child. The facts and circumstances of the parties in each family law case are different, which is why these cases are equitable proceedings in which the court must have the ability to exercise discretion to achieve fairness and equity. It is for this reason that the author of the child support statute, later in the same legislative session in which it was adopted, ushered in another bill making clear "that it was not the intention of the Legislature to eliminate family law judges' traditional discretionary authority to adjust child support orders in individual cases where fairness requires it." (See Summary of Sen. Bill No. 1614 (Hart) (1991-1992 Reg. Sess.), attached hereto as an appendix.) This makes clear that the court, in child support cases, is not just supposed to punch numbers into a computer and award the parties the computer's result without considering circumstances in a particular case which would make that order unjust or inequitable. (See, *County of Lake v. Antoni* (1993) 18 Cal. App. 4th 1102 [22 Cal. Rptr. 2d 804].) Otherwise, there would be no need for a judge; all you would need would be a computer." *In re Marriage of Fini* (1994) 26 Cal.App4th 1033.

Apologies for the long digression, but it is important to understand how frustrated judges and parties are about the calculation of "Guideline" child support. In the Legislature's effort to be uniform in the application of the child support laws, the Legislature lost sight of the fact that every story and every family is different, and that we call upon judges to decide difficult matters and not just to sit there like automatons, punching numbers into a computer. It's so boring that not only do judges not understand it, often they do not even get it correct. Many judges just rely on child support services attorneys to tell them what number to order.

Good lawyers find it so boring that sometimes they won't even deal with child support orders, instead sending their clients to an already overworked Department of Child Support Services, where clerks sit in front of a Title IV Commissioner who reads information out while they punch it into their computers. No one understands the support calculation whatsoever . . . and no one cares to understand it. I am continually surprised at how just a slight change in a child support computer program calculation can reduce or increase support 30-40%.

This is even stranger when you consider that child support is the longest and most drawn-out payment most people will make in their lifetimes, excepting their 30 years mortgage or perhaps their pension contribution. It often gets set quickly, without care or understanding, and although virtually everyone can seek to modify it at some point during the length of the child's minority, most do not. It is a number that is at once too low and too high. Everyone believes they were screwed by the child support number but learn to live with it in resignation.

Below are the categories in the child and spousal support computation computer program, which will help you to understand the input variables in the program used to calculate support. This will give you some power to manipulate the variables[9]. I do not ever recommend that you evade your duty to support your children, but it's very important that you understand that this is simply a computer program. If it receives garbage in, it will spit garbage out. Most lawyers and every single person representing themselves (and most judges) have no blessed idea how the program works. They simply type in a few numbers and hit Enter.

If you are representing yourself, you may be able to buy the program for your iPad or your Android device for about $40. It will not be the full and complete lawyers' edition, but it will suffice. Sit with your ex's paystubs and tax returns and play with the numbers.

---

9   Just to make the confusion more palpable, while writing this book, the computer program called "Dissomaster," which had been the main way of calculating child and spousal support, went out of business. I understand that "X-Spouse" will take its place. Perhaps. More grist for the mill.

Take some time with it. I think you will find that you really benefit when you do. If you deal with the most complex input variables, you will know more and do more than 99% of everyone who walks into the Courtroom, including the judges and the Family Law Specialists.

Remember that if the input variable is one that gives you a tax advantage or more money, you will correspondingly pay more in support (unless it's your new spouse's income—which counter-intuitively results in a higher tax bracket for you and less in support). If it is something that is a dollar-for-dollar reduction in your income with no corresponding tax benefit, it will make less income available for support and reduce your payment. And as I harped on in the last chapter, the more time you have with your kids, the less you pay.

1. Tax Filing Status and Number of Exemptions

There is always an afterthought fight over the children's tax exemptions. For many W2 families, the tax return is an annual bonus they receive from the federal government. There is plenty of writing about how when you do that, you are simply giving Uncle Sam an interest-free loan that he pays you back in April each year. The tax return, though, is based on certain deductions and exemptions. The claiming of the children as exemptions is one of the major ways for parents to receive a discount on their tax returns. So, invariably, it comes up as a discussion point after we calculate child support.

I point out to the paying spouse (or recipient) that the tax advantages of claiming the children are calculated into the support program. Since you receive a personal exemption for the children, the computer program assumes that you have monthly additional income when you get the exemption. It then factors that into the support calculation. Thus, if you have the children as an exemption, you pay more in support. If you split the kids, then the computer gives you both the tax advantage associated with each. In most cases there is very little difference each month in the calculation:

you either pay for it monthly in the form of child support (and then get money back at the end of the year) or you pay less support but lose the annual exemption.

There are exceptions, of course, which are based around the basic tax rules. Lawyers hate talking about taxes because we are every bit as mystified by the tax code as you are, except that you pay us to give you good advice.

Whether you file Head of Household or Married Filing Jointly has a large impact on child support. From a child support perspective, filing Single 1 is usually the costliest way to file. Even lawyers often make the mistake of listing both as Single 1 even though they may be filing as Married Filing Separately or Married Filing Jointly. Also, be careful of lawyers who intentionally make "mistakes" in entering data into the program, each of which coincidentally benefits their client.

The computer program we use defaults to Single status, so it's not uncommon for a lawyer to simply forget to put the right filing status into the computer program. It is worth double checking, but you should understand the basic movement of child support liability: if you get more back from the IRS (or pay less) then the program will know that you have more money (or less) available for support.

2. Timeshare Percentage

The Family Code still refers to "visitation." Regardless, "timeshare" is perhaps the second most important element of the Dissomaster calculation (with earnings being the most important). A timeshare percentage change of 10% can have a major impact on the child support payment, and the difference between a 20% "standard" plan (every other weekend and a dinner visit each week) and a 50% plan (alternating weeks or a 2-2-5 schedule) can be well over 50% of the total payment.

For most people, however, wages don't change. The calculation "is whatever it is." If you and your spouse are W2 wage earners, the likelihood that there is going to be any major revelation or change in income is slight. The biggest variation in the calculation will come in the timeshare percentage with the children.

We play a strange game with judges regarding timeshare percentage. Judges do not like it when they think the parties are negotiating a timeshare percentage based on reducing (or increasing) child support. The policy of the state of California is that each parent should provide support to their children, meaning both paying support and taking care of the kids. Typically, the non-custodial parent pays the larger support amount because the custodial parent is taking care of the kids. Each is contributing to the children's upbringing and needs, even when an actor making $3 million per year has to make sure that the mother of his child has $10,000 per month to keep her home that the children do not visit.

Calculating timeshare is its own beast. You are trying to maximize the amount of time you are awarded to reduce or increase your support payment, while trying to seem like you don't care about how you count it. Courts typically do not like it when parties "count hours" to figure out the exact timeshare percentage, although they allow the Department of Child Support Services to do it when they calculate support. The reasons probably have to do with the Court only seeking to maximize child support when there is money to be collected to repay public assistance money received by the custodial parent (versus counting hours to get more or pay less support by two parents who are not on government assistance).

At any rate, the counting hours method is where the court literally divides the total number of hours the noncustodial parent has with the children by 168 hours in a week. I use 336 hours over two weeks because it helps to account for a Week 1/Week 2 schedule like alternating weekends, etc. . . . Lawyers use a sort of shorthand that says every other weekend is 20%, two nights per week is 28%, 5 nights out of 14 is 36%, and 6 nights out of 14 is 42%.

The support-paying parent often pays for hours when the children are in school or in day care, which can lead to a type of double-dip where the support payor is not only paying for half of the childcare or school expense, but also paying support to the ex-spouse for time when the kids are in school or daycare. Many dads ask me, "Why can't I get credit for those hours since the child is in school anyway?" The Court has opined on this issue several times, always stating that the person who gets the credit should be the one who will have to pick them up if they need to come home from school early because of sickness or some other reason. The person getting the credit is the one who is responsible for them when they are in school. It is imperfect with double-income families where everyone is doing the best they can to manage where the kids are going to be and how they are going to get them there. This is an area where there is potential growth in the timeshare percentage. It amounts to around 35 hours per week. If you are the parent who stays home when the child is sick, even when it's not your day, you might be able to pick up extra timeshare for this.

I'm in favor of rethinking some of the guideline calculations of support. If I were drafting new child support regulation, I'd probably look at finding a way to split the support from the timeshare. I'd suggest picking a percentage such as 35% or 38% and using it as the timeshare number in all cases. Then I would follow through with the rest of the computer program inputs, giving the court some wider discretion on determining child support orders, such that a deviation from the guideline would be more reasonable (such as in cases where there is a true 50-50 split, or where a parent receives very little time share). I think this would lead to a drastic reduction in child custody battles, which are often about child support.

In any event, many courts are moving toward shared parenting. Modern psychology tells us that continued contact with both parents is very important to kids; the "tender years" doctrine is dead. Fathers are spending much more time with their kids and taking quite a bit of pride and joy in fatherhood, including taking the kids to the doctor, going to school functions, participating in extra-curricular activities, and preparing home cooked meals. Women are increasingly becoming a force in the market, and traditional "women's professions" in the service fields (nursing and teaching) are becoming increasingly high-paid. Women are also becoming more dominant in the professions of law, engineering, technology, and entrepreneurship. Courts are also increasingly recognizing that both parents, especially in two-income families, are contributing to the upbringing of the children.

From my perspective as a divorced dad, there is nothing more important in your divorce than the establishment of the timeshare on good terms for both parents. There is nothing more important than spending time with your children. Plus, it drastically impacts the bottom line.

Let's be honest for a moment: your kids are the most important thing in your divorce. But money is also the most important thing. You need stability for your kids and money provides a good deal of that stability. Both parents need enough money to rent a place to live, buy food and gas, and do something fun besides watching kids' soccer games periodically. Both parents also need enough money to do things when the kids aren't around, up to and including finding a new partner or someone to have sex with. (Those things usually take money too.) It is simply better for everyone when there is more money. Proxy battles over money should not be viewed as evil because people are fighting to ensure their own stability, which is natural and normal. The problem is that the battle is being fought over the kids rather than over money, and because judges hate fights over money, money is an unspoken taboo that is not dealt with until the very end.

I tell dads especially to ask for more time with the kids but *not* to change the support order. Mom gets what she needs, which is enough money to stay stable, and Dad gets what he wants, which is more time with the kids. It's win-win.

I can't count the number of times I've been in a courtroom arguing whether the timeshare is 33% or 37% for support calculation purposes. A simple formula for support calculation will produce many more settlements in the custody and visitation arena, which is where most of the money is spent for the least amount of value. Lawyers put on a show for their clients about the custody issues. They say all kinds of brutish things about the spouse. For example, I just had a trial where the other lawyer beat my client up for an hour over his marijuana use and his "dead end" job, and then called his boss as a witness and asked her if she was bothered that he smokes marijuana around heavy machinery. Meanwhile, his client was forced to admit that she hasn't had a job in four years, started and stopped going to school two different times, moved to Arkansas for four months last year, and married an Airman who is now being transferred to Oklahoma. Plus, she confessed that she smoked marijuana with my client. (And since marijuana is legal for recreational use in California, what was the point in raising the issue?)

The judge later dressed both lawyers down (correctly) for taking cheap shots at two people who are just trying to figure out what to do with their kid. The judge was right, but my complaint with him was that he allowed it over my objections. Once opposing counsel went for the throat, I felt obliged to do the same or my client invariably would have said, "You aren't fighting hard enough for me like her lawyer is doing."

The excesses of two parents attacking each other in open court is one reason why I suggest to many dads who make decent money (or get remarried to a wage earner) that they offer to pay support on a smaller timeshare in exchange for receiving a larger timeshare. Remember the *Cryer* case above—housing stability is probably the most important part of paying support.

3. Income – Wages

The computer program distinguishes between income from employment (W2 income) and self-employment income. The program generates tax and support factors (including income tax and employment tax). If one of the income taxes does not apply to you, the program gives you an opportunity to exclude those taxes from the calculation. The more information you feed into the program, the better it can calculate the amount of income you have available for support. All income that is subject to employment taxes go into this category. The easiest way to do this is to use your "Medicare wages" as your wages.

You can get your Medicare wages by dividing the Medicare tax by 0.0145 (which is just the Medicare tax rate of 1.45% as a decimal). Unlike FICA, which has a ceiling, there is no upper wage limit for Medicare. That is why you can just look for the Medicare wages. The Medicare box and the calculated Medicare wage should match up.

There isn't much to say about income available for support if both of you are wage earners. The most likely number to use for income available for support is your W2 wages. The Court uses gross numbers (much to people's chagrin) and then gives you a bunch of additional deductions and additions based on payments you make for certain things, such as deductions for health insurance, mandatory retirement and union dues, but adds back depreciation, vehicles provided by your employer and cell phones paid by your employer. 401(k) or IRA contributions are mixed because they are pretax income.

W2 income has the advantage of being relatively certain. (Of course, there are raises and the possibility of losing a job, which complicate things.) People lose jobs during a divorce at a slightly higher rate than those who aren't going through a divorce—adding insult-to-injury. It's probably because divorces can be so stressful that performance decreases. I wouldn't say it's a large percentage, but in cases that drag on it can happen. Wage earners who are seasonal workers should pay attention to ensuring that a Court does not calculate their income on a 12-month basis at their high season earnings. If you are a teacher, professor, wildland firefighter, involved in any business where there is a harvest, or you work at a tourism-based business in a seasonal job, make sure that this is clear to the Court when discussing the issue. In the past, with truly seasonal workers, we've treated the income as an annual average—meaning that in some months, you've barely got enough to cover the payment, and in other months, you are flush with cash. The most common way to do it is to pick a baseline number and carve out a sort of "overtime percentage," in which you pay a percentage of your overtime to your children's other parent as a type of bonus. The benefit of this, called an *"Ostler-Smith"* bonus (yes, based on a case with those names), is that you only pay more in support when you work overtime – the downside is that it reduces the incentive to work overtime because you have to pay a percentage of it to your ex-spouse.

The only exceptional thing regarding W2 income is overtime. The Court cannot make you work more than a full-time week, but if you are going to work overtime the Court can (and should) make you pay support based on what you actually earn. Thus, if you have the type of job where you work overtime regularly (cops, firefighters, prevailing wage earners on big construction projects, Highway Transportation workers, nurses in hospitals, etc.) you will want to exclude overtime income from the calculation of support and use an "overtime" table to calculate your payment when you work overtime. There is good caselaw on this.

An *Ostler-Smith* order comes from *In re Marriage of Ostler and Smith* (1990) 223 Cal.App.3d 33 in which the court sets a percentage of actually earned overtime or bonuses to be paid out as child and spousal support. It is roughly 14% of gross earnings for each child and your spouse (capped at around 40%). *Ostler/Smith* orders are a pain in the ass because you must continually provide evidence to your spouse of what you have earned and "true up" this income and your support payment roughly every 90 days. However, they are fair because you don't have to pay each month when you don't have the overtime or bonus money coming in.

Some clients tell me they have decided not to work overtime anymore after a divorce. They say they worked the overtime to provide for their families or to buy a house or pay off certain debts. They decide they would like to work less and spend more time with their children. This is noble; yet almost 0% of the ones who say it actually do it. I think there are certain people whose identity is based around their work and working less messes with their sense of self. Nevertheless, if your choice is to work less, the Court *cannot* make you work more than 40 hours per week. Argue hard for an *Ostler-Smith* overtime table and then don't work the overtime hours. Your support will be based on your base wages with a percentage of overtime for the times when you cannot avoid it.

Conversely, there are others who work more overtime after the initial support order so that they can try to keep a semblance of their former lives. This is fine too; although my caution to the overtime worker is that once you start working overtime there is always a chance that your support will increase because of it.[10]

4. 401K Contribution

The more you contribute to your 401(k), the more the computer program makes you pay in support. Since the contribution is pre-tax, the software program counts the contribution as income not subject to employment taxes.

5. Self-Employment Income

For the purposes of calculating income available for support, self-employment wages are where the fun really starts. At its most basic form self-employment income is just business profits after expenses—the number on the 1040 that transfers from Schedule C. The computer program then generates income tax, self-employment tax, and guideline income from the entry. Since self-employment taxes are roughly double employment taxes for the same amount of income, a wage earner has more discretionary income (and a larger support payment) than someone who is self-employed.

But self-employment income is a bit of a moving target because divorce lawyers and judges (along with CPAs) are aware that self-employed business owners write many things off their income as "expenses" that would be considered "perks" if a wage earner received them from their employer. For example, every small business owner writes off their car payments, cell phone and internet bills. You would have these items if you did not have a small business and you would not be able to write them off. If your wage paying boss provided them for you for personal use, that would be a

---

10 There are practicalities and possibilities. The practicality is that a person who takes extra shifts to try to pay the child or spousal support award is unlikely to be punished by the Court for doing so. There is a basic understanding that people have to live and that true fighters do whatever it takes to continue to live. The possibility is always there, however, that if you get an initial support order for $1,036 per month based on your wages of $60,000 per year and then earn $10,000 per year in overtime to make up for some of the loss, your payment could increase to $1,218 to account for the extra earnings of $833 per month (21% of your overtime gross.)

perquisite that would be subject to income taxation. You essentially get a perquisite provided by your small business when you include them, even if you use them for work as well.

Other deductions that reduce self-employment income are meals and entertainment expenses, car leases and loans, mileage deductions, home office expenses, and travel. For example, you wrote off that trip to Hawaii you took with your new paramour because you stopped into the pro shop and bought some golf clubs for your best client? It may pass muster with the IRS (I repeat, I am not a tax lawyer so this example may be bunk), but it creates a real problem in family court when your income available for support is reduced by a travel expense for a trip you took with a new romantic partner. Another big moving target is depreciation. In any business where you can depreciate assets, you are basically getting money for nothing.

All the action happens when the Court decides what it will "add-back" into the income available for support. This is sort of a wildcat way of doing this. Most judges are not adept at using the detailed nuances of the computer program and do not know that there are places where itemized deductions can be added back into the program, so they will look at bottom line income. If you are a real estate broker showing gross revenues of $200,000 on commissions, but after expenses are showing profits of only $60,000, opposing counsel or the Judge will inquire about what is giving you the big write-offs. Inquiry is not the same as judgment. You may have real write-offs that should be included in your business expenses—advertising expenditures in a brutally competitive market, sales associate whose salaries you are guaranteeing, the need for a hot car, or wining and dining potential high-end clients at the country club—but most judges will "add back" certain deductions that double as personal benefits. Meals and entertainment, vehicle expenditures, mileage, and depreciation are major targets.

But don't get too excited about how nuanced the process will be. In one case, Husband made $850,000 per year. He had a good accountant who (with a straight face) wrote it down to $17,000 per year in taxable income. There were deductions for a Bentley, a $150,000 deck put on his "home office," and a $100,000 "50th Work Anniversary" party he threw himself. The trial court judge accepted these deductions. In another case the trial court judge reviewed the tax return and said, "I'll give him half his vehicle lease, all of his cell phone bills, none of his meals and entertainment, all of his advertising, half of his rental expenses, and half of his office expenses." No real rhyme or reason to it. I asked the $850,000 per year guy with the Bentley whether he takes his son out to lunch on the business expense account and writes it off: "I write everything off." I asked, "Do you use the deck for personal entertaining?" "I use the deck every day, all day." I asked, "Did you buy a $200,000 Airstream? Did you write that off as a business expense? Have you ever used it for business?" "Yes. Yes. No." The judge did not care. He let him write it all off. Admittedly, that was an extreme position. It's much more likely you will get the judge who reviews the tax return and says, "I'll give him this, half of that, and none of that."

Family court is not in the business of telling you how to file your taxes and, frankly, it isn't interested in whether you are fully transparent about your expenditures with the IRS. Assuming you've been taking higher-risk deductions for years, your spouse will have signed the returns along with you. Family court is a place where, in theory, no one is in trouble; it's a place to resolve problems. Nevertheless, expect to be able to defend your Schedule C to the Judge or to opposing counsel.

·············· **PRO TIP** ··············

Add up all the possible "add backs" and run the support calculation that way. Then analyze each add-back as a percentage of the total amount of personal vs. Business use. If you rely heavily on your car and phone as many real estate professionals do, you may be entitled to the full deduction, or at least a larger percentage of the deduction than a lawyer who leases a BMW to drive back and forth to the courthouse. If you are a commercial plumber, you may have a much larger Cost of Goods Sold or a need for a heavy-duty work truck to move tools and equipment between jobsites. Make sure the Court knows the difference between a work and personal vehicle. Most courts spend about 5 seconds on these line items, so you will want to be prepared to answer quickly. Any perks you can get credit for on your self-employment income are a win for the support payor.

··

The support recipient should be prepared with counter arguments. If your ex is a "paper contractor" with a Ford F-350 King Ranch fully-loaded dually that cost $110,000 off the lot because she likes to pull her horse trailer but would never carry a toolbox, make sure you tell the Court that her job could be done in a Toyota Prius. Same if your ex is deducting cell phone bills for his new girlfriend and her kids.

In some instances, a spouse will accuse the other spouse of cheating on their income taxes, or a lawyer will try to convince a judge that the self-employment income is understated. Thankfully, there is good caselaw to assist the tax reporting party:

> "[G]ross income, as stated under penalty of perjury on recent tax returns, should be presumptively correct. Returns are, after all, ultimately enforced by federal and state criminal penalties." *In re Marriage of Loh*, 93 Cal. App. 4th 325, 332 (Cal. App. 4th Dist. 2001).

On occasion, the IRS has asserted that a taxpayer's lifestyle belies their reported income – under the theory that the taxpayer is underreporting income. (E.g., *United States v. Gellman* (11th Cir. 1982) 677 F.2d 65 [burden on United States to prove that taxpayer willfully did not file returns where prosecution was based in part on lifestyle evidence].). There are established ways the IRS goes about computing income based on the contention that a taxpayer's manner of living is inconsistent with his or her reported income. *In re Marriage of Loh*, 93 Cal. App. 4th 325, 332 (Cal. App. 4th Dist. 2001).

A few photos of an ex-spouse with assets owned by the ex-spouse's new spouse or "nonmarital partner" would not be sufficient in tax court and they are not sufficient here. In the absence of tax returns, the only evidence as to Petitioner's income is her own testimony and her income and expense declaration." *Id.*

The party alleging the underreporting must prove that the reporting party has falsely underreported her income.

This is a high burden to meet. A colleague of mine once had an investigator stake out a hot dog cart in a busy tourist area to count cash sales. There were no credit cards processed—everyone at the beach knew that if you wanted a hot dog and a cold drink, the only way to pay was cash. My colleague successfully showed that the operator was bringing in a little over $1,000 cash each day, and because the vendor was not being honest about his reporting, the Judge allowed my colleague to extrapolate that daily income to an annual income of over $200,000 per year. When the vendor protested that his busiest cash days were all clustered during the summer, the Judge told him he wasn't credible because he had lied about his income previously.

But that case is an oddity because cash is difficult to prove. As one of our retiring judges says, "I'm in the evidence business!" You must be in the evidence business, too. If you want to prove under-reported cash sales, you need to do more than produce lifestyle evidence with photographs and text messages. You MUST find the money. Period. Otherwise, the Court has no basis to decide other than the documents submitted to the Court (the Income and Expense Declaration) and the Tax Returns.

6. Other Taxable Income

This is the "catch all" category for income. It is everything else besides employment or self-employment income that you include on your tax returns. There are categories for short- and long-term capital gains, rental property income, farm income, and income from other sources. Its key importance is that although it is not subject to employment taxes, it is subject to income taxes or capital gains taxes. If this rather exhaustive list of options does not include your option, you can use the "other income" slot for your inputs.

7. TANF plus CS Received

This is Temporary Assistance to Needy Families. It has no direct bearing on child support, but it does help the judge understand the overall income picture for each of the parties.

8. Other Nontaxable Income

This is where it's a good idea to get creative (or not if you are trying to reduce your support payment). Nontaxable income could be certain disability or VA payments, but it can also be job perquisites that are not reportable income on your income taxes (or income at least that you do not report). Sometimes someone who gets caught by their ex-spouse with a certain amount of unreported cash income finds that income being slotted into the nontaxable category by the Judge. The Judge does not care if you report it to the IRS, but the Judge does want to include it as income. The best place to calculate unreported cash income is "nontaxable" income, which causes you child support payment to increase because you don't pay taxes on it.

You can also use this option for tax advantages that someone gains, such as a credit for a hybrid vehicle or the use of a vehicle as part of a person's job. I've also seen it included when someone is renting out a room in their home, but the rental payments are not included in the tax return as income.

9. New Spouse Income

This one is often a complete shock to people. New spouse income actually has a counter-intuitive impact on support payment. The new spouse has no obligation to support your children or your ex-husband, but they do have an impact on your income. When you get married to a new partner your tax filing status changes. (You get an advantage in filing MFJ v. filing Single.) You also receive a second exemption, so you are filing MFJ 2 instead of Single 1, which increases your support payment because it makes more income available for support since you are paying less income tax.

On the other hand, if your new spouse has income in addition to your income, your tax bracket changes. The more your new spouse earns, the less money you have to pay in support (or the more you receive in support).

A case I had in the last year had a father (my client) with a 35% timeshare of his teenage daughter. He had a small business as a landscaper and worked part-time for one of the larger package delivery services. He earned about $3,500 per month between the two jobs. His ex-wife, one of the most unsavory characters I have ever come across in my entire career, was a high school teacher with a master's degree. She said awful things to him and about him. She felt like she was the ant, and he was the grasshopper (a lot like the LDS Hippie case). This was probably true, but he was a really funny guy and fun to be around. She was one crappy sourpuss. Anyway, she managed to rope another man into her life—a former cop with a disability pension of around $50,000 per year (nontaxable income) who was also a high school teacher. (She had an affair on campus, but my client was the bad guy? ... Usually, I get over these things but this one is obviously still bugging me.) Both her and the former cop earned about $90,000 per year.

At a 35% timeshare with his income at $42,000 per year and hers at around $90,000 per year, there would have been no child support payment (if she claimed the child exemption) or a very minimal one from the mother to the father. But when you added in the new spouse income, an increase of $90,000 per year, plus his $50,000 nontaxable pension, the payment from my client to her jumped to around $300 per month! I argued vigorously for this guy that the Court should discount the new spouse income to $0 based on the equities of the situation. It did not make sense that he had to pay more child support because the new spouse made more money and pushed the ex-wife up a tax bracket. He was paying more in child support to the ex-spouse because she married a richer husband.

Family Code section 4057.5 sets forth that you cannot use new spouse income to set or modify support. At least not directly. Family Code section 4059, however, says you can use it to determine the actual tax consequences on the parent's responsibility.

County of Tulare v. Campbell (1996) 50 Cal.App.4th 849 is a killer when it comes to arguing this issue:

"When a parent has married a wage-earning spouse with whom he or she is filing a joint tax return, accurate calculation of the parent's actual tax liability is not possible unless the couple's combined gross income is considered. The new spouse's income is merely included in the calculation of the parent's actual federal and state liability; while that inclusion may, depending on the circumstances, affect the "bottom-line" child support amount, we do not perceive this indirect effect as being at odds with section 4057.5. Rather we interpret section 4057.5 as prohibiting direct consideration of a new spouse's income in determining proper support, absent extraordinary circumstances. Thus, the trial court is not authorized to raise or lower child support because a parent has remarried. However, this does not preclude determination of a parent's actual tax liability based on the combined gross income of the parent and his or her new spouse. This tax liability may then be taken into account in order to accurately determine the parent's real net disposable income."

This is a true bullet for anyone dealing with a person who is in the counter-intuitive situation of remarrying wealthy and finding themselves entitled to more child support. I argued that the consideration of new spouse income in this instance was unfair (but lawyers hate to argue fairness when law dictates a different outcome). How could it be that a father with 35% timeshare on $42,000 per year was paying child support into a home where the gross income was $230,000 per year? The caselaw doesn't help you out in this situation because the legislature has built a basic inequity into the Family Code in the Family Code section 4057.5 and 4059 distinction. The parent receives the benefit of the shield provided by 4057.5 (where new spouse income isn't factored into the calculation because there is no obligation to support your new spouse's child) but gains the advantages of having the new tax status accounted for from 4059 (which permits factoring new spouse tax brackets into the equation). The Courts have not liked this. The Court in *In re Marriage of Romero* (2002) 122 Cal. Rptr 2d 220 balked at the inequity of the situation in which Husband's new wife had a great job while Wife's fortunes completely failed. He was able to get his support reduced in the meantime.

I was forced to argue equity and unfairness. I repeated loudly that it was unfair at the most basic level that this dad who had joint physical custody of his teenage daughter—who needed a bedroom, clothes, sports team fees, high school activities, etc. —on an only slightly better than subsistence living in Santa Barbara County, was going to write a monthly check to a household with four times as much income.

I resorted to equity. Equity (fairness) is always available in any case, but judges prefer law (cases and statutes). You can ask for a deviation from guideline support as the Court in *County of Lake v. Antoni* (1993) 18 Cal.App.4th 1102 authorized a deviation from the guideline support calculations if the circumstances warrant it. But although everyone wants to argue in favor of a deviation, there are limited circumstances for it. The *Antoni* court upheld the consideration based on a large consumer debt and additional children the father was supporting, but it also noted that his child support payment tripled rather than quadrupled as the computer program said it should.

In any event, we lost that issue. We did get a reduction in support from the $556 per month my client was paying to around $230 per month, and even pulled a little off the guideline support calculation with our equity argument. My client had a new baby on the way and the court factored that into the calculation under hardships (below). Still, I was disappointed to lose the legal argument on that one.

10. Adjustments to Income

The adjustments to income slot is for deductible expenses from the tax return. These do not reduce income available for support, but increase it because of the advantaged tax treatment.

11. Child Support Paid – Other Relationship

This is a guideline deduction, but there is no positive or negative tax treatment for the payment of child support.

12. Spousal Support Paid – Other Relationship

This is a guideline deduction, but it is a tax adjustment to income.

13. Health Insurance

This is both a guideline deduction and an itemized tax deduction. There are options available in the computer program to make sure you get the correct treatment. Self-employeds enter the information into the "paid by party" column, while wage earners enter it into the "wage deduction" column. There is a column for pre-tax contribution as well.

14. Itemized Deductions

This is an important one, but again, counter-intuitively so. The greater your itemized deductions, the higher your support obligation (or the lower your need) because you have more income available for support. Normally the major itemized deduction is for mortgage interest, property taxes, and insurance. However, you can be industrious and search through your tax returns looking for additional itemized deductions to increase the support obligation if that is what you are trying to do. My experience is that most lawyers (and almost all judges and/or parties) have no idea how to work their way through the more complex areas of computer program calculations. So, if you are trying to reduce support, focus more time on your spouse's itemized deduction entries than on your own.

15. Mandatory Retirement

For PERS and STRS recipients particularly, you want to remove the FICA and social security tax settings but enter your mandatory retirement contribution. If it is "qualified," the computer program treats it as a tax benefit to you—an Adjustment to Income. If it is "not qualified," the computer program removes the benefit to you but also treats it as not available for support.

16. Hardship Deductions

There are two types of hardship deductions: 1) direct reductions of income available for support due to statutory expenses like extraordinary medical expenses, and 2) a "hardship children" calculation.

For direct statutory expenses you add these into the calculation directly as a dollar amount. These might be catastrophic medical care expenses or something similar. For example, I have a very wealthy client who is basically bedridden and has incontinence issues. We are fighting over whether the $15,000 monthly payment for her around the clock health attendants counts as catastrophic medical needs for purposes of this calculation. Because the Husband earns on the order of $800,000 per year, the result will mean the difference in a spousal support payment of $36,000 per month (if it is not catastrophic) and $48,000 per month (if it is).

The hardship deduction for "hardship children" (which sounds like a sad movie to me) is calculated in such a way as to match the Presumed Child Support (plus basic add-ons) on a per child basis. The hardship for each "hardship child" is set equal to the presumed child support order. It can add or reduce child support obligations depending on which side of the line it falls.

A hardship child is one-half if the other parent is involved in the matter. A recent case frustrated me to no end because the Judge wanted to give the mother a full hardship for a child whose father was not seeing her, but who was local and could have been made to pay more support. They had an agreement that the father did not have to pay support (or very little) if he would just leave them alone (not my favorite order, but supposedly he was a pretty bad dude, so maybe it was better that way). My point to the Court was that my client (the newly divorcing stepfather) should not have to support the child because the Mother refused to go after the biological father for more support. Our judge told us that he was more interested in what was actually happening than in speculation on what could happen, so he gave her the full hardship. It changed support $75 per month on a $3,300 per month support payment because my client was a high earner.

17. Other Guideline Deductions

The amounts you enter as other discretionary deductions reduce income available for support dollar-for-dollar. In addition to actual discretionary deductions, you can use this line to adjust guideline nets due to program limitations.

18. Child Support Add-Ons

There are certain statutory add-ons. Some are mandatory, like childcare costs so that a parent can work, and unreimbursed health insurance; and some are discretionary like payments for educational or extra-curricular activities. These can be added to the support calculation (payable directly to the parent incurring the costs) or they can be payable directly to the provider.

Childcare costs are confusing because it might seem like the parent already gets a lot of support and should have to pay childcare costs on their own. However, the theory is that if they are not working, they shouldn't have childcare costs, and if they are working and need childcare to be able to work, the supporting party is actually getting a benefit from it in the form of reduced support. Thus, the supporting party should be liable for half the cost of the childcare.

19. Tax Settings

I already mentioned it above, but you can modify the tax setting for anyone who does not pay all employment taxes—meaning FICA, social security, Medicare, etc. Teachers, firefighters, law enforcement, public servants, some nurses, correctional officers, in short, anyone who works for a public entity likely doesn't pay one or all of these. Make sure you go on the special screen and uncheck the boxes. (Or make sure you don't if you don't want to pay more support and you can hope that neither the lazy judge nor the lazy opposing counsel will catch it). A client I inherited from another lawyer came into the office recently. She is a high school teacher who makes a little over $100,000 per year. She does not pay FICA or Medicare. Lazy lawyering by two lawyers, and a completely uninterested Judge, led to them failing to uncheck the FICA and Medicare boxes—but they still gave her credit for her mandatory retirement contributions. This led to an under-award of child support by over $400 per month, and led to a "no payment" of spousal support that should have been around $150 per month. In total, failing to check those boxes cost the Husband about $550 per month. As we discussed the $187 per month payment she was ordered to make, we also considered leaving the order alone uncorrected (as mad as she was to be paying it). Predictably, the previous lawyers made other mistakes as well—misstating her income, undercalculating her health insurance payment, failing to include her union dues (all things that would have reduced her support burden) but none of them were as serious as the issue of the failure to uncheck the FICA and Medicare boxes. Those are employment taxes that she does not pay; thus, represent income available for support that no one calculated.

If you are handling your divorce or child custody matter on your own, you will want to review each of the inputs to see if there are helpful additions you can make. Ordinarily, anything that will save you money in tax obligations, anything that you are required to pay by law, or anything that provides more net spendable or discretionary income for you means that you will pay a higher support payment (or receive a lower support payment). Conversely, anything that tends to increase the other parent's net spendable income or reduce their tax obligation will result in a reduction in support you pay.

As you calculate support payments, follow the basic principles (and their corollaries):

1) Anything that increases your net cash flow as against your tax liability will increase your support.

2) Anything that you are obligated to pay, whether health insurance premiums, taxes, child or spousal support from another marriage, or children that you take care of from another marriage, will impact your net spendable income negatively and will reduce the amount you have to pay.

3) Any mandatory costs, such as unreimbursed health care or childcare costs (but not premiums) are added on at 50 cents on the dollar.

4) Your child support is for daily living, and does not include school clothes, shoes, athletic team fees, field trips, etc., so make sure that you contribute to those things as well. Only assholes tell their children, "I already give your mom money, she has to pay for that stuff!"

5) Discretionary deductions from your paycheck for 401K contributions, HAS contributions, or charitable deductions are not considered mandatory and may impact your support payment if they are pre-tax contributions because they are income you do not get taxed on.

6) Mortgage payments are generally beneficial to the payor because of the mortgage interest and property tax deductions in the tax code, so paying more may shield more income and increase your support payment.

Finally, remember the counter-intuitive principle that new spouse income will decrease the support payment to the payor because new spouses have no obligation to support their new spouse's children, so their income is not available for support. However, because the added income may increase their tax bracket and result in higher taxes on the payor's income, it may reduce income available for support. Remember my $3,500 per month income landscaping client who ended up paying child support to a household with more than $200,000 in income ($50,000 of which was a tax-free pension) because the new spouse's income pushed the total household income into a higher tax bracket.

CHAPTER 14

Spousal Support

SPOUSAL SUPPORT HAS become a more pressing topic in the last ten years than I realized during the first eight years of my family law practice. Perhaps I simply don't have enough historical perspective, or maybe the more experienced lawyers (who still refer to me as "the new guy," by the way) would argue that it has always been a significant issue. I perceive it as particularly salient as women increasingly out-earn men.

I don't have a lot of citations in this book, mostly because I didn't want it to bog down with a ton of footnotes. Even most case names are without case citations, under the theory that you can just drop the case name into an online search tool and find the case. If it's a case that has a common name like *Marriage of Brown* you can just add "time rule" to the search and it will come up. So, when I cite statistics, they are a) for illustrative purposes only – it truly doesn't matter if it is exact or not and b) I presume you can look them up, same as me.

A 2022 or 2023 Pew Charitable Trust study found that in 55% of heterosexual marriages, husbands earn more than wives, in 29% of heterosexual marriages, husbands and wives earn about the same, and in 16% of heterosexual marriages, wives earn more than husbands. Ten years ago, 98% of men and women who came to my office for their first consultation believed that the man would pay alimony to the woman, regardless of earnings.

"How bad is my alimony going to be?," the typical man would ask, and I would inquire about the earnings between them. They would be shocked to learn that spousal support isn't a given and it's definitely not a gender-specific term. I do note that men are much more likely to believe they will have to pay spousal support and much more likely to have come to terms with it before they walk into my office than women are.

In fact, I would venture to say that any time a woman is sitting across from me and I tell her that she has spousal support liability, it is the equivalent of one of those super anti-heroes who gets mad and sets off a nuclear fusion reaction. Women, in my experience would rather burn down the world than pay spousal support to a man. They get so mad. They hate it so much. But why?

I was interviewing a potential new client recently who is a nurse. She was a doctor in her native country, came to the United States with nothing, fleeing civil unrest and got a job as a nurse's assistant. She went to school to do a nursing degree in the U.S. because she needed to work quickly. Got an R.N. degree and went to work. She now makes close to $200,000 per year. Her husband is from the same country as her. He, she said, has "been a lifetime student, sitting on his ass and never deciding what he wants to do for the last 18 years!" He recently moved to Brazil to go to medical school, leaving her with three teenagers.

All he wants, right now, is to have her file taxes jointly with him. I started to talk to her about spousal support liability, dividing her CalPERS pension with him, her 401(k) and half the equity in their house. I thought she was going to burn my office down. I understand being mad, I really do. It really hurts to give up half your stuff and 38% of your income to your spouse. Men have been doing it for generations too.

It used to be that doctors or lawyers, or other professionals would come to my office, just understanding that they had to pay alimony (alimony and spousal support are synonymous and not gender related. "Palimony" is support paid by unmarried couples and isn't something we cover in this book). More recently, men will come to my office and complain that their wives underearn and that they have educational backgrounds that would support them with full-time earnings. Just as they want to share the child rearing, they want to share financial responsibility with their wives.

Both sides want to tell me, in the last ten years, about how lazy their spouse is and how they don't do anything and they have to do everything and etc. But I tell them, "stop saying that! You are making their argument for them!" In other words, your marriage is your marriage. No one cares how you do your marriage. I have clients with open marriages who film themselves having sex with other people and watch together and clients who live on different coasts and clients who have "traditional Christian families" and clients who cheat and clients who gamble and clients who do all of the drugs together or separately and clients who have mental health problems and PTSD and everything you can think of. The Court does not judge. I do not judge.

But, when it comes to paying alimony, the high earner pays the lower earner. Start with that as the general rule. Yes, there is a whole body of caselaw and perhaps some statutes that support exceptions to these rules, but you can be pretty sure that if you are the high-earner (and I don't mean nominally high-earner – if you are the high-earner by $25,000 or more per year – you will be paying spousal support, male or female to a male or female partner).

That means that when you say "all he did was lay around all day while I busted my ass" or "he's a lifetime student who didn't help out," all you have told the Court is that "for 17 years I was OK with him being a lifetime student and now I am finally sick of it." The law and the Court assume that you approved of his behavior or her lack of work by not divorcing sooner. I know that hurts, but the truth is, whether she did or didn't work (even though she has an MBA or JD or contractor's license) is a product of your marriage. You always have the option to divorce. You vote with your feet. If you do not tell your spouse that she must work or you will divorce her and keep your word, the Court will assume that you were fine with her not working. People don't work outside the home during marriages for all types of reasons and the Court is not really going to engage in the question of why the person did not work during the marriage (although, Family Code 4320 does give us some things to question) (i.e., did one spouse do domestic duties so the other could work? Did one spouse put the other one through school? Was there documented domestic violence?)

In other words, the argument that the other spouse was lazy helps them more than it helps you, especially if they were long-term lazy. If they were long-term lazy, it looks like you agreed to it. And people unfairly call each other lazy all the time, so really ask yourself if it was laziness. If your spouse was capable of earning $20/hour and you are able to earn $300,000 per year and you decided as a family that he would stay home and raise kids so you can work, that is not laziness, that is a sound financial decision, even if it means at divorce that you have to pay alimony. I was surprised at the number of female lawyers with whom I went to law school who came out commanding excellent salaries and then married artists or temp workers or people with much lower earning potential. But, it was certainly a thing. We could wax philosophical about grasshoppers and ants and why it is that some ants love grasshoppers or we can start accepting reality that the high-earner will almost assuredly pay the low earner spousal support.

The law suggests that if the marriage is less than 10 years, spousal support is for half the length of the marriage. The rule is that you are trying to get the former spouse to be self-supporting by giving them a lifeline. There is no reason why support must last half the length of the marriage or, in the case of a long-term marriage, indefinitely. Spousal support terminates when:

A) The supported spouse gets remarried,
B) Either party dies, or
C) Further order of the Court (normally when someone retires or has a change of financial circumstance – such as when she finishes medical school or he passes the state bar).

Too often, spousal support is treated as a boondoggle for the receiving spouse and a cost or punishment for the paying spouse. It's truly meant to be a way for the receiving spouse to get on their feet and work toward becoming self-sufficient. Spousal support, like child support, is always too much for the payor to pay and less than if the payee goes to work. Everyone loses with long-term spousal support because it consigns the recipient to a life of just-barely-making it and takes enough out of the payor's pocket to keep them from ever getting ahead. It is always better, if you can, to get a job and develop a career – you will get more money than you lose in alimony.

A) *Pendente Lite* Spousal Support

Pendente lite spousal support or "temporary spousal support" is support calculated by the computer program. It uses all of the same input variables as the child support calculation, so I am not going to repeat them all here. Most counties use the computer program to come up with the presumptively correct calculation. There are different settings by county. My counties use Santa Clara County's formula, but I have practiced in Alameda County as well and it has its own slightly different calculation. There are a half dozen or so different formulas. If you don't own the computer program, which you wouldn't if you aren't a lawyer, you can use the California Child Support Calculator and tick the bubble at the very bottom for which county you are in. If you don't see your county then ask your favorite search engine to tell you which formula your county uses.

It is based solely on the need of the supported spouse and the ability to pay of the supporting spouse.

An award of temporary spousal support generally is "based on 'a showing of two conditions: the moving party's needs, and the other party's ability to pay." (*In re Marriage of Dick* (1993) 15 Cal. App.4th 144, 159; see also *In re Marriage of Murray* (2002) 101 Cal. App.4th 581, 594 [temporary spousal support may be ordered in any amount "subject only to the moving party's needs and the other party's ability to pay"].) "Ability to pay encompasses far more than the income of the spouse from whom temporary support is sought," and thus, "investments and other assets may be used for... temporary spousal support." (*In re Marriage of Dick*, supra, at p. 159.) In addition, the trial court "may properly look to the parties' accustomed marital lifestyle as the main basis for a temporary support order. [Citations.]" (*In re Marriage of Wittgrove*, supra, 120 Cal.App.4th at p. 1327.)

The typical formula is 40% of the net high earner's income minus 50% of the net lower earner's income. The computer calculates net high earner's income and net low earner's income using all of the sophisticated tools it uses for child support with all of the various input variables. I wish there was a better way of explaining it.

Here's a very rough example. Wife makes $180,000 per year ($15,000 per month) as a nurse. Husband makes $60,000 per year

($5,000 per month selling real estate). Wife nets about $10,000 per month and husband nets about $3,300 per month. The very rough formula is: $10,000 * .40 - $3,300 * .50 = $2,350 per month. This carries through with the $0 wage earner too. Roughly, $4,000 per month when high-earning Wife earns $15,000 per month as a nurse and low-earning Husband has no income from his work as a "lifetime student." $4,000 per month is a back breaker on $15,000 per month income. Wife needs Husband to finish medical school and get to work.

This is true across the board. It is a brutal fact early in the divorce litigation because parties are trying to figure out the money situation and there usually is not enough of it in the early stages, particularly, while each side is hiring lawyers with $10,000 retainers and trying to figure out a second rent payment and utility bills and food budget and the like. Wife will no doubt scream bloody murder about having her income reduced from $10,000 take home to $6,000. Husband will point out that he went from $10,000 per month income to $4,000. It's ugly all around.

The judge is not allowed to use the computer program when calculating spousal support, so I usually advise my support-paying clients to get on with the divorce as quickly as possible, because, at a minimum, we would expect to see support payments drop somewhere between 20% and 35% at trial. If I represent the supported spouse I argue for a 20% reduction and if I represent the supporting spouse, I argue for a 35% reduction at trial.

Permanent Spousal Support

Permanent spousal support is more involved. The Court looks at Family Code 4320 and analyzes a host of factors that help answer the question of how much permanent spousal support to grant. One of my judges often says, "spousal support determinations are where I have the most power. I can basically pick any number I want." While that is not entirely true, it is also not entirely untrue. The judge is not supposed to even look at the computer calculations to make the determination of permanent spousal support, but the reality is that picking a spousal support number isn't easy and the computer is as good a tool as any. I expect that the judge is going to at least look at the calculation when thinking over what number to pick.

Family Code 4320 (called "the 4320 factors"), are 13 different factors that go into the analysis of what permanent spousal support should be.

Family Code 4320 says:

"In ordering spousal support under this part, the court *shall consider all* of the following circumstances:

(a) The extent to which the earning capacity of each party is sufficient to maintain the standard of living established during the marriage, taking into account all of the following:

(1) The marketable skills of the supported party; the job market for those skills; the time and expenses required for the supported party to acquire the appropriate education or training to develop those skills; and the possible need for retraining or education to acquire other, more marketable skills or employment.

(2) The extent to which the supported party's present or future earning capacity is impaired by periods of unemployment that were incurred during the marriage to permit the supported party to devote time to domestic duties."

The first step is to figure out the marital standard of living and figure out how each party can contribute to both parties being at or near the marital standard of living post-divorce. Most families cannot afford to do this. This says look to marketable skills and how much time and expense it will take to develop marketable skills.

"(b) The extent to which the supported party contributed to the attainment of an education, training, a career position, or a license by the supporting party."

The Court analyzes whether or not the supported spouse basically took time away from their career to support the other spouse's career. This could mean doing domestic duties and it could mean working while the supporting party went to school (i.e., Wife works as a nurse to put Husband through medical school but does not go to medical school herself).

"(c) The ability of the supporting party to pay spousal support, taking into account the supporting party's earning capacity, earned and unearned income, assets, and standard of living."

Here, the Court looks at the ability to pay spousal support, taking into account not only current earnings but whether the supporting party could earn more (earning capacity), earned and unearned income (actual pay versus deferred compensation and stock options), assets (including passive income-producing assets and dividends) and standard of living. This is essentially to say, income from all sources.

"(d) The needs of each party based on the standard of living established during the marriage."

The marital standard of living provides the baseline from which the Court should make its spousal support decisions. The ability to pay is the "key" factor in determining spousal support (*Marriage of Cheriton*). (c) and (d) are the most important factors. The needs of each party and the ability to pay of each party.

"(e) The obligations and assets, including the separate property, of each party."

The Court can look to separate property assets of each party and also income-producing community property assets.

(f) The duration of the marriage.

(g) The ability of the supported party to engage in gainful employment without unduly interfering with the interests of dependent children in the custody of the party.

(h) The age and health of the parties."

These are pretty self-explanatory.

"(i) All documented evidence of any history of domestic violence, as defined in Section 6211, between the parties or perpetrated by either party against either party's child, including, but not limited to, consideration of:

(1) A plea of nolo contendere.

(2) Emotional distress resulting from domestic violence perpetrated against the supported party by the supporting party.

(3) Any history of violence against the supporting party by the supported party.

(4) Issuance of a protective order after a hearing pursuant to Section 6340.

(5) A finding by a court during the pendency of a divorce, separation, or child custody proceeding, or other proceeding under Division 10 (commencing with Section 6200), that the spouse has committed domestic violence."

It is not exactly clear what this means in terms of outcomes of spousal support calculations. There is a general proposition that survivors of domestic abuse should not pay spousal support to their abuser. This may be what this is referring to, but there is already a statute in place that creates a presumption against paying spousal support where there has been a criminal conviction. I think this likely is overplayed by so many people filing DVROs in order to gain a spousal support advantage. My thought is that if a supported spouse has been the survivor of domestic violence, they will be less likely to be required to get employment more quickly because of the anguish the violence has caused them. And if a supported spouse was the perpetrator of domestic violence, there may be cause to reduce the term or amount of spousal support they receive.

"(j) The immediate and specific tax consequences to each party."

After the 2019 Tax Bill eliminated the deduction for spousal support payors, this is a little bit iffy. However, there may be tax consequences such as capital gains taxes from liquidating separate property assets to pay support. There may also be tax consequences of early withdrawals from IRAs and 401(k)s, although I have almost never seen a court order spousal support from these types of assets except from Required Minimum Distributions.

"(k) The balance of the hardships to each party."

It is tough to consider what the balance of hardships might mean, but we can use some examples. If you have a health condition that will require ongoing care and treatment or if you have a dependent child or children from this or a different marriage or if you have a dependent parent, you would assume there would be a change in spousal support obligations if you are the supported spouse or supporting spouse. In other words, reasonable hardships that would have affected the community during the marriage will be considered in making spousal support awards. If Husband has Parkinson's Disease and cannot work or cannot keep the same work hours, we would expect a reduction in support if he is the paying spouse. Similarly, if Wife's elderly mother has Alzheimer's and needs care, reducing her ability to work, the support amount or the length of the award might be increased.

Here, again, the Court has tremendous power to do whatever it wants. Courts have the ability to balance hardships as they see fit. It is almost never overturned on appeal when they analyze hardships and make decisions based on that analysis.

"(l) The goal that the supported party shall be self-supporting within a reasonable period of time. Except in the case of a marriage of long duration as described in Section 4336, a "reasonable period of time" for purposes of this section generally shall be one-half the length of the marriage. However, nothing in this section is intended to limit the court's discretion to order support for a greater or lesser length of time, based on any of the other factors listed in this section, Section 4336, and the circumstances of the parties."

Whenever you read the term, "court's discretion," you should hear the legislature saying, "the Court has a ton of power to do whatever it wants." That's what this section says. In general, spousal support awards rarely get overturned on appeal because the trial court has so much discretion to determine the size of the spousal support award. The Court can make it longer or shorter than the general proposition that it be half the length of the marriage in short-duration marriages and can make it longer or shorter or put an end term on it in a long-duration marriage. Even Family Code 4336, which sets forth that a court retains jurisdiction indefinitely over spousal support in a long-duration marriage unless the court terminates its jurisdiction or the parties agree otherwise, gives the Court discretion to make a determination that a long-duration marriage is not of long duration if there were periods of separation and to make a short-duration marriage a long-duration marriage if it sees fit. In other words, even though there is law and it provides guidelines, the trial court has a ton of power to make exceptions to the guidelines and insert its own determinations.

"(m) The criminal conviction of an abusive spouse shall be considered in making a reduction or elimination of a spousal support award in accordance with Section 4324.5 or 4325."

I mentioned in my comments on section (i) that I was not sure what this meant in the context of spousal support awards because section (m) and Family Code 4324.5 and 4325 both create a presumption eliminating spousal support payable by the survivor to the abuser. It is clear that the legislature does not want survivors to pay abusers. It is not clear the effect of documented domestic violence that did not result in a criminal conviction on a spousal support calculation. Needless to say, no one wants survivors to pay abusers.

We are seeing a flowering of high-earning women filing DVROs against lower-earning men. I am not saying here that the claims are not good ones, but I do think we are seeing more such claims because women hate paying spousal support to men and this is a way to potentially get a reduction.

"(n) Any other factors the court determines are just and equitable."

And again, with the discretionary power of the Court to do just about anything it wants under the circumstances. As long as the Court says why it believes it is just and equitable to make an award that deviates from the norm, it'll be almost certainly upheld on appeal.

Need-Based Attorneys Fees and Costs

This is a large body of law, too large to cover in detail here. There are two fee-shifting statutes in Family Law based on need. The traditional "American Rule" is that each side pays its own attorneys fees. The American Rule has exceptions whenever parties contract around the rule (i.e., when a contract has a prevailing party attorney's fees provision) or when the statutes provide for attorneys fees. In courts of equity, particularly family law courts and probate courts, there are statutes that provide for attorneys' fees under certain conditions. Both Probate and Family Law courts have fees as sanctions for bad behavior or obstreperous lawyering.

But we are concerned here with need-based fees. Family Code 2030 and 2032 provide that the high-earner contributes to the low-earner's fees (2030) or the person with the larger separate property estate contributes to the smaller separate property estate owner's fees (2032). The factors are similar to the spousal support analysis except that the Court, to make an award must receive a *Marriage of Keech* declaration that sets forth what the fees were spent on so that the Court can analyze whether or not fees were expended judiciously (no pun intended). New caselaw in *Knox v. Knox* tells us that Courts must consider fee requests and cannot wait until the end of the litigation to make fee awards. Many judges liked to wait until the very end to pay lawyers. The fact that I am a lawyer will give away that I hated it when judges did that because it put me at risk of getting paid or not getting paid at the end. It also requires me to "carry" the case, paying my own staff to work on the case while I hope to get paid at the end.

Anyway, between *Knox* and *Keech*, the high-earner should expect to contribute some fees to the low-earner. It may not be at the beginning of the case, but it is likely coming at some point.

Strategies for Success

If you are the higher earner by a lot, you have some strategies that can help you minimize the pain from having to pay spousal support. The first and foremost thing is that you want to avoid a court-ordered *pendente lite* spousal support payment if you can. You can run the numbers as easily as the Court can run them.

Massage them a little bit, but bite the bullet; you are likely to be paying. The last thing you want to do is have the Court run the numbers for you and use numbers that do not benefit you and stick you with a big payment early in the litigation. That payment will end up becoming the *status quo* and when you get to trial, you will be arguing for a big reduction from that amount. Even if you get a big reduction, you will have overpaid support for a period of time. And if you get a small reduction at trial, it will have been set against a baseline number that is high.

There are ways to do this. Figure out your liability early and honestly. Know what your worst-case scenario is and your best-case scenario. In the *pendente lite* phase, it is likely that your spouse will be imputed some income if they do not have income and they have an employment history, but do not count on that being a big number. Minimum wage full-time is a likely bet. Smaller than that if you have school age children and you are a high-earner. It won't move the needle very far anyway.

I like reasonable sharing of bank accounts at an early phase. There is no reason to start depositing your check in another account unless you really cannot trust each other to spend wisely. This won't last forever, but it will save you from all sorts of future pain. A spouse who loses the high-earner's paycheck starts to panic. Panic leads to emergency motions. Emergency motions lead to judges in a snit. Judges in a snit lead to orders you will not like. Go slowly and be methodical even if you are mad as hell. This will lead to far less pain in the long-run. Trust me that you will thank me for it later.

If you follow the shared bank account plan and your spouse drains the account, then you will file an emergency motion, the judge will be in a snit in your favor and you will get good orders that you can live with. Setting your spouse up for success with a shared bank account for about 90-120 days is a good plan. Let them know that you are planning on depositing your paycheck in the account for the 90-120 days and that before you stop depositing the check in the account, you will give ample warning and that you will be contributing money to that account, but that you need a little time for the two of you to figure out how much money that should be when you get your own place, etc. Do this off books for as long as you can. The longer your spouse goes without asking the court for spousal support, the more it seems like he or she has things under control financially. If he or she comes to court in 180 days after filing and says: "I need spousal support." You can say: "I've been giving them an agreed upon amount of spousal support for the last 6 months. We finally had to come to court to get an order." Or you can just make the offer. In any event, the Court will see you as even-tempered and caring, even in the face of tension. If you've underpaid a little bit, it's likely to be forgiven – no guarantees of course, but this is the much better approach, and it keeps things calm. Calm people make agreements. Good agreements save you tens of thousands of dollars. You keep this off the Court's radar for as long as possible.

The next idea is to divide an asset early. Sell the house, liquidate some stock, or find another source of funds that you can give your lower-earning spouse early in the case. As opposed to the shared bank account, you do this with a written agreement signed by the judge and made into an order. The idea is that a signed agreement memorializes that you have made an agreement so that it doesn't bite you in the ass later, but it does much more than that. By having the judge sign off on the agreement, she will know that you have made an agreement. When Wife comes to court later to ask for support, the judge will have a record that she signed an agreement you made to divide an asset. The first question the judge will ask at the spousal support and attorney's fees hearing is: "Ma'am, did you receive the funds from the agreement I signed?" That will signal that the judge knows that you freed up cash for your spouse and that the need is not likely as dire as your spouse is making it out to be.

That said, the law says your spouse should not have to live off of their property settlement when you have available income or assets for support. So, you are playing the odds here. A thoughtful family law judge (of whom there are very few) will know that your spouse should not have to spend down their property money to pay for their living expenses and attorney. A not very thoughtful family law judge (of whom there are very many) will see that your spouse got $100,000 in cash 3 months ago and will wonder why they need more now.

I got a $60 million case a few years ago. There were hotshot lawyers on both sides – big Beverly Hills law firms billing millions of dollars in fees. I came on four years into the case. Husband started the case by liquidating a $15 million asset and giving Wife half. So, she had $7.5 million and no income. Husband had income of close to $2 million per year. Wife did not ask for spousal support or attorney's fees for four years until I got involved in the case as Wife's lawyer. Then she got $35,000 per month in spousal support and $200,000 in attorney's fees. To be fair, we asked for about double both numbers, but the point was that she did not ask for support or fees because she had $7.5 million. After four years, she had spent most of this on her home and her prior attorneys. No one got her spousal support or attorney's fees. What a shame. What a masterful play by Husband to bite the bullet early on and give her the cash so that she would not come around and ask for more cash. He probably saved himself $1.5 million in spousal support by doing so.

Finally, remember your best- and worst-case outcomes and do not get suckered into the trap of trying to find experts to jack your spouse's earning capacity up. You will spend tens or even a hundred thousand dollars trying to prove she can work as an ER nurse when she has been an aesthetics nurse for the last 8 years. I had this exact case where Wife had been a high-earning ER trauma nurse during the first part of the marriage. Husband was a firefighter. Both were earning around $150,000 during the marriage. Wife had attended a music festival and witnessed a grisly mass murder scene that made national headlines. She could not work in trauma anymore. She got work that worked for her and allowed her to use her RN degree. It paid about half. Husband hired experts to prove that she could earn more money as a trauma nurse. He got suckered into the trap of believing that he was going to prove that she should be earning $200,000 per year with her level of experience. He spent $25,000 on the expert report. She hired professional psychologists and had her own psychologist prepared to testify that her PTSD from the mass shooting made it impossible for her to work in trauma nursing. It was awful. Ultimately there was a standdown by both sides and the case resolved on the eve of trial, but not before each side had gone into their parents' inheritances to pay fees and experts. The difference in spousal and child support was about $1,000 per month. I did the math at one point and pointed out to them that they had spent more than $200,000 arguing over about $58,000 in potential child and spousal support liability. That is, if Husband won, it would have saved him $58,000 payable over 6 years at zero percent interest. He spent more than $100,000 in today's money on his attorney and experts to fight for this. They finally settled on some number in between but who cares, the damage had already been devastating.

They were so angry with each other, even years into a never-ending divorce that neither party could take a breath to see that they might lose the argument at trial. They both were so convinced of their righteousness that they refused to see a worst-case scenario outcome for them. I helped by explaining that both sides had substantial risk and that an angry judge could punish them both for bringing this to court when it should have settled years ago. If I knew the judge at all, I am certain that she would not have given either of them something that would look like a win. She would have reduced support by imputing wages to Wife and then made Husband give it back to her in attorney's fees. Or she would have pumped up the support and then made Wife pay it to Husband in attorney's fees. Even the lawyers were running on fumes heading into what was going to be a multi-week trial.

The point is, before you get enraged and start spending stupid money on stupid results, ask: what is my best-case scenario if I win what I am asking for? What is the real chance of success I will have with it? The reality in the nurse-firefighter case is that the judge did not like either party and did not like the case. She also knew that Wife did not have the money; any order for her to pay support based on imputed wages would have been met with failure. She could not have paid. Husband should have known that going in. Wife should have known that the judge did not like her especially and the chances that the judge would have ordered him to pay her anything more than a nominal amount were slim.

You do not litigate based on hope. Hope is not a course of action. Stay tight in the areas where you know you can win. You can certainly press in at the margins that Wife should have a better job where she earns more money, but if she was at Music Festival massacre, it is a waste to spend a week of trial trying to convince a judge to treat her like she can still be a trauma nurse. At the same time, his best argument would have been to say that she should stop trying to work for herself and get a job as an aesthetics nurse at a higher-end boutique med-spa where her income would have been about 40% higher. That's where the smart money would have been. Not trauma nursing after a massive trauma.

CHAPTER 15

Applying the Three Property Rules of Family Law to Property Division

> A) Dividing Pensions: The "Time Rule."
> B) Dividing Businesses: The Business Valuation.
> C) Ownership and Reimbursements in Property
>   a. Moore/Marsden – Community Property Ownership Interests in Separate Property.
>   b. Family Code 2640 – Separate Property Reimbursement Rights in Community Property.
>   c. *Watts/Epstein* Reimbursements
>   i. Paying Rent for Exclusive Use of Community Property
>   ii. Getting Reimbursed for Paying Community Property Debts

A hard truth about divorce is that half your stuff is going away. We may as well just rip this band-aid off at the outset of the chapter. Nothing about this is easy. Aside from the emotional toll of divorce, the loss of the edifice you have built during your lifetime of working – whether on your own or for someone else – is painful. For the high earner, in my experience, this can almost be as painful as the loss of the marriage itself. From the perspective of this book, it is easier to know what is coming so that as you negotiate, you understand what 50% means.

This chapter provides some hypotheticals to explain the law. I have already given you the Three Property Rules in divorce several times, but this chapter puts them into perspective so you can better understand them in action. Although family law can be broken down into relatively simple parts, the devil is in the details. It is easy enough for me to say: "1) all property acquired before marriage is yours, 2) all property acquired during the marriage is ours, 3) except inheritances and gifts," but this can get very complex very quickly. This chapter does not try to give all of the subtle nuances of how to put these rules into place, but it does give you an overview of how to conceptualize them so that you can do a deeper dive in your own particular circumstances.

It covers several different cases that bring the Three Rules into focus. Each of the cases is a play on the Three Rules, interpreting them in particular context. We can say that we know what we mean when we say "separate" or "community" property – we know that separate property is property you had before marriage, after separation or that you received as a gift or inheritance during the marriage. But there are complexities within this that are where lawyers earn their money...by taking yours. Understand these rules and save money and spend your time and effort where it matters.

Many assets take on a "mixed" character – such as assets you owned before marriage, but contributed to with community property funds during the marriage, or payments on community property obligations that you made with post-separation separate property earnings. There are pensions to which you contributed before marriage and then kept your same job during the marriage, making the same contribution during the marriage that you made before it (the "time rule"). There are homes that you owned before marriage, but paid the mortgage with your community property earnings (Family Code 2640 and *Moore/Marsden*). There is the home that you bought together but when he moved out, you continued to live there, and he contributed to the mortgage (*Watts/Epstein*). There are businesses that need to be valued and profits to be shared (*Pereira/Van Camp*; perhaps *Marriage of Geraci*).

Dividing Pensions: The "Time Rule"

How do we divide a pension earned partially in the marriage and partially before the marriage? Remember, we are following the Three Rules. You get what's yours from before the marriage, the community shares what you earned during the marriage, except gifts and inheritances. That means that the portion of your pension that you started earning before marriage – which is a type of compensation for your work – is yours, but whatever you contributed during marriage belongs to the community. How do we figure out the math?

Hypothetical 1: Pensions and Retirements: The "Time Rule"

Wife works as a union carpenter. She's been a member of the Carpenters' and Drywallers' union for 30 years. She was married to Husband for the last 18 years she was a union drywaller.

First, a pension is a thing of value. Second, a pension is a type of compensation to the worker. We know from the property rules that anything earned during marriage is community property. To put it bluntly, all compensation you receive from work the day before you get married is yours. But from the day of your marriage all the way to the date of separation, all compensation you earn from work is community property. That is because the community is entitled to all of your labor. So, whether you have your own business or you work for someone else, everything you receive as compensation for your labor – including, but not limited to, stock options (vested or unvested), deferred compensation of any sort, perquisites (vehicle use, gas card, per diems, BAH/BAQ if you are in the military, etc.), pension contributions, 401(k) and 403(b) contributions, employer matching contributions to any retirement plan and just about anything else you can think of that counts as compensation – is community property.

There are a number of different types of compensation that commence before marriage and continue on throughout the marriage – depending on your work situation. This hypothetical uses the pension (or what's referred to as a Defined Benefits Plan – where you get service credits that are converted to an annuity paid out monthly for your lifetime after retirement – to help describe how to handle a community property interest in deferred compensation.

Question 1: Is the pension a thing of value (to be divided)?

Answer: Obviously, yes.

Question 2: Doesn't Wife just keep it because she hasn't started receiving money from it yet and she earned it?

Answer: No, because she has already earned the right to receive the money from her pension by working at the job. If she left now, she could begin collecting it, either now or when she gets to be a certain age. Pension is another form of compensation.

Question 3: Should Husband get half the pension, or should he get something else?

Answer: Something else. Why? Because when they got married, Wife already had 12 years of service into her pension. It is the same as if she a bank account with $400,000 in it when they got married. Just because they put in another $600,000 into that account after marriage, doesn't change the fact that Wife had $400,000 in it when they got married. Remember the Three Property Rules—she gets what she brought *to* the marriage, and they split what she brought in *during* the marriage.

The way to divide the pension is by the "time rule," which comes from a case called *Marriage of Brown*. The formula for the time rule division of any assets that have a mixed character (except certain real property) is to divide the total years of contribution during the marriage by the total years of service. Here, 18 years of married service is divided by 30 years of total service.

Community Property (CP) Interest = Years of Contribution During the Marriage/ Total Years of Contribution. 18/30 = 60% CP.

Separate Property (SP) Interest = Years of Contribution before Marriage or after Separation/Total Years of Contribution. 12/30 = 40% SP

The Community has an ownership interest in 60% of the pension, and Husband will get one-half of that. Based on our three rules above, Wife owned 12 years of service credit when she got to the marriage, and together they earned another 18 years of service credit; thus, the community owns 18 out of a total of 30.

This is a very clean way of doing it. It uses round numbers and supposes a plan in which there are service year credits given rather than cash contributions. But the conceptual framework is there, and you can use that framework for any retirement division.

Cash contributions to a retirement account such as an IRA or a 401(k) are handled a bit differently, but with the same basic principle. Instead of dividing by total credit years, you do a fraction where you analyze the total amount on deposit at the beginning of the marriage, plus the earnings (positive or negative) on the premarital principal balance during the marriage. The separate property portion is the premarital balance on the date of marriage plus any market-driven gains or losses.

The community property portion is the contribution during the marriage plus earnings (positive or negative) on the community property portion.[11]

Check in on the Rule of Reasonability: seems fair doesn't it? She keeps what she brought to the marriage and he shares in what they made together. If you are the pension holder, you may not think that it's fair that your spouse gets half the pension you earned by working.

Suffice it to say, although you were working to earn the pension, your spouse was doing other things for the community or forgoing income to the community while you contributed to your pension. Your spouse may have been contributing his own earnings to the community, taking care of the home or children, or just forgoing income that was being paid to your retirement rather than to the family. Dividing a pension is not only fair and reasonable—it is the morally correct thing to do.

Ownership and Reimbursements in Property

    a. Family Code 2640 – Separate Property Reimbursement Rights in Community Property

Hypothetical 2: Real Property Owned Before Marriage (The Property Reimbursement Rules) Family Code 2640.

Husband owns a house when he and Wife get married. He has $100,000 in equity on the date of marriage. To let Wife knows he loves her, he puts her on title, thereby "transmuting" the property into community property. A transmutation is the conversion of property ownership from community to separate property or from

---

11 It gets more complicated if there are withdrawals from the account, but typically withdrawals during the marriage up to the date of marriage principal balance are community property if they are used for community property purposes, and withdrawals beyond the date of marriage principal balance are separate property.

separate to community property. On the date of separation, the home has $200,000 in equity. How should we divide it?

Look back at the Three Rules and the Rule of Reasonability. Husband had something worth $100,000 on the date of marriage. ($100,000 in the bank, in his pension, or in equity on a home. It's all the same: a thing of value that goes into the "of what?" column.) Husband keeps his $100,000 and the community splits the other $100,000. H gets $150,000 and W gets $50,000.

Family Code 2640 does not allow Husband to receive any growth on his original investment of $100,000. When Husband puts Wife on title, he agrees that Wife gets to share in any increase in value of the home equally with him with no benefit to him regarding the growth on that investment.

This is not equally true of a 401(k). In the 401(k) situation, if Husband has $100,000 in a 401(k) plan on the date of marriage and then contributes an additional $100,000 during marriage, we have to analyze the rate of return on Husband's original $100,000 invested in the Plan and then analyze the rate of return on the additional $100,000 invested in the plan. Thus, if, at the date of division of the Plan, there is $300,000, Husband will receive the $100,000 initially invested and all of the growth associated with that $100,000. Husband and Wife will split the $100,000 invested during marriage and the growth on that $100,000. Thus, Husband may receive $175,000 (the initial $100,000 + $75,000 in growth on that investment. Husband and Wife will then split equally the $100,000 contributed during marriage and $25,000 in growth.

I do not care for Family Code 2640, as it is applied to real property. The likely reason for the difference between real property and 401(k) contributions is that, Family Code 2640 assumes that Husband transmutes the real property from his separate property from before marriage to community property. He says: "Baby, I love you so much, I am going to give you half of my house; that way, if I die, you will get it all." Family Code 2640 has problems both directions.

In nearly 100% of cases, Husband and Wife believe that when Husband puts Wife on title, he is giving her 50% of his home. That means both of them believe that Husband is also giving Wife one-half of the equity in the home whenever it is that he puts her on title. But Family Code 2640 says that Husband actually keeps his equity interest in the home when he does that. So, if the home has $100,000 in equity, he gets that back first. Then he and Wife split the additional equity in the home after she is added to title. Husband does not get any value for the additional growth on his $100,000 investment, unlike the 401(k) where he gets growth on his initial investment. Perhaps this has to do with transmutation – when Wife is added to title of the home, Husband has given her something of value, which he is allowed to do without Wife giving him anything back (the legal way of saying this is that spouses can give each other gifts without "consideration"). With a 401(k), the Plan interest is owned by Husband from beginning to end. His contributions to the Plan are community property contributions to his otherwise separate property 401(k). Spouses do not transmute a 401(k), by definition. Instead, there is a community property contribution to a separate property asset, thereby increasing the value of the separate property asset. Since no spouse can gain an advantage at the expense of the other spouse (or the community), we give the community credit for what is contributed, but we do not take away the spouse's separate property investment.

The difference seems to be in the transmuting of the asset. This is also true in the *Moore/Marsden* context, which is how we calculate Wife's interest in Husband's separate property home if he never puts her on title, but instead just uses his earnings to pay the mortgage principal, interest, taxes and insurance (PITI).

I said that I do not like Family Code 2640 above for two reasons. The first reason is that when Husband adds Wife to title of his separate property home, both he and Wife believe that he is giving her half the home. I do not like a situation in which someone has given the other a gift that the gift-giver and the gift-receiver both believe is one-half of the home, including the equity in the home and then, when they divorce, Husband and Wife each find out that the gift was only in the future equity growth of the home. That seems like Husband "lucks out" at Wife's expense.

On the other hand, transmutation aside, I also do not believe that it is just that, if Family Code 2640 is going to give Husband his equity in the home back, that Husband should not get growth on his original investment. *Moore/Marsden*, below, shows that if Husband never puts Wife on title to the home, he gets his original investment on the home back plus all of the growth in that original investment in the home and the community only gets growth on the contributions during marriage (more like the 401(k) Plan).

Other than deeding the property to Wife during the marriage, there is no other basis for this. By signing the deed transmuting the property to community property, Husband should either be giving Wife one-half interest in the home, including all of its equity, or Husband should be keeping his equity and all of the growth on his equity investment. Family Code 2640 unabashedly splits the baby on this one and gives Husband his equity back but then does not allow him any growth on it. This is a stinker of a rule that was poorly conceived and really just does not serve either party in a legally consistent manner.

Nevertheless, Family Code 2640, in very general, even if inconsistent with other rules, terms, follows the guidelines we set out above. H gets back what he had when they got married, and W gets to share in the growth from the date he changed its ownership from separate property to community property. I don't like Family Code 2640 as it stands and yet, although I think it is a terribly written rule, I admit that it follows the Rule of Reasonability and the Three Rules set forth above.

The only way to waive a Family Code 2640 right is through a written waiver in which a person writes, "I fully understand that I am entitled to a Family Code 2640 reimbursement for the equity in my home, but even though I know that, I intend to give half of the equity to my spouse as a gift."

You know how many people have done that? That's right. 0. Even when lawyers draft Family Code 2640 waivers (or Transmutation Agreements) the Appellate Courts still overturn them. Earlier, I referenced my unpublished Appellate case called *Marriage of Vanherweg* (2019) 2d Civil No. B292651 where the court did just that.

The point is that, even when the parties waive their interests specifically and fully, the Court can still overturn it if the party says they did not understand it. That just sucks and if you think that I am having a hard time explaining it here, imagine how it felt to explain it to my client.

Family Code 2640 also includes any separate property paydown of the community property mortgage or any improvements to community property with separate property. The old rule was that if a Husband contributed separate property to paydown a community property mortgage or improve the property, there was a "gift presumption" that Husband gave this money to the community. There was no corresponding rule for Wife. Husbands managed the community finances until the mid-1970s (I know, right?) and therefore any investment of Husband's separate money in the community was considered a gift and any investment of Wife's money required her to be paid back.

So, any investment of separate property that leads to the "acquisition" or "improvement" of community property gets paid back without growth or interest to the person who invested the money. My position is that people should be free to give the gifts they give. No one thinks, during marriage, that when they use an inheritance to pay down the mortgage, they are going to get the inheritance money back. They think they have just reduced the mortgage. They think is a gift to the community. Just the same as when Husband adds Wife to title of his premarital home. I do not believe in "bail outs." My view is that: "if you give a gift, you have given the gift. No take backs."

Family Code 2640 is a "take back" law. I don't like it. But it is the law.

Now, don't get me wrong, the sexist "gift presumption" in the 1970s that only applied the gift presumption to Husbands should and could never be permissible in the gender-equal world we live in now, but when both the giver and the receiver believe they have given or received a gift, the gift should be completed, not later discovered that the gift-giver gets to take the gift back.

So, Family Code 2640 is bad in both directions. 1) It is bad because it is a "take back" law that permits the giver to renege on his or her gift, only when some lawyer later tells them that the law gives them their money back. 2) It is bad because, if it is not a gift at all, but an investment into the community property, then the investor (not gift-giver) should get return on their investment just like they would in a *Moore/Marsden* situation that I describe in the next section. Why would Husband invest his separate property money in community real property in such a way as to pay down the mortgage without getting a return on his investment any more than he should get to take his gift back after giving it?

    b. *Moore/Marsden* – Community Property Ownership Interests in Separate Property

Hypothetical 3: The *Marriage of Moore/Marriage of Marsden* Reimbursement Rules.

California has two cases (*Marriage of Moore* and *Marriage of Marsden*) that make more sense than Family Code 2640 reimbursements, but there are problems with these rules as well. But before the problems, let me describe the law. In the Family Code 2640 case, Husband placed Wife on title to his separate property real property and "transmuted" it from being separate property into community property.[12]

My criticism of Family Code 2640 is in two parts: first, that when the transmutation occurs, both parties believe that Husband is gifting Wife one-half of the equity, only to find out at divorce that Husband was not gifting Wife anything other than title ownership and future growth in equity. If the house went down in value, Husband would get all the equity and if it went up in value, Husband would get "his" equity back first before Wife received anything. The second part of my criticism is that if Husband is gifting Wife future growth in equity, why doesn't he receive growth on his initial investment the way he would with a partially separate property 401(k) Plan? Family Code 2640 is inconsistent because it tries to solve a problem with a legislative pronouncement but does not follow the general rule very well – even if it sort of follows the rules a little bit.

---

12   A "transmutation" occurs when one party owns property separately and converts it to co-ownership as community property. It may also occur when the parties jointly own community property and convert it back to one spouse's separate property. This normally happens with an "interspousal transfer deed" or a "quitclaim deed." The Family Code allows for both types of transmutations, but the "fiduciary duties" require a very strong amount of proof that there was no undue influence or pressure exerted on one spouse to give the other spouse their property.

In the *Moore/Marsden* cases, Husband owns real property before the marriage as his separate property. The parties move into it, but he never puts Wife on title -even though she is his wife and he loves her very much, he does not love her enough to add her to title – maybe he says: "this house is for the children of my first marriage when I die." (which is also wrong, as we will see). But, he is not above using their community property income to pay down "his" mortgage. Her income and his income.

The *Moore/Marsden* cases say that the community begins acquiring a property interest in the property by paying down the mortgage principal. Principal payments are relatively small as a percentage of the overall value of the property. Husband gets to keep all of his down payment and value in the home and the community gets a small property interest with each payment it makes.

At the time the community begins paying the mortgage on the property, Husband is entitled to all the equity in the home on the date of marriage and any growth that occurs on that equity, while the community (i.e., one-half to each party) is entitled to the amount of principal paid down during the marriage and any growth on that.

This is like a 401(k) case where there is $100,000 in a 401(k) in Husband's name alone on the date of marriage. During the marriage Husband continues to put money in "his" 401(k). At divorce, Husband has put $100,000 in "his" 401(k). The 401(k) has $250,000 in it because of the market-driven gains in the 401(k). Husband gets $100,000. The community gets $100,000 (Husband and Wife each get $50,000). And then we determine how to divide the increased money from the market by how much the $100,000 in the 401(k) from before the marriage earned during the marriage, and how much was earned from the $100,000 that went into the 401(k) during the marriage. This is essentially *Moore/Marsden* applied to a house; it is just more difficult because most people do not appraise their homes on the date of marriage.

The community property percentage ownership interest in the home can be either small or large depending on the length of the marriage and the principal payments. But it also conveys an ownership interest that is not simply a reimbursement right. The community ends up owning a portion of the house, which in this example might extend to Wife having the right to live in the house over Husband's objection; or Husband owing Wife fiduciary duties regarding the house (in a way that he would not if it was purely separate property); or Wife could possibly even be able to force a sale of the home if her interest in the home is larger than Husband can afford to buy out.

To be fair, the community interest is normally not very large. Walking through it with fake real numbers, we can see how *Moore/Marsden* plays out in practice.

Numbers for Examples Below:
1. Purchase Price: $500,000.
2. Down payment: $100,000.
3. Value on Date of Marriage *(Bono v. Clarke)*: $600,000.
4. Mortgage Principal Date of Marriage $300,000.
5. Total Equity on Date of Marriage: $300,000.
6. Mortgage principal Date of Separation: $250,000.
7. Community reduction in principal: $50,000.
8. Value of Property on Date of Separation: $700,000.

9. Value of Property on Date of Trial[13]: $800,000.

Moore/Marsden Community Property Interest Analysis

$700,000 (DOS value) - $6000,000 (DOM value) = $100,000 (appreciation during marriage).

Community mortgage paydown = $50,000.

Community interest in appreciation: $50,000 (principal reduction) divided by $600,000 (DOM value): $50,000/$600,000 = **8.3%**

Community interest in the appreciation is 8.3%* $100,000 (appreciation During Marriage) = $8,300.

Plus, the $50,000 paydown of the mortgage principal during marriage.

In addition, because the community paid the mortgage down $50,000 during marriage, the community is entitled to reimbursement of this $50,000. In total, the community has a $58,300 interest in the real property, of which Wife is entitled to one-half or $29,150. Husband's interest in his separate property home worth $800,000,

---

13 Date of separation or date of trial? There is a split of authority between *Moore/Marsden* (date of trial) and *Bono v. Clark*, which is a later case that departs from date of trial value in favor of date of separation value based on Family Code 771:

"the relevant statute dictates crediting the separate property estate with post-separation appreciation. (See, Fam. Code § 771, subd. (a) ["The earnings and accumulations of a spouse . . ., while living separate and apart from the other spouse, are the separate property of the spouse"].) For these reasons, the right of the community to share in the property's appreciation begins with the funding of improvements and ends as of the date of separation." *Bono v. Clark*, 103 Cal.App.4th 1409, 1427 (Cal. Ct. App. 2002). *Mohler v. Mohler (In re Marriage of Jodie)*, 47 Cal.App.5th 788, 794-95 (Cal. Ct. App. 2020), a much more recent case, follows *Bono v. Clark*: "Thus, during a marriage, only the portion of community assets that is used to pay off loan principal is relevant to establishing the community interest in the property. After separation, however, the earnings and accumulations of a spouse are that spouse's separate property. (Fam. Code § 771, subd. (a).)"

Because both *Moore/Marsden* and *Bono v. Clark* (affirmed recently in *Mohler v. Mohler*) are both still good law, you can argue whichever is better for your position, although, as you will see, in most cases, it really won't amount to much difference in value).

on which Wife was never added to title is: $770,850; Wife's interest is $29,150.

If we use the Date of Trial value of $800,000 (rather than Date of Separation value of $700,000), the Community Property (CP) interest increases $8,300 (of which Wife gets half or $4,650). This is why I noted that it really does not have a large impact on the community property interest whether you use the date of separation or date of trial value (unless it is a really long-term marriage).

The Community Property (CP) interest under *Moore/Marsden* (adding in *Bono v. Clark*) gives Husband credit for the value of the home at the date of marriage and then stops giving the community credit for any increases in value after separation. It's a calculation that is mostly complicated by the fact that most people do not get these values when they are getting married because most people do not think that their separate property homes will have a community property component. If they did, they might make them community property from the get-go by adding Wife's name to title at the beginning of the marriage.

Let's do an analysis using the same numbers as we used in the *Moore/Marsden* calculation under Family Code 2640, but imagine that Husband had added Wife's name to title of the home on the date of marriage.

Under Family Code 2640, Husband gets credit for the value of the property on the date Wife is added to title, in this scenario, he adds her to title incident to marriage. Husband gets his $600,000 interest back at divorce, but he and Wife equally share the increase in value to the date of trial, which is $800,000. Husband's Family Code 2640 interest is $600,000. Husband and Wife split $200,000. Each takes $100,000. Husband gets $700,000 and Wife gets $100,000. We use date of trial value rather than the date of separation value because the home was transmuted to community property when Husband added Wife to title. Husband does not get any credit for the increase in value of the property based on his $600,000 initial "investment" in ownership of the house.

This rule seems "slightly fairer" to me than Family Code 2640, because once you get married your income is community property. It would be unfair for community property income to be used to benefit only one spouse, which is what would happen if the property remained separate property with no community ownership. Husband and Wife are using their community property income to pay down Husband's mortgage for Husband's benefit. The family law does not like this.

"Slightly fairer" aside, there are several things not to like about *Moore/Marsden*.

1) Unwittingly to both parties, Wife gets an ownership interest in Husband's property. Using our above example, Wife gains ownership over Husband's property and neither party is aware. In Family Code 2640 there is a gift that is not really a gift, because Husband can "take it back" at divorce, while under *Moore/Marsden* Wife is gaining a property interest that neither party knows about. Here, Husband deliberately does not add to title to "his" house and the parties go forward (Wife being at least marginally OK with not being on title to Husband's house because, well, she married him), and no one thinks that Wife has any interest in the home. Then, upon divorce, Husband and Wife discover, lo and behold, Wife actually owns some of the home.

Think about what Husband may have said to Wife about the house: "this house is for my children of my first marriage, but we can live here." In fact, it turns out, that he is incorrect about this. He will leave most of the house to his children, but not all of it, because the community takes an ownership interest in the home. In the above example with fake numbers, this is a small amount, but if the second marriage is 30 years long, the community can own the entire interest without ever changing title. In my appellate case called *Wilkin v. Nelson*, the Court found that the home that was solely titled in Husband's name had become 100% community property during the marriage. Thus, the house that was for "his children," had become 100% community property. The agreement that the parties had where Wife kept her separate property home as a rental and Husband and Wife lived in Husband's separate property home so that each would have something for their children, failed because Moore/Marsden converted the home to 100% community property over the years. (Husband kept the home anyway for other reasons).

In Family Code 2640, everyone thinks Husband has made a gift to the community by paying down the mortgage (or adding Wife to title), but it turns out he gets a "take back" at divorce. In *Moore/Marsden*, no one thinks Husband has given Wife anything and in divorce, Wife actually owns a portion of it, including the increase in value on her portion due to the increase in value of the property. How can it be that Husband's Family Code 2640 "gift" receives no return on investment, when Wife is on title with him and Wife gets return on investment when both parties agreed that the house belongs to Husband? These rules do not square.

2) Husband can step into a fiduciary duty trap by doing things with his property without Wife's consent, because he does not know she owns any part of it. Husband may unwittingly breach his fiduciary duties to wife by selling, transferring, or encumbering what he thinks is separate property, only to find out later that there is a community property interest and that he owes Wife certain duties. He may unwittingly step into a breach of fiduciary duty trap and could face sanctions, or at the very least have to pay his wife's attorneys' fees for acting with his own property that neither he nor Wife thinks Wife has any interest in.

3) Wife lives in Husband's separate property home, and although she acquires an interest in the home it is small relative to the payments made. Wife lives in the home with Husband, making payments on Husband's mortgage, and she pays property taxes, mortgage interest and principal and all she gets credit for is the measly $600 per month in mortgage principal reduction. It can take 5 or 7 years to paydown mortgage principal $50,000, and how many times do people take out a second deed of trust on their homes the minute they have equity? The second deed of trust is community property and it eats up all of Wife's small amount of equity in the home.

It seems unfair to the Wife that she would live in the Husband's house during their marriage, struggle to help pay the mortgage and all of the maintenance and upkeep on the home, and end up with a $29,150 interest in the home after all those years. Worse, Wife's lawyer is going to charge her $22,500 (or so) to make the argument for her because even good lawyers don't know *Moore/Marsden* very well, and they will spend more than $10,000 fighting over whether to use the *Moore/Marsden* date of separation value or the Bono v. Clark date of trial valuation, which in this case, is worth $8,300.

Yes, we must do the *Moore/Marsden* calculations, but for God's sake, do them quickly and get it over with. Lawyers love to spend thousands of dollars fighting over things that have relatively little meaning or value that make judge's eyeballs roll back in their heads.

Let me give a real-life example: I recently settled a case that had been going on for 9 years over a 4 year and 7-month marriage. One lawyer represented Husband for all 9 of those years, but Wife had had a parade of lawyers. I got involved when Husband sued Wife's parents because of some ownership they had in the house in question. There was a *Moore/Marsden* issue that seemed to be holding the entire case up because Wife's separate property house was in Santa Barbara and worth a small fortune. However, there was almost no mortgage on the home when Wife inherited it and Husband was never added to title.

Husband and Wife each had very good lawyers. I was hired by Wife's parents. It became apparent to me very quickly that a) the parties' lawyers hated each other and b) that neither lawyer, as good as they were, understood *Moore/Marsden*. The home was worth $1 million on the date of marriage. They paid the mortgage down $50,000. The community interest in any appreciation was 5%. That means, for every $100,000 increase in value, the community received an additional $5,000. The fight was over *Moore/Marsden* date of trial or *Bono v. Clark* date of separation value. Date of separation value was $1.4 million. Date of trial value was $1.8 million.

Worst case for Wife was that the community was entitled to 5% of $800,000 and best case was 5% of $400,000. That means the spread from best to worst case was between $20,000 and $40,000, of which Husband was entitled to half (plus the $50,000 paydown of the mortgage of which Husband was entitled to half). Do the math in your head: Wife was going to owe Husband between $45,000 and $65,000. The fight over the *Moore/Marsden* valuation brought in my elderly clients (one who died during the litigation and the other who ended up with a form of cancer we thought would kill her before it killed him). My involvement lasted two years. I kept saying to everyone that if they would do the simple math, they would see that this was a $20,000 spread. "Split the Goddamned difference and call it a day!" When it was over, I gave my remaining client her money back and told her that I could not charge her for the obstinacy of the two parties who would not settle over a $20,000 spread.

Watts/Epstein Reimbursements

Here are another series of cases, *Marriage of Watts* and *Mar-*

riage of Epstein. Still following the Three Rules, the law says that any time you pay a community property debt with your separate property post-separation earnings, you are entitled to reimbursement. Why? The community owes the debt jointly. If you service the debt or pay down principal on the community, you are entitled to reimbursement of half (you have to pay your share and your spouse has to pay their share). This is called an *"Epstein* credit." An *Epstein* credit is when you pay community credit card obligations, vehicle loan payments, mortgage payments and the like, including unreimbursed health care costs (including elective procedures that are financed on a payment plan). You should tally these up to get reimbursed at trial.

Watts charges work like a piston with *Epstein* credits. When you use a community property asset, there is a use value to the asset. We might call that the "Fair Market Rental Value," (FMRV) which is another way of saying, "what could you rent the asset for on the open market?" We could get really technical, down to the micro-level of detail with *Watts* charges., but normally we do not. That is, we could measure the use value of the couch and dining room tables in your home, but generally speaking, we do not do that. Most things, we assume the FMRV is either negligible (the couch and dining table) or that the rental value matches the cost (most vehicle payments). The real action in *Watts/Epstein* reimbursements has to do with the family home.

It's pretty simple to calculate *Watts/Epstein* reimbursements for the family home. Find FMRV by asking a real estate appraiser or a real estate broker or property management agency to say what the house would rent for. You already know the mortgage payment because you either are paying it or have paid it previously. If the house would rent for $3,000 per month and the mortgage (principal, interest, taxes, and insurance and HOA dues) is also $3,000 per month, we can calculate the *Watts/Epstein* reimbursements simply.

If Wife lives in the home, she owes Husband $1,500 per month for one-half of the FMRV.

If Wife pays the mortgage, Husband owes Wife $1,500 per month for one-half of the mortgage.

This "washes out."

If Husband and Wife equally share the mortgage, even though Husband does not live in the home, then Wife owes Husband $1,500 per month for FMRV and there is no *Epstein* credit because each party is meeting their obligation to pay the community debt.

If Husband moves out but pays the mortgage, Wife owes Husband $1,500 per month for FMRV and also Wife owes Husband $1,500 for one-half of the mortgage payment. This means Wife owes Husband $3,000 per month.

This can get dicey when the mortgage payment is much less than the FMRV, even with Wife paying the mortgage and living in the home. If the FMRV is $3,000 per month but the mortgage is $1,000 per month, if Wife lives in the home and pays the mortgage, then, Wife owes Husband $1,500 per month for one-half of FMRV and Husband owes Wife $500 per month for one-half of the mortgage. Thus, Wife owes Husband $1,000 per month.

For one or two months, this may be small potatoes, but Husband can move out of the home in January, file for divorce the following January and get to trial the following January. 24 months have passed, and the *Watts/Epstein* reimbursement is $24,000.

As you probably expect, I have several problems with *Watts/Epstein* reimbursements.

1) Husband moves out unexpectedly leaving Wife with a mortgage she can't pay. Husband continues to pay the mortgage. Wife does not ask for spousal support because Husband is paying

the mortgage. What happens? What can happen is that Wife has no money to move out of the house and does not realize that by paying the mortgage and not living in the home, Wife is racking up a huge debt to Husband every month that she lives there. Wife's much better solution is to ask for spousal support to move out of the home or pay the mortgage herself. In a 24-month separation and divorce, at $3,000 per month, Wife will owe Husband $72,000.

I do not like this scenario and it happens all too often. It happens when people do not understand the law. And no one understands this law until they are sitting in a lawyer's office and they get delivered the bad news that they owe their spouse $72,000 in *Watts/Epstein* reimbursements because they lived in the house without requesting spousal support and allowed Husband to keep paying the mortgage.

OK, in reality, a reasonably good family lawyer could argue their way out of this. There are cases such as *Marriage of Jeffres* that provide that if a spouse is paying the mortgage in lieu of paying support, what would look like the *Epstein* credit can be transmogrified into a support payment. This argument gets better when the support payment would include spousal and child support rather than just spousal support – in other words, the Court is unlikely to order Wife, who gets stuck in the family home with no ability to make the payment and no divorce pending (hoping perhaps that she and Husband will reconcile or waiting for a better time to file for divorce, while Husband lives in an RV or at his parents' home) and has the parties' two children the majority of the time, to make a *Watts/Epstein* payment to Husband.

Judges truly hate *Watts/Epstein* credits for just this reason. It just sounds ugly. And everyone hates it. "Jude, you mean I have to pay him rent to live in my own house?!?! He moved out!" But, *Watts/Epstein* is the law of the land and is something to be taken seriously.

2) Husband moves out of the house, leaving with a mortgage she cannot handle on her own. One of them had to move out of the house and neither really makes enough money to pay the mortgage on the home, which is also their biggest asset, on their own. Husband and Wife are just doing the best they can. Husband continues to contribute to the mortgage while Wife lives there, although she pays a portion of the mortgage as well. Let's say for a moment, Husband is doing exactly the right thing. Wife lives in the home for the initial separation and the kids stay with her most of the time, trying to minimize the shock of divorce on the children as much as possible. Husband gets a small apartment he can afford while contributing to the mortgage, big enough at least so that the kids can stay over on the weekends, but not really so that they can live there half the time. Is this really a situation in which we want Wife to owe Husband an *Epstein* credit?

In a recent case, there were no kids. Husband moved out in a rage. He kicked in Wife's bedroom door, breaking it off its hinges, and stole her dog, got in his car and left the state. Wife came to me after deciding to file for divorce about two months after he had left. Neither of them could handle the mortgage on their own. Husband was an angry drunk. He was a veteran suffering from PTSD. The house was on his VA loan. Mortgage rates had spiked. Wife did not want to keep the house. And she had gotten a good job out of the area. She was waiting for her job to start and she thought he would want to come back to the house because his son from a prior marriage was in the area.

I asked her if she wanted to keep the house and she said no. I asked her if she was willing to move out immediately and she said she was. So, in the first letter I wrote to Husband about the case, I told him that she was willing to list the house for sale or move out immediately, she just needed him to tell her which he preferred.

He refused to answer her. Another month went by and by then Husband had counsel, so we sent another letter asking if Husband wanted to buy or sell the house. He refused to answer. After the third request, with Husband refusing to answer, we filed a motion to sell the house. The Court ordered the house sold.

This strategy was very successful in stopping the court from ordering *Watts/Epstein* credits because Wife offered multiple times to move out of the house. The Court reasoned that Husband had months to make a decision and Wife offered to move out repeatedly. The Judge did not believe it would be equitable to let Husband sit on his rights and then demand a payment from Wife.

3) Wife moves out and Husband continues to live in a house with no mortgage, delaying the case indefinitely. This one buries the lead, because this one is the one I think is the biggest problem with *Watts/Epstein* credits. Here, there is no mortgage on the property. Husband won't move out because he knows there is no mortgage. Wife moves out when the situation becomes unbearable. Husband then delays the proceedings indefinitely.

I switched the genders here because in all my years of practicing, it is only Husbands who stay in low- or no-mortgage houses and delay proceedings. In fact, arguably, this is the one time I would violate my own advice in this book, which is generally to get your divorce done as quickly as you can. The reason is that, if you have a low- or no-mortgage situation, you may later owe *Watts* charges in the form of half of the FMRV of the house, but the cost of living in the home is very low. Wife essentially subsidizes Husband's rent during the time he lives there because *Watts/Epstein* credits are trial issues. Husband delays the trial as long as possible so that he can keep living in the home for low- or no-mortgage.

The Family Code does not provide for prejudgment interest (some unpublished cases say the Court could award it in very limited circumstances). So, my criticism of *Watts/Epstein* in the low- or no-mortgage situation is that Husband has a disincentive to get the case to trial. He has every reason to delay. Why? When the trial comes, he will have to pay Wife *Watts* charges for FMRV during the time he lived in the house post-separation. Wife does not have any (or very little) corresponding *Epstein* credits to offset the *Watts* charges. The longer Husband delays the trial, the longer he delays the big payment to Wife and the more he buys himself time to negotiate a smaller *Watts* payment. Nonetheless, he is borrowing money from Wife each month, each month the amount of money owed to her growing. But, because there is no prejudgment interest on the amount he owes her – he gets an interest-free loan from her every month he lives in the house.

Let me give two short examples:

Husband is living on the community property estate worth $16 million in Montecito, CA. FMRV is $60,000 per month. The divorce is in year 5. Husband owes Wife $30,000 per month for not only tying up FMRV income that Wife could have used to sustain herself, he also ties up a $16 million asset that could be sold. Husband stalls the divorce with discovery motion after discovery motion. After 60 months, he owes her $1,800,000 in *Watts* charges. Each month another $30,000 without interest. Why would he go to trial when that $1.8 million is coming out of his pocket? The longer he stays there, the more he owes her, but he gets a $60,000 per month, $16 million estate with no monthly payment (fine, upkeep is enormous on a property like that), that includes his own private vineyard for his "sugar baby" girlfriend's wine label, a 16-car garage for his classic and supercars, and all of the prestige of owning an estate of that caliber. Sure, Wife was not suffering in her own $6 million home, but the point was that Wife was ready to sell both homes for $22 million and take her $11 million and be done with the case. In that case, Husband was able to ultimately settle around the $1.8 million paying only a fraction of it. I was involved in this case as Wife's attorney for two years, but, for various reasons, not during settlement negotiations.

The other example is less egregious, but here Husband also delayed for four years and then settled around the issue. FMRV was $7,600 per month for a Los Olivos ranch property. Mortgage was $3,000, which was being paid with Community Property funds. *Watts* of $3,800 per month. After four years, Husband owed Wife $182,400. No offsetting *Epstein* credits. In the end, the case settled around the issue with a single lump sum payment.

We got a lot more than we expected to get in the Los Olivos settlement, and Wife lost big time in the $16 million estate case that did not involve me in settlement, but in each case, Husband had far superior bargaining leverage because he had separate property resources that would allow him to absorb an unfavorable trial ruling better than Wife could.

In assessing our trial risk, we knew that if we ran the table at trial and won the majority of our issues, the upside would be enormous, but if we lost a couple of key issues (where losing was a definite possibility), Wife would suffer a huge loss. In the Los Olivos Ranch case, we were well-within the Range of Normal Outcomes, but Husband was able to live in the home for almost no rent and then settle his way out of it later.

In my view, Courts should entertain motions that deal with *Watts/Epstein* credits as a pretrial issue, along the lines of spousal and child support. Upon a noticed motion, the Court should quickly determine whether *Watts/Epstein* credits apply and then make orders regarding monthly payments of the difference between them.

Dividing Businesses: The Business Valuation

Dividing businesses follows the same Three Rules. But, of course the three rules as applied to a separate property business have their own quirks. There is also the problem of community property business profits post-separation. This book is already long enough without me giving an exegesis on the complexities of business valuation. I want to give you the weeds, but a detailed analysis of business valuations is beyond the scope here. already long enough without me giving an exegesis on the complexities of business valuation. I want to give you the weeds, but a detailed analysis of business valuations is beyond the scope here.

I am going to try to hit the highlights so that you can see the way the Three Rules works in practice.

Separate Property Business Valuation

Separate property businesses are, like any asset, a business owned before marriage by one spouse or inherited by one spouse during the marriage. Income earned from working (as opposed to passive income from separate property sources) is community property. That means, if Husband owned a plumbing contracting business before marriage, the business is his business, but to the extent that he works as the plumber in the business (or even as the manager of a fleet of plumbers), his income is community property.

The law attempts to distinguish between the goodwill value of the business that stems from the separate property nature of the business and the income from the business based on Husband's work in the business. In other words, how much of the business profits are based on Husband's premarital efforts to build the plumbing business and how much of the business profits are income from Husband's efforts during the marriage?

The family law wants to know if the separate property business-owning Husband paid himself enough for his work during the marriage or if he used money that should have been marital income and invested it back into his business.

This sounds a lot like the "time rule" pension division and *Moore/Marsden* calculations. The community should receive fair return for its investment of Husband's time running the plumbing business and the plumbing business value should not be increased at the expense of the community. It is complicated because as Husband runs the business, he both increases its value (if it was sold to a third party) and takes a profit (paycheck). The community gets the paycheck, including profits based on his invested time and efforts during the marriage, and a share of the increase in value of the business due to Husband's marital time and effort. Husband, however, has a separate property interest in the business that will naturally grow as a result of Husband's premarital investment of time and effort into the business.

So, there are some complex accounting moves that have to be done to get the actual value of the business on the date of marriage and the value on the date of separation. There is also an analysis of whether, essentially, Husband paid himself enough or invested what should have been community property salary into plumbing trucks and commercial storage yards and the like.

If we can ascertain the value of the business at the date of marriage and give the business a reasonable rate of return on that value, we can ascertain Husband's separate property interest in the business. In so doing, we can also ascertain the community property interest in the value of the business.

There are two methods of doing this and they are both ancient (well 100 years old feels pretty ancient).

In *Pereira v. Pereira*, a 1909 case!, the Court determined that a personal skills and efforts business (like a law office or a small construction company) should be apportioned between separate and community property by valuing the business on the date of marriage and assigning a reasonable rate of return, as though that value had been invested. The rest belongs to the community. The theory is that, in a personal services business, the growth of the business can be attributed to the personal skills and effort of the "in spouse" during the marriage. The community is entitled to the skills and effort of each spouse during the marriage. Therefore, apply the reasonable rate of return on the initial investment and apportion the rest to the community.

This tends to square with *Moore/Marsden*, which gives the separate property-owning spouse growth on the initial investment in the real property and awards the community a property interest in the portion of the investment made by the community paying down the mortgage principal. The more value added to the asset by the community, whether by paying down the mortgage or by investing time, skill and effort (even through the business owning spouse alone), the more interest the community has in its growth.

In *Van Camp v. Van Camp*, a 1921 case!, the separate property business was essentially a factory canning fish (e.g., tuna). Because the business growth was based on the nature of the business itself, rather than its management, the court set a fair salary for the business owning spouse. The fair salary is what the community is entitled to. Everything above that fair salary is separate property. The reason for this is that the court treats the initial premarital investment in cannery factory equipment as the reason for the business. The only question is whether the managing spouse paid themselves enough salary or invested that money back into the business, which must then be disgorged.

Unlike *Moore/Marsden*, there is no corresponding property interest in the business from this investment, just a reimbursement to the community. So, for example, if, under a *Van Camp* analysis, Husband pays himself $100,000 per year to manage a cannery that is otherwise his separate property and then invests $200,000 per year back into the business to buy more fish and tin cans, thereby increasing the value of the business by $400,000, and the court determines that Husband's fair salary for managing the business is $300,000, Husband will owe the community $200,000, of which he will get half back. But, he will keep the increase in value in the business.

Like *Watts/Epstein*, *Van Camp* creates a disincentive to pay oneself appropriately (and instead invest the money back into the business), because this becomes a no-interest reimbursable loan payable to the community at trial. Yes, Husband will owe Wife $100,000, but his $200,000 investment into the business returns $400,000 in business value, plus he gets half of the $200,000 he reimburses to the community.

In simple terms:

"*Pereira* accounting —> increased value primarily due to community labor: Value of business at beginning + fair rate of return = SP, the rest is CP.

***Van Camp* accounting —> increased value due to the unique nature of SP asset**: Fair salary for community labor x years of marriage − salary already received − amounts already paid to community expenses = CP, the rest is SP."[14]

---

14   This was borrowed from a Stanford Law School "Community Property Checklist" downloaded from a Wikipedia reference. I thought about trying to change these formulas around to make them "mine" but they are elegant means of stating the rules, so I use them here in their entirety. The "checklist" has no author associated with it. Having been to law school at Berkeley myself, it looks like exam or bar review notes put together by one of the faculty members on a crib sheet.

How do you know if your business falls under *Pereira* or *Van Camp*? There's no good answer to that. Like so many areas of family law, you make the best argument you can on whichever position you support. And then, even then, great lawyers (and almost all judges) get it wrong all the time. The truth is that almost any business, except obvious one-person operations, can find a way to fit under either approach. In theory, anytime your business is dependent on your skill and labor to run and manage it such that you are irreplaceable, it should fall under *Pereira* and any time its success is dependent upon market forces or capital investment rather than time and effort, it should fall under a *Van Camp* analysis.

If you have a separate property business that has any real value to it, it makes sense to consult with a family law forensic accountant to give you advice about how to argue this.

················ PRO TIP ················

Most lawyers and judges do not understand this type of analysis at all. Go to a forensic accountant and have them give you the value for your business under the best approach to valuing your business and have them write a report that is very official sounding and looking and unless the other side takes the opposite but same approach, you will almost assuredly prevail. Judges love when accountants do math for them. Lawyers were not usually trained in math and judges do not attend accounting school as part of their training. Sometimes, the prettiest expert report wins, especially if your expert sounds very sure of themselves on the witness stand. If this is an important issue in your case, do not try to do this type of accounting on your own. Hiring an expert is even more important than hiring a lawyer for this, but if you have the money for an expert and it is worth it (meaning the analysis will have a real effect on your bottom line), you should have a lawyer too.

···

Final note on this: the out-spouse does not get a property right in the business. We have a good case that is directly on point: *Patrick v. Alacer,* which dealt with the Emergen-C fortune.

This was a multi-faceted tale of woe that went back and forth to the Appellate Court many times. The basic outcome was that the Court expressly rejected applying the *Moore/Marsden* property interest in the business context. Wife gets no ownership interest in Husband's separate property plumbing business. She gets apportionment under either *Pereira* or *Van Camp* (in this case, the Court used *Pereira* – which probably benefitted her a great deal, but it did not give her shares of stock or an ownership interest in the business; she got what the cases require, compensation for Husband's efforts to increase the value of the business during the marriage). Apportionment, in this case, just meaning that she got a portion of the increase in value of the business due to Husband's marital efforts at increasing its value.

Community Property Business Valuation

There are few areas of the family law where a person can really get burned. Valuation of a community property business is one of those areas; it is fraught with problems.

Essentially, business valuation, to be fair, includes all of the tangible items owned by the business – from trucks to office equipment to computers – all of the cash on hand, and all of the business liabilities. It also includes a reasonable salary for the spouse buying the business. It also includes the business "goodwill," which is an intangible asset that is essentially, the likelihood of future profits.

The action in divorce business valuation (and business valuation in general) is around calculating the intangible business goodwill value. It would not be fair to value the business based only on the stuff it owns, when it also generates income and profits. So, we have to figure out the goodwill value, which is essentially the likelihood of future profits and then use that value over a period of several years to get the total value of the business.

The most commonly used method of valuing goodwill is the "excess earnings" method, which is essentially how much profit the business earns each year after deducting reasonable business expenses and hypothetical reasonable salaries divided by something called the "capitalization rate." The cap rate is a number smaller than 1, so when you divide by it, you are actually multiplying. More on this below.

For the most part, we can value tangible assets like stuff and cash and debts. We can also get to a reasonable salary pretty easily. The salary definition takes a little bit of work, but you have a reasonable idea of what it would cost to hire a person to do what you do and, using a "cost of replacement" analysis, we can get to a reasonable salary for you and, if your spouse was involved, the reasonable cost of replacing their work in the business.

················· PRO TIP ·················

The larger your reasonable salary, the smaller the business goodwill valuation. If your spouse worked in the business, the larger their cost of replacement, the lower the business goodwill.

One thing I have seen over the years is Husband and Wife arguing over Wife's involvement in the business. Wife says "I was a huge part of creating and running this business" with an air of self-importance. Husband says "no she wasn't. I built the whole thing by myself," with his own air of self-importance.

Counter-intuitively, these people are arguing for business valuations that benefit the other spouse. The reason is that "goodwill value" which I talk about below, is focused on "excess earnings above reasonable expenses and reasonable salaries." If Husband contributes $150,000 in reasonable salary and Wife contributes $0, then there is no cost to Husband to replace Wife in the business and when we calculate profits, we calculate them with no cost of replacement for Wife. Total reasonable salary is $150,000. Then, if net profits after reasonable expenses are $300,000, we deduct Husband's $150,000, then business excess earnings are $150,000.

However, if Husband agrees that replacing Wife will cost him $75,000 (because she did so much work for the business), then with $300,000 net profits before salaries, we find "excess earnings" to be $300,000 - $150,000 - $75,000 = $75,000. As you will see below, when we use a capitalization rate to determine the value of the business goodwill (which ends being a multiplier because the capitalization rate is expressed as a percentage smaller than 1) the reduction in excess earnings drastically decreases the total goodwill value.

For some reason, I see capitalization rates around 33% on a regular basis. So, using that as an example: $150,000/.33 = $454,545 while $75,000/.33 = $227,272. If Husband just says, "replacing Wife in the business will cost me $75,000 per year," he has reduced his business goodwill by 50%. Remember that Wife is going to get 50% of the business goodwill.

In an acrimonious divorce, you really really want to make your spouse look terrible. One easy way of doing that is to say "she just sits around all day and does nothing while I work my ass off!" Then she says, "that's not true! I am invaluable to his business. I manage contracts and do billing and clean toilets and and and...." These are the exact wrong arguments for each side to be making because they bolster the other side's argument. If you are the "in spouse" (the one keeping the business), always argue that your spouse's involvement was substantial and that replacing your spouse will cost money from the bottom line so that when you calculate goodwill, you do so with a hypothetical cost of replacement for the out-spouse.

There, I just saved you $250,000 with one page of this book.

•••

Goodwill is a painful concept. "OK, Jude, I get it, she gets all the trucks, equipment and cash and all I get is my good name?" Yes. Maybe. I mean you get the trucks, equipment and cash and your good name. You also get future business profits forever.

I can see both sides of the business goodwill issue, and I have represented parties on both sides with big and small businesses. I can tell you that no one is happy with the outcome of business valuations and divisions. Most people who own a business are essentially running a paycheck company. They do work on a contract basis for clients who need them. They make enough money to have a job where they are their own boss, but other than that, there really isn't much goodwill value in the business to speak of.

Using my plumber example above – in the classic tradesperson business, there is the license holder (like the plumber or lawyer or accountant) doing work for people who hire them. They make enough money from the business that they do not have to work for anyone as a captive employee. They set their hours and their rates, and they do the job they were hired for. That's it. They have good years and bad years. There are also all kinds of small businesses that are shops and restaurants, catering trucks and real estate brokers, trash haulers and florists and home organizers and anything else you can think of. America, they say, is run on small businesses.

•••••••••••••••• PRO TIP ••••••••••••••••

If your business is really just a paycheck machine, then goodwill is probably $0. That is, if a plumber normally makes about $150,000 per year and your business makes about $150,000 per year, there are no excess earnings. The earnings of the business are essentially a job and a paycheck.

• •

A community property business is an asset. I had a crane operator instructor case where the Husband ran this business training people to operate cranes. He made a small fortune each year – maybe not a "1%er" but certainly a "5%er." He had no employees and he didn't even own a crane. He would get gigs all over the country and go there and train people to operate the very cranes they would be using. Smart business. He had been a crane operator when he met my client and he made a good living doing that…$65 per hour and more when he worked a prevailing wage job. But, he was his own man, and he didn't like someone telling him where to go work, so he and Wife sat down with Wife's father and said they had an idea. Wife's father pitched in $80,000 to get him started in business training crane operators. It took them two years to pay Wife's father back with business income. Then, he went on to make about $500,000 per year doing the job. At trial, he testified that he was "always working" because he would wake up at 6 AM and talk to East Coast clients and be talking to clients in Hawaii at 10 PM.

There was no question that this was a community property business, but he was the person who managed and operated it. They did not have any employees and almost no overhead. 95 cents of every dollar that came in, came in to the family. Wife needed to get half of the business value because it was a community property asset and she also needed spousal support for the income Husband received from operating the business. The question was how do we value this thing?

Husband argued that if he got sick or died or injured, there was no one who could operate the business without him, so the business had no "sale" value. Wife argued that that is not the question when determining the value of the community property business. Like all assets, the valuation of the asset does not require building in a cost that you don't pay. In this case, Husband hadn't died or been injured or gotten sick. He was operating the business. It was true that the likelihood they could sell the business was very slim. Husband was a good trainer, he had a lot of connections and he worked ridiculously long hours.

Valuing the goodwill value of a business that you pour your blood, sweat and tears into for many years is really painful. The basic way we normally look at a business is to examine what it would cost to replace you (the reasonable salary) and then look at "excess earnings," which is a fancy way of saying "profits above reasonable salary." Excess earnings are essentially everything that is left after reasonable business expenses are deducted from gross receipts and the hypothetical salary it would cost to replace you.

I have seen hundreds of small business owners' tax returns (maybe thousands). I know that the items your accountant (or you) deduct from your small business expenses are not always truly business expenses. You deduct the deck you built in the backyard for your 50th work anniversary, the payments on your wife's Lexus, your phone and internet bills at home, food you buy for the office and a number of various other expenses that are perfectly reasonable for the IRS, but get added back in for purposes of calculating business profits under this excess earnings approach. Family law accounting does not track IRS accounting. And so, for example, my case where the headhunter generated $900,000 per year in gross receipts and then ran every single expense through his business and wrote his income down to $15,000 and then came to court on a child support motion and said he was broke, did not fly with the court. The court, in that case, added back a reasonable salary (not enough in my opinion). In other cases, the court will add back specific items (the headhunter had added a $150,000 deck in his $6 million Los Olivos ranch and the judge gave him credit for that as a business expense because it was to be used for his work party one time!). But, you cannot rely solely on your tax return to tell the court which of your business expenses is reasonable to be deducted from your gross earnings to get to profit.

.... PRO TIP ....

Having just said above that you cannot rely on your tax return to tell the court what your reasonable profits are, I have to qualify that statement. There is good caselaw that says a tax return is presumed correct because you sign under penalty of perjury and face criminal charges if you lie to the IRS. So, if you are a high earner (or even a medium-earner) and you have a very aggressive accountant who takes your $900,000 per year in gross receipts and, even though you have no staff and no office other than the office you use at your $6 million ranch and even if you admit on the witness stand that your only bank account is your corporate account such that when you take your son to lunch or to the Maldives on vacation or buy a $200,000 Airstream or put in a $150,000 deck in your backyard, you should still come to court with a straight face and tell the judge your tax return is accurate. First of all, you already signed it as accurate under penalty of perjury. Second of all, the caselaw (*Marriage of Loh*) says that the signed tax return is presumed accurate, which shifts the burden to the other side to prove it is inaccurate. Third, likely your spouse signed off on your tax return as well, which makes it very difficult to for your spouse to come to court and say that it was inaccurate – in fact, most judges will not allow that testimony under one of two theories: estoppel – this says once you have stated something under penalty of perjury you are estopped from saying something else; 5th Amendment right against self-incrimination – most judges are not going to let your spouse accuse you or herself of a crime (and tax evasion is a crime) in open court under oath.

So, if there are no forensic accountants involved in computing your reasonable expenses, go to court with your Schedule C and say loud and proud that it is accurate. *Marriage of Loh* says there is a presumption that the tax return is correct. That is not a "conclusive" presumption, it just means that the burden shifts to the other side to prove that it is incorrect. Sometimes this is easier than other times. In the case of the headhunter with the deck and the Airstream trailer, we got the judge to add back in the Airstream trailer but he let the deck be a reasonable business expense. I actually thought it should have gone the other way because Husband testified that he was a germaphobe and he didn't like staying in hotels so he used the Airstream when he went on work trips – and my client, Wife, agreed that this was true of him. Judges have a ton of power to use their discretion to decide what is a business expense and what is not; because they are not experts in tax matters, they will defer to your accountant as much as they can.

But, also, do not be surprised if some of the deductions your accountant takes on your tax return get "added back in" to your income.

• •

The excess earnings are supposed to tell us how much more than a "job" this business actually is. But we do not leave it at an analysis of how much profits the business earns above a reasonable salary; we also look at this profitability over a period of time. This is called a "capitalization rate," which is based on an analysis of how much risk is in the industry, how much competition there is, and how the business compares to other business of the same type. Basically, the "cap rate" is the likelihood your business will continue to generate the same or greater profits over a period of years. It is expressed as a percentage and it is the denominator in a fraction that looks like this:

Valuing Business Goodwill Using the Excess Earnings Approach:

Excess Earnings (= gross receipts – reasonable business expenses – hypothetical reasonable salary)

Capitaliz*ation Rate (expressed as a percentage)*

Using this formula, you can see that the larger your reasonable expenses or the larger your reasonable salary (and also the larger the cost of replacement for your spouse's salary), the lower the goodwill value of the business.

It may have been a little while since you did high school math, but when you divide by a percentage (smaller than 1), you are basically multiplying. So, when the cap rate is 33%, for example, you are essentially multiplying the top number by 3. The smaller the cap rate, the longer the period of time that the valuation of the business includes your business profits. A good rule of thumb is that the goodwill of the business is roughly 3 years' of net profits after paying reasonable expenses, including a reasonable salary for you. A higher reasonable salary to you means more alimony, but less value for the business. You will "get to keep" one-half of the business goodwill and your spouse will get the other one-half of business goodwill.

In the hypothetical example above of a business with net earnings before salaries of $300,000 per year, Husband's reasonable salary is $150,000. If the cost of replacing Wife's role in the business is $0, then with a cap rate of 33%, the business goodwill value is $150,000/.33 = $454,454. If the cost of replacing Wife is $75,000 per year, then the business goodwill value is $75,000/.33 = $227,272. You can play around with these numbers, but if the cap rate is 25%, then the goodwill value of the business is $150,000/.25 = $600,000.

I truly believe calculating the capitalization rate is voodoo magic by the accountants, but when two accountants do their work, they normally come very close in their cap rate calculation, so maybe there is more to it than that, and I don't mean to offend accountants by saying that. The accountants say they have tables that will give them baseline percentages to use to determine the capitalization rate and I am sure these have been vetted by national and international academies of accountants who say these are good numbers.

Basically, the value of the business is going to include all of its capital (money), its equipment and tangible goods (what it actually owns) and tangible liabilities (debts), and its "goodwill" value (the likelihood of future business profits based on past success and future growth projections).

Essentially, the capitalization rate is a multiplier that extends the profits over a period of years. If the crane operator trainer business generated $500,000 in income each year, but to hire a good trainer would cost $200,000, then the excess earnings (profits above reasonable salary) are $300,000 per year. Then, you determine how many years to multiply these profits by to determine how much of the success of the business was due to the crane operator trainer's ingenuity and skill and connections and business acumen – all of which belong to the community during the marriage, including the time invested in learning how to do the job well, cultivating clients and building the business model. After determining excess earnings, then the accountants multiply this by a period of years to value the business "goodwill."

I have dealt with probably 300 business valuations over the years, and they almost always use a capitalization rate of between 27% and 33%, averaging out to about 30%. What this meant for the crane operator was that we would use the annual business income of $500,000 and subtract $200,000 cost of replacement to get $300,000 in annual "excess earnings." Then we would divide $300,000 by 30% ($300,000/.30) to get $1,000,000.

If you think that the Husband did not come unglued when I said the business was worth $1 million and he owed Wife $500,000, think again. He screamed that that was more than twice as much as he earned in a year. He didn't own any trucks or cranes or equipment. He only had a few contracts at a time. If he got sick, no business got done. If it rained and he could not work, he did not get paid. How could he owe her half a million dollars when the business was really him just working 16 hours a day to try to make a living?

And he is not wrong. But also, my client is not wrong. The thing of value was created during the marriage, which makes it community property subject to division. It would be patently unfair to value the business on the basis of its office equipment and cell phone alone because, as a going concern, it will continue to produce income and profits after the marriage is over. I see this problem both directions – both the crane operator trainer and the crane operator trainer's wife have cause to be upset with valuing a business based on its future profits over a defined period of time.

The crane operator trainer Husband says, "it is patently unfair to value a business as though I could sell it when I am perhaps one of 10 crane operator trainers in the United States and I train all over the United States and without me personally doing the training, there would be no profits. Plus, the only way to make this business run is for me to work essentially every waking minute."

The crane operator trainer's Wife says, "I invested money from my father into this business. When we started it, our son was 5 years old. While my Husband worked 18-hour days, I took care of our son, the household, and all of the things that allowed my

Husband to work those hours. As a family, we forewent a steady $65/hr. paycheck that was all but guaranteed and afforded us home ownership, newer cars, trips to Disneyland and a full pantry so that Husband could start this business. We had lean times while he built it. We had years where it seemed like he was never home. When he suffered, I suffered with him. I took care of his mom when she got sick and died. This was our business. And now, after 15 years of building this business together as a family, I will get, essentially one-half of the profits for 3 years and he will keep it going forward forever."

In other words, both sides are mad. Both sides feel like they are getting screwed. Husband because he will owe Wife $500,000 for a business that relies 100% on him and the market could change, he could get sick or the laws could change. Wife because she sees the $500,000 per year in profits as something that will only stay the same or grow for the next 10-20 years and she will only get half of 3 years.

But there is also the "double dip" problem that will upset each of them even more.

Community Property Business Profits: the "Double Dip" Problem

To me, the most insidious problem with community property business valuation is the "double dip" problem. It will not be enough for the crane operator trainer to pay Wife one-half of the profits for three years. Remember, the business value is one-half of profits for three years. That means we are dividing the business as an asset, the same way we divide your 401(k) or your home equity as an asset. It's just easier to get values for 401(k)s and homes than it is for businesses. The value of the business, we established, using very rough numbers, is:

Community Property Business Value Formula (Most Common):

All Tangible Assets and Liabilities + (Excess Earnings/Capitalization Rate) = Community Property Business Value

Excess earnings, we said, is the profit after paying all reasonable expenses associated with the business and a hypothetical salary for the spouse running the business. Everything above that amount is "excess earnings" (or what most people would call "profits").

OK, here is where it gets crazy and I cannot tell you how many people have lost their tempers in my office when I explain this next part, so brace yourself.

Let's go back to the crane operator trainer for a moment. Husband and Wife start this business with Wife's start-up capital and Husband's ingenuity. Wife had always hustled during the marriage up until the business started doing really well and Husband started being gone so much and making so much money that her part-time jobs actually cost them more with her being gone than they helped the family with her income. Whether by mutual agreement or not, Wife stopped working outside the home. Ten years went by. Wife had no college degree and had no work history to speak of for those ten years and only minimal work experience before that (part-time yard duty at their son's school kinds of jobs that pay a little more than minimum wage but only 12 hours a week and mostly for convenience). She had initially done some office work for the crane operator training company, but her involvement in the business led to arguments and it was easier for all of the if Husband managed his own scheduling and billing.

So, we value the business. In this case, there were no tangible assets or liabilities (cell phone, home office, laptop computer, etc.), so we used $300,000 in excess earnings with a 30% discount rate: $300,000/.30 = $1,000,000. Husband owes Wife $500,000 *for the division of the business asset.* The piece of property that is the business.

However, although Husband is dividing off Wife's share of the business, this is not spousal support and it is not income to Wife, despite the fact that we have used profitability as the measure of the value of the business. Her interest in the business is a property right; something the Court must divide in half to properly divide the community estate (remember, in California, the court must divide the estate equally). The business's intrinsic asset value is the profits of the business over a period of years. So, he owes her the $500,000, as though there was $1,000,000 in equity in the home and he needed to give her half of it.

But, this was a long-term marriage and Wife was entitled to spousal support. So, here's the double dip. Husband is paying $500,000 for the business and he also has to pay spousal support based on his business income. Remember that we calculated "excess earnings" by taking Husband's hypothetical reasonable salary off the net profits after reasonable business expenses and we divided that by 30% to get a business value. But now, when it comes to spousal support, we need to use Husband's total income, which = reasonable hypothetical salary + excess earnings (profits). A spousal support order where Wife has no reasonable income and Husband earns $500,000 per year is around $12,000 per month. You can imagine that Husband was fuming mad about this. He asks: "how the *%$&! am I supposed to give her $500,000 and $12,000 per month and keep running this business?" How indeed?

The double dip problem is pervasive. Do an online search for "double dip in California divorce" and you will find hundreds of articles about it. *Marriage of Blazer* suggests that you cannot include a future income stream as a value for the business and then order spousal support based on that future income. The Husband in

Blazer argued on appeal that the Excess Earnings approach uses future income streams to calculate business value. The Appellate Court disagreed, stating that just the use of Excess Earnings was not sufficient evidence that the calculation included future earnings. But, if you look at our formulas above, you can see that Excess Earnings almost explicitly uses future earnings to value the goodwill value of the business.

What we know from where we currently sit is that *Blazer* does permit a business owning spouse to retain earnings (profits) to reinvest in the company or to have capital available to diversify or expand. That means in the case of the crane operator trainer, if Husband were to have argued (or argue in the future) that he was getting older and needed to hire staff to both do his billing and scheduling as well as to train other crane operator trainers and that those costs would come out of the bottom line, he would likely have been able to point to these as reasonable business expenses. In *Blazer*, the court disagreed with Wife's argument that every nickel of profit should be considered income for spousal support purposes (she went from roughly $57,000 per month in spousal support to a paltry $20,000 per month in spousal support) because Husband successfully argued that his brokerage firm required capitalization to operate effectively. However, the *Blazer* Appellate Court also rejected Husband's argument that the Excess Earnings approach was an impermissible "double dip" on its face.

"To sum up, California authority offers no basis for treating husband's earnings from his ongoing business differently from income generated by other assets divided at dissolution, for purposes of determining spousal support," the *Blazer* court held, and declined to adopt any prohibition against the double-dip in divorce.

················ **PRO TIP:** ··················

The double-dip is the only place in a divorce where I believe a spouse can get royally screwed. But, just saying that does not make me feel better. Isn't the out-spouse also getting screwed if there is no double-dip? When a business is divided as an asset in a divorce, the out-spouse is undergoing a forced sale with imaginary numbers. The business was generating an income stream. If the crane operator trainer Husband could pay $500,000 for a future income stream of $500,000 for as long as he continued to be successful in business, and the only reason he was awarded the business was because he was the one who could train crane operators, isn't that unfair to Wife? Wouldn't we all pay $500,000 now for a business that will generate $500,000 per year in income into the foreseeable future? This seems like a good investment.

So, since I represent both in-spouses and out-spouses, I feel the pain of this. I have also gotten divorced and had my own business when I did so and saw how I could get double-dipped as well. Imagine how I felt thinking that I built my law firm from nothing into a firm with 4 lawyers and 4 paralegals and two additional staff, with high gross receipts, on 80-hour workweeks and brutal days in trial, dealing with completely uninterested judges, vile opposing counsel, death threats and state bar complaints and my own clients refusing to pay their bills all to see myself in the situation of having not only to buy my spouse out (who did not have a law degree) and pay spousal support on my earnings? I hated it too.

But, I also see the point of the double-dip, which is that even if you purchase an income-producing asset, you still have income available for support.

The *Blazer* trial court, and the crane operator trainer court, did what I think was the right thing, which was to base the spousal support not on "net profits" (hypothetical salary + excess earnings), but on hypothetical salary alone. This would be to say that the court recognized that Husband had bought the future profits of the company with the Excess Earnings approach to buyout Wife. But, remember that we deducted hypothetical reasonable salary to determine goodwill value. That makes the reasonable salary available for support even if the in-spouse pays for the future profits.

I think this method is a good one because of the incentives it creates. Let's say that there is truly no market for crane operator trainers. We cannot really pick a good number as a reasonable hypothetical salary for the crane operator trainer because there are only ten of them in the United States. We cannot tie his income to his work hours because anyone who has owned a small business knows that you could never hire someone to have the same devotion to the success of your business that you have. Cost-of-replacement is truly a hypothetical model to use to get reasonable salary. Husband's reasonable salary could have been $500,000 per year. That would have reduced the value of the business to $0, because there were $500,000 per year in profits. We got to a $1 million value by setting his reasonable salary at $200,000 and dividing the remaining excess earnings of $300,000 by 30% to get to $1 million.

If Husband's reasonable salary was $500,000, then deducting that from the $500,000 in net revenues, we would have had excess earnings of $0/30% = $0.

But, under the *Blazer* trial court approach (not necessarily the appellate court approach) and the crane operator trainer approach, he would have had to pay support on the $500,000 in reasonable hypothetical income. Therefore, we incentivize Husband to not game the system by overstating reasonable hypothetical salary in order to reduce the value of the business, because the court will use that salary to calculate spousal support. This creates a proper incentive to balance reasonable hypothetical salary (for future support calculation purposes) with excess earnings (for valuation of the business).

The state of the law is still in flux, and you should not base how you approach the arguments on this alone. *Blazer* left the law very unsettled with its final comments:

"To sum up, California authority offers no basis for treating husband's earnings from his ongoing business differently from income generated by other assets divided at dissolution, for purposes of determining spousal support."

This is also true of pension division, so be very careful here too. Normally we divide a pension by the "time rule" as I noted above. If you had 30 years of service and were married for those same 30 years, each of you will take one-half of the pension. When you retire, your spouse will receive (or should) exactly the same amount of money that you receive each month. If you were paying spousal support while you were working, because of your higher income, then when you stop working, your spousal support payment would be set based on the differences between your pension income and your spouse's pension income. In the hypothetical 30-year marriage/30-year pension contribution, you both have the same income available to you for support. The spousal support payment should end.

In the case of a 30-year pension contribution and a 10-year marriage, however, you will receive 25 years worth of pension contributions and your spouse will receive 5 years of pension contributions. This means that you will have asymmetry in your pension payments. Assuming this is the only income, your spousal support payment will decrease for sure, because you will be earning less money after retirement and your spouse will have increased income from the pension, but you will still likely have some spousal support payment to make. It is common to return to court to reduce or terminate spousal support at retirement.

But, it is also common to trade your spouse's interest in your pension for some tangible good now. The old most common trade was the house and all of its equity for the pension. That seems like a good trade for both parties, if they are getting what they want. Pensions, however, are usually very valuable, much more valuable than you think. So, it is not always a good trade – it is worth valuing your pension at its present value to know what it is worth when you are negotiating.

When you trade keeping your pension in exchange for the something that is valuable now, like a house, you would think that your pension income should then be excluded from future spousal support calculations. The present value of your pension includes the payments you will receive at retirement based on your actuarial lifespan. So, it seems inequitable that if you use your pension, as a thing of value, to trade for another thing of value (particularly one that has value now since there is no secondary market for pensions – meaning you cannot sell your pension to someone else for cash now the same way you can sell your house), that later your pension income can be factored into a spousal support calculation. But, the appellate courts have left this open, in *In Re Marriage of White* ["...the flaw in the "double dipping" argument is that spousal support considerations are separate and distinct from property division concepts."].

Ouch. Ouch. Ouch. They are separate and distinct from each other, but how can it be that if you purchase an income producing asset from your spouse in the divorce, that you should also have to pay spousal support on the income it produces? Isn't the future income stream the value that you paid for? You forewent access to cash now (selling your house, for example) in exchange for a future income stream. This delayed gratification may be an indicator of intelligence and determination in young children, but it turns out that in a *Marriage of White* situation, you could be on the hook for paying spousal support based on the income stream from the pension that you bought from your spouse based on a value that was based on the very income stream that you are now asked to pay support on.

Things you can do:

1. Get a *Marriage of White* waiver. I am not sure that this works for businesses, too, but I would try. When people are in settlement negotiations, they are most likely to agree to things. And when you are dangling $500,000 in cash to your spouse, they are more likely to waive future support based on the income stream. People get emotional in their negotiations and this is the time to get your *Marriage of White* waiver that says something like: "I understand that this asset is income-producing and I am waiving my right to seek spousal support based on that future income as part of this trade of my house for the pension or the business."

2. I tell my support-paying clients that they have to undertake a risk calculus regarding their spouse's future marriage prospects. Spousal support terminates upon remarriage or your inability to work. Property settlements stay around forever and they collect interest at 10% per year. If you have a property payment to make, you have to make that until its paid off. If you have a spousal support payment, you make it until your spouse remarries or dies, or you retire or become incapacitated. So, you have to think about the business valuation and excess earnings versus salary/income. Spousal support can be very long-term. Let's look at the crane operator trainer case again to help

game this one through.
- a. If Husband states that his reasonable hypothetical income is $500,000, then the business has no value. But he will pay about $12,000 per month in spousal support until Wife marries or dies or he becomes incapacitated or retires. Let's assume that he will work for 12 more years. That means 144 payments of $12,000 per month = $1,728,000 in spousal support payments. But they are payable monthly and without interest and they end if he dies, she dies, she remarries or he retires.
- b. If Husband states that his reasonable hypothetical income is $200,000, then the business is worth $1,000,000, of which he owes her $500,000 now. Plus, he will have a spousal support payment based on the $200,000 of about $3,500 per month (maybe $4,000). Again, assume 144 months of payments = $504,000 in spousal support payments plus $500,000 now = $1,004,000.
- c. Obviously, option A is much more costly, but if Wife is hot and heavy in a new relationship or has cancer or Husband is closer to retirement age or he has cancer, then a property payment is a guaranteed payout, one you have to make, one even your estate will have to make if you die and one you will have to make to her estate if she dies. Spousal support payments are payments you will have to make so long as you are working, she is not earning as much as your are and she is not remarried.
- d. There is no easy answer to the question of whether to push up the value of the business, so that you know exactly what you will owe her and have a timeline to pay her or to reduce the value of the property payout and take the bet that something will happen in the future that will

reduce or eliminate her need for support.
  e. At least one court has referred (in a slightly different context) to the "macabre gamble" that spouses play with each other when it comes to lifelong support awards.
  f. I settled a multi-million-dollar case where my client was going to remarry, but Husband had substantial spousal support liability. Husband, however, was 80 years old and suffering from advanced Parkinson's Disease (which, itself was not going to kill him, but which reduced his quality of life). Wife had assets she wanted to keep and she was going to lose spousal support almost assuredly whether she remarried or he died. We needed to use the threat of spousal support as a hammer to get a support buyout with the property she wanted. We got less cash than we wanted because Husband was hoarding cash to pay for his medical needs, but we got the property she wanted and we got a $500,000 term life insurance policy. That life insurance policy was the kicker because instead of getting spousal support while Husband was alive for only as long as Husband was going to live, Wife got the guaranteed payment of $500,000 at his death (plus $600,000 in cash now, plus her multi-million dollar lake house out-of-state, which is what she really wanted). Both parties thought they got completely screwed in the settlement, but I actually think the other lawyer and I (and the fabulous mediator we used) came up with an ingenious solution. And I had to point out to Wife that she was going to remarry and her ex-Husband was not going to live as long as she was (almost certainly – she was 10 years younger than he was and in great physical health).
3. Remember to think about your spouse's role in the busi-

ness. Was it really nothing? I think there are two benefits to acknowledging the role your spouse played in your business. I used both to my advantage in my divorce.

It reduces the value of the business because Excess Earnings is the amount you earn less reasonable business expenses and hypothetical salary. If you have to hire someone to do what your spouse did for your business, that is a reasonable business expense. The Excess Earnings approach uses a multiplier in the form of the capitalization rate. So, even if you have to pay someone $50,000 per year at a 30% cap rate, this reduces the value of your business by $166,666.

I have said this earlier in the book, but I will say it again: when you say nice things about your spouse, it goes a tremendously long way in reaching agreements. If you compliment your spouse by saying: "this business needs her input. I am going to have a very difficult time doing the work I have to do without a person of her caliber and character and her commitment to the company," she feels like a million bucks. She may hate your guts because you had an affair or whatever, but this small compliment may save you months of legal bills. Plus, it will reduce the value of the company when it comes to buying her out of it.

· ·

If you are wondering about whether the price for this book and the investment in reading this far into the book was worth it, and you own a small business, this chapter will have saved you tens of thousands of dollars, perhaps a million dollars. Thank me by writing a nice review online and telling people to read the book and take my classes. If I can help you for $50 or $2,500 by giving you tips, it is worth it to me. But I gotta make a living too.

Community Property Business Profits

This Property Division Chapter has turned into its own book on its own right. I thought of snipping it down and giving it to you in a separate volume, but I think it's better that we push through it here. I am not trying to hold information back from you and I want you to read this book and be armed with everything I can arm you with.

There is another business problem that comes up repeatedly. What do we do when there is a community property business that the in-spouse is running after separation? The law says that post-separation earnings are the separate property of the spouse earning them. What if those post-separation profits are from a community property business?

Let me give three quick scenarios where this might play out.

Husband and Wife start a business together during the marriage, so it is all community property.

1. Husband and Wife incorporate the business and are equal shareholders in the business, or if its an LLC, they are equal members.
2. Husband incorporates the business and is the sole shareholder or member.
3. Husband and Wife operate the business as a sole proprietorship.

What do we do, in any of these scenarios, with post-separation profits? Does the scenario matter for purposes of discussion? I have had each of the three scenarios, sometimes all at once. The prevailing wisdom is the in-spouse keeps all of the money and pays spousal support. But that makes no sense even purely from a corporations perspective. Why should the in-spouse keep all of the profits from a business that is jointly owned with their spouse?

In a case called *Marriage of Garaci* the trial court held Husband accountable for one-half of the profits of the community property business. The Appellate Court reversed, although it did not get to the issue of the community property profits. It found, instead, that the business was not community property. So, the case that could have helped us resolve the issue of what to do with community property profits, didn't.

The problem I see is one of incentives. In the same way that receiving a no-interest loan from your spouse in the *Watts/Epstein* analysis (where Husband lives in a mortgage-free community property house) leads to disincentive to settle the case because he will owe Wife a large Watts charge for Fair Market Rental Value, not having to share business profits with the spouse during the separation leads to a disincentive to resolve the business valuation. Actually, with business profits, the disincentive is even more perverse. Here, Husband gets to keep all of the profits from the business without sharing with Wife. Wife has to continue to pay taxes on corporate profits as though it is her income (if she is a shareholder or member and gets a K-1). Assuming the business is an S-Corp or an LLC, she will receive equal distributions as Husband at least on paper for their taxes, since the IRS recognizes only one class of stock. And Husband gets to delay the business buyout.

Business valuation takes time, and I expect a case with a community property business to take an additional 8-12 months for resolution by trial or settlement. In addition to the 6 months required to resolve a California divorce case.

Here is what happens when a case takes 18 months to resolve and Husband has been permitted to keep all profits from the business for those 18 months. We know that the Excess Earnings approach to valuation gives Husband a reasonable hypothetical income and deducts that from net revenues to get to Excess Earnings (profits). Then, we divide by a capitalization rate, usually between 27% and 33%. I will use 33% here because it makes it easier to explain, not because that is a standard number. That means, when we value the business, we are essentially utilizing 3 years of profits to get the goodwill value. (because we take one year of excess earnings and divide it by .33 or multiply by 3). Remember that the Blazer court did not find that Excess Earnings was a measure of future profits (even though we know it is). Husband then owes Wife one-half of 3 years of expected profits (that's not exactly an elegant phrasing for what is happening in strictly legal terms, but it is good enough). If excess earnings are $330,000 per year and we use a 33% capitalization rate, the value of the business is $1,000,000, of which Husband owes Wife $500,000.

If Husband is able to run the business and keep all of the profits for 18 months before trial, without having to share any profits with Wife, then he will have kept $495,000 in profits from the business, of which the joint business owner, shareholder or member, under IRS regulations, would be entitled to half of $247,500. The Corporations Code and the Internal Revenue Code each require an equal shareholder or member to take half of the profits of the business. Remember that we are not talking about reasonable hypothetical salary here. Husband is getting that too. We did not calculate that into the value of the business. If the business generates $530,000 and $200,000 of that is reasonable hypothetical salary, then we have $330,000 in excess earnings.

Why doesn't Wife get one-half of the Excess Earnings? In fact, many cases with business valuations take 3 years to resolve because of fights over business valuations, getting books and records, doing interviews with the CPA/business evaluator, conferring with forensic accountants, and etc. If we extend the above example out to 3 years, Husband will have received $990,000 in profits, of which Wife would be entitled to half as a joint shareholder or equal member or general partner under the Corporations Code and the Internal Revenue Code. Instead, Husband keeps all of the profits. Then, when he has to buy the business from her at the $1,000,000 valuation after trial, he is using her $495,000 to pay for her own share of the $1,000,000 business valuation.

This is a scam. It is a con. The law is dead wrong on this. Blazer could have and should have fixed this.

How can it be that the Internal Revenue Code and the Corporations Code treat the out-spouse better if she was "only" a shareholder or member, than the Family Code treats someone who is a spouse?

Whenever the law creates a disincentive to settle or try a case, it will be exploited.

Family Code 771(a) says: "The earnings and accumulations of a spouse and the minor children living with, or in the custody of, the spouse, after the date of separation of the spouses, are the separate property of the spouse."

Question: why do we treat earnings and accumulations of a spouse working in a community property business during the post-separation period differently when we look at business profits during separation, then we do when we value the very same business?

The Court should adopt a similar Excess Earnings approach to business profits. I have argued several times that the way to do this is to pay Husband a reasonable hypothetical salary and have the parties equally divide the profits from the business. I do not think any of the three scenarios I outlined above (that is the corporate entity status) matters for these purposes, because ownership is ownership. In Scenario A where Husband and Wife are equal shareholders or members in the company, each holds stock. In Scenario B, where Husband is the sole shareholder, Wife is entitled to half his stock as community property. In Scenario C, where it is a sole proprietorship, it is still community property. In fact, the most accurate way of describing Scenario A is that the community owns 100% of the stock shares that have been allocated between

Husband and Wife. Husband owns 50% of Wife's 50% and Wife owns 50% of Husband's 50%. The point is that the entire thing is community property.

If Husband and Wife were business partners only and there was no Family Code 771 to bother us, Husband would need to pay to Wife 50% of the profits of the company. She would get a K-1 statement showing that she had received these distributions and pay taxes on them.

Family Code 771 seems to fly in the face of this. But I just think the caselaw and our trial judges misread Family Code 771. I think the better approach is to give Husband the reasonable hypothetical salary – this can come as part of the business valuation process – and then give Wife half of all of the Excess Earnings. This could come as a "pendente lite" order (i.e., during the litigation where it would be much fairer) or it can come as a trial order once we have established Husband's baseline income for running the business, where it will be less fair to Wife, who has to wait for it, and much more painful to Husband, who in the above 3-year-divorce example, will need to pay Wife $500,000 for her half of the business plus $495,000 for her one-half share of the community property business profits during the divorce.

But, if we do this, then Husband's spousal support should be based on his hypothetical reasonable income and on his share of the distributions and on Wife's share of the distributions. In other words, if we use the number $530,000 per year in net earnings, $200,000 of which is hypothetical reasonable income, then Husband's income is $200,000 plus one-half of $330,000 or $365,000. Wife's income is $165,000. That will generate a spousal support payment based on the $200,000 gap between their incomes, although Husband will have an argument that Wife has much less need for income because she is receiving corporate profits.

Imagine a scenario in which Husband drags the divorce out for four years. He is living in the home with no mortgage, and he is operating the community property business without sharing profits. Wife is "loaning" him money by subsidizing his mortgage each month at no interest and she is waiting to receive her one-half share of business profits, which she has not received, even though she is receiving a corporate K-1 each year and paying taxes on it (even if the business pays her taxes). Why would Husband do anything besides delay the outcome as long as possible? He will have to pay her the *Watts* charges and her share of the business valuation whenever he settles or tries the case and there is no guarantee that when the trial happens, he will have to pay either.

In fact, I think it is highly unlikely that Husband will have to pay one-half of the business profits at trial because there is no authority for the proposition that he owes it to her.

I have tried a couple of different strategic approaches to push to divide corporate profits in the divorce, particularly one that is dragging out for a long time.

1. Join the corporation to the lawsuit (or the LLC or the sole proprietorship) and allege that as a shareholder, member or general partner you are entitled to one-half of the profits of the company under the Corporations Code and the Internal Revenue Code. Alternatively, file a Complaint in civil litigation against the Corporation, LLC or sole proprietorship to assert your rights as a shareholder, member or general partner. This is called a derivative shareholder suit. You can do this when you join the corporation to your divorce by filing a pleading on joinder that will allege that the corporation has violated its fiduciary duties to its shareholders and needs to not only disgorge the profits paid out as distributions but also must pay your attorneys'

fees for trying to collect what you are owed.
2. Argue Family Code 760, the community property presumption, and note that all income from community property is community property. This is equally true of community property 401(k)s (in which the community shares in the up/down market values), real estate values (although not when the real estate is separate property and *Bono v. Clark* requires a date of separation valuation), and real estate income from rentals (you almost assuredly will split the real estate income after expenses, including management fees).
3. Argue breach of fiduciary duty under Family Code 720-721 (which incorporate the Corporations Code regarding general partnerships), Family Code 2100-2107 (which are information-sharing and business opportunity sharing statutes) and 1100-1101 (which provide for specific breaches of fiduciary duty and the remedies for violation). Any retention of money that belongs to the community, which is money generated by a community property asset in the form of profits above reasonable hypothetical income belongs to the community.
4. Argue *Marriage of Loh*, which says that a tax return is presumed correct. If Wife is receiving a K-1 that says she got $165,000 in distributions, she should receive $165,000 in distributions. If the Internal Revenue Code and Corporations Code require that it be done, the Family Code should also require that it be done.

By definition, spousal support is not equal to profit sharing. It's about 38% of profit sharing. So, it is not equivalent to say that the out-spouse is getting spousal support based on the profits from the business, because the spousal support payment will be in the 38%

range when the out-spouse is entitled to 50%. Add to that issue, what happens when the out-spouse makes a good living on their own? Spousal support will be determined by each party's respective incomes.

If the in-spouse generates $530,000 per year in income from the community property business and $200,000 is the reasonable hypothetical salary, then there is $330,000 in excess earnings, of which $165,000 should go to each party from the community property business profits above the hypothetical reasonable salary. If Wife also earns $530,000 per year as a stockbroker, then she will not get a spousal support payment from Husband. But Husband will be keeping her share of the community property business profits.

The fact that Wife makes a lot of money does not impair her ability to make more money from her community property business investment. In fact, what should happen is that Husband should get his $200,000 reasonable salary plus $165,000 in business profits. Wife should get her $530,000 in salary as a stockbroker and $165,000 in community property business profits. Husband then earns $365,000. Wife earns $695,000. Husband gets spousal support from Wife based on the $330,000 differential in their incomes.

·················· PRO TIP ··················

I hate writing Machiavellian pro tips, but I have done it previously, and here it is again. I assume that the person reading this book is either the high-earner or the high-earner's lawyer. I assume that the high-earner is more likely the in-spouse when it comes to the business, more likely to be the one in the home with no mortgage and more likely to be the one paying spousal support. I have not done it necessarily as a pro tip earlier in the chapter, but I have said that I think the business profits issue is a scam. That does not mean you should not use it to your advantage. There is no reason why, if you are keeping all of the business profits and paying spousal support on those profits rather than sharing the profits equally with your spouse, you should not delay. I normally urge people to push to resolve their divorces quickly and without paying lawyers. If you have the business profits (and tax deductions) and you have the house with a lower mortgage than the FMRV, you might want to put your lawyer on delay. This is the one time where you have all the cards. Delay benefits you at every turn. Yes, you will have attorneys' fees gathering and you may be on the hook for your spouse's attorneys' fees, but this is a rational calculation that you have to make.

I am typically anti-delay when it comes to divorce, but I also believe that you have to use your leverage where you have it. A few discovery motions are not going to break your back financially and they may keep you in your house on a rent-free basis for longer or they may allow you to make full use of the corporate profits without having to buy your spouse out. You may be able to save enough corporate profits by delaying long enough to use your spouse's own share of the community property business profits to buy out their interest. I've seen it done. I don't like it. I think it's ugly, but all is fair in love and war, and the family law appellate courts have had opportunities to fix this problem, and they have refused to do so. Their refusal to fix it is your advantage. Take it.

· ·

End of Property Chapter

This ended up being much longer than I had anticipated, but it is important to cover these issues. I know that sometimes this book is a presentation of what the law is and sometimes it is a presentation of what is wrong with the law.

My confession is that I came to law through a discipline called "Law and Society," where the core books are about how law works in society and how society works on the law. I am an organization theorist by training (besides law school – that's the Ph.D. part of me) and my work has been about organizational structural issues in the law. Much of the law and society literature focuses on decision-making in legal contexts of all sorts – my dissertation work was on how nuclear weapons lab scientists make safety and security decisions in a legal context at high-tempo.

The point is that this book uses family law to teach decision-making under uncertainty. It wants you to think not only about what the law says but what its logical consistencies and inconsistencies are. That way, you can reason to the right conclusion. I have said previously that I think that when you give 10 people a legal problem 9 of them reason to the right conclusion and the 10th one is not far off. That is because law is based around guiding principles.

The Three Property Rules are just a set of guiding principles to deal with the division of property. It isn't all that complicated. It's just a timeline or "time rule" that says you get what you had before marriage, the community gets what you got during marriage, except gifts and inheritances. When you know that, even in the context of complicated mixed character assets (like post-separation income from a community property business or Fair Market Rental Value for a home), you can more or less reason to a correct conclusion.

Because I am, at heart, an academic who got stuck for 18 years doing divorces, I got a first-hand look at the inconsistencies in the law. I took a lot of cases to the Appellate Court that are cases of first impression, where I was pointing out a gap in the law or a logical inconsistency in the law. The Appellate Courts mostly disappointed me, even though I respect my former colleagues who are on the bench. I went to elementary through high school with the daughter of one of the former justices, practiced in front of one of the former justices and went to law school with one of the current justices. I know them to be smart, thoughtful people who hate family law just as much as any other judge. I have tried to tell them when I believe they have the law wrong. I have also tried to tell them when their decisions will impact many, many people in ways they cannot predict. Most of the time, they have disappointed me. Here's hoping that if this book finds it's way onto one of their bedside tables for light evening reading before bed, they will see the errors in their ways.

I have a reverence for the law, but I am not enamored by it. I think law evolves over time in ways that sometimes do and sometimes do not make sense. Family law is so interesting because it is at the bleeding edge of social and political change. But, we still have work to do.

PART IV

Stepping Back Just Enough to See the Forest *and* the Trees

CHAPTER 16

Getting What You Want in Your Divorce
Intangibles and Strategies for Success

WHAT I HOPED to Accomplish with this Book:
A) Teaching What I know About the Law.

This book has attempted to give you an overview of not only the Family Law "system," such as it is, but to help you think about how to make decisions in an uncertain legal environment; along the way, I hoped to have taught you how to think about the dynamics of the law. The book was not designed to teach you how to file forms or format pleadings; it was designed to give a way to handle what is likely to be the most expensive thing you've ever done and deal with what is perhaps the most stress you've ever been under.

My own Ph.D. and post-Doctoral research and writing focused on the operators of high-risk, high-tempo technical systems, who face uncertainty and have almost no time to make decisions. I worked in the field of organizations and the law and wrote, in part, about how people interpret legal rules on the fly, with little or no legal knowledge or expertise, but, like you, a whole lot hinging on each decision they make. It dawned on me during that research (and while I was studying for the bar exam) that most of the law is built on the basic conceptual framework of "reasonability." Reasonability is a mix of subjective (what do I think is right?) and objective (what would a reasonable person think is right?). This is as true in nuclear safety regulations and disaster management as it is in the Family Code.

Most people do not have facility with the law. And when they are facing high-stress decision-making environments, they are not particularly adept at slowing their brains down and deciding from a place of calm and mindfulness. The last thing they want to do when they are feeling so much stress on them, is slow down and read and try to understand what the law says they must do. They get angry, sad, ashamed, or guilty and they let that anger, sadness, shame or guilt infiltrate their decision-making apparatus. Adding to that is that so many people have been through divorces and have their own, often totally unrelated, divorce stories to share. These divorce stories come with common tropes that play out repeatedly: "fight for your kids," "don't let her take your stuff," "don't let that [name your expletive] win!" Like good-intentioned cheerleaders, they stand on the sidelines and urge you onward. But just because they urge you onward, that does not mean that they are urging you in the right direction. The cheerleaders rarely understand what is going on with your case specifically and, even when your cheerleaders are other lawyers, they rarely have knowledge of the facts as your lawyer sees them. That is because, most of the time, the person relaying the facts, you, does not do a very good job of capturing the nuances of the case when they explain it elsewhere. I do consultations with people who already have lawyers all the time. I hear all of the complaints the clients of the other lawyers bring to me, and unless they are complaining about a lawyer who I think is malpracticing on a regular basis, I try to use the consultation to show them that even though I might take a different approach, I am not going to sharpshoot their current lawyer's approach because I will rarely know all of the facts as the other lawyer knows them. In addition, the consulting client often relays to me all of the bad things they feel their current lawyer has done and I spend much of that consultation telling them why the client does not have all the information necessary to understand what's going on.

I asked myself this question yesterday: "Did going to law school teach me how to teach law to my clients?" How am I expected, as a lawyer, to not only perform the law via litigation, but also to explain the law to my clients so that they can make informed decisions? I believe in informed consent. Clients should be able to make their own decisions with full information; but teaching the vagaries of the evidence code or helping someone interpret a judge's on-the-record words or squaring legal decisions with the law as I read it, is not an easy task. In fact, I have been a lawyer since 2005. It is 2024 as I write this. Many if not most lawyers who've been practicing since 1985 would say that I am only really just beginning to learn about the job. This job takes an entire career to learn. How then can I teach my own clients everything I know over the course of one particular case? This book is a start. I am imagining additional books: *The Art of Declaration Writing, The Divorce Financials Workbook, Prosecuting and Defending Domestic Violence Cases,* and *The Move-Away Petition*. But, odd as it is to write about writing about books that have yet to be written, it may be that by the time you get to this section, the books are already on your shelf. In any event, I thought this was the best way of teaching what I know.

B) Stop Listening to the Cacophony of Voices Telling You What to Do.

In a recent case with one of the most difficult clients I have ever worked with (because she was so untrusting), I got a text message around midnight from the client. She told me that she talked to another lawyer and he questioned everything I had been doing in the case. He had told her about the "American rule" (in the United States, parties to a lawsuit pay their own fees unless there is a statute or a contract that modifies that – in family law there is a "fee-shifting" statute). He said she should never give up her ex's pension. He said the ex should not have 50-50 with the children. He said, "your lawyers are not doing anything for you and they should be ashamed for how much they've charged you."

We were on the eve of a 3-week trial. I had been preparing for this trial for almost 3 weeks. I blew a gasket. I was not proud of myself for my response, but I had had enough and even though I try to keep my Zen however and whenever I can, this was too much for me.

I had a very good idea that the other lawyer was an 80-year-old personal injury lawyer who I had known for perhaps ten years and with whom I'd had a falling out. I told her: "Fuck Jack. If Jack wants your case, I have the trial binders prepared for him. He knows damned well where I live and he can come pick them up tonight." Then, as I calmed down, I wrote her a text message and said: "Please call Jack up and read this word-for-word to him:

'Dear Jack, you have not had anything to do with this case despite knowing my client for all 8 years of this divorce (as you know, I've only been involved and known my client for 18 months). You are a personal injury plaintiff's lawyer and former DA and you've never billed an hour in your life and never stepped into a family law courtroom. My client was found guilty of contempt for alienating the children from their father – she should be glad to still have 50-50 custody. The marriage was 4 years long (and the divorce is approaching its 9th year!), so the most interest she has in the pension is 2 years. She has a house with Watts charges and Moore/Marsden credits of more than $200,000 and we are trading

those for two years of pension. The American rule does not apply to family law because the family law has fee-shifting statutes where the person with more property (my client who owns a $2 million home free and clear) pays the other party's fees. The court has already found my client to be a liar and has said so on the record. She is facing a 3-week trial that will cost her $10,000 per day. Do you still think we should go to trial over 2 years' of pension?"

She promised to read it to him. And after hearing it, he seemed to quiet down. As he should have. The client was untrusting and the case was filled with her continually trying to go down unrelated paths – the trial was over financial issues and she was fixated on talking about child custody and visitation, issues that had already been resolved (and there was a question of whether the judge would send her to jail for 5 days for each of four counts of contempt of court). Every time we focused the issues on the financials, she would derail the case with discussions about how bad of a co-parent the father was and how none of her three children wanted to be around him. It was a mess. But on the eve of trial, for me to get a text message from this 80-year-old lawyer who knew nothing about family law and talked about the god-damned "American rule" (a term I had not heard since law school), it was completely out of bounds.

That case was the worst type of excess because the judge had already found that both of the parties were bad actors who could not be trusted to tell the truth under oath. She said neither party was credible and she thought both parties manipulated the children against the other parent and both parties were hiding income. The lawyers knew that a 3-week trial was going to be a complete disaster. We averted disaster as best we could. The clients agreed because we explained the risks of spending $200,000 apiece and still losing. Then, my client sends me the text message from her "lawyer" friend who was trying to sharpshoot my work and undo everything we had put together to save her from oblivion. Yes, we could have won out across the board, but the husband was essentially judgment-proof, so any victory would have been illusory. What I mean by this is that Husband had already said he was going to file for Bankruptcy protection after the case resolved, so, even if we won out across the board, we still would not win anything because he was going to bankrupt the debts I said he was "essentially judgment-proof" because although you can bankrupt some marital debts (as against third-parties, thereby shifting responsibility for those debts to your spouse), you cannot for the most part bankrupt debts you owe to your spouse – this is a subject for another day. Needless to say, we did not feel that even if we "won" all issues, we would actually receive anything. We settled the case not only because we were not confident that we could get anything if we won, but also because the risk of losing with a client who has been called a liar (before my time in the case) by the judge and held in contempt of the judge's orders was very high. I am not a miracle worker. I cannot fix bad facts. Well, actually, I did work a miracle in that case – I got an efficient resolution of the case that saved a 3-week trial that we likely would have lost by trading $200,000 in *Moore/Marsden* and *Watts* reimbursements for 2 years' worth of pension payable in 20 years. I thought it was a miracle of a deal. And this 80-year-old lawyer who had never been in family court (nor had he billed a billable hour) in 56 years of law practice, was attempting to undo it over martinis in a Santa Barbara steakhouse.

My point is that, all-too-often, well-intentioned outsiders say things without the slightest level of understanding about your case. They have no idea of the real facts, in large part because you do not know how to tell them the real facts and even when you do, you will almost assuredly leave out very important facts that anyone analyzing your case would need to know. My client did not tell this personal injury lawyer that she had been found in contempt of court for parental alienation or that the judge had said she wasn't credible or that the pension she was "giving up" was *only* 2 years' worth of pension (and, I forgot to mention, she was keeping $100,000 in her 401(k) and saving $200,000 in reimbursements). To even say the words "the American rule" aloud is laughable. No one says the phrase "the American rule" except courts of appeal and law school professors and perhaps naive first year law students.

C) Settlement Before Trial. Way Before Trial.

When you have a lawyer locked in on going to trial, it is highly unlikely that any new lawyer or lawyer-friend or friend-who's-been-through-a-divorce will be more knowledgeable about your case than your lawyer.

That said, there is no better time to think about settlement than with a trial date looming. I'd say about 40% of cases settle with no trial looming. The other 60% settle within days of a trial beginning. Why? Most lawyers are only partially focused on your case months before trial because they have other cases that are set for trial and taking up their time. When a trial date is set, the lawyers become supremely focused on your case and they really learn the insides and outsides of your facts. Then, they start seeing ways of settling they hadn't seen before.

Many cases settle at the courthouse with a judge getting ready to start the trial; in fact, of the cases that settle on the eve of trial, I'd say 90% settle in the hallway outside the courtroom. By then, the lawyers know their good and bad facts, have exchanged briefs and evidence and they are both ready. It's actually a great time to settle. But, it would be really nice to settle your case well before then because you'd save a boatload of attorney's fees on trial preparation. Armed with the tools in this book, you can perform so much of your own analysis that you can save tens of thousands of trial preparation dollars and have an early settlement conference.

That's what I am after. Settlement before trial. Settlement way before trial. You can do this if you get serious about your case issues and concerns early on and start doing the work ahead of time.

D) Comporting Yourself in Court (and at Settlement Conferences and in Your Pleadings).

I had always conceived of this chapter as a exegesis on how to behave in court. As time has gone by, it's been reduced to a sub-chapter, but I do not want to diminish its importance.

Trial judges are watching you. Courtroom clerks, court reporters and bailiffs are watching you. Your ex is watching you. When you walk into a courtroom, you have to assume that everyone has eyeballs on you. Clerks, judges and bailiffs talk to each other during the breaks. They know when you've held the door for someone and when you are angry enough that you slammed a wall in the hallway outside of court. They see you sitting next to your ex in court. They see you yelling at your lawyer in the hallway.

Once I was in the hallway screaming at another party who was not represented and said "Do it now. Right fucking now! Do it fucking today!" Then, sheepishly, I had another case and had to go into the courtroom after being told by the bailiff and then the judge that they heard everything I said in the hallway.

One of my judges told me that he learns more from watching a party talk to their lawyer during argument than from reading all of the pleadings. A party who talks over their lawyer or whispers animatedly into their ear or demands that the lawyer keep saying things, is noticeable and the judge is forming opinions. I tell my clients to write things down for me to read so that a) I can listen to what is being said and b) so that the judge sees them as calm and thoughtful.

1. Dress for Court.

So, for Court, you can wear whatever you normally wear to work so long as: 1) the pants and sleeves are long and cover your legs and arms, 2) the clothes you are wearing are clean – I do not mind when my clients wear their farmworker shirts and jeans or a mechanic's jumpsuit, or a military uniform (not their dress uniform although that can be fine too if the military allows it), their nursing scrubs or what have you. But I tell my clients that these outfits should be clean and pressed.

You do not need to wear a suit. In fact, I often tell my clients not to wear a suit. The lawyers are wearing suits. You can dress more casually, but you need to send a signal that you take being in court seriously. In an era of Zoom appearances, a lot of decorum was lost. I recall the Zoom camera switching to a party sitting in a white tank top blowing out a huge vape cloud. The judge said "Mr. Johnson, can you not smoke? It's inappropriate." We were all on edge at that time and I don't think it cost Mr. Johnson anything that he was vaping on camera, but needless to say, I hope, don't do it.

In my rural-urban crossover community, jeans and a tucked in button down shirt with a belt and dress shoes or boots is fine. For women, the same outfit will work but slacks work too. No need for dresses or skirts unless you feel more comfortable.

If you are a beautiful woman, tone it down. That sounds shitty but it's true. I think both male and female judges are intimidated by beautiful women. Understate your makeup. I was in Court one day and the most beautiful woman was being represented by a power-hitter of a lawyer. She was almost regal looking. It turned out she had been on Maxim's 10 hottest women list for several years and was a part-time actress on a sci-fi show that I had actually watched (although I didn't recognize her). Even though her husband was a professional baseball player with a Stanford MBA who had decided to stay home and raise kids, the judge did not go easy on her at all. She'd have been better off dressing down. I also had a Russian model and pianist as my client. She was so beautiful that other lawyers actually tried to high-five me. I pointed out that she was my client and not my girlfriend so, sweet Jesus, what was wrong with people? But, still, I did point out to her that we were going to do better if she dressed like a pianist and not a model. She did so, and shockingly, was one of the very best witnesses I have ever had on the witness stand. I believe that with her beauty, our argument that she needed three additional years of not working so she could finish her PhD in Musicology at UCLA would have fallen flat.

Court is a great place for modesty. It's a fine place to be who you are as well, just be the most modest version of that person. If you have neck tattoos, fine. But I'd wear long sleeves to cover the arm tattoos to go with the neck tattoos. If you design clothing or jewelry and you want to wear it, also fine, but wear the more modest ones. I am not trying to hold anyone to a corporate America sense of style or trying to make us all look the same. I have tattoos and I wear silver and turquoise jewelry (including belt buckle) and boots with my suits. But the point is, I still wear a suit. Dress "smart casual" to court, as our British friends might say. Tone down your beauty (and if you are a man, do the same, but it's a double-standard world and handsome men do not get mistreated by judges in the same way that beautiful women do – it's bullshit, but we aren't trying to change the world right now, we are working on YOUR particular case and giving you the best chance to win.

  2. **Your Behavior Matters: When They Go Low, You Go High; Speak the Queen's English and No Matter What You See the Lawyer-Sharks Doing, Stay Calm.**

     "We don't let mad people make us mad."

Look, it's easy to get upset in a family law hearing. I've done it a million times. I've also really worked on keeping my cool. I've taken to writing the above phrase at the top of my hearing notes in every single case. I like the phrase because "mad" can mean "angry" or it can mean "crazy." You can play that phrase out any way that fits with those two definitions of the word "mad." Angry and crazy people tend to do badly in court.

You basically only get a few shots at standing in front of a judge. I do it for a living, so I get more chances than you do. That means I can call on righteous indignation from time to time, but when I really lose my temper, I am not doing good for my client or my reputation. I am definitely a better lawyer when I am calm. You will be a better client (or your own lawyer) if you stay calm and clear-headed. This can be tough especially when you have either your ex or your ex's lawyer saying things about you in a courtroom full of people that are untrue or inaccurate.

Staying calm is the mainstay of good advocacy. And it is also why Abraham Lincoln famously quipped: "The man who represents himself in Court has a fool for a client." I've represented myself before and this is true. To a fault. If you must represent yourself in Court, you have to be better than good.

Start by dressing clean and smart. Hold the door for people as they enter the Courtroom. Use the water glass in front of you to keep yourself as calm as possible. Have good notes and even though I have written above that you may read your notes, try not to. Stay laser focused on what you are asking the court to do. If things get off track, you can say "I'm not prepared to talk about that today. I thought we were only here to discuss 'XYZ'."

Always refer to the Judge as "Your Honor," never as Sir or Ma'am. Court is theater and in this theater, there are certain formalities that must be kept. Remember that even if you do not like your judge or

Chapter 16 • Getting What You Want in Your Divorce | 453

your judge does not like you, you are giving respect to the bench and the flags that stand behind it.

This is not a personality contest. Let me say that differently: if you make it a personality contest, you lose. The Judge is the person who matters most. Your job is respectfulness, politeness and honor. You can respectfully disagree comments made by the other side. You say: "Your Honor, may I please be heard on this issue?" I will tell you that there are times when decorum is the only thing holding me back. "Your Honor, may I please make my record for appeal?" The Court: "No you may not." Me: "Your Honor, I have a right to make a record for appeal." The Court: "You've already been given your chance." Me: "Your Honor, respectfully, I have not been given a full opportunity to make my record. All I am asking for is another couple of minutes." The Court: "Denied."

OK, what can I do?

Me: "Respectfully, Your Honor. I disagree."

The Court: "Take it up with the Appellate Court."

Me: "You can bet I will."

But, you see, other than the hint of snark at the end, I upheld my decorum as much as I could in a hearing in which the other lawyer blatantly and with no evidence whatsoever, called me dishonest and a liar. I was on Zoom, but I can tell you that I wanted to come through the screen and start screaming right there in court. But I kept it together. As a side note, I think that judge is one of perhaps the dumbest humans I have ever met in this job. How they are a judge is beyond me. And that is another reason to settle.

There are certain other items: do not call names – do not call anyone a "liar" (despite the last little anecdote in which I was called a liar); needless to say, I hope, do not call your ex-wife a "whore" or impugn her moral character. Do not raise your voice at the Judge. Do not speak over other speakers. Let them finish even if your blood is boiling. I will, at times, deliberately speak over another lawyer when they are speaking gibberish or spewing lies, but you should not do that. I have more leeway in some courtrooms than others.

It will always be the case that women get away with more bullshit than men in family court, but you can use that to your advantage, by saying "Do you see what I have to deal with?"

Write somewhere where you can see it: "We don't let mad people make us mad." Internalize the message.

I try to help my clients see that I am going after what they tell me they want and will do anything legal to get it – I'll take the blame and fall on my sword, I will scream until my jugular is popping out my neck, I will write long briefs, I will work until 3:00 A.M. day after day, but the very most effective strategic arrow in my quiver is to be myself – I use a mixture of humor and calming energy to soothe the judge into my way of thinking. I always ask for what is "reasonable," which is the 50% my client wants plus a little bit of icing on the cake. The other side is so unreasonable most of the time, and by unreasonable I mean they ask for things that the law just doesn't support that my reasonable approach to 50% + say 3-6% more, seems so downright fair that we almost always win. The only time I feel like we stand a chance of losing is when the client wants a slugfest. "Me (constantly): Judge, as you know, two weeks ago this case turned into a massive blowout right here in this courtroom. The Bailiffs are still talking about it on their coffee breaks (laughs, because I know the bailiffs don't give a crap about it and they know I know). But I am trying to keep today from going sideways. I'm turning over a new leaf with Attorney X. If they want to throw acid all over the case, that is on them. We came here to seek a reasonable outcome, and we have it. Let me tell you, calmly, what it is." I cannot say enough for a rational, well-thought out, calm delivery. I am famous, secretly with my clients for having my voice get softer and more soothing as a hearing goes on. My daughter calls it my "sleepy voice." I used to teach at Cal Poly San Luis Obispo, at UC Berkeley (as a graduate student) and at Louisiana State University. I probably lulled 40 people to sleep once a week at least. That's probably my second gift. Nevertheless, I developed this strategy when defending a particularly nasty situation in which my client was wrongly accused of domestic violence (which needs its own chapter as well). They wanted to say my client was a loudmouthed hothead who could not control his outbursts. As his representative, then, I took exactly the opposite approach. I told him not to say a word and I did the entire hearing in the calmest sleepiest voice I had, the other side ranting and raving the whole time. The wife ended up looking like the abuser in the relationship.

3. The Same Decorum Applies to What You Write.

A very well-known former LA Superior Court judge who teaches continuing education classes for lawyers told his class one day that he has a plaque behind the bench that only he can see that says "Don't say it." This is fabulous advice especially in your written submissions to the Court. Calling your ex-wife a "whore" or accusing her of abusing the kids without documented proof will do two things:

    a. It will make her mad in a way that you can probably never repair. And remember that even though today you are in a war with her, one day this will be over and you will need to co-parent or get an agreement and if you've written terrible things about her, she can never unread them.

    b. The Judge will think you are a jerk.

I tell my clients to focus on the good in their lives in their declarations. You always make the other side draw first blood. Your first written declarations should be about what makes you a good parent and what you have to offer your children. It should compliment her on her parenting and remind the Court that each of you is involved in your children's lives or that she has earning potential with her master's degree and real estate broker's license.

You can defend yourself by playing defense if you need to but only after she has gone after your character. Then, you say, "do you see what I have to deal with? I was trying to channel Michelle Obama and go high even when she goes low, but now I have to defend myself." Then defend yourself. But I have read eyeball bleeding declarations that accuse the other party of high treason, tax evasion, being a literal prostitute, physical abuse, drug abuse, pornography "addiction," and so many other things. I have never heard of a judge paying any attention to any of these types of allegations. You know who does pay attention to them? My client. My client never forgets reading their ex-husband's declaration detailing the threesome she had at his request with lines of cocaine and a video camera. *Who. Gives. A. Fuck*? Knock it off and don't air dirty laundry. If you were doing cocaine with her and you consented to having another man in your bedroom, shut the fuck up about it. This is true of the four martini dinners where you both got into the car drunk (and thank God you didn't hurt anyone) and affairs and all of the gobbledygook.

Reign it in tiger. And for that matter, you aren't out there talking about prescription medications or therapist diagnoses either. What's wrong with people who do this? You learn a lot about your spouse. You are in or were in a relationship of trust and confidence. Now you are going to go into Court and spew all of the secrets your spouse told you? Defectors get mistreated by the countries they defect to. Why? Everyone hates a traitor.

Don't be a traitor. Focus on yourself. What you do good. What you do right. If you've had a DUI or arrest or you've made other mistakes, own the mistakes and give the Court a plan for how you've worked on yourself.

"I know I haven't always been the best communicator, but when we separated I joined a men's group or started going to AA and working my program with a sponsor or started therapy."

"I've had issues with substance abuse in the past, but I've been sober 6 years or 6 months."

"I've worked hard on my relationship with my teenaged child – I had hard time at first when they announced they were nonbinary/gay/queer, etc."

"I always had a learning disability and remain dyslexic to this day, but I can help our children with their homework and if I can't I will get them tutors."

"I like camp and fish with my kids. I want my girls to grow up unafraid of the dirt."

"I've always been a horsegirl at heart and my boys have learned respect for animals by grooming the horses."

"We are a gun family. My dad taught me to be safe with firearms and to this day, I believe in the safe use of firearms and have already begun teaching our children gun safety."

It's your story. Tell it. Tell about yourself and your siblings and your children's cousins and grandparents and your love of travel or camping or horror movies or surfing and how you want to share this with your children. I had a BMW mechanic who became a garlic farmer. His son was on the spectrum. My client loved working on cars and tractors. His son was obsessed with bugs. He fought it for a while, telling the court and me that he wanted his son to love cars. But, at some point, I got through to him and he said: "Here's how I am going to nurture my son's love of bugs. We are going to plant a huge garden and I want my son to figure out how to keep the bugs off the plants without pesticides. He will identify all the bugs and caterpillars and tomato worms and together we will figure the good and the bad ones and make a plan to grow our garden together."

And guess what? His son adored him and the Court rewarded him. He also got an awesome new wife who his son loved and that did not hurt. And then, from this garden the father learned to love to grow things and – while it may have seemed a huge leap – he bought land in Gilroy, CA and became a garlic farmer. And although his son went away to college, I hear from the father that their bond has never been better.

So, I write this because happy endings are important. So much of what I've written about in this book has to do with the various types of unhappy stories – divorce, subjectively, is a sad thing for many people (probably most people), but they do it with a sense of optimism that there will be something better. My experience is that people's lives do get better if they do the work on themselves and with their families to make space for a better life. That means, though, doing the therapy and self-searching to be ready for new love or being good with being alone.

So, back to declaration writing for a moment: you should want to hold your head up high and take pride in your behavior during what is undoubtedly one of the worst times in your life. That means to focus on what you do well and good and what you have contributed to your marriage and your family. Going low serves no one. You can always say: "See what I have to deal with?" You can also always say: "I refuse to go low, Your Honor. I am here to tell you what is good with our family and why I should get what I am asking for, not at my ex's expense, but for the good that can result from me getting it."

E) Conclusions

This book started out with the idea of teaching some very basic truths about the law and how to make decisions "in the shadow of the law." I wanted to introduce the concept of reasonability and the Range of Normal Outcomes. I wanted to teach about the range of best-case and worst-case outcomes to help you develop this range. I have pursued the concept that you should always work to settle your case in the Range of Normal Outcomes and if you get an offer to settle within that range, you must take it seriously. I have not said you must take any offer within the Range of Normal Outcomes, just that you must take such offers seriously.

Taking an offer seriously means considering it fully. What would it mean for you down the road if you offer to let your ex-wife live in the family home for two more years? What would it mean for you to pay or receive spousal support indefinitely? Are you willing to trade retirement for the house? What will a day-to-day schedule look like with the children?

I have also said that only you (and your ex and to some extent your children) will live with the outcome of your case. You should not make an agreement that you cannot abide in the middle of the night. If the dogs mean the world to you, you cannot give them up. But, also, you should recognize what you will not be able to get from any court and then you must release your desires and get serious about what outcomes actually can come to fruition.

I have talked about "good negotiation" as getting to a point where you discern what matters most to your ex-spouse and what matters most to you and then seeing where there is overlap and where there isn't. I am always surprised that gun owners divide guns so easily. Everyone knows whose gun is whose. It's that way with cars as well. My ex-wife and I had a F-150 (mine) and a Toyota Prius (hers). We both paid for both but we also both knew whose is whose in our divorce.

Fundamentally, the things that are personal items go to the person who they belong to, even if we are going to divide the stuff later. I have a case right now where the husband is a lifetime farmer and rancher. He exudes farmer and rancher. They have a good chunk of property 101 acres in San Luis Obispo plus three other city slicker properties. The wife, I've met her a few times, is a sourpuss if there ever was one. I've rarely ever seen a party so angry at the other and so spiteful where there wasn't an affair, and there wasn't in this case. She's more city slicker than rancher herself. They've got 40 acres of avocado trees and a pond stocked with trout. She hasn't picked an avocado or baited a hook in 50 years. All the husband wants is the ranch. The wife has made clear that they are going to have to pry her cold dead body out of there because she doesn't want him to have it. But even though they each live on the ranch about 20 acres apart, that's also too close for her. She wants him off the ranch altogether even though they have 7 adult children and a dozen grandchildren all coming and going from the ranch all the time.

Sometimes a person will be spiteful, but the reality is that a dead-in-the-water negotiation can get jumpstarted if one person makes a small gesture. In a recent case that was going to be grandparent funded all-out war, I communicated to the other lawyer that my client wanted to compliment his client on how attentive and loving he was being to their daughter. She wanted him to know that she thought he was a good father. All the ice melted, and we reached an agreement about 30 minutes later. Good negotiating is understanding that you are going to give up some things to get some things and that it's not only about the things. Showing your ex-spouse that there is still some attentiveness and care can go a long way to resolution. I will talk about why I think mediation is not productive and should be avoided, but why I believe firmly and strongly in negotiated agreements.

Mindfulness, I think, is an overused word. It has so many meanings that it is vague, and it is so overused and cringe-worthy to people who see it that I might as well be writing the word God (nothing against either mindfulness or God as a practice and way of being, just the overuse of the term without any real definition). I'm upset with so-called mindfulness because it has become an amorphous topic that no one can put their finger on, but everyone is talking about. I am partial to Eckhart Tolle's Power of Now version of mindfulness on a meditation level. I try to mediate 15-20 minutes a day. But I also write and I am teaching myself to paint, so I have some meditative kinds of practices. My paralegal is always teasing me that I put my headphones on and "listen to whale music" but I do listen to binaural beats and calming music. I think that a mindfulness practice, or Judeo-Christian-Muslim prayer, or nature walks (especially nature walks), putting your feet in the wet sand below the tide line, going for a long loud ride on your Harley, shooting guns (at the range for God's sake), going fishing, having sex, playing your guitar/piano/saxophone, painting, writing or reading are all ways to calm the mind. Many of them can get us into a state of "flow" where time stands still. This can happen in mindfulness meditation – I like Tolle's work because the way he teaches it, you can be mindful for 30 seconds while you wait in line at the grocery store. Anyway, I urge everyone to get a therapist and/or take up some sort of meditative practice when you start a divorce. It cannot hurt. But still I hate the word mindfulness, even though I have used it a lot in this book.

I think mindfulness is directly relevant to keeping yourself in check – I believe that emotions are key to successfully navigating divorce, but that runaway expressions of emotion can be damaging. There is a difference between not feeling things (impossible in a divorce fraught with so many emotions from anger to feeling of failure to guilt) and letting the feelings you feel eat you alive to your detriment.

Of course, the book has covered a lot of other material, some of it with relative depth. I have argued that, as California, New York and Texas go, so goes the country. Even though the ground-level view of the law in this book comes from California law, I argue that many of the lessons California law teaches are applicable across community property and equitable distribution states. While California's child and spousal support calculators may be unique to California, the application of the general principle that support increases (to the payor) with the presence of more available cash to the payor is applicable across jurisdictions. Fiduciary duties between spouses are generally applicable across jurisdictions, even if other jurisdictions don't call them fiduciary duties – everyone still knows that it's a bad look to benefit personally at the expense of your spouse.

I have also tried to pepper the book with both anecdotes and "pro tips" to help give you additional ways of thinking about real life examples – and for entertainment purposes.

It is my sincere hope that as you internalize what you've read, you take home the fundamental lessons that a) being done with your divorce has a value and only you can monetize that value, b) that if your lawyer wants to file a motion, you should understand it, what it's going to cost and what your chances of success are, c) that family law judges rarely understand or care about family law, so if you are focused on esoteric arguments, you will almost always lose them, d) you should put your own kid through Stanford rather than your lawyer's kid, and e) spending your efforts on getting tomorrow's $1 is a far better use of your resources than spending your efforts (and money) fighting over yesterday's $.50. If you have to spend ten cents to get fifty cents, you only get forty cents. If you can focus on tomorrow's earnings to get an entire dollar (and still get the 40 cents plus some of the ten cents you would have spent to get it), you are being smart with your time and money.

In the end, most cases can settle completely and all cases can settle mostly. Don't be the guy allowing your lawyers to set 15-day divorce trials. This is about the worst use of money you can imagine.

Not only is it stressful and embarrassing, it serves almost no one but the lawyers, particularly because your judge almost assuredly will not take your case anywhere nearly as seriously as you do.

Finally, finally, finally. When they go low, you go high. A divorce is an opportunity to do good and just things by the person you spent many years of your life with and may even have had children with. This is your story. In five years, you will be sitting with your new spouse at a dinner table and someone will tell you that they are going through a divorce. You will tell them about your divorce. How do you want to feel about that? There is nothing so awkward as hearing a story about how much fighting there was during your divorce. Your interlocutor will excuse themselves as quickly as they can and hope the conversation does not return to the topic. Remember also that your children – maybe minors now, but who will one day be adults – will learn the story as well. This is their mother or father. They will want you both at their weddings and graduations, but only if you aren't a complete ass during the divorce. Get it done quickly; get it done fairly; and be good.

ABOUT THE AUTHOR

Dr. Egan is a Certified Family Law Specialist, Certified by the State Bar of California Board of Legal Specialization. He holds a Ph.D. and J.D. from the University of California, Berkeley. He has practiced family law, including probate and trust law, since 2008. He has published widely on family law issues in the popular press and legal journals. He is a world wide expert in decision-making in high-stress environments.

He is available to consult on family law and probate matters, to work as an expert witness, particularly on probate matters involving community and separate property, and on appeals. To read his other publications and ongoing blog, or to reach him, his website is: www.judeeganlaw.com.

www.ingramcontent.com/pod-product-compliance
Lightning Source LLC
Chambersburg PA
CBHW021148230426
43667CB00006B/296